4

MW01059051

THE PROFOUND TREASURY
OF THE OCEAN OF DHARMA

VOLUME ONE
The Path of Individual Liberation

VOLUME TWO
The Bodhisattva Path of Wisdom and Compassion

VOLUME THREE
The Tantric Path of Indestructible Wakefulness

Published in association with Vajradhatu Publications, a division of
Shambhala Media. www.shambhalamedia.org.

VOLUME TWO

THE PROFOUND TREASURY
OF THE OCEAN OF DHARMA

The Bodhisattva Path of Wisdom and Compassion

CHÖGYAM TRUNGPA

COMPILED AND EDITED BY

Judith L. Lief

SHAMBHALA • BOSTON & LONDON • 2013

Shambhala Publications, Inc.
Horticultural Hall
300 Massachusetts Avenue
Boston, Massachusetts 02115
www.shambhala.com

9 8 7 6 5 4 3 2 1

First Edition
Printed in the United States of America

♾ This edition is printed on acid-free paper that meets the
American National Standards Institute z39.48 Standard.
♻ Shambhala makes every attempt to print on recycled paper.
For more information please visit www.shambhala.com.

Distributed in the United States by Random House, Inc.,
and in Canada by Random House of Canada Ltd

Designed by Dede Cummings Designs

LIBRARY OF CONGRESS CATALOGING-IN-PUBLICATION DATA
Trungpa, Chögyam, 1939–1987.
The profound treasury of the ocean of dharma / Chögyam Trungpa;
compiled and edited by Judith L. Lief.—First Edition.
pages cm
Compilation of Chögyam Trungpa Rinpoche's
Vajradhatu Seminary teachings in three volumes.
Includes index.
ISBN 978-1-59030-708-3 (hardcover: alk. paper; set)—
ISBN 978-1-59030-802-8 (hardcover: alk. paper; vol. 1)—
ISBN 978-1-59030-803-5 (hardcover: alk. paper; vol. 2)—
ISBN 978-1-59030-804-2 (hardcover: alk. paper; vol. 3)
1. Buddhism—Doctrines. I. Lief, Judith L., editor of compilation. II. Title.
BQ4165.T75 2013
294.3′4—dc23
2012022795

CONTENTS

EDITOR'S INTRODUCTION

THE FOUNDATION OF HINAYANA
AND THE TRANSITION TO THE MAHAYANA

The Bodhisattva Path of Wisdom and Compassion is the second of the three volumes of *The Profound Treasury of the Ocean of Dharma*. This volume focuses on the mahayana path. In the previous volume, Chögyam Trungpa Rinpoche presents the hinayana path of individual liberation, and in the final volume he introduces the vajrayana, or the path of complete awakening. By presenting the dharmic path as a natural progression that begins with the hinayana, expands into the mahayana, and reaches its fruition in the vajrayana, Trungpa Rinpoche provides the reader with a complete map of the spiritual journey from confusion to enlightenment.*

In teaching about the three stages of the path, Trungpa Rinpoche presented each stage as having its own integrity and power, and taught his students to see each stage as complete in its own right. He especially cautioned students not to denigrate the hinayana or skip the mahayana in favor of what they might consider the more powerful or exotic vajrayana, but to see the three stages, or *yanas,* as an interconnected whole, and as one continuous journey.

Trungpa Rinpoche went so far as to rouse his students from their sleep for a spontaneous talk late at night during the 1986 Seminary in order to

---

* For a brief overview of the three yanas, see volume 1 of the *Profound Treasury,* "Editor's Introduction."

drive this point home. In this pithy and impassioned talk, he remarked, "[The hinayana] is to be understood as the life force that carries on whether you are going through the hinayana, mahayana, or vajrayana. . . . The hinayana should be regarded as life's strength."*

Trungpa Rinpoche made it clear that hinayana teachings are not just introductory, but reverberate throughout the path; they are the foundation on which the entire path is built. The logic in beginning with the hinayana is that if you would like to help others, you must first be willing to work on yourself.

At the same time, although working on yourself is essential, according to Trungpa Rinpoche it is not enough. Sooner or later you need to start thinking about others. The world is vast and it needs help. Therefore, it is important to take the further step of entering the mahayana path of inseparable wisdom and compassion, and to balance your own individual training with service to others.

READING THE DHARMA

According to Trungpa Rinpoche, "You should try to connect what you study to your personal experience. Each aspect of the dharma is based on personal experience, so you can relate the dharma to what you experience on the spot."† So in studying these teachings, you could deepen your understanding by balancing your intellectual study with meditative practice and personal reflection. Scholarship without practice is of limited value, as is practice without scholarship; but the combination of the two is both powerful and transformative.

THE STRUCTURE OF VOLUME TWO:
MAHAYANA

1. Awakening the Heart

The opening section of this volume is about the transition from hinayana to mahayana. There is an introduction to basic concepts of the mahayana, such as *bodhichitta*, the mind / heart of awakening; *maitri*, or loving-

---

* See appendix 1, "Never Forget the Hinayana."

† "Egolessness and Compassion," Vajradhatu Seminary, Lake Louise, Alberta, Canada, January–March 1980, talk 18.

kindness; *karuna,* or the noble heart of compassion; and *upaya,* or skillful means. This section includes a discussion of the relationship between bodhichitta and *tathagatagarbha,* or buddha nature. Throughout this section, the reader is reminded of the essential importance of the hinayana, and particularly of *shamatha* and *vipashyana* (mindfulness and awareness practice) as preparation for entering the mahayana path.

2. Buddha Nature

This section focuses on the fundamental human qualities that make it possible for one to practice the mahayana. Trungpa Rinpoche refers to the innate tendency toward growth and awakening as "enlightened genes." He also introduces the concept of "basic goodness," the fundamental state of our consciousness before it is divided up into "I" and "other." Although the potential for awakening may be hidden or stained, Trungpa Rinpoche points out that such stains are temporary and can be removed.

3. Preparing the Ground

In this section, having had a glimpse of the potential for awakening, one is given instructions on how to expand that glimpse and prepare oneself for making a formal commitment to the mahayana path. The reader is directed to draw upon and strengthen the hinayana training of mindfulness and awareness, and to develop sympathy and a deeper understanding of egolessness. In order to awaken one's potential, or enlightened genes, four methods are explained: love, compassion, joy, and equanimity. At this point, it is essential to work with a mahayana teacher, known as a spiritual friend, or *kalyanamitra.*

4. Making a Commitment

Having prepared the ground, one is ready to make a formal commitment to the mahayana path, also referred to as the bodhisattva path. This section is about preparing for and taking this profound vow to liberate all beings. It introduces the concept of the bodhisattva, or awake being, as a compassionate warrior of awakening. There is a discussion of ultimate and relative bodhichitta, of the aspiration to become a bodhisattva, and the implications of following the mahayana path.

5. Emptiness and Compassion

This section is about the view of the mahayana, which is that of emptiness and compassion, or *shunyata* and karuna, which are said to be inseparable. It is about developing *prajna,* or transcendent knowledge. There is a detailed discussion of the egolessness of self and the egolessness of dharmas, or phenomena. In addition, the doctrine of the two truths, relative truth and ultimate truth, is introduced. There is an emphasis on contemplating emptiness as a way of awakening unfabricated perception, and therefore experiencing reality fully and completely, without fear or distortion.

6. Bodhisattva Activity

Once one has taken the bodhisattva vow and had a glimpse of emptiness, it is time to put one's understanding into practice, and engage in bodhisattva activity. The way to do so is by means of six techniques of nongrasping, called *paramitas,* or transcendent virtues: generosity, discipline, patience, exertion, meditation, and prajna (knowledge). The six paramitas provide the bodhisattva with guidelines for both practice and daily life.

7. Mind Training and Slogan Practice

Here mind training, or *lojong,* is presented as a way to undermine aggression and awaken bodhichitta, both ultimate bodhichitta and relative bodhichitta. It includes a discussion of *tonglen,* or sending and taking, and the idea of exchanging oneself for others. In this section, Trungpa Rinpoche comments in detail on the fifty-nine slogans of mind training, which were compiled by Geshe Chekawa, and are attributed to the great Indian master Atisha.

8. The Bodhisattva's Journey

This section gives a map of the bodhisattva's journey from beginning to end. This is presented according to two related models: the five paths and the ten *bhumis,* or spiritual levels. The author concludes with a description of the eleventh bhumi, called "complete radiance," the attainment of unsurpassable enlightenment.

NOTES ON FOREIGN TERMS AND DEFINITIONS

Tibetan, Sanskrit, and other foreign words and phrases are italicized on first appearance in these volumes. Tibetan terms are spelled phonetically in the body of the text. The glossary contains definitions of all terms, as well as transliterations of Tibetan terms. A special thank you to the Nalanda Translation Committee and to Ellen Kearney for preparing and editing the extensive glossary. Please see the credits page for a list of further acknowledgments.

DEDICATION

*May the ever-expanding wisdom and compassion of the
    mahayana
Draw us out of our complacent self-concern
Into the liberating and challenging playground of the peaceful
    bodhisattva warrior.
May the world enjoy peace, and may all beings be freed from
    ignorance and suffering.*

PRONUNCIATION OF
SANSKRIT AND TIBETAN

SANSKRIT

Sanskrit words may seem intimidating at first sight because they are so long. However, once they are broken into syllables, they are easy to pronounce. Sanskrit follows very regular rules and contains no "silent letters" such as those in English.

Vowels

In general, vowels are pronounced as in Italian or Spanish. Sanskrit makes a distinction between long and short vowels in the case of *a*, *i*, and *u*. However, in this text they are not represented differently. Therefore, it is acceptable always to pronounce them as if they were long:

a as in c*a*r.
i as in f*ee*t.
u as in l*oo*t.

The following vowels are always considered long in Sanskrit:

e as in d*ay*
ai as in p*ie*
o as in g*o*
au as in h*ow*

Consonants

Most consonants are pronounced as in English. The aspirated consonants (*kh, gh, ch, jh, th, dh, th, dh, ph, bh*) are pronounced as the consonant plus a noticeable aspiration of breath. In particular, note that the consonants *th* and *ph* are not pronounced as in the words *thing* and *photo*, but as in po*th*ole and she*ph*erd. The letter *g* is always pronounced hard as in *go*, never as in gem. The letter *h* is pronounced as a breathing sound at the end of a word.

Accent

In classical Sanskrit, each syllable received approximately the same emphasis; vowels were lengthened rather than stressed. Although today we tend to stress syllables, it should not be so emphatic as in English. Accent is placed on the next-to-last syllable when this contains a long vowel or ends with more than one consonant (not including *h*). Otherwise, it is placed on the last previous syllable that contains a long vowel or ends in more than one consonant. If none exists, the stress is placed on the first syllable.

TIBETAN

In this text, Tibetan words have been spelled to reflect pronunciation as accurately as possible. As in Sanskrit, the consonants *th* and *ph* are not pronounced as in the words *thing* and *photo*, but as in po*th*ole and she*ph*erd. The letters *ü* and *ö* are pronounced approximately as in the German words *über* and *möglich*, or as in the French words *connu* and *oeuvre*.

Note that the letter *e* is always pronounced at the end of a word. In some cases, words ending in *e* have been spelled with a hyphen in order to prevent mispronunciation: shi-ne, Ri-me.

Part One

AWAKENING THE HEART

I

A Glimpse of Wakefulness

The mahayana brings greater vision and greater action. Heroism,
celebration, and excitement are all solidly a part of it. . . . You begin
to like your environment and, as egoless as you may be, you begin
to like yourself. The appreciation of the world outside is called com-
passion, and the appreciation of yourself is called maitri. Unless
those two are working together, it is a dead end.

THE GREAT VEHICLE

The mahayana is called the great vehicle. It is also referred to as the
bodhisattva path, which means the path of the awakened beings. *Bodhi*
means "awake," and *sattva* means "being"; so a *bodhisattva* is an "awakened being." As the second of the three vehicles, or *yanas*, the mahayana
is known to be a great and powerful journey.* Why is it so powerful? Its
power comes from the realization of your own potential; it comes from
the realization that you are a worthy person. You have the potential to
be without aggression or passion, to be a person without problems. You
could be thoroughly, utterly, completely good. You could be a person with
basic sanity and goodness. It is possible.

In the word *mahayana, maha* means "great," or "powerful," and *yana*
means "vehicle," or "palanquin"; so *mahayana* means " great vehicle." The
Tibetan word for yana is *thekpa*, which means "that which lifts you up."

---

* Trungpa Rinpoche usually uses the term *three yanas* to refer to the three stages of the
practitioner's journey—the hinayana, mahayana, and vajrayana—rather than to the differ-
ing schools of Buddhism.

Anything that lifts you up and takes you to your destination is a yana. So a yana is a form of transportation. For instance, an elevator, a car, a train, or an airplane could be a yana. In the Buddhist sense, the term *yana* is used in a more subtle way to refer to the path itself or to the practitioners.

Once you step into the mahayana, you do not have much control. It goes by itself and there is no reverse, none whatsoever. Everything goes forward. Furthermore, there are no brakes and no steering wheel, and the vehicle does not need any fuel. In fact, the road moves rather than the vehicle. We could also say that about life: life itself moves rather than you moving through life. So once you get onto the path, the path moves and you are stuck with it. There is no way of getting off or taking a break. The journey takes you over.

THE DISCOVERY OF BODHICHITTA

The mahayana begins with the discovery of *bodhichitta,* the heart or mind of awakening. *Bodhi* again means "awake," and *chitta* means "heart," or "mind"; so *bodhichitta* means "awakened heart." In Tibetan it known as *changchup kyi sem. Changchup* means "awake," *kyi* means "of," and *sem* means "consciousness" or "cognitive mind"; so *changchup kyi sem* means "mind of awakening." The question is, what are you waking from? You are waking from the three poisons: passion, aggression, and ignorance or delusion. Passion leads to possessiveness, and it is connected with the attachment to pleasure. You never want to eat at home, but you always want to go to restaurants, or you constantly want to watch television. Aggression leads you to use all your energy fighting others and becoming somewhat macho. Ignorance creates a feeling of general dullness; you begin to spend all of your time in bed. Those three principles are the problems you face, and you have to overcome them.

However, passion, aggression, and ignorance are not regarded as deep-rooted problems; they are simply phases we go through, like any other phase. But although they are simply phases, they are obviously obstacles. The problem with such situations is that they occupy your time and space, so they prevent you from being in a state of wakefulness.

RELATIVE AND ULTIMATE BODHICHITTA

There are two types of bodhichitta: relative bodhichitta and ultimate or absolute bodhichitta. Relative bodhichitta is called *kündzop changchup-*

kyi-sem in Tibetan. *Kündzop* means "relative," *kün* means "all," and *dzop* means an "effigy," or "outfit," and *changchup-kyi-sem* means the "mind of enlightenment," or "bodhichitta"; so *kündzop changchup-kyi-sem* is an "effigy of bodhichitta," or "relative bodhichitta." Kündzop is like a scarecrow; it is an outfit that fits the world. Kündzop is a kind of facade or medium. If you are a painter, you use paint as the medium, not the meaning. You could represent things much better if there were a greater medium, but since there is not, you use what exists around you. In any communication, you use whatever medium is available, so in a sense your presentation becomes a facade or superficial.

Relative bodhichitta is the common practice of involving yourself in the world with benevolence, fearlessness, and kindness. It is the manifestation of your friendliness and deliberate training, and it is helped a great deal by the experience of *vipashyana,* or awareness, which brings reminders of all kinds.

Ultimate bodhichitta is called *töndam changchup-kyi-sem. Dam* means "ultimate," and *tön* means "meaning"; so *töndam* means "ultimate purpose," "ultimate meaning," or "ultimate goal." *Changchup-kyi-sem,* again, means "bodhichitta"; so *töndam changchup-kyi-sem* means "ultimate bodhichitta," or "absolute bodhichitta." This type of bodhichitta is based on an enlarged sense of egolessness. It is based on emptiness, or the *shunyata* experience. In basic egolessness, you have a sense of nonexistence, but it is still a conceptualized notion of nonexistence. You still have a nonexistent but changing world around you. But with ultimate bodhichitta there is no world outside, no world separate from yourself. From the point of view of ego, there is a total nonexistence of personality. That ultimate understanding of egolessness comes from your vipashyana experience becoming more outrageous. You are more willing to be brave, heroic, and crazy.

True bodhichitta combines spaciousness, sympathy, and intelligence; or shunyata, compassion (*karuna*), and knowledge (*prajna*).* In order to be exposed to intelligence, or prajna, you have to understand that it is not worth struggling, that you have to give up ego fixation. In order to be exposed to sympathy, or compassion, you have to give up territoriality, possessiveness, and aggression. And in order to relate with spaciousness, or emptiness, you have to realize that there is no point trying to use

---

* *Spaciousness, sympathy, and intelligence* are an alternate and evocative way of referring to these three principles, more commonly referred to by Trungpa Rinpoche as emptiness, compassion, and knowledge.

metaphysical analogies or the language of nonreference point as another reference point; you just need to relate with yourself.

Bodhichitta is fundamental to the teachings of the Buddha. It is the basis of being awake and open. Without bodhichitta we cannot survive, we cannot function. In the mahayana we are acknowledging that such a quality exists in us. It is not particularly mystical, or something that we have not experienced before. We are not impotent, but we are capable of expressing our affection to ourselves and to others. Bodhichitta is what we want to plant in our mind and in our existence. It is the foundation of the mahayana.

A Taste of Enlightenment

With bodhichitta, the heart or chitta comes first, and bodhi comes later: the heart awakens. So we begin by developing a particular kind of heart, one that is not connected with personal longevity, personal entertainment, or egotism. First we develop heart, and then we develop what heart is all about, or enlightened heart. Enlightened heart is expansive and awake. It is not territorial, and it does not demand that we gather our own flock of egotistic companions. When we look into that quality of basic wakefulness beyond our own territoriality, we find ourselves having a taste of enlightenment for the very first time.

In the hinayana, we may have had a glimpse of gentleness, goodness, and precision, but we never had a taste of the mind clicking in and awakening on the spot, as it should. That has not yet happened. But in the mahayana, it is actually happening. That is why it is very important for us to join mindfulness and awareness, or *shamatha* and vipashyana.

In *shamatha-vipashyana,* the process of training takes place in your heart. It is not an athletic approach. You are training yourself so that you can be awakened from drowsiness, deep sleep, and the samsaric world. But you are awake already, which is why it is possible to notice that you have fallen asleep—and you can tune yourself in to this awakened state of being by the practice of rousing bodhichitta. Shamatha brings *maitri,* a simple and kind attitude toward yourself, and vipashyana brings *karuna,* a compassionate attitude toward others. So joining shamatha and vipashyana brings about the realization of bodhichitta. When concentration and awareness are working together, for a fraction of a second you may have a taste of what enlightenment might be.

Such a glimpse is highly possible, even by suggestion. You might find yourself with no discursive thoughts. When you discover that your unwholesome discursive thoughts have been pacified and subjugated, there might be a gap. A pure gap of the absolute, ideal state of mind might occur to you. This is not hypothetical, but real. When discursive thoughts are liberated, you may try to cover up that gap, disguising it as absentmindedness. But you may be unable to cover it up, which is lucky, for you are having an actual glimpse of bodhichitta. For everyone, without exception, such a glimpse is always possible. And at some point, you realize that it is more than a glimpse, more than a possibility. You realize that bodhichitta is not a theory or a metaphysical concept, but a reality. It is more than rain clouds gathering in the sky—it is the actual rain.

APPRECIATION AND HUMOR

One of the basic principles of mahayana is learning to include others in your world. That process begins with the realization of complete bodhichitta. You do not have to attend to or cultivate the awakened state of being as something new in your system. You realize that you already possess that awakened state of freshness. Anything that you can appreciate and enjoy in your life, such as seeing a beautiful flower, experiencing exquisite situations, or hearing beautiful language, teachings, or music, comes out of that awakened state.

One problem we have had for a long time is that we do not appreciate ourselves fully. We don't appreciate that we are capable of seeing, hearing, and experiencing. We think that if we buy something expensive, it will do the trick. But when we do buy something, we get tired of it very soon, and in a lot of cases it leads to disappointment. We may have managed to acquire everything we can think of to experience the world at its best, but we still cannot experience things completely and fully.

The notion of bodhichitta is that we have the faculties to experience the world at its best. We can see things beautifully, we can hear things beautifully, we can experience things beautifully. The only requirement is that we let go of all our struggling and searching, all of our shopping, so to speak. When we do so, we might be left feeling as if we have given something up. But as we relax further, more and more, we realize that our appreciation is growing. It becomes a natural experience to have an appreciation of the beauty of things as they are.

The main obstacle to bodhichitta is aggression. Aggression may come from too much learning, too much success in life. You might be a fantastic calligrapher, you might be a fantastic driver, or you might be highly skilled in changing flat tires, for that matter. You might have your skill worked out, everything is fine, and you know what you are doing. The aggression is not in having such skills, but in your attitude of self-confirmation. But all those confirmations go down the drain at this point.

Bodhisattva heroism is an entirely different type of heroism. It has nothing to do with how highly sophisticated you are. Even if you are sophisticated, you still are not making yourself into a potential bodhisattva. What is the obstacle? The obstacle is aggression. Aggression is precisely what made Buddha's cousin Devadatta unfit to be his student. Devadatta was too proud, and according to the story, he finally fell down into a crack in the earth.* Bodhichitta is absolute nonaggression, the epitome of nonaggression. It is peace without reward, and openness without feedback. You are simply open. The quality of gentleness and peace in the bodhisattva's approach is absolutely devastating.

Compassion or warmth actually possesses a lot of humor. Prajna also possesses a lot of subtle jokes, such as that the world is curving in and it is just about to get to square one—and square one is looking at itself as well, which is not the end of the world. The reason bodhisattvas can actually work so hard to relate with reality is because of that quality of delightfulness and humor. There is a willingness to be an adolescent rather than a grown-up. A sense of humor runs through all three yanas completely. It does not happen much in the first yana, but in the second and third yanas, you are definitely willing to be an adolescent rather than a completely hard-core, business-deal type of person. You are willing to be childlike.

Bodhichitta is not much of a fanfare, but at the same time, it may be a spiritual atomic bomb. In order to become real Buddhists, it is necessary to give up the past. You could say that the past has been good and successful, but that particular past needs some kind of cleaning. Why don't you put your past into a steam bath or a washing machine? Your past could be cleaned up, and come out as good as the present. That is what you do with your clothes: your clothes are worn in the past, you put them in the wash-

---

* *Devadatta* was the Buddha's jealous cousin, who is said to have caused a schism in the *sangha,* or spiritual community, through his arrogance.

ing machine, and they come out clean in the present, so they are wearable in the future. That's a great idea.

Bodhichitta has to be discovered and realized, and the way to do so is by appreciating both the phenomenal world and yourself. In the mahayana, there is an emphasis on working with what you have rather than what you will be. You become more and more softened, rather than being a hard-core meditator or a hard-core scholar. Hard-core practitioners believe that what they think is right, and they are not open to any information or experience other than their own. That tendency toward dogmatism, no matter how small it may be, is an obstacle to developing bodhichitta.

The mahayana brings greater vision and greater action. Heroism, celebration, and excitement are all solidly a part of it. You begin to like the world around you. You are aware of the activities and phenomena happening during your meditation and postmeditation experience, and you develop an appreciation for the phenomenal world. You begin to like your environment and, as egoless as you may be, you begin to like yourself. The appreciation of the world outside is called compassion, and the appreciation of yourself is called maitri. Unless those two are working together, it is a dead end.

DEVELOPING FEARLESSNESS

The greater vision of the mahayana brings tremendous exertion and patience. You are not particularly afraid of the pain of samsara, or tired of being in samsara. You are not planning to run away from it, but you are willing to sacrifice yourself. You are willing to develop yourself and stay in samsara for the sake of others as long as you are needed. Therefore, you are fearless in developing your own strength and asceticism, or hard work. That kind of patience and exertion is a mark of waking up.

On the whole, the approach of mahayana is one of not taking time off or looking for relief. You are not looking for a way to take a break, or to comfort yourself by running away from the challenge. You just stay put; you are on the spot. You stay with the pain or the discomfort, and you continue to carry on with exertion and the vision and joyousness of wakefulness.

The starting point is that you do not regard your life as boring, nor do you try to escape from your life by any means whatsoever. You do not run after entertainment or substitutions of any kind. You are honest and direct, and you face the facts of life, not only for your own sake, but for the sake of others. You would never let anybody down, or let go of anybody in order to seek pleasure for your own sake. That is what is known as being a fearless bodhisattva warrior.

As a bodhisattva warrior, you are fearless because you hold to certain principles. You may be terrified of getting stuck in samsara forever, but at this point you have to be willing to stay there. Fearlessness means that you are willing to get stuck, which is marvelous. And strangely, if you are willing to get stuck, you never do get stuck. That is the logic. But to begin with, you have to recognize your own cowardice. You do not have to condemn yourself for being cowardly, but when you see how cowardly you are and how fears come up in your mind, you will begin to realize that fear is your working basis. So you stay with it, and you keep working with it.

Opening to Messages

The point is simply that you just keep going. Once you keep going, there will be messages coming to you from the universe about how far you are or are not going. You don't need to talk to your teacher, particularly; the universe is always very good at giving you messages. Even the weather can give you messages. As long as you are open, you find reference points everywhere. Once you are willing to open yourself up, to work hard and do something, you will get feedback. You may get very bad feedback or very excellent feedback. If you do not react either badly or excitedly to that feedback, but just keep going, you are beginning to get somewhere.

Any confusion you experience has within it the essence of wisdom automatically. So as soon as you detect confusion, it is the beginning of some kind of message. At least you are able to see your confusion, which is very hard. Ordinarily people do not see their confusion at all, so by recognizing your confusion, you are already at quite an advanced level. So you shouldn't feel bad about that, you should feel good about it. You should not be terrified of your confusion, but you should look into it further. You should push into it instead of closing yourself off. In that way, you just keep opening and unfolding, like flowers in the summertime. Even though they are exposed to the weather, to the wind and rain, flowers still keep unfolding themselves, until finally they bloom at their best. You could be like the flowers: you could let the bees sit on you and take your honey away, and that would be fine.

You should not take time off from your confusion, or from the inconvenience or embarrassment of seeing that confusion. It is better not to stop, for you are about to see something. If you stop, you stop seeing, so you have to keep going. Obviously, what you see may not be the greatest thing, but it is not necessarily the most terrible, either. Whatever you see has its own openings and unfoldings. In any case, it will be a great contribution to your path. And gradually, stitch by stitch, step-by-step, you will finally become a good bodhisattva.

2

Love, Vision, and Warriorship

You are not poverty-stricken. In the mahayana, you have to expand yourself, to feel more expansive than you are. Bodhisattvas are known as warriors because they are visionary. They are not confused, and they do not shy away from others.

WHEN WE enter the mahayana, we should not disregard the general truth of hinayana as a reference point. We should have a foundation on which we can begin to build the building itself. We cannot look down on the hinayana as something optional, or something that you can either take or leave. The hinayana is like having a body, and the mahayana is like the outfit that goes with it. The hinayana requires a quality of mindfulness, which involves paying respect to your basic existence, and out of that arises awareness. So in entering the mahayana, the previous vehicle cannot be ignored or discarded, but at the same time there is an expansion of vision. The bigger vision of mahayana is a natural expansion of our path.

SKILLFUL MEANS AND KNOWLEDGE

The ultimate meaning of mahayana is that it is the great vehicle that brings out one's bodhi mind, or bodhichitta. In the application of bodhi mind, skillful means and prajna are combined. Skillful means are naturally accomplished by allowing yourself to relate with life in general without strategy or speed, and prajna is based on developing tremendous intelligence and an intuitive, awakened state of mind.

Bodhi mind is wakefulness. It is not just like waking up from sleep, but it is total openness. You are so awake that you cannot find out who is waking up. When you put wakefulness together with mind, it means that the consciousness is thoroughly and properly trained. That is the definition of enlightenment, in a sense. You are thoroughly accomplishing the awakened mind and the two components of skillful means and prajna.

PASSIONLESSNESS

Out of bodhi mind and the development of skillful means and prajna arises passionlessness, not in the sense of frigidity, but in the sense of not trying to possess anything. In Tibetan, passionlessness is *chakpa mepa*. *Chakpa* means "desire," "wanting," or "lust," and *mepa* means "without," or "not"; so *chakpa mepa* is "without passion," or "passionlessness."

Passionlessness is necessary in order to develop loving-kindness and compassion. If you have passion, you cannot develop loving-kindness toward yourself and compassion toward others; you have to be completely passionless to work with others.

The passionate state of being is an obstacle because you always want to grasp onto either yourself or others. When you are in a passionate state of mind, you cannot afford to allow space to develop between yourself and others. But when passionlessness takes place, you begin to create a lot of space. You can afford to have loving-kindness for yourself, and you can also afford to be compassionate to others, because there is lots of room.

The idea is that passion should be transmuted into compassion for yourself and others. This is possible because passion without reference point, goal orientation, or aggression *is* compassion. When passion is transmuted into compassion, you do not abandon your existence, but you are able to be gentle and nice. Since you are not substituting such behavior for your actual self, you do not feel particularly lost or deprived of your capabilities. Beyond that, you can expand to others as well. So you are full, but at the same time, you are empty.

Passionlessness is what enables you to practice the dharma and to quiet your body, speech, and mind. It is related to the development of fearlessness and egolessness. The reason egolessness is necessary is that the idea of self-existence, or ego, creates tremendous self-hatred, which automatically projects out to others. In contrast, when there is kindness to oneself and others, this automatically creates a quality of workability. It creates immense space or emptiness.

THE INTERPLAY OF EGOLESSNESS AND COMPASSION

The mahayana is based on friendliness and compassion. Such compassion is not goal oriented and it is not based on striving. You are not looking for feedback or confirmation. Compassion is without reference point.

In order for friendliness and compassion to take place, we work with the notion that others are more important than ourselves. We begin to realize the notion of egolessness. Accordingly, we begin to manifest generosity, discipline, patience, exertion, meditation, and prajna (knowledge).* With egolessness, there is both space and a great sense of celebration. Because of that, we can be kind to others. Our original problem is that "I" exists; therefore, "am" exists; and therefore, there is no room to help anybody else. But if we have no "I" and no "am," there is room to help others constantly. So egolessness is the basis of compassion.

Compassion occurs because there is room to help others, not because you have been made to feel guilty. Compassion is not based on guilt, but on having mahayana vision. Because you have mahayana vision, you can afford to be compassionate. Even if you become completely steeped in vajrayana practices, you should always reflect on mahayana vision. Otherwise, you will find yourself becoming completely ego-centered, without compassionate action of any kind. The point of dharma is not to produce egomaniacs, but good people.

The connection between compassion and egolessness goes both ways. When we let go of the self, we are more inspired to work with others; and when we are generous to others, we realize that the self is lost. We begin to lose our ego fixation. So when we are generous to *that*, we begin to lose *this*; and when we have lost *this*, we become more capable of dealing with *that*. At that point, the shedding of ego is a mutual situation.

---

* A reference to the six *paramitas*, or transcendent virtues of the bodhisattva path. The paramitas are discussed in detail in part 6, "Bodhisattva Activity."

TWO ASPECTS OF LOVE

The soft heart of mahayana can only develop by paying attention to your existence and your state of being by means of shamatha and vipashyana. Mahayana experience evolves from being in a state of tranquillity as well as by gentleness to yourself and others, and the only way to develop that is by being fully aware and mindful. So the state of compassion and love grows out of awareness. In the Buddhist tradition, we do not usually use the term *love*. Instead, we use the two terms *maitri* and *karuna*.

Maitri / Loving-Kindness

The primary glimpse of experience that is closest to love is maitri, or loving-kindness. In Tibetan it is *champa*. *Cham* means "tender," or "gentle" and *pa* makes it a noun; so *champa* is "tenderness" or "loving-kindness"; it is being kind and gentle to oneself. Maitri arises as the result of shamatha discipline. When we begin to be very precise with ourselves, we experience wakefulness and gentleness.

At the hinayana level, your attitude toward discipline is very acute and precise, but at the bodhisattva level, you begin to relax. That relaxation is a form of maitri, or loving-kindness. When you are free from ego fixation altogether, you gain some kind of relief. You realize that you don't have to be all that intense and tight. When you let go of ego fixation, you develop freedom and relaxation, and as an automatic response to that freedom and relaxation, you develop gentleness and compassion.

With maitri you are actually trying to confront the ego directly, to insult the ego. That may seem aggressive, but it is always good for you to insult your ego. Maitri is known as the source of all dharmas, because maitri is the basis of losing the ego. By losing the ego, you automatically give birth to kindness toward yourself and gentleness toward others. It is important to understand that by losing the ego you are becoming benevolent. You realize that caring for others is intrinsic. Once you have removed the fixation on "me" and "my-ness," behind that fixation you discover a general and natural kindness toward others. It is like removing the skin and flesh from the body and discovering the bones and the marrow. With maitri, it is possible for even ordinary people to appreciate enlightenment.

Because of maitri, you can begin to awaken your buddha nature. You can awaken your ability to be in love. Everybody is capable of falling in love; everybody is capable of being kind to others. Everybody who has an ego can reverse their ego fixation and rediscover their buddha nature. You may not achieve complete liberation right away, but you can begin the occasional back-and-forth journey from confusion to freedom. Anybody can make that journey; anybody can have a taste of freedom. That is always possible. If you want it, it can be done. It doesn't mean that you are going to become a living buddha on the spot, but you could still experience a taste of enlightenment. That taste of enlightenment makes you nostalgic; it makes you want to go further and to practice more. The Black Crown Ceremony is an example of such a taste of enlightenment.* It gives you a taste of how to be open and to experience oneness. In this ceremony, you are in a gigantic hall with the Karmapa, the head of the Kagyü lineage, and you just dissolve. When you identify with that experience, enlightenment ceases to be a fairy tale, and begins to become real.

Maitri is based on being gentle with yourself, and at the same time respecting yourself. Often people suffer from depression and other psychosomatic problems because they are unable to respect themselves. They kill themselves because they hate themselves. The idea of maitri is to have sympathy and a gentle attitude toward yourself, to feel that your own existence is worthwhile. You are a would-be buddha, and you have the inheritance of buddha nature already, so you don't need to feel poverty-stricken.

With maitri you begin to experience a quality of delight. You feel that you are worthwhile and delightful in spite of your little thingies. You begin to feel that you can stick your neck out. Your attitude toward yourself begins to lift like a cloud, and you feel as if you have been freed

---

* In the *Black Crown Ceremony,* the Karmapa, as the official head of the Kagyü lineage, holds a black crown on his head. This ceremonial crown is a replica of the one given by the Chinese emperor Yung-lo (1360–1424) to the fifth Karmapa (1384–1415). The original crown was said to have been made from the hairs of *dakinis* (female deities who protect the teachings) after Yung-lo had a vision of the crown on the fifth Karmapa's head. As the Karmapa holds the crown on his head, he slowly recites the mantra of Avalokiteshvara, the bodhisattva of compassion. It is said that during those few minutes, he brings to earth the transcendent form of Avalokiteshvara and radiates the bodhisattva's pure egoless compassion.

from twofold ego completely.* You begin to have fewer hang-ups and less aggression. This experience is not earthshaking, it is just a little shift whereby you begin to feel that you are capable and that you have no reason to hide in your depression. At that point, you are ripe and ready to take the bodhisattva vow and formally enter the mahayana path.

Karuna / Compassion

The second aspect of love is karuna, or compassion. In Tibetan it is *nying-je*. *Nying* means "heart," and *je* means "noble"; so *nying-je* means "noble heart." Nying-je is connected with dealing with others. Because we feel gentleness to ourselves, we are able to feel compassionate to others. We begin to experience vipashyana, to be aware of our environment. We see that our friends, relatives, and the people around us are suffering, and they need help. We see that our building is beginning to have cracks in its walls and leaks in its plumbing, and we have to fix it. So we first learn how to love ourselves with the help of shamatha discipline, and from that we begin to develop vipashyana, so that our attention is not stolen by distractions or surprises. Therefore, we begin to develop good compassion.

Traditionally, maitri is connected with the desire to join the path of the bodhisattva, and karuna is connected with actually going along the path. Maitri is the way to overcome aggression; it is the mentality of egolessness. Karuna liberates us from ignorance so that we know how to conduct our affairs, and know how to relate with the world at large. So first we tame ourselves, and after that we develop bodhichitta. But we have a long way to go. Until we have maitri and karuna, loving-kindness and compassion, it is not possible to experience bodhichitta. Therefore, we need to work with shamatha and vipashyana. So hinayana discipline is the preparation for realizing mahayana vision. Without that preparation, we cannot experience what mahayana is all about.

THE UTTERLY VISIONARY QUALITY OF LOVE

According to the mahayana, love is entirely without aggression. Love includes accepting others and being noble, reasonable, openhearted,

---

* Twofold ego includes both the fixation on self and the fixation on phenomena as solid, independent, and real.

Calligraphy by Chögyam Trungpa Rinpoche.
Ocean turbulent with innumerable waves of emptiness.
"The source of energy which need not be sought is there; it is that you are rich rather than being
enriched by something else. Because there is basic warmth as well as basic space, the Buddha
activity of compassion is alive and so all communication is creative."

resourceful, and free of possessiveness. With love, you are totally gentle, utterly kind, thorough, wise, fearless, and willing to commit yourself to any situation. You are warriorlike, industrious, tireless, and never take time off for yourself. When you need to give your help to others, you are always willing to do so. I think that covers the Buddhist version of the word *love*. Love is very noble, elegant, beautiful, resourceful, and utterly visionary. It is the starting point or foundation of the mahayana.

Being utterly visionary has a touch of humor and a lot of fearlessness. You are willing to jump in, and you are entirely free from panic. You are resourceful and willing to get into any projects that might arise. You have long-lasting vision and effort. Moreover, you are selfless, so you are willing to do whatever is needed in a situation. You enjoy what you are doing, but not just because things are entertaining for you or because you are on a big ego trip.

Mahayana vision is straightforward and honest. It contains and needs a lot of fortitude. The idea of mahayana vision is that you are not trapped in any small, localized, or selfish situations. You are not poverty-stricken. In the mahayana, you have to expand yourself, to feel more expansive than you are. Bodhisattvas are known as warriors because they are visionary. They are not confused, and they do not shy away from others.

3

Doubt and Delight

The birth of mahayana spirit begins with a combination of distrust and the possibility of good news. It is a very powerful emotional experience, a sweet-sour feeling. That quality of joy and delight is wisdom, or jnana, and the doubt or distrust is compassion. Doubt and compassion are both very direct. . . . There is a sense of something touching your heart, and it is painful.

POSITIVE GROUND

In the hinayana we are working with ourselves to achieve goodness, based on the practices of mindfulness and awareness. We are aware of the suffering that exists within us, and we are trying to overcome that suffering by means of individual salvation and a real understanding of truth and of peace. The hinayana notion of peace is based on the cessation of grasping or holding on to the phenomenal world through our sense consciousnesses. It is based on renunciation. We are actually paying attention to every detail in our lives: how we hold our pen, how we pour our cup of tea. Everything is scrutinized down to the very basis of our lives, and we find that every situation brings pain. So we try to overcome that pain, which started from ignorance, uncertainty, and bewilderment.

We cannot develop bigger vision, mahayana vision, with the sloppiness of our basic confusion. It is necessary for our sloppiness to be cut through by hinayana discipline. We need to take a clean-cut approach at the beginning in order to sweep out any unnecessary garbage or attachment and bring out our potential. When we begin to get into meditation practice, we uncover both garbage and inspiration, but the level of garbage is greater than the inspiration. We see that we carry gigantic loads of garbage on our backs constantly. But step-by-step, we learn how to wash ourselves and clean up.

Hinayanists would say that you could become good. They say that you are neither good nor bad, but you have possibilities of both. Mahayanists would say that you are intrinsically good already, and any obstacles and problems are temporary. The hinayana approach is the good-student approach, and the mahayana approach is that of the good warrior. According to hinayanists, Buddha was an ordinary man, and he achieved ordinary enlightenment. They think that because the Buddha got a splinter in his foot, this showed he was still an ordinary human being who had to die as an ordinary human being as well. They saw the Buddha as a fellow elder, as a good person rather than heroic. But according to the mahayana, the Buddha is the Victorious One. He actually conquered confusion and became a king.

The hinayana is based on repetitive practice. But each time you practice, you connect in a new way to what you are doing. For instance, even though you have spent ten years with the person you love, each time you kiss it is slightly different, and at the same time it is very ordinary. In hinayana monasticism, in particular, there is practice taking place all the time, so the everyday situation is great. That constant repetitive practice makes hinayana monasticism fantastic.

DELIGHTFUL DOUBT

The precision of shamatha and the greater awareness of vipashyana provide the practitioner with a sense of positive ground. The development of both peace and greater awareness produces the possibility of something else, a delightful doubt that you may have the buddha seed in you. You may have been approaching practice impersonally, but something personal may be involved after all. There is a hint of buddha nature, which can only be brought about by accomplishing shamatha-vipashyana practice.

Seeing such a possibility within you is a pleasant surprise. This discovery is not only possible at advanced levels of the path, but it could develop early on, at the beginning of the path. Mahayana practitioners have advance warnings of such pleasant surprises and the possibility of having buddha nature. Not only could arhats, bodhisattvas, and higher beings have that kind of hint, but ordinary laypeople could as well. The discovery of buddha nature is the result of constant meditation practice, extreme diligence, faith, energy, and so forth.

When you begin to sit and discipline yourself a great deal, there is a gradual awakening in spite of any neurosis that comes up. In other words, we could quite safely say that out of hopelessness, greater hope begins to arise. That is the promise of the mahayana path. The discovery of buddha nature is not regarded as a myth and it is not based purely on blind faith, but it could become very real. Discovering this and working with it means you are relating with nonduality. The possibility of a split reality no longer exists, and the factory of karma-making is no longer useful. The past still means a great deal to you. You cannot forget your past with its emotional hang-ups and memories, but you are approaching things in an entirely different way.

When you have completely accomplished the shamatha-vipashyana practice, you have a sense of reward. You experience joy in the possibility of buddha nature, but you may still feel skeptical. Although you begin to feel that buddha nature is a possibility, you think the whole thing may be a hoax. You begin to doubt the teachings. The idea that you already have a built-in buddha in you is something that you cannot quite imagine. It seems to be too good to be true, and you begin to feel that maybe it is not true. You think that the whole thing may be a big put-on, a big joke, a lie.

The birth of mahayana spirit begins with a combination of distrust and the possibility of good news. It is a very powerful emotional experience, a sweet-sour feeling. That quality of joy and delight is wisdom, or *jnana,** and the doubt or distrust is compassion. Doubt and compassion are both very direct. Compassion is somewhat more spacious, but the pain of doubt and compassion is the same. There is a sense of something touching your heart, and it is painful.

---

* Chögyam Trungpa usually referred to prajna as "knowledge," or "transcendent knowledge," and to the related term *jnana* as "wisdom." Prajna, the sixth paramita or transcendent action of the mahayana, is *sherap* in Tibetan. *She* is "knowing," or "knowledge," *rap* is "superior," or the "best"; so *sherap* means "superior knowledge." In Tibetan, *jnana* is translated as *yeshe,* or "primordial knowing." However, at times Trungpa Rinpoche used the term *wisdom* to refer to prajna, particularly in the context of indivisible *upaya* and prajna, or skillful means and wisdom, a key teaching of the mahayana path.

At this point, you have the possibility of wisdom and compassion, but they are not completely finalized. It is like a fetus whose limbs are not quite formed. It is as though you are pregnant with buddha nature: you realize that something is happening even before the baby begins to kick. However, this pregnancy is different from ordinary pregnancy. Unlike a fetus, buddha nature is not a foreign body, it is a part of your whole being. You cannot have an abortion because it is too powerful to get rid of. You have to accept the whole thing.

The eighth-century Indian Buddhist scholar Shantideva said that an ordinary person's attitude is like a dead tree, and a bodhisattva's attitude is like a growing tree.* A bodhisattva's commitment, merit, and development continuously advance, even while you are unconscious or while you are asleep or eating. While you are doing ordinary daily work, the inspiration of the bodhisattva continues to grow in you.

As your practice becomes more strenuous, and you become more and more industrious, you would like to identify yourself with this particular inspiration and doubt. In doing so, the doubt tends to become less hostile and more soft, and the joy less intoxicating. As the joy becomes less intoxicating and more solid, you feel more rooted. It is like a mother who at first feels that pregnancy is a joyful thing, but further along sees that the pregnancy is a responsibility. She begins to approach it in a very business-like way by going to the doctor, taking the right vitamins, or what have you. So joy begins to transform itself into acceptance and solidity, and doubt begins to become more like a playful complaint.

At this point, the birth of buddha nature is still at a very elementary level, and your experiences of it are temporary. Flashes of buddha nature happen, but then more ordinary things happen as well. But over time those flashes become much more predominant. The only way to acknowledge your buddha nature as a reality is to commit yourself to the path of the bodhisattva. You need to think back and identify yourself with the buddhas and bodhisattvas of the past, who also experienced it. You cannot complain too much, because you begin to realize that you belong to the same family, the family of the Buddha. You have inherited the genes of the Buddha, so you have no choice.

---

* Shantideva, *The Way of the Bodhisattva*, translated by the Padmakara Translation Group (Boston: Shambhala Publications, 1997).

INTRINSIC ENLIGHTENMENT

At the mahayana level, our garbage has already been somewhat cleaned up as a result of hinayana discipline, so we begin to feel a quality of space. We no longer have to struggle with our garbage, so we can sit back and breathe. There is a sense of relief. It is like abandoning a big load, then sitting down and saying "Whew!" That relief comes with a reason. We have something up our sleeve, something else in store, a quality known as *tathagatagarbha,* or buddha nature. It is because we have that intrinsic basic nature that we have the intelligence and guts to say "Whew!"

In the hinayana path of individual salvation, we are transcending both harming others and the basis of that harm, which is aggression. At the bodhisattva level, we not only transcend harm and causing harm to others, but we begin to create situations where we can be helpful. In our attempts to be helpful, one outstanding and harmful problem that comes up is imposing our views on others. That is what we are trying to cut in the mahayana approach to reality. The reason we impose our own values on the world is because we actually do not care all that much for others. In fact, we really do not care for others at all. We may speak in the name of caring for others and find ourselves in helpful positions such as being a teacher or volunteer, but what we really want is a confirmation of our own existence. When we help someone, it is for our own success and glory alone.

That attitude has become a big stumbling block. You are taught that you are supposed to develop your talents in order to be useful in society, but if you do so purely to build up your own individual ego, that causes problems. In such an atmosphere, it is impossible to experience bodhichitta. The ability to be helpful to others and at the same time to yourself requires a real and genuine journey. It is not simply like getting a credential, or a PhD, and it is not based on wanting to build yourself up or keep others down. Instead, there is a genuine desire to say or do something for your own development as well as for others' benefit. When you have that attitude, you are a potential bodhisattva. You are inspired by the concept of the bodhisattva, a person who is brave in the search for bodhi, or awakening. Along with that potentiality, you have an element that already exists within you completely in your own mind: you possess tathagatagarbha.

Buddha nature means that we each have intrinsic enlightenment, which reacts to the chaos of samsara and aspires to wakefulness. Buddha nature is like a gene, a mind gene or psychological gene. It is like a gene in that the essence of existence can be transmitted from one generation of your physical body to the next. You transmit that gene from one life to the next, rather than from father to son, or mother to daughter. So consciousness goes on continuously, although it is also discontinuous. You have a kind of flow taking place from one body to the next, like electricity that is transmitted from one thing to another, but is at the same time different and separate. It is a psychological process of mind, which is very delicate and insubstantial, and at the same time it is substantial because it is so fickle.

Buddha nature exists constantly. It is your intrinsic essence. You are who you are, and nothing can prevent that. But it could be exaggerated; you could evolve further. The difference between buddha nature and the hinayana idea of enlightenment is that in the hinayana tradition, the emphasis is on developing enlightenment by working toward it with exercises of all kinds. It is like saying that if you do more gymnastic exercises, you might make it to the Olympics. In the mahayana we say that Olympics-ness exists in you already. The hinayana idea that enlightenment is something that you can achieve through training is somewhat removed from the mahayana idea that it is an instinct that already exists in you. According to mahayana, what you are has further potential, but you still are what you are. Rather than becoming a better person, you are what you are. However, you may have never had the chance to experience or work with what you are—and what you are is true wakefulness.

THE NATURE OF THE BODHISATTVA PATH

At the mahayana level, you are inspired to help others, based on the idea that you are less important than they are. It is an obstacle to becoming a mahayanist if you do not have enough sympathy for others and for yourself. According to ordinary logic, you cannot develop the motivation to help others unless you yourself feel good, so you always need some kind of rehearsal. But in this case, no rehearsal is necessary. So the bodhisattva's approach is entirely different because it is based on warmth, and when there is warmth and compassion, territories do not exist.

In the bodhisattva's warmth and friendliness, there is no need for reference point or feedback, because it is beginning to take place within the greater vision of shunyata, or emptiness. It has been said that emptiness cannot exist without compassion, and compassion cannot exist without emptiness—they work together. In contrast, in ordinary neurotic friendliness, there is still a need for feedback. There is no heroism or celebration. It's more like putting on a Band-Aid when you have cut yourself, which has a slight air of patheticness.

The basic attitude of a bodhisattva is to be willing to admit your problems, to be willing to be a fool. A bodhisattva wouldn't say, "I did silly things yesterday, but it was purely because I got drunk. I apologize for what I did, but today is a different world, and everything is okay. So let's forget it." It is the mentality of a real person rather than a fake. There is room for other people to look at you, sneer at you, laugh at you, and work with you. Something is left showing. You are not so completely guarded that nobody can do anything with you. You go through the experience and discipline of the bodhisattva path by yourself, but it is largely based on cooperation.

Becoming a bodhisattva means you automatically become a potential helper or teacher, and people would like to work with somebody who is understanding. You are willing to cooperate with the phenomenal world instead of making enemies with everything. You are not constantly blaming your environment, but you are willing to work with the world. If you have a flat tire, you don't just call a cab, but you are willing to get down and change the tire. And if someone wants to help you, you don't say, "Go away. Don't insult me," but you bring them in. You are willing to say, "Please come and help, I've got a flat tire." Sharing a problem with somebody becomes a promise of enlightenment. You are actually willing to work with people, willing to open, willing to bend a little bit if necessary.

The mahayana path is extremely broad and vast. As a practitioner of mahayana Buddhism, you are asked hundreds of questions, and you are expected to do all sorts of things. While you are being a boat, you might be asked to be a bridge. While you are being a bridge or a boat, you might be asked to be a highway. While you are being all of them, you might be asked to be a reservoir. You are asked to be all sorts of things, and ideally you are ready to accommodate them all.

CONFUSING EGO'S LOGIC

The virtue of the hinayana is its immense dedication. Whether you are slightly goal oriented or not, there is still a quality of dedication that continues all the time. That dedication, simplicity, and directness are the virtues of the lower yanas.* But that goal orientation still speaks the language of ego, which might become a problem. Because of that, people begin to step toward the mahayana path. The reason mahayana is regarded as a greater vehicle is because of its larger thinking, its greater vision. Greater vision means not having any goal. That greater vision of not having any goal and just doing the discipline for its own sake rather than because of any promises that arise is very important.

Doing something for its own sake tends to confuse the regular logic of ego. You begin to get very confused and wonder, "If I'm doing this for nothing, what on earth am I doing it for? Why do I have to be nice to somebody or open myself if I don't feel like it? Why should I sit or develop bodhichitta? What is the logic behind it?" Naturally, a lot of complaints come up, but that is not regarded as regressing from your original intention. It is regarded as the process of ego beginning to get confused and unhappy because something does not go along with its regular logic of tit for tat. Ego's logic is that whatever you spend, you should get your money's worth. You can blame that logic for the feeling of antagonism you have when you feel you are being cheated or used. But the obvious question in this case is, "Used by whom?"

Ego's logic somehow does not work. Usually our feelings of being exploited and other complaints of that nature are merely the squealing of ego and nothing more. All kinds of problems of that nature come along, and from the bodhisattva's point of view, this is regarded as great news. Finally, we are getting to it! Finally, we are cracking down the old-fashioned fortification of ego's castle. It is beginning to be fundamentally shaken. It is like a people's revolt against the monarchy: when the subjects of a particular king cease to pay taxes, the king's own financial situation

---

* The *lower yanas* refer to the two yanas of the hinayana path: the *shravakayana*, or the path of hearers, and the *pratyekabuddhayana*, or the path of solitary realizers. For more on these yanas, see volume I of the *Profound Treasury*, chapter 61, "Shravakayana: The Yana of Hearing and Proclaiming," and chapter 62, "Pratyekabuddhayana: The Yana of Individual Salvation."

becomes shaky. It is possible that he will be unable to live in as rich and wealthy a manner as he would like. So finally the king, or the ego, begins to be shaken by this revolt. In this analogy, the fact that the subjects are boycotting the possibility of further entrapment because they have been conned in the past has quite a lot to do with egolessness. Egolessness comes from non–goal orientation. Transcending goal orientation brings not only the egolessness of individuality alone, but the egolessness of dharmas as well.* So egolessness becomes very well-grounded and much more realistic and definite.

Oddly, we find that a student of the bodhisattva discipline who has transcended goal orientation can nevertheless speedily attain enlightenment. In fact, this happens much faster than it does for goal-oriented people, who are trying too hard. Students of the bodhisattva discipline have given up the possibility of getting anything for themselves; therefore, they get a lot. That is a kind of joke. It is supposed to be just a footnote, rather than being presented in the mainstream of textbooks, but I think it is worth mentioning. The interesting point is that the actual reason we are prevented from attaining enlightenment right now, at this very minute, is because we want to attain it. Once that situation is changed, once it is completely switched around, we have no further obstacles to go through. We have no obstacles other than that.

---

* Egolessness is said to be twofold: the *egolessness of individuality,* or self, and the *egolessness of dharmas,* or phenomena.

Part Two

BUDDHA NATURE

4

Enlightened Genes

Fundamental enlightened mind or essence exists in us all the time. It is there right at the beginning, although there is no beginning. Before any kind of perception occurs, wakefulness is already there—beyond concept, beyond limitation, beyond anything measurable. We can all awaken—that is the hope and the potential.

BUDDHA NATURE AND BODHICHITTA

According to the mahayana, we are basically wretched, soaked in our own egotism, neurosis, and confusion, but at the same time we possess what is known as tathagatagarbha, or buddha nature. *Tathagata* means "one who has gone beyond." It refers to the buddhas of the past, present, and future, who have all gone beyond fixation. *Garbha* means "womb"; so *tathagatagarbha* means the "womb or essence of one who has gone beyond," or "buddha nature." Just as milk has the possibility of producing butter, as human beings we have the possibility of producing enlightenment in ourselves. That basic fact or possibility was discovered by the Buddha, and it has been actualized and promulgated throughout the twenty-six hundred years of his reign. So at this point we know that all sentient beings possess buddha nature.

Bodhichitta is a natural state of being awake, tender, and genuine. You feel that you are capable of opening yourself up to others, and you can express tenderness and affection to others and to yourself. Traditionally, it is said that even the most vicious animals are capable of expressing affection to their young. So tenderness is not a foreign thing; it is definitely inherent. You might say that the whole world hates you, but that is not

31

true. You might say that you are not capable of falling in love or being tender, but that is also not true. If you were not capable of such a thing, you would soon perish.

Tenderness is what keeps you functioning throughout your whole life. Tenderness makes you a genuine and lovable person. Tenderness is magnetic; it causes the softening up of your environment altogether. Tenderness brings about wakefulness in yourself and others. It is what inspires you to comb your hair and wear clothes. We often forget such simple logic, but because of tenderness, you are capable of talking to others and working with them. You are capable of opening and closing a door, or taking a walk in the fresh air. You are capable of smiling. Those are all aspects of tenderness or bodhichitta.

Bodhichitta means the "heart of awakened mind," but buddha nature is more than the heart. It means that your whole makeup, your whole nature, is based on buddhahood. The idea of buddha nature has been condemned by some as a distortion of Buddhist philosophy because it could be regarded as a form of ego, but I don't think that particular charge makes sense. We could say very simply that bodhichitta is like a heart transplant: it is as if a new heart is being transplanted into you, something better than you had before. But you already have buddha nature, which is more important. It is your essence, which goes beyond your heart alone.

In another analogy, the difference between bodhichitta and buddha nature is described as approaching a cloud from the city's point of view, or from the sun's point of view. People in the city would say that the sun is behind the cloud, and the sun would say that the city is behind the cloud. That difference of perspective is an interesting and important point. When city people see the sun disappear behind a cloud, they need reassurance that the sun is not going to go away forever. They need to know that it is not going to go from being more and more clouded over to finally becoming completely nonexistent. That is the basic point of transplanting bodhichitta: it reassures people that the sun is always there, even if it is behind a cloud. The concept of buddha nature is the sun's point of view, as the sun unveils itself to the city one cloud after another. So bodhichitta and buddha nature work together.

The mahayana symbol of indestructibility is a tablet, and in the vajrayana, the symbol of indestructibility is a *vajra,* or scepter. That tablet is buddha nature, which consists of both prajna and karuna. It is like the monolith in the film *2001: A Space Odyssey.* That symbol of the monolith was somebody's brilliant coincidence. Very mysteriously, in that film somebody clicked into possibilities of human nature that cannot be captured, but are manifested even from the ape level. That monolith is precisely the notion of bodhichitta or tathagatagarbha. It is the soft spot, whose meaning is monolithic. So a basic monumental experience occurs, which is yours, which is inside you. But when you try to lay your hand on that experience or to touch it, it does not happen. You cannot grasp it. Such an experience is unreachable; it goes and comes at the same time.

Bodhichitta, or buddha nature, is monumental and always there, like the tablet. It is indestructible wakefulness. Buddha nature is based on tenderness toward others. We all have some kind of tenderness toward others, otherwise this planet earth would have dried up a long time ago. People would be killing each other, or simply not caring for one other. However, this planet earth has been able to continue for many billions of years. The reason for that is quite magical: it is a result of buddha nature. Without any doubt, there is buddha nature everywhere.

On the whole, in spite of our nastiness and aggression, we still always project warmth and compassion toward others. You can argue otherwise and try to refute this fact. Nonetheless, if the world were all that aggressive and terrifying, if no one related with sympathy and love, we would not have anything at all. People do not create businesses or go to work just to survive or to make money alone. Let us give everybody a little bit more credit. It is time to respect the world. We cannot say that people do not have gentleness and sympathy in them. They might be quite shocked if we told them so, but it is the case that there is always a certain amount of individual warmth and tenderness taking place. That is why the teaching of the Buddha, or *buddhadharma,* is seeping into the world. It is because of its integrity and its egolessness.

The possibility of realizing buddha nature comes from mindfulness training. When you are eating, for instance, it comes from knowing how to hold your bowl, how to pick up your chopsticks, how to eat properly with good posture. By developing mindfulness of eating, you are actually doing yourself a favor. You no longer need to eat aggressively or just gobble everything up.*

---

* Trungpa Rinpoche placed great emphasis on mindful eating. In the 1980 Vajradhatu Seminary, Trungpa Rinpoche introduced his students to the practice of *oryoki,* a formal meal ritual he adapted from the Zen tradition. Since that time, oryoki has continued to be a component of seminaries and of group meditation retreats such as *dathüns* (one-month-long practice intensives). For more on oryoki and mindful eating, see appendix 2, "The Practice of Oryoki."

Sometimes you might flop, but even then you do not lose your buddha nature. It is always there. If you were a dog, would you lose your claws when you went to sleep? When you flop you don't lose your buddha nature, but you do lose your bodhichitta awareness. You lose your rays, but you do not lose your sun. Bodhichitta is in your heart always, but when you are sloppy you do not communicate with it. You find something else to entertain yourself with. But you can always step back and reconnect with your bodhichitta. You could take an upright posture and expand yourself, then you could conduct your business. Working with bodhichitta has to be a natural process; you cannot strategize it on the spot. It is a question of how much at home you feel in your world. If you make your world homey, then you have no problem. You find that everything is hospitable. Even if you went to a hectic place like the New York Stock Exchange, with all the frantic people running around, you could sit down and make a decision about your investment.

When you develop full mindfulness-awareness like the Buddha, you automatically become a king or queen. In fact, one epithet for the Buddha is *vijaya,* meaning the "Victorious One." The image of a king or queen with a scepter signifies that you are always going to work, from the beginning to the end, for the sake of sentient beings. Following the example of the Buddha, you are going to be a leader of the six realms.* On one hand, the Buddhist nontheistic approach is based on the notion of not having a ruler or a god to worship. On the other hand, the medieval symbolism of a monarch continues in the Buddhist tradition. That notion of becoming a king or queen might raise the problem of egotism, but holding on to your ego is the complete opposite of the Buddhist nontheistic tradition.

Basically speaking, the starting point of the mahayana is being capable of extending love and affection to yourself. You begin by being gentle to yourself and not punishing yourself. In the process of becoming gentle to yourself, you first need to have a good understanding of shamatha. Next you need to have good vipashyana and proper postmeditation experience. Finally you look at yourself and find that you are not as bad as you

---

* The samsaric world is said to comprise six realms of existence: the god realm, the jealous god realm, the human realm, the animal realm, the hungry ghost realm, and the hell realm. For more on the realms, see volume 1 of the *Profound Treasury,* chapter 9, "The Painful Reality of Samsara."

thought. In fact, you find that you are a quite delightful and worthwhile person. That is the three-step, how-to-like-yourself technique.

THE FORMING OF THE SAMSARIC WORLD

Buddha nature refers to a basic seed or inheritance we possess. It could be considered a form of enlightened genes. However, although we possess enlightened genes, we have never experienced perfect clarity. At the very beginning, when consciousness first began in our state of mind, it took a different form in us. As ordinary human beings, when we woke up, we woke into a nightmare, and experienced desires of all kinds. That is how the samsaric world was formed.

The beginning of the nightmare we call "samsara" is stupidity and the willingness to dwell in ignorance. From that, we start to spin samsara. We spin out the twelve *nidanas* and all the rest of it.* The original split took place already, and we continue to pile things up, one after another. Our stupidity and bewilderment become very comfortable and easy for us, so we keep piling up passion and aggression, this and that, all sorts of things. Then all these things begin to bounce around, and we begin to evolve in this world. We try to fight others or to seduce them. We dedicate our lives to warfare, hoping to perpetuate our existence by destroying others. That process is what is called samsara.

But the original split can be recovered. By tracing things back to the original split and beyond, you can actually experience who you are and what you are, right at the beginning—or who you are *not*. There is a quality of wakefulness that has no fixation and no sense of entity. It is egoless. We could call this genes of wakefulness, or genes of emptiness. Wakefulness is not a game or a technique. It is clear and spacious, very basic and ordinary, with no self-consciousness.

The Buddha grew up in the samsaric world, just like ourselves. He realized the nature of confusion and made his journey back, undoing his samsaric world until finally he reached square one. The Buddha followed the path all the way to the final achievement of enlightenment. The term *enlightened genes* could seem to imply that you merely have potential

---

* The *twelve nidanas* refers to the chain of interdependent origination that fuels the karmic patterning of samsaric existence. For more on the twelve nidanas and karmic conditioning, see volume 1 of the *Profound Treasury*, chapter 9, "The Painful Reality of Samsara."

buddhahood, rather than already having within you a fully realized buddha. But the teachers of our lineage say that buddha nature is like having a statue of Buddha in your heart, fully developed in all its faculties and possessing all the enlightened marks. Although, like the Buddha, you are treading on the path, you possess buddha nature even before you become a student.

Stained and Unstained Buddha Nature

There are two types of enlightened genes or buddha nature: stained or conditional buddha nature, and unstained or unconditional buddha nature.

Stained or Conditional Buddha Nature

In the first type, stained buddha nature, you are yearning toward wakefulness, so it is similar to relative bodhichitta. You yearn to develop gentleness, softness, and virtuousness. At this level, you simply are guessing that you will be good one day. You don't actually acknowledge that your existence is all that good—you just guess that you are good, guess that you are beautiful, guess that you have possibilities.

Stained tathagatagarbha is deliberately manufactured, like relative bodhichitta. If your grandmother told you that you should enter the mahayana and become a bodhisattva, you might become religious about bodhisattva-ism. But that would just be conceptualization or religiosity, not quite the true thing.

Stained or conditional buddha nature is called "conditional" because although even dogs, cats, and worms possess intrinsic buddha nature, that potentiality is covered over by samsaric veils. Conditional buddha nature is not discovered directly; it is discovered indirectly by uncovering these veils.

There are said to be five types of students, depending upon the thickness of their fog, veil, or blanket. These could be referred to as the five veils, or five types of genes: immediate, *pratyekabuddha*, distant, dubious, and very distant.* The first type of gene, immediate, refers to people who aspire to the mahayana, and who have a sense of compassion, openness,

---

* These five categories are often referred to as five families. Trungpa Rinpoche preferred the term *gene,* saying it had fewer connotations of individualism and a greater emphasis on intrinsic potential.

and celebration. The second type, pratyekabuddha, refers to people who strive for personal salvation and have been able to cut through their own egotism and attain the first level of egolessness.

The third type, distant, refers to *shravakas*. For shravakas, as for pratyekabuddhas, personal salvation is important, but the veil is much thicker.*

The fourth type, dubious, refers to people who are sometimes able to cut through their resistance and sometimes not. There is a quality of uncertainty and gullibility. You are questioning life, trying to find the meaning of life, to find truth, but it is uncertain whether you will be pulled off course or whether your understanding will be provoked. The fifth type is known as cutoff, or very distant. For such people, the possibility of realizing their buddha nature is cut off, but they are not completely cut off, just very distant. You may be preoccupied with your lifestyle or livelihood, or you may have never heard of the dharma. You have a long way to go to cut through the thick fog that exists between you and your realization.

In discussing the five veils, we are not evaluating buddha nature itself. Enlightened genes are pure, and capable of expressing their intrinsic nature. They are only considered to be conditional, to be good or bad, because of their covering, their particular neurosis or fog. So nobody is fundamentally condemned as completely bad. The point is that the thickness of the veil depends upon how much we try to trick the world and cover up our deception.

Unstained or Unconditional Buddha Nature

The second type of tathagatagarbha is unstained or spotless tathagatagarbha. It is like ultimate bodhichitta. At this level, your notion of awakened essence is not just as a potential, but as the fully grown existence of tathagatagarbha that is already in you. The difference between spotless and stained tathagatagarbha is that in the spotless approach, having seen that you have the potential of wakefulness, you do a double take. You think, "I have possibilities of being spotless. But wait a minute!

---

* In the nine-yana system of Tibetan Buddhism, the hinayana is divided into two aspects: the *shravakayana*, or path of the hearers, and the *pratyekabuddhayana*, or the path of the solitary realizers. This volume of the *Profound Treasury* is based on the third yana, or mahayana, and volume 3 is based on the six tantric yanas. For more on shravakas and pratyekabuddhas, see volume 1 of the *Profound Treasury*, part 5, "The Hinayana Journey."

Maybe it is not just a possibility. Maybe I am already utterly spotless."
With spotless tathagatagarbha, you recognize the very powerful and vivid
possibility of tathagatagarbha in you already, free from case histories and
habitual patterns as to what a good person should be. Independent of
all that, such a thing as tathagatagarbha could exist in you really, utterly,
and fully. You begin to realize that cultivating tathagatagarbha is not the
point—acknowledging fully the existence of tathagatagarbha is more
like it.

Tathagatagarbha is based on gentleness and the absence of twofold
ego, the ego of self or individuality, and the ego of dharmas or phenomena. It is based on compassion, but not the kind we might expect from the
reference point of ego. Tathagatagarbha is pure because it does not refer
back to memories or to a conceptual case history of the past. With pure
tathagatagarbha, there is no reference point to the past or the would-be
future. It is very open. Since it is without fear, you do not need to defend
anything at all.

What pushes you from just feeling that tathagatagarbha is a possibility to realizing that tathagatagarbha is an actuality, is trust in your
own intuition and trust in your teacher, your spiritual friend. When that
begins to happen, a lot of unfolding takes place. So you jump first to the
possibility of tathagatagarbha, and then you begin to realize the actuality of tathagatagarbha. In Buddhism, nobody is expected to do a perfect
job. People begin as amateurs, and then build up. There is no problem
with that; nobody is expected to be absolutely good at the beginning. In
fact, trying to do so is a form of theism. According to our philosophy of
nontheism, human conditions are taken into consideration.* We include
people's inadequacies.

Unconditional buddha nature is spontaneous. It is not regarded as
anybody's product. Such a mind cannot be produced by parents or by
two other minds—mind is simply mind. Unconditional buddha nature is
beginningless. It has already occurred nowhere; therefore, it has occurred
everywhere. According to the vajrayana, at the beginning there was a split

---

* The contrast between *theism* and *nontheism* is a recurring theme in Trungpa Rinpoche's
teaching. He uses the term *theism* to refer to the belief in an external deity who might save
or punish you, and in particular to deity-based religious traditions such as Christianity or
Hinduism. More generally, he uses *theism* to refer to the co-opting of any tradition, including Buddhism, as fuel for one's ego aggrandizement. For more on theism and nontheism,
see volume 1 of the *Profound Treasury*, chapter 6, "Achieving Sanity Here on Earth."

into two categories: confusion and wakefulness. But at the same time, there was no split. The beginning occurred because there was self-existing energy where things happen very straightforwardly. According to both the mahayana and vajrayana, samsaric confusion and chaos are just a gust of wind that swirls over our wakefulness. That wakefulness is going on all the time, right from the beginning. From where does it come? From nowhere. It is just wakefulness, simple and straightforward.

Fundamental enlightened mind or essence exists in us all the time. It is there right at the beginning, although there is no beginning. Before any kind of perception occurs, wakefulness is already there—beyond concept, beyond limitation, beyond anything measurable. We can all awaken: that is the hope and the potential. That self-existing potential has the capability of proclaiming and propagating the enlightened dharma because it has no beginning, and no time when it actually took place.

Unconditional buddha nature is beyond our conceptualized mind's measure. In that way, it is similar to the notion of *dharmata*. *Dharmata* means "dharma-ness," or the "isness of dharma." Mahayana is a vast space, a vast experience, but when we realize the vastness of it, we begin to feel that we are being squished. We ask, "How am I going to survive? How am I going to breathe my air?" That experience, which is both vast and claustrophobic, is dharmata.

5

Basic Goodness

*There is a basic state of existence that is fundamentally good and
that we can rely on. There is room to relax, to open up. We can make
friends with ourselves and with others. That is the fundamental
virtue of alaya, or basic goodness. It is the basis of the possibility
of absolute bodhichitta.*

As we tame our mind by means of shamatha-vipashyana, we begin to
be thoroughly and properly processed, which in Tibetan is called
shinjang. We develop shinjang, but we also begin to find certain problems.
Shinjang is the realization that our state of mind is workable. It is said
to be like thoroughly processing cotton into batting: the mind becomes
soft and weeded out. So when we sit on the batting, if there are any little
prickly thorns in the middle of it, we find those thorns quite noticeable.
Likewise, when we practice the discipline of shinjang, we notice our subconscious gossip and the distractions caused by sight, sound, and bodily
feelings. We notice any movements of the mind that distract us from perfect concentration. The softness is shinjang, and the thorns are temporary
obstacles that make us feel we may not be as good as we think.

As we practice, we find that there is an edge. That edge is not regarded
as problematic; it is regarded as our working basis. Having processed
our state of being, further inquisitiveness takes place. We ask ourselves,
"What next?" That question does not mean we are ignorant, confused,
or misled—it expresses intelligence and wakefulness. Asking ourselves
what we should do after waking up is like sitting on the cotton batting of
shinjang, and feeling something prickling us and asking, "What is this?"

At that point, the possibility of further learning is taking place. We are doing more than just tagging along and trying to be courageous for lack of a better choice; instead we experience something in ourselves that inspires us to learn further, to be continuously interested in pursuing the dharma.

SUGATAGARBHA

What is that something? It is *sugatagarbha*. In Sanskrit, *su* means "perfect," or "complete," *gata* means "gone," and *garbha* means "womb" or "essence." In Tibetan, sugatagarbha is *dewar shek-pe nyingpo*. *Dewar* means "pleasure," or "well," in the sense of "well done"; *shek* means "gone," *shekpa* is "those who have gone," *pe* makes it "of those who have well gone," and *nyingpo* means "essence." So *sugatagarbha* or *dewar shek-pe nyingpo* means the "essence of those who are well gone," or the "essence of those who have passed into the state of liberation joyfully and easily."

In the related term *tathagatagarbha, tathagata* means "those who have gone," whereas *sugata* means "those who have gone easily and joyfully." The "going" in this case is not so much a tearing away from what you have; rather, you are going on a journey that is joyful. The idea is that somebody has done it joyfully, and you can, too. It is like the Buddha saying, "Well done." When people asked good questions, the Buddha would say, "Well done! Look at this person who has done so well. Why don't you all do so?" That is the idea of sugatagarbha—sharing the vision with everybody.

Sugatagarbha is indestructible. It is the ancestor, or parent, of *alaya.**
It is pre-alaya, but it encompasses alaya as well. Alaya has basic goodness, but sugatagarbha has greater goodness. It is wakefulness itself. From the sugatagarbha point of view, alaya could be said to be a kind of awareness, or even a form of samsaric mind. Sugatagarbha is beyond that. It is what makes the veils and obscurations only temporary obstacles.

We all have sugatagarbha. That is why we can follow the mahayana path. Although we may try to keep ourselves away from possibilities of wakefulness or dharmic situations, once we have sniffed the air of dharma, our sugatagarbha will begin to awaken. It is like raising tigers: even if we keep tiger cubs on a vegetarian diet for years, at some point or another

---

* Alaya is the basic ground that gives rise to both samsara and nirvana.

they are going to smell blood, and at that point they are going to want to eat meat right away. We cannot prevent that from happening. So one of the greatest messages of the mahayana is that we have the potentiality of wakefulness and that we can actualize it constantly.

THE NATURAL VIRTUE OF ALAYA

The basic goodness of alaya transcends both the cotton batting and the thorns, the shinjang as well as your irritation. Beyond the delight of that early shinjang level, you develop greater friendliness to everything, and your early irritation and aggression has been processed by mindfulness and awareness, and replaced instead by basic goodness. This is described in the Kadam texts as the "natural virtue of alaya."* It is an important point to understand. A state of perfect, complete gentleness does exist and can be understood. The shinjang-and-thorn principle is path oriented, but basic goodness is fruition oriented. There is a state where everything is cotton batting, not just in terms of shinjang, but from the point of view of the natural, original hammock.

The technical term for basic goodness is *künshi nyangluk kyi gewa*. *Kün-shi* is the Tibetan word for alaya. Like alaya, künshi can also have the sense of a vast range, as in the word *Himalaya,* which means "snow range." *Kun* means "all," and *shi* means "base"; so *künshi* is the "basis of all." *Ngangluk* means something like "basic style": *ngang* means "natural state," and *luk* means "its own style." *Kyi* is "of," and *gewa* is "goodness," or "virtue"; so *künshi nyangluk kyi gewa* is the "natural state of goodness of the künshi, the basis of all." The alaya or künshi is the fundamental state of our existence or consciousness before it is divided up into "I" and "other," or into the various emotions.

Starting from the basic alaya principle, we then develop consciousness, which makes distinctions. We begin to create a separation between this and that, who and who, what and what. That is the basic notion of self-consciousness, distinguishing who is on our side and who is not. The basic alaya principle is called natural virtue, because it does not have any bias. It is basically just *it,* just neutral. It is neither male nor female, so there is no

---

* The *Kadam* tradition of Tibetan Buddhism was founded by a disciple of the great Indian Buddhist master Atisha (982–1054), and is known for its teaching on bodhichitta, mind training, and stages of the path.

question of courting. In contrast, the *alayavijnana,* or alaya consciousness, is somewhat biased.

The virtue of basic goodness exists naturally in the alaya. That state of mind is very benevolent and quite possibly naive. However, the notion of basic goodness is not exactly a Pollyanna approach. It is that in spite of our personal, individual paranoia and our discriminating awareness that looks for danger and separates everything into what is acceptable and what is unacceptable, there is a basic state of existence that is fundamentally good and that we can rely on. There is room to relax, to open up. We can make friends with ourselves and with others. That is the fundamental virtue of alaya, or basic goodness. It is the basis of the possibility of absolute bodhichitta.

POSITIVE NAIVETÉ

Once we have been inspired by the precision of shamatha and the wakefulness of vipashyana, we find that there is room for total naiveté in the positive sense. The Tibetan term for naiveté is *pagyang,* which means "carefree," or "let loose." We can be pagyang with our basic goodness. We do not have to scrutinize it or investigate it to make sure, but the basic goodness of künshi can be cultivated and connected with quite freely and naturally. We can be carefree in our basic goodness. We can develop a sense of relaxation and release from torment and paranoia—and from *this* and *that* altogether.

With pagyang, we can actually look at our basic goodness literally and straightforwardly. We begin to recognize that state of mind because of our wakefulness, our mindfulness and awareness. As a result of practicing good posture and the techniques of shamatha and vipashyana, we see that our basic state of mind, which is naive, or pagyang, did not come from anywhere. It was never born. So our basic state of mind is unborn, unmanufactured. We also see that it does not dwell anywhere: it is nondwelling. It is difficult to capture, and we cannot seize it and sit on it. Because the basic goodness of künshi is unborn and nondwelling, we cannot theorize its existence by saying it is this or that. We discover that basic goodness is free from pigeonholing, free from any particular concept or reference point we might have.

When we look at our mind, the only thing we can find is sense consciousnesses or sense perceptions. We see that there is an intelligent mind working, but if we look deeper than that, we find that it is like a pool of milk and honey: it is good, soothing, and fundamentally harmless. It is not even harmless—it is just completely good and willing to create the effects of goodness as well. That good state of mind can be referred to as *rapkar gewa,* which means "white virtue." The word *white* means unstained, so white virtue is unstained basic goodness. That unstained basic goodness is the starting point of the Buddhist path of loving-kindness. All human beings, even the most vicious, possess that possibility. That kind of caring, softness, and gentleness exists in everyone. There is always some white virtue. The bodhisattva path is not moralistic or puritanical, and it is not about trying to be good in the name of virtue or for somebody else. In the case of the bodhisattva path, it is because we have goodness already in us that we can afford to be good.

In shamatha-vipashyana, we look at our basic state of mind and experience it fully, and we regard any obscurations or obstacles as temporary. Instead of looking for trouble or for problem areas, we look for that naive state of existence that we always possess. Whenever we take care of ourselves by taking a shower or combing our hair, or even putting our glasses on our face, that is our naive way of treating ourselves better. We do not always behave as if we were on a sharp edge looking out for an attack, but there are occasions when we treat ourselves better. That tendency to treat ourselves better seems to indicate that a tendency toward goodness exists. Obviously, basic goodness goes beyond that—it goes deeper than that to goodness itself—but those occasions when we don't deliberately hurt ourselves, when we deliberately treat ourselves well, could be seen as expressions of pagyang. And as we go on, we could then develop into realizing basic goodness on the spot; we can recognize basic goodness naturally. That is how we begin to develop the possibility of absolute bodhichitta. We do so by realizing that our basic state of mind, or the natural virtue of alaya, is unborn, dwells nowhere, and is unconditional, open space.

TEMPORARY STAINS AND THE FIVE CATEGORIES OF MIND

According to the mahayana, our mind includes stains or obstacles as well as sugatagarbha. In the Buddhist tradition, we have lots of words for mind or consciousness, all of which are connected with the possibility of the mind being stained or free from stains. Nonetheless, all of them have the suggestion that such stains or hang-ups are somewhat temporary. In the mahayana, and even at the early level of hinayana, your mental stains and discursive thoughts are not regarded as permanent problems. In Tibetan, the term for temporary stain is *lobur gyi trima*. *Lobur* means "temporary," "abrupt," or "sudden," *gyi* is "of," and *trima* means "stain"; so *lobur gyi trima* means "temporary stain." Because your stains are temporary, your situation is altogether workable.

Sem

The first term for mind is *sem*, which means "that which minds the other." We have an expression in Tibetan, *yul la sem pena sem*, which means "mind is that which can project toward an object." Sem is the process of minding, like the English expression "Mind your own business." You are minding the situation, minding the day and minding the night. It almost becomes a verb: you are "sem-ing." Sem is that which proclaims itself for no reason, like a fish jumping out of the water, and then projects to the other. You think, "Aha! This is red, this is green, and this is yellow," or "I am happy, I am sad. I am this, and I am that." That is minding, or sem.

Lo

The next term for mind is *lo*. Lo comes out of the sem principle, but with lo you have more discrimination. Lo is slightly more intellectual than sem. It is found in words like *lodrö*, or "intellect." Sometimes lo is connected with prajna and the quality of being smart. Actually, the best translation of *lo* may be "smart." Basically, you can distinguish between fish and fowl. But in general, when we go from sem to lo, we are going to a slightly better grade of mind.

Shepa

Another term for mind is *shepa*, which means "consciousness." *She* means "familiarity," "knowing," or "comprehending," and *pa* makes it a noun; so *shepa* means "consciousness." It is slightly better than lo, which is still somewhat instinctive and naive. Shepa is beginning to become much more intelligent. It is that which is capable of *she*, or knowing. *She* is the root for *sherap,* which means "prajna," and *she* can also be found in *yeshe,* which means "wisdom."

Rikpa

The next term, *rikpa,* means "insightfulness," or "able to be touched by a situation." *Rik* means "insight," and *pa* makes it a noun, so *rikpa* means "insightfulness." *Rikpa* goes beyond knowing and feeling. It is a more advanced state of the mind's capability.

Tokpa

Beyond rikpa, we have what is known as *tokpa,* which means "comprehension," or "realization." *Tok* means "comprehend," and *pa* makes it a noun, so *tokpa* means "comprehension." With tokpa you are finally able to perceive and realize the phenomenal world, to see things as they are and to comprehend them. You are no longer confused, but you have insight. That insight may not be a spiritual discovery at a high level of wisdom, but when you begin to *tok,* you actually make a connection to the phenomenal world. *Tok* is also the root for *namtok,* which means "thoughts," or "concepts." When you have thoughts, you begin to label things. You say, "This is an enemy, that is a friend." Tokpa is connected with intuition; it is the intuitive level of your relationship with the world.

To review, first there is the mind that perceives the phenomenal world, that perceives the other, and then there is the mind that puts labels on it. Then there are levels of mind that not only label, but also think intelligently about the world. And finally, there is the mind that actually perceives some kind of reality. It is like waking up from sleep: First you open your eyes, and you realize where you are. Then you have to get up. You probably think about whether to take a shower or put on your bathrobe. After that, you think about what kind of breakfast there will be. Then you think further about what you are going to do next. It is that kind of growth. You begin at the beginning, and continue until you have actually faced so-called reality. That is how the five levels of mind take place. And as you work with those states of mind, you begin to clarify your existence. You become more precise, and are able to clean up habitual patterns connected with past activities or behavior.

In working with the mind, the temporary-stain part is the imperfections and problems you have collected and put in your pouch. But at the same time, you have collected insight. When you learn, you learn accurately, which is an expression of purity—but you learn with your own version of accuracy. For instance, you may hear the statement "Form is empty." You learn that form is empty, but then you add something else to it, which gives you something to hang on to. The training would be to eliminate that stain, that extra thing. Having done so, what is left is sugatagarbha.

All aspects of mind possess stains as well as intelligence. It is possible for us to train our mind because we have all those faculties to work with. In each aspect of mind, one part has the possibility of sugatagarbha, because there is intelligence taking place, but another part is marked by temporary stains. It is said that if you put a tortoise into a bowl of milk and water, the tortoise will be able to separate the two and drink the water because the tortoise has certain chemicals in its lips that curdle the milk. That analogy applies to us: once we have understood that we have a mind—and we are sunk into our mind already, in any case—we begin to realize that part of our mind is sugatagarbha, and part of our mind is temporary obstacles. When we are able to see those two aspects quite clearly, we can then train our mind.

When we train our mind, we are training all those categories of mind at once. But before we do so, we have to know that the mind has particular areas with particular functions. In talking about mind, basically what we are referring to is the double vision of what is known as duality, which causes us to say, "I am so-and-so." When we say "I" and "am," there is the duplicity of our mind, which is sem; there is our basic awareness, which is lo; there is our intelligence, which is shepa; there is our insight, which is rikpa; and there is the collective mechanism that stores information in our mind, which is tokpa. All five aspects contain sugatagarbha as well as temporary stains, and we go through all of them thoroughly and properly. We cover all the possibilities, so that we have no further questions as to which part of us is left behind. It is like going through a gate: you don't just go through the gate right away, but you consider the whole process. You realize that your eyes, nose, head, shoulders, arms, legs, and whole being need to go through this gate. The whole thing may seem very complicated, but each part is very simple and workable.

You have mind and you have problems; therefore, you can train yourself. In other words, if there were no potential for failure, there would be nothing to train. You can't train someone who has been trained already, and if there is no potential for success, there is also no way to do so. Therefore, the basic logic is that you are trainable. We have both potential success and potential failure in our state of mind; therefore, we can develop ourselves. But before we discuss the training itself, we need to try to understand our mind. We need to see that we have sugatagarbha in us already, and that because of that seed, we can work with ourselves.

The five aspects of mind seem to be a slightly once-removed expression of alaya. They are not fundamental alaya, but the product of alaya consciousness, or *alayavijnana*.* They are active, so they are more like the limbs of the body than the body itself. Nonetheless, those limbs have a connection with the alaya principle and how to get back to it. So they act as intermediaries, like a fuse as opposed to an actual explosion. The five aspects of mind are the thinking or watching process, or *semjung*, which is the idea that the mind is actually relating with the phenomenal world. However crude and heavy-handed the five aspects of mind may be, they could still connect with the root, the basic alaya principle. Although they might be nasty and have their own little tricks to play, nonetheless they came from the original nature. They have their origin in absolute bodhichitta.

---

* Trungpa Rinpoche distinguishes *alayavijnana*, or alaya consciousness, from alaya, which is the fundamental ground that gives rise to both samsara and nirvana, or the basic split. *Alaya consciousness* is the base, or storehouse consciousness, which is the basis of duality and of all mental activities. It is also referred to as the eighth consciousness. For a discussion of the eight kinds of consciousness, see volume 1 of the *Profound Treasury*, chapter 37, "Rediscovering Your Own Mind."

Part Three

PREPARING THE GROUND

6

Cultivating Wholesomeness

*If you have awareness in whatever you do, you always have a sense
of basic decency. You do not cheat. You do not do things just because
they are traditional, and you don't just do something this year simply because you did it last year. You always try to practice your
discipline as genuinely and honestly as possible—to the point where
the honesty and genuineness begin to hurt.*

IN THE mahayana there is a quality of wholesomeness, which comes
from shamatha, vipashyana, and the union of the two. Shamatha leads
to freedom from aggression; it brings gentleness, maitri, and kindness to
yourself. Vipashyana leads to freedom from ignorance; it brings clarity
and intelligence. The combination of the two produces wholesomeness.
That is how to develop an enlightened person.

Shamatha-vipashyana practice is utterly important in all three yanas,
so you should not drop it. Otherwise, you might find yourself behaving
calmly in the hinayana, kindly in the mahayana, and then freaking out in
the vajrayana. With mindfulness practice, you do not behave differently
in each yana. It is not that you graduate from the first grade and then get
into the second grade and the third grade. It is more like making butter
out of milk. In the hinayana, when you make butter from milk, you find
that you have something called buttermilk left to drink; in the mahayana,
you drink the milk; and in the vajrayana, you enjoy the butter itself.

Joining shamatha precision and calmness with vipashyana awareness
brings the realization that the world is not attacking you. The world is no
longer an obstacle; in fact, the world is actually helpful to you. This is the

beginning of entering into the mahayana, which brings the possibility of egolessness. Instead of hanging on to yourself, trying to grasp "me" and "my-ness," you could let go by means of shamatha and vipashyana. You could begin to loosen up a little bit more.

MINDFULNESS: FREEDOM FROM AGGRESSION

When you practice mindfulness at the mahayana level, instead of simply trying to be mindful, you also have to tame your aggression. The more you tame your aggression, the more mindfulness you develop. If you are so energized that you are unable to concentrate or have difficulty paying attention to details, those problems are a result of underlying aggression. Generally speaking, aggression tends to come up in the form of boredom. Because you are bored, you want to find some way of occupying yourself other than what you are doing on the spot, whether it is watching your breath, eating your food, or whatever you are doing.

Aggression is an obstacle to mindfulness. If you are pushed to follow your breath or to watch your thoughts, you are bound to get angry. Such aggression is completely inevitable. Aggression affects your span of attention; it is the reason you cannot sit still for more than a few minutes, why you fidget, why you are irritated, why you have to bring up the pain in your back or your knees. Triggered by aggression, the intelligence of boredom is manifesting itself. Your subconscious gossip tells you, "Don't obey any of those rules. You should be an individual. Do anything you want." That is the voice of aggression, manifesting through impatience and boredom. But with mindfulness practice, you can develop gentleness and nonaggression.

AWARENESS: FREEDOM FROM IGNORANCE

Vipashyana is trickier than shamatha because in order to pay greater attention to more details, you need to expand yourself further. To be aware of what is around you, you have to become less self-centered. The conventional approach to awareness is based on the idea that if you do your best, you can win a gold medal. But in the mahayana, we don't think of awareness in terms of having a particular purpose. You are simply trying to pay more attention to the environment around you. For example, in oryoki practice, you learn to be fascinated by your napkin, your bowls, your spoon, and your chopsticks. Paying more attention to them is better than paying attention to yourself, to good old Joe Schmidt. You do not have to handle two things at once. Hopefully, while you are cleaning your bowl, Joe Schmidt is completely forgotten. While you are eating in that way, there is no ego of self. At least on a simple level, that is one way of realizing egolessness.

If you have awareness in whatever you do, you always have a sense of basic decency. You do not cheat. You do not do things just because they are traditional, and you don't just do something this year simply because you did it last year. You always try to practice your discipline as genuinely and honestly as possible—to the point where the honesty and genuineness begin to hurt. In fact, such hurting is regarded as good. If you begin to get hurt by being genuine, it is the beginning of warriorship. It is the level at which you are capable of exchanging yourself for others.

7

Expanding Your Practice

At the mahayana level, there is greater vision. Dedication becomes not just dedication to yourself and your own liberation, but an expansion of openness, love, and compassion. There is a quality of dignity, which is not especially localized, and the path begins to expand beyond one's own individuality.

THE HINAYANA journey is travel oriented or achievement oriented, but in the mahayana, you view the journey less as traveling and more as a way of life. So your attitude toward the path begins to change, and there is less emphasis on striving to achieve something. At the same time, I would like to make it quite clear that you cannot reach the level of mahayana teachings without first having realized and understood the hinayana. But having done so, you take a completely different approach. You feel that you no longer have to roll along the road in an airtight coach, but you can be more exploratory.

You could describe the difference between hinayana and mahayana as the difference between being a Boy or Girl Scout and a real soldier. When you are in the Scouts, you obey orders and try to do the right thing. You learn how to make a fire, how to cook food, and how to conduct the business of basic survival. That training is very useful, because when you actually become a soldier, you still need to know how to make a fire, how to tie your shoelaces, and how to respond to emergencies. The same kinds of problems still take place, and that training continues to apply. But when you become a soldier, you use real guns instead of toy guns.

At the mahayana level, there is greater vision. Dedication becomes not just dedication to yourself and your own liberation, but an expansion of openness, love, and compassion. There is a quality of dignity, which is not especially localized, and the path begins to expand beyond one's own individuality. The mahayanist attitude or outlook is based on immense prajna, or knowledge, and immense compassion. Due to immense prajna, you are able to see through twofold ego completely, and due to immense compassion, you want to work with other sentient beings, and you do not get tired of doing so.

In the mahayana, your compassion is not based on desire. You do not want to save somebody because you will get a gold star or win The World's Kindest Person Award. Instead, compassion is a natural instinct without concern for the end product. When you do not work for personal achievement and are not solely dedicated to yourself, you begin to develop a more expansive vision and more natural communication. You realize that working on yourself is not the biggest project of all. You see that relating with others is more important and real.

BASIC TRAINING

To work for others, you first have to develop composure. If you have no basic stability, when you try to help others, they will not benefit from your help. If you are trying to prevent someone from falling out of a window, you will both go out the window together. To prevent that, you have to stay inside so you can pull them back. In order to do this, training in shamatha and vipashyana is absolutely necessary. With that basic training, you are able to maintain yourself properly. This is why it is so important to develop hinayana self-discipline first, before going on to mahayana vision. You can then learn how the whole thing works, and watch yourself progressing.

Shamatha and vipashyana, or mindfulness and awareness, allow you to be stable and precise. Mindfulness allows you to become stable, to develop tranquillity and peace; awareness allows you to be precise, to be able to pay attention to details. Out of that stability and precision, there naturally arises a quality of gentleness and kindness, an attitude that you will never cause harm to others or create the basis of such harm. When you carry that attitude slightly further, you begin to develop the mahayana view that not only will you refrain from creating harm for others, but you will actually try to benefit them. You try to create a helpful attitude in yourself, and at the same time perform helpful actions for others. So the ground of mahayana comes from training in shamatha and vipashyana.

Through shamatha and vipashyana, you become like a young thoroughbred horse, somewhat responsive and well trained. You have an understanding of egolessness and the four noble truths,* and you have achieved a relatively good state of control over mental distraction. But it is possible that you lack real conviction, so you are unable to fulfill the practice completely. You do need to have mental discipline and control over your mind, but in the mahayana, it is necessary to develop a greater level of commitment. No matter how contemplative the practices of shamatha and vipashyana may be, there is still an element of mechanicalness. Therefore, it is absolutely important to be awakened and to be encouraged to join the mahayana path. Shamatha-vipashyana experience and treading on the mahayana path are complementary to one another and equally important.

As a result of shamatha and vipashyana, you are shinjang-ed, or flexible. You can climb rocks, you can swim—you are capable of doing anything. When you are no longer rigid and tough, when you stop trying to hold on to things, when you stop trying to make everything meaningful to you, when you no longer want to do everything in your own original samsaric style—when all that has fallen apart—you become very soft, gentle, and pliable. In fact, you are so soft that you become almost wormlike. Once you are soft, there are many ways to connect with sentient beings, and there are all kinds of sentient beings you could work with. You could work with very tough ones or very mushy ones.

Hinayana discipline, the inspiration of taming the mind, never dries up. It has been around quite a long time, twenty-six hundred years, and it is still going on. You have to work with your own training first. If you want to become a professor, you must first learn to read and write. Even someone like Mozart had to go to school to learn about music in order to wake up his talent. Likewise, although tülkus, or "incarnate lamas," may be very highly developed, they still have to go through an extremely

---

* For a discussion of the *four noble truths,* see volume 1 of the *Profound Treasury,* part 4, "The Four Noble Truths."

excruciating, painful training—even more so than other people. That was my personal experience as well.

Sitting practice is important, but attachment to sitting practice can become a danger. There can be too much emphasis on the heroism of sitting practice and on the idea that there is nothing to do but meditate. Basing your life on sitting practice alone may be a true approach, straight from the books and the experience of your teachers. Nevertheless, you cannot just look at practice in that way. There is a greater world than your little meditation world, your little meditation hall, and your little meditation cushion. There are other seats—there are saddles and chairs and green grass you can sit on. Everywhere you sit does not have to be a meditation cushion.

In the hinayana practice of taming the mind, you are working with the various forms of unmindfulness. In the mahayana, since your mind has already been tamed, you can work on training the mind. Having domesticated your mind, you can make further use of it. It is like capturing a wild cow and domesticating it to the point that the cow becomes completely willing to relate with its tamer. In fact, the cow likes being domesticated; it becomes a part of your household. So first you tame the mind by means of shamatha discipline, and then you train the mind by means of mahayana contemplative practices such as *tonglen,** or exchanging oneself for others, as well as by the actual fieldwork of helping others.

PUTTING YOUR TRAINING INTO ACTION

When you have been thoroughly tamed by the practice of shamatha and when you have developed vipashyana insight, you know how to hear the teachings. You have begun to develop a complete understanding of the dharma. You also have begun to develop an understanding of how, in your particular state of being tamed, you can relate with others. You have a sense of sacred outlook and are willing to work honestly, without being egocentric. Therefore, genuine practice is taking place. You may also have encountered teachers who show you by their example that you do not

---

* *Tonglen,* or sending and taking practice, is the practice of breathing in the suffering of others (taking), and breathing out to them your own healthiness (sending). It is also referred to as exchanging yourself for others. Tonglen practice is described in detail in chapter 37, "Point Two: Training in Relative Bodhichitta."

need to lock yourself in a closet and hide, but you can actually expand out. You can walk out and relate with others, who are in tremendous need of help.

The confirmation of your training is in your actions. It is like the saying, "The proof is in the pudding." But first you have to be willing to eat the pudding! It is necessary to get your hands dirty before there is any possibility of being confirmed. You actually have to do something: you have to follow the example of your teacher and work for others. When you do that, both you and other people benefit. On the mahayana path, the wheel of your chariot must always touch the road, otherwise it would be impossible to travel.

In the mahayana you need to work with others, but the desire to help can be problematic. It gives you gratification, a personal recognition of your ego. You might go so far as to think of yourself as the next world leader, or a great savior like Jesus Christ. You might think of yourself as the sole hope for the world, if only everybody would listen to you. People have all sorts of crazy ideas like that; this sort of personal gratification is exactly what people are looking for. Therefore, it would be very helpful to work on the side of inconvenience, to sacrifice your pleasure and your desire to be private. You cannot shy away from discomfort; you have to be willing to work with inconvenient situations. You should not preserve your privacy, but be willing to open constantly, to be exposed. That attitude is the factor that will destroy any temptation to build yourself up. On the whole, you always have to refer back to your basic hinayana discipline. That is a tremendous saving grace, the greatest saving grace, in fact.

When you feel that you need a break, not just for the sake of taking a break, but because you are tired of working for others, at that point you have to extend yourself a little bit more. You have to be a completely steady person, and at the same time a completely energetic person. Once you are able to bring those two things together, once you join the essence of hinayana and the essence of mahayana, then you are about to do something very good. You are about to bring about the vajrayana, which comes next on the path.

When you realize that not only can you achieve individual salvation, but you can be awakened further, you are joyous and you look forward to such wakefulness. You realize that you can awaken from the need to put so much emphasis on the preservation of your own ego, and you can develop greater compassion. Wakefulness is the loss of ego. It is the loss of your self—the "me-ness" of it, the "I-ness" of it. When you lose that ego-centeredness, you naturally and automatically develop an awareness of others; and when you are more aware of others, you develop a more sympathetic attitude toward them. You have a keenness for others, a liking for other people. Therefore, you do not feel that you need your privacy, or that you have to lock yourself in a room alone to enjoy yourself. Instead, you prefer to enjoy yourself by being with others and by helping them. You are not helping others because you feel sorry for them or to confirm that your existence is important, but because you have developed a quality of upliftedness.

8

Cutting Ego Fixation

By understanding the implications of egolessness, you develop a quality of genuine sympathy and softness. . . . That combination of sympathy and egolessness makes you a perfect candidate to enter the bodhisattva path.

REVIEWING THE LOGIC OF THE HINAYANA

In order to realize the meaning and purpose of the mahayana, it is necessary to review the logic of the hinayana. Going back and finding out more about what you have already studied helps a lot. It is like combing your hair: when you comb your hair, you don't comb just the ends of your hair, but you start from the beginning, from your scalp. So going back again and again and again is very important. It makes a thorough job. In turn, you begin to realize the basic geography and logic of the whole situation.

When you enter the bodhisattva path, you become a more hinayana person, and when you become a vajrayana person, you become a more mahayana person. That is how the whole thing works. Everything complements everything else. Each time you think you are ahead of yourself, you find that you are behind yourself. So the best vajrayana practitioners could be at the most pure mahayana level, and the best mahayana practitioners could be at the best hinayana level. That is how it works.

The hinayana approach of individual salvation is the ground that prevents you from relating with the wider vision of the mahayana purely as egotism or as the excessive emotionalism of trying to help everybody. Hinayana also provides you with the necessary ground for understanding the meaning of nontheism. If you follow the sequence of the five *skandhas*

60

and the twelve nidanas, it becomes absolutely crystal clear that the world is not made by someone else, but is of your own making.* It is also clear that when a group of individuals influence each other and create a society, their world begins to take shape in a particular way—with growing passion, aggression, and ignorance. You realize that the world is in chaos, and in order to control or work with that chaos, you have to begin by working on yourself. There is no other way. Having worked on yourself, you can then begin to branch out into the greater vision, expansion, intelligence, and cheerfulness of the mahayana.

The bodhisattva path is the path of the warrior, the fearless path. This highly disciplined lineage has been handed down from generation to generation, up to the present. You take up the bodhisattva path with the attitude of working for others first, which means that you begin to give up your own personal struggle to survive and maintain yourself. Beyond that, you can expand further and develop into an ultimately genuine and good person. The reason you can do so is because you do not put your own situation first; you put others first. Therefore, you become more reasonable.

The transition from hinayana to mahayana is an evolutionary process. When you enter the mahayana, you have already abandoned the notion of taking refuge in external gods. You have understood that nontheistic discipline is based on working with yourself. At the same time, you have also begun to realize that you need further input and further vision, but this further vision also comes from you. You can't ask anybody else to give you that vision; you have to work on it yourself. So in the mahayana, there is still a quality of individual salvation. You can't ask for any support, but you can make friends with someone who has done it already. You can rely on the *kalyanamitra,* or spiritual friend, as an example rather than a savior.

In approaching the mahayana, we are trying to work with the theoretical level and the practical level at the same time. We are taking an approach of practical realism. There are certain things I can describe or tell you how to do, but there are other things that you have to experience yourself. My obligation, my vow, is that certain experiences in your practice have to be your own discovery. By definition, a spiritual friend is

---

* The *five skandhas* refer to five aspects of what we take to be the self. For more on the five skandhas, see volume 1 of the *Profound Treasury,* chapter 2, "The Frozen Space of Ego."

someone who will push you, but who will not push you too much. They will let you experience what is happening.

THE NATURE OF EGO

As a would-be bodhisattva, you are expected to be an ideal hinayanist already. You are expected to understand egolessness. But in order to develop your understanding of egolessness, you first have to understand the notion of ego altogether. In the hinayana, you dissect your ego and divide it into its components. You divide the ego into five skandhas, and study the case history of ego in the form of the twelve nidanas and the notion of interdependent origination.

But there is a problem with that approach. Even though you could become proficient in the logic of the five skandhas and know the nidanas inside out, your ego could continue to function as usual. So simply learning about the five skandhas does not particularly help; you have to work on each individual skandha, step-by-step.

You are also taught that in order to free your mind of desire, you should reflect on the different parts of the body. You reflect on your lover's body, thinking of it in terms of flesh, bones, mucus, hairs, internal organs, and so forth. However, although that approach might have worked at one time, in modern times it is problematic. Highly accomplished physicians know the body inside out; nonetheless, they do not stop falling in love. So working with desire is not all that simple.

The question of what ego is all about can only be solved by understanding the mahayana view of ego. According to the mahayana, and buddhadharma in general, ego is the tendency to hold on to your own survival and to defend it against anything that might interrupt it. Ego or egotism is known in Tibetan as *dagdzin. Dag* means "oneself," and *dzin* means "grasping," or "holding"; so *dagdzin* is "holding on to oneself." In the English language, we do not usually use the term *egomaniac* to refer to ourselves; we use it to refer to somebody who is extremely egocentric. But from the Buddhist point of view, whenever we are holding on to ourselves, we are expressing egomania. So we are all egomaniacs; we are all holding on to ourselves.

Ego is an instinct that we share with the animals, but on a slightly more sophisticated level. Instead of barking, we talk, and instead of perching, we sit, but there is not much difference beyond that. Ego is a kind of basic crudeness that exists in us. Usually it is the very first thought that arises. Whenever there is any challenge, any incomprehension or dismay on a smaller or larger scale, we always think, "How am 'I' going to deal with this?" We always begin with "me." It doesn't have to be large-scale warfare. Even if it is only a small inconvenience, like running out of hot water or running out of toilet tissue, our first thought is, "How am I going to wipe my bottom? How am I going to take my bath?" That is the first thought, but it is not particularly the best thought. In fact, it is the worst thought. Whenever the slightest edge occurs in our life, we think of ourselves first. We think "me."

This does not mean that we should stop taking care of ourselves. The point is to recognize that there is a quality of psychological panic, which starts with "this," "here," "me," "my-ness." It starts with apprehension, with bewilderment or confusion, and quite possibly leads us to resort to aggression. When worse comes to worst, that is our only choice. Aggression is what we resort to, even in the most sedate situations in our lives. When we find that things are not convenient, when things don't happen according to our expectations, we complain to the manager, or we make a phone call, or we write a letter of complaint. We would like to just jump up and strangle somebody, if we could. We have preconceived ideas of how things should be, and when things do not happen as we expect, we begin to feel doubtful. Roughly speaking, that is what is known as the survival mentality of ego.

With that mentality, you see the idea of compassion as a threat to your personal territory. You think, "If I follow the mahayana, will I have enough freedom? If I give up my privacy and surrender my whole being for the benefit of others, it might be like joining the Salvation Army, or even worse." You question how far you are willing to go—and your first thought is about how to preserve your own comfort. But once you become involved in the mahayana path, you should not be thinking about comfort at all. In the hinayana, there may be some comfort in the precision of shamatha and vipashyana. But in the mahayana, your own comfort is out of the question. You do not actually have such a thing as privacy or personal comfort, but you are purely dedicated to the welfare of others.

Your parents, psychiatrist, and other responsible people will say that you should be careful, that you should try to build up your ego and have self-respect. In fact, Buddhism has received complaints and criticism from people who say that it is a nihilistic religion, and that you have to give up your self-respect. But we still continue to teach about egolessness, which is more respectable than self-respect, if I may say so.

TWOFOLD EGOLESSNESS

When you enter the mahayana, you are expected to have already developed an understanding of what is called one-and-a-half-fold egolessness. The first fold is the egolessness of self. Having understood that, you go on to the second fold, the egolessness of external phenomena, or dharmas. But at this point your understanding is only partial, so it is referred to as one-and-a-half-fold egolessness. You have realized the egolessness of external phenomena, but not the egolessness of the perceiving itself. So you have not completely cut your belief in the world's crude manifestation. At the mahayana level, you need to be willing to open up and work with other sentient beings much more vividly than is prescribed in the hinayana. You need to be willing to take a step further into twofold egolessness.*

At this point, we are talking simply in terms of inspiration, which plants a seed. There may not be a one-hundred-percent experience of egolessness. Perhaps just tokens of such a possibility are happening. But talking alone does not help, even though you might have theories about it, and sitting practice does not help all that much either. You need to have the experience of dealing with day-to-day life situations in the world. The point is that in entering the mahayana, a good understanding of twofold egolessness goes a long way, because then you could teach yourself and hear the teachings at the same time.

FUNCTIONING WITHOUT EGO

In the hinayana, you are provided with the idea of shamatha and the merits of mindfulness. Once you have developed mindfulness, then you are able to go further, to the development of vipashyana, or awareness. The combination of shamatha and vipashyana brings you greater intelligence, or prajna. With that intelligence, you begin to realize the hideousness of

---

* The realization of *twofold egolessness* is divided into three stages. First is the egolessness of self, the first fold. Second is the egolessness of phenomena, described as a partial understanding of the second fold. Third is the egolessness of the perceiving itself, which completes the second fold.

believing in your self. You see how your habitual patterns make you thick and stupid, and you realize the problem of ego.

The problem of ego even shows up in our language. In the English language, you may be about to say something intelligent, but your first word has to be *I*, as in "I am about to say something intelligent." In order to be grammatical, you have to use this word *I*, so at the grammatical, verbal level, your intelligence is already obscured. If you say, "I have a good idea," where did that good idea come from? Should there be "I" in it at all? Why can't you just say, "There is a good idea"? So the problem of ego seems to be inherent in our English language and our grammar.

In the early stages of human linguistic life, we are also taught to say "me" and "mine." That may be all right in terms of learning to speak the language, but beyond that there are continual problems with the notion of possession. The point of mahayana is to overcome that notion of possession and the ongoing impulse that things should belong to you first, and only afterward to others. According to the mahayana, things do not have to belong to you in order for you to enjoy them.

When you realize the obstacles that arise from the belief or habit of ego, you also begin to realize the opposite possibility of overcoming those obstacles and working with them. You realize that you actually possess a state of being that is not centralized in "me," in "my" beliefs, in "my" profession, in "me" as an ego-person. You see that there is another side to you, that you have the potential to experience gentleness and peace. You begin to discover your soft spot. That discovery comes from the experience of vipashyana, or awareness.

We could quite safely say that everybody possesses a soft spot, and everybody can function without ego. We all possess a basic soft spot, which is not ego. Some people might think it strange if you tell them that you are practicing a discipline known as egolessness. They probably think you are on your way to becoming a vegetable. But according to enlightened vision, it is possible to live fully without ego. Ego is, in fact, stupidity. It is fundamental thickness. It sets up obstacles or veils that prevent you from developing any form of intelligence at all.

By understanding the implications of egolessness, you develop a quality of genuine sympathy and softness. You begin to feel relaxed and easy. That combination of sympathy and egolessness makes you a perfect candidate to enter the bodhisattva path. Why? Because at each and every step you are losing your ego, and as you shed more layers of ego, you realize that there is something beyond that. So your fixation on ego, or ego-clinging, no longer plays an important part in your life. You have no idea why or how it happens, but further intelligence and greater possibilities are taking place in you.

With the understanding of egolessness and the help of the spiritual friend, you experience a feeling of great sadness. You feel humbled and sad that something has been lost. In ordinary life, you may have gained all sorts of charisma, but now all that charisma is gone because it was based on aggressively conquering territory. It was an expression of twofold ego. When you begin to lose that, you develop depression and a feeling of loss. You begin to panic, thinking, "Now what? Where am I? What am I?" When you have lost your grasp on the ego of dharmas and the ego of individuality, you begin to feel empty.

When you have understood the first egolessness, the egolessness of self, you are said to have understood grasping but not fixation.* In terms of twofold egolessness, when "you" begin not to exist anymore, you are halfway through; and when you realize that, there is a yearning for the egolessness of dharmas. There is a yearning to go beyond struggle—to go beyond hunger, thirst, duty, and the idea that some kind of relief or letting go will take place. Although you may not yet have a complete understanding of twofold egolessness, you have expanded beyond the level of individual salvation. You realize that the individual salvation you have experienced so far has become tenuous, and you have developed greater sympathy for other people. Where did that come from? It came from realizing that fixation on dharmas does not help.

When you begin to lose the ego of self and the ego of phenomena, you start to feel that you are not professional at anything. You are not a professional con man and you do not need to sell yourself, but you transcend salesmanship. You could still have your little business ventures, but the salesmanship of selling your ego is impossible. As a student of the mahayana, or a would-be bodhisattva, you take the bodhisattva vow because you have a yearning to go beyond such salesmanship and charisma.

The approach of individual salvation is very simple. You know what you are, and you know how to save yourself. Your only dependence is on an elder, a learned person who tells you what to do. But that is only

---

* Twofold ego can be described in terms of grasping onto a self and fixating on phenomena.

a little help; you can do most of it yourself. Shamatha-vipashyana can be conducted in years of solitude. You can just keep doing it, with occasional references to that wise person. Your relationship with the elder is like consulting your grandfather about your business, or paying respects to your grandmother. There's not much surrendering involved.

If you tried to carry the approach of individual salvation into the mahayana, it would be like immigrants who keep taking care of their families back home. When you enter the mahayana, grasping and fixation are transcended, and you go beyond the hinayana attitude of individual salvation. From the clarity of individual salvation, you develop further, so although you are getting into completely new territory, you are no longer dealing with such immigration problems. Instead of clinging to the past, you develop a better, healthier problem, the problem of having expectations.

RENUNCIATION AND FAITH

Having understood the egolessness of dharmas and the view that there is nothing to hang on to, nothing to work on, nothing to grasp, you begin to understand the notion of simultaneous openness and fullness. With that understanding, you begin to develop faith. You are going beyond the business-deal mentality of trying to get a return on your investment. You are developing simple faith or trust. You have trust in something without expecting anything in return. In the crude world of spirituality, faith is based on some kind of return, but in the bodhisattva path, genuine faith is faith without any expectations. Such faith brings about a quality of loneliness. You begin to feel alone and lonely, not knowing whether you are giving or whether you are gaining. Quite possibly you are both giving and gaining, but it is also possible that you are neither giving nor gaining.

The day-to-day problems and complaints that individuals manufacture come from not being able to work with twofold egolessness. In order to develop true faith, you have to become less aggressive, less demanding, and less involved in justifying your ego fixations. You need to develop renunciation, including renouncing the notion that you were going to get something out of following the path of dharma. Renunciation is particularly pointed toward giving up aggression. When renunciation has begun to occur in your system, there is a possibility of developing indivisible emptiness and compassion in your heart.

Emptiness is based on faith, but faith without the idea of getting anything in return; and compassion comes from giving up clinging. Having given up clinging to any situation in your life, you begin to develop sympathy, because you do not have to buy or sell anything. With real renunciation, you do not want to cultivate yourself for the good, the great, and the glory. Instead, with a very genuine and gentle process, you could cultivate bodhichitta in yourself. That is altogether the important point of mixing your mind with the dharma. When the flow of mind is becoming completely mixed with that of the true dharma, it brings about fundamental gentleness and tremendous beauty.

The extent to which you are actually willing to be gentle depends on how awake to yourself you are. You need to be able to catch yourself, and you need to be able to see yourself on your own mental screen in order to know how far you have gotten with the ego and egolessness. You need shamatha and vipashyana. That is the way to mix your mind with the dharma completely.

The problem in being unable to do such a thing is that you keep trying to mimic the dharma while trying to justify yourself at the same time. You may simply want to be the best, which becomes clumsy, awkward, and absurd. Although you may be somewhat well trained, you might still be simply mimicking the dharma. The blindness of not being able to watch yourself, and therefore going too far and making too much of your own abilities, is always possible.

You can sense when a person's mind is somewhat mixed with or dissolved into the dharma. Some people might say, "I think I know the dharma. My mind is very much mixed with the dharma, but I don't think yours is quite so much as mine." Such people have less dissolving taking place, and it shows in the level of their arguments. Other people might try too hard and become too rigid and frozen; such people are also far from mixing their minds with the dharma. It is absolutely possible to know the level of mixing from the way a person picks up a cup of tea and speaks, the way they handle their mouth, handle their face, handle their arms, legs, neck, and shoulders. Strangely, the way we do those seemingly insignificant little things reveals how far we have merged our mind with the dharma.

9

Awakening Your Enlightened Genes

There is no limit as to how much you could develop loving-kindness
toward yourself or compassion toward others. You can go all the
way. It is like the atmosphere, which has no boundaries. You can
achieve complete freedom; you can experience vastness.

GENUINE WAKEFULNESS is possible constantly. We all have the
potentiality of wakefulness within us. Even those with cut-off
genes have this possibility. As long as they can tune in to the dharma,
there is always a way that they can be brought back. In the big vision of
the mahayana, nobody is rejected.

The mahayana message of wakefulness is designed to make you feel
claustrophobic, because there is no turning back. Once you have heard
the message that everybody has enlightened genes, sooner or later you are
going to wake up. There is no chance to panic, and even if you do panic,
it is too late. On one hand, the whole thing is completely hopeless, even
somewhat terrible. On the other hand, it could be delightful. It is a mixed
blessing for beginners, and a full blessing for those who are proceeding.
And for those who actually achieve it, it is a great blessing—whatever that
"it" may be.

SIGNS OF THE ENLIGHTENED GENES
BEING AWAKENED

There are two signs that the enlightened genes are being awakened: maitri, or loving-kindness, and a lack of deception. With maitri, you are gentle
toward yourself and you do not give yourself too hard a time. When the

69

enlightened genes begin to wake up, it is very genuine. Sunshine begins to come out of your heart. But when that happens, you may try to cover it up. You may begin to deceive yourself as well as others. The level of your deception is dependent upon your commitment to the dharma. When you have less commitment to the dharma, you deceive much more, and when you have more commitment, greater genuineness takes place. If you cover yourself up, there is no way of shining out, no way of enlightening, no brilliance of any kind. If you are afraid of brilliance, you try to insert some kind of filter. You apologize for the whole thing. You are shy and you do not want to give up territory, because when you do so, there is the possibility of genuine compassion. But in the mahayana proclamation of buddha nature, something tremendous takes place. You do not have to be worried about your existence. You do not need to ask, "How am I going to survive if I don't have my little ego?"

Signs of the Enlightened Genes Not Being Awakened

There are two signs that the genes are not being awakened: being unable to react to suffering, and not having bigger vision. The first sign, being unable to react to suffering, is quite straightforward. Some people just keep hanging on to their own pain; they do not give it up. Pain is their home, their security, their lover, their friend, and their parents.

The second sign, not having bigger vision, is that you shy away from anything big, anything large scale. Relating to that kind of vision makes you feel awkward and wretched. For instance, you might decide to go out into your backyard and enjoy the snow. But suddenly you think, "I can't go out there! It's too cold!" So you decide to retreat to your bedroom. But inside, things are very constricted; there is no room to stretch out or expand. There is no fearlessness in that approach.

Obstacles to Awakening Enlightened Genes

There are both psychological and situational obstacles to awakening enlightened genes: intrinsic slavery, being without awareness, taking part in evil activities, and sleepiness.

The first obstacle is enslaving yourself, or intrinsic slavery. You set up your life in such a way that you do not even have time to think about it. You have sold yourself to somebody, and there is no time for anything else.

The second obstacle is being without awareness. Without awareness, your intrinsic genes cannot be awakened. If you do not pay attention to your world and to yourself, things become extremely naive and ordinary. There is no sacredness without awareness; everything is too casual.

The third obstacle is taking part in evil activities. You are lured into activities that destroy your wakefulness and mindfulness. This could include indulging in the wrong occupation or wrong lifestyle. It could mean that rather than cultivating wakefulness, you are doing something that is against spiritual practice, that is degrading, or that perpetuates what is called "setting sun" vision.*

The fourth obstacle is sleepiness. You are asleep to your life, so successive *kleshas*, or conflicting emotions, of all kinds are taking place in you.

These four obstacles to awakening enlightened genes are very destructive.

SITUATIONS CONDUCIVE TO AWAKENING ENLIGHTENED GENES

There are also situations conducive to the awakening of enlightened genes: waking up at the right time, and taking an interest in dharma practice. The first is an outer situation. It is that you are actually waking up at the right time, a time when dharma can be heard. The second is an inner situation. Your interest in dharma practice becomes a prominent part of your enthusiasm.

METHODS FOR AWAKENING ENLIGHTENED GENES

We have two methods of awakening our basic genes: the four *brahma-viharas* and the four limitless ones.

---

* Trungpa Rinpoche uses the phrase *setting sun* to refer to a degraded and small-minded outlook on life, one without vision, dignity, or upliftedness.

The Four Brahmaviharas

The first method, the four brahmaviharas, is used at the hinayana level, before entering the bodhisattva path. As a beginner, you may not yet have formally connected with a spiritual friend, but you have made contact with an unofficial spiritual friend, such as a parent or teacher who can guide you. *Brahma* is the ultimate god in the Hindu tradition, and *vihara* means "dwelling place"; so *brahmavihara* means the "dwelling place of Brahma." It has the sense of behaving like Brahma, behaving like a god, so it is similar to the Judeo-Christian concept of godliness. The four brahmaviharas are: love, compassion, joy, and equanimity.

LOVE. The first brahmavihara is love. In Tibetan it is *champa,* which means "gentleness." Here love does not refer to romantic love, but to the notion of love as it is understood in the Hindu tradition, which is a feeling of goodness, brotherhood, and harmony.

COMPASSION. The second brahmavihara is *compassion,* having a sympathetic attitude to others. In Tibetan it is *nying-je,* which means "noble heart." You are merciful and you do not inflict your aggression on others.

JOY. The third brahmavihara is *joy,* or celebration. In Tibetan, it is *gawa.* You appreciate who you are and what you are, as well as your surroundings. There is an absence of aggression and complaint.

EQUANIMITY. The fourth brahmavihara is relaxation, or *equanimity.* In Tibetan it is *tang-nyom. Tang* means "let go," or "release," and *nyom* means "equalize"; so *tang-nyom* means "equanimity," or "equality." You are not constantly fighting, and you are giving up tit-for-tat mentality.

The four brahmaviharas are at the level of ordinary decency and good manners. They are practiced by nontheistic Buddhists, who don't believe in ego, as well as by theists. But the term *theism* does not simply apply to Jews, Christians, or Hindus. It means maintaining an attitude of self-preservation, as opposed to giving up the self. When you take the bodhisattva vow, you are ready to be less concerned with self-preservation, ready to be more open to others. That is the beginning of the mahayana.

On the mahayana path, you have to mash yourself like a potato so that the ego begins to soften. The so-called ego, which doesn't actually exist, is very gullible and credulous. It is always looking for security. So when the possibility of buddhadharma is presented to the ego, it buys that as well. But in the process of buying, the ego could be twisted around and it could begin to dissolve. Love or gentleness to oneself, compassion or gentleness to others, joy, and equanimity or equilibrium are all designed to thaw out the ego by a natural process, rather than a fight.

By working with the four brahmaviharas, you are keeping the world in good order and trying to be a good person. In order to wake up your enlightened genes, you have to develop decency. Otherwise, it would be very difficult to awaken that psychological inheritance of softness, brightness, and goodness.

The Four Limitless Ones

The second method of awakening our basic genes is called the four limitless ones. The four limitless ones are also comprised of love, compassion, joy, and equanimity. These are the same four qualities as the brahmaviharas, but in this case they can be developed to a much higher level. The four limitless ones are called "limitless" because they are not bound by ego intention. Since they are practiced after you have taken the bodhisattva vow, you begin to develop a nontheistic approach to the whole thing. The brahmaviharas are still somewhat limited by goody-goodyness, but with the limitless ones, there is no end, only continual expansion. There is no limit as to how much you could develop loving-kindness toward yourself or compassion toward others. You can go all the way. It is like the atmosphere, which has no boundaries. You can achieve complete freedom; you can experience vastness. The four limitless ones, particularly equanimity, have a quality of transcendence.

LOVE. The first limitless one is called love. It is maitri, or loving-kindness. You are beginning to realize that your buddha nature has woken up, so there is no reason to hate yourself anymore. You actually begin to feel good about yourself, and there is some sort of wakefulness. At the start of a new day, you do not just feel that you have to face another day, but there is a quality of rejoicing and delight. You develop an intrinsic appreciation of yourself in spite of all the obstacles you might face.

At the brahmavihara level, love is still somewhat self-centered, but at the level of the four limitless ones, love is not self-centered or a perpetuation of your ego. You simply realize that you have gentleness in you already, so everything is workable. Everything is possible, even more than possible. You are surprised how gentle you can be to yourself, and you realize that you don't have to torture yourself.

When you are in pain, you feel lonely and distant, cut off from the world. You have no friends to talk to, and nobody understands you or how terrible you feel. It is as if the world has given up on you. But that feeling of loneliness can actually provide gentleness. You notice how soft and raw you are, and you feel the painfulness of your own ego. That rawness is the starting point of loving yourself and having compassion for others.

The theistic traditions carry with them the idea of punishment. The theism of the East teaches us how dirty we are, and the theism of the West teaches us how wicked we are. To overcome our impurity, we have to wear white and eat *sattvic* food.* To overcome our wickedness, we have to be sweet and nice to everyone. However, the Buddhist nontheistic tradition is not based on having to prove yourself or change your lifestyle. According to Buddhism, gentleness simply exists in you, so you can afford to be good and to feel inspired. You can trust yourself. That trustworthiness is maitri.

COMPASSION. The second of the four limitless ones is compassion. The missionary's style of compassion is based on feeling sorry for the natives. Feeling sorry for them makes you also feel sorrowful, so you ask the Red Cross to send supplies. With nontheistic compassion, although you may feel sorry for somebody, you are not disturbed and you do not necessarily shed any tears. You just act nobly in order to help others help themselves. The gentleness that you feel for yourself is expressed in turn to others, so your compassion has nobleness and dignity. With a noble heart of compassion, you understand people's pain, but you still keep your composure.

JOY. The third limitless one is joy. Nontheistic joy arises as a celebration that you possess enlightened genes. You have tremendous personal dig-

---

* In the Hindu *kriyayoga* tradition, *sattvic food* refers to food that is pure, clean, and wholesome.

nity, which arises out of maitri, and you have tremendous public dignity, which is inspired by karuna. When you put them together, you develop joy and humor. In this case, humor does not mean laughing at jokes or making up puns. Humor is being able to see clearly, to see through things. With humor, you begin to appreciate the workings of your mind and the situations that are given to you. You have a quality of natural celebration, based on the goodness, wakefulness, and vastness of mahayana vision. You are inspired by the healthiness and togetherness of maitri, and the openness and possibilities of karuna. You have settled into your world and you are not threatened by possibilities of other worlds, so you can perform your activities freely, beautifully, and wholesomely.

EQUANIMITY. The fourth limitless one is equanimity. You do not hold on to your territory, but you equalize situations, so there is no bias. You have had a glimpse of egolessness, so you do not expect compliments and you do not work for a personal reward of any kind. You just open your heart; you open yourself altogether. In the *Bodhicharyavatara*, or *The Way of the Bodhisattva*, the eighth-century Indian teacher Shantideva says, "Please use me. I prefer to be a bridge, a ship, a highway, a swimming pool, a chariot. Please use me in the service of all sentient beings. I have no hesitation. Whatever my situation may be, I am willing to do good for others."* That openness is very genuine. It is not just a goody-goody approach, but is based on letting go of twofold ego.

Aims of the Four Limitless Ones

The aim of loving-kindness, or maitri, is to experience peace and to cause others to become peaceful. The aim of compassion, or karuna, is to separate the cause of pain from the pain itself. The aim of joy is to help people experience pleasure without causing themselves pain. It is to bring about a lessening of the kleshas. The aim of equanimity is to free people from passion and aggression so that they can see beyond the bias of close and

---

* This is a reference to the type of vow a bodhisattva makes, as found in the *Bodhicharyavatara*, or *The Way of the Bodhisattva*. See Shantideva, *The Way of the Bodhisattva*, chapter 3, "Commitment," translated by the Padmakara Translation Group (Boston: Shambhala Publications, 1997).

distant. When you are too distant, you couldn't care less about others, and when you are too close, you care too much about them.

Causes of the Four Limitless Ones

There are four causes or ways to evolve love, compassion, joy, and equanimity: buddha nature, the spiritual friend, confidence, and discriminating awareness. The root cause is buddha nature. It is the natural tendency of your enlightened genes to evolve further rather than continue your particular style of nuisance and confusion.

The second cause comes from outside of you; it is the spiritual friend. When you meet a spiritual friend or teacher who demonstrates that such a possibility exists in you, it is like two flint stones rubbing together: there is a spark of wakefulness and connection.

The third cause is confidence. You are developing the confidence that the four limitless ones are possible and that you are up to it.

The fourth cause is discriminating awareness. You see the virtues of practicing the four limitless ones and the problem with not doing that. Your prajna is becoming activated.

The Natural Progression of the Four Limitless Ones

In our aspiration to become detached from our fixations and awaken our enlightened genes, the more keen our attitude, the more heroism and greater vision can take place. In the four limitless ones, there is a natural progression from love to compassion to joy to equanimity. With maitri, or loving-kindness, we begin to like ourselves. With karuna, or compassion, we begin to like others. Then, because we like both ourselves and others, we experience celebration or joy. Finally, with equanimity, we begin to feel that the atmosphere is clear, free, and fantastic. We feel that we could settle down and work with others. We could do anything with them.

According to the mahayana, everything we confront has those four levels. We could relate them to whatever we do.

THREE LEVELS OF ACCOMPLISHMENT

In awakening enlightened genes, there are three levels of accomplishment: the four brahmaviharas, the four limitless ones, and twofold egolessness.

The first level, that of the four brahmaviharas, is based simply on doing good. This level is common to both theists and nontheists.

On the second level, your experience of the four limitless ones is based on one-and-a-half-fold egolessness: the egolessness of self, and half of the egolessness of dharmas. This is the level of shravakas and pratyekabuddhas.

On the third level, you have a hint of twofold egolessness. You begin to experience nondwelling and complete nontheistic vision. Egolessness of self, which comes first, is quite victorious, but it is still very close to theism. With the egolessness of dharmas, you leave theism completely behind. You have achieved two-hundred-percent nontheistic enlightenment.

10

The Spiritual Friend

When we discover the spiritual friend, we begin to realize that our endeavors to discover the mahayana path must be completely genuine. There is no way to cheat, to short-circuit, or to pretend. Everything has to be very genuine and straightforward. That is the duty of the spiritual friend.

RESTORING GENUINENESS

Once we have realized the need to give up aggression and ego, we can give birth to gentleness and a kind attitude toward others. We can wake up our enlightened genes. But the question then is, how are we going to continue further? It is like discovering that we have good soil and good seeds, and wondering what we need to do next. The answer is that we need a good farmer, someone who knows how to plant the seeds in the soil. That farmer is the spiritual friend. We are the soil and we have the seeds, and the farmer knows how to plow and how to plant those seeds properly in us. So discovering a good spiritual friend is one of the best ways to develop bodhisattvahood.

The discovery and development of your buddha nature depends on the spiritual friend. You need a good friend who will point these things out to you. That person is the kalyanamitra, or in Tibetan, the *ge-we shenyen*. *Ge-we* is a form of *ge-wa,* which means "virtue," or "that which is fine," *she* means "companionship," and *nyen* means "friend"; so the *ge-we shenyen,* or spiritual friend, is a virtuous and very close friend or companion.*

THE ROLE OF THE SPIRITUAL FRIEND

The role of the spiritual friend is to tell you how bad, how wretched, and how miserable the samsaric world is, and how fortunate you are to be able to see this and attempt to come out of that world. Because you have discovered how the pain and neurosis of samsara brings constant torment, you feel compassionate and try to help others. The role of the spiritual friend is to show you how you can help yourself and others, but the actual helping itself has to be done by you. The role of the teacher is to bring up trouble for you, and your role is to have to deal with it. In that way, the teacher-student relationship is workable and becomes a delightful dance. The teacher might play the music, and you might dance to the rhythm. That is the principle of the spiritual friend.

At the mahayana level, there is a greater need for leadership than in hinayana. What is needed is not heavy-handed leadership, but leadership by example. You need personal communication with someone who is actually practicing the bodhisattva path. The spiritual friend serves as a reference point of somebody who has done it and succeeded. He or she is someone who has actually attained some level of buddhahood, although such a person does not have to be a completely realized Buddha.

Your first reaction on meeting the spiritual friend is feeling welcomed, so a strong connection is established. You need that kind of connection to begin with—and after that you have to get into the nitty-gritty of the situation. You need to look into what needs to be solved, what should be dropped, and what should be cultivated. In fact, one of the functions of a spiritual friend is to interrupt your life. For example, if you are about to kill yourself, your friend will come along and say, "You idiot! Stop it!"

---

* In Trungpa Rinpoche's discussion of the mahayana, the phrase *spiritual friend* refers specifically to one's spiritual teacher or guide. More generally, spiritual friends can refer to sangha friends who support you in your practice.

and save your life. That's what real friends do—only fake friends like to indulge you.

Relating with a spiritual friend is not particularly therapeutic. You have to watch very carefully for that attitude. It is not therapeutic, but practical, absolutely pragmatic—and in the mahayana, when things become very pragmatic, they can become very heavy. But in fact, it is not something heavy coming at you—it is your own fixation that is being revealed. There are so many things you don't make friends with in your life, even such simple things as brushing your teeth, but you cannot blame mahayana doctrine for your own fixations. You are actually tripping yourself. Spiritual friends are very earthy and ordinary, and at the same time they are very practical and powerful. They may tell you to cut out certain things, but over time you will begin to understand their logic and why they are telling you to do that. It is quite straightforward and basic.

The role of the spiritual friend is not to advertise or to talk students into anything, and it is not to convince students to join the Buddhist tradition. It is not a missionary approach. I myself encountered that kind of missionary approach when I was a refugee in Kalimpong in northern India. The Presbyterian missionaries there used to give powdered milk to all the Tibetans every Wednesday morning. The Tibetans came because they liked the milk, but they were given religious literature at the same time, which they couldn't care less about.

When we discover the spiritual friend, we begin to realize that our endeavors to discover the mahayana path must be completely genuine. There is no way to cheat, to short-circuit, or to pretend. Everything has to be very genuine and straightforward. That is the duty of the spiritual friend. Discovering a spiritual friend is a tremendous help to us in restoring reality and genuineness and in dispelling hypocrisy, such as the hypocrisy of thinking that we could get away with hiding our habitual patterns, or with secrecy of any kind. There is no secrecy on the mahayana path at all. When we discover the spiritual friend, our path becomes much more straightforward and basic.

A good spiritual friend allows us to maintain our bodhisattva path by helping us to refrain from previous habitual patterns that may not be wholesome or necessary. The spiritual friend allows us to refrain from the bad habitual patterns and obstacles we have developed from birth, through our upbringing, and in the way we relate with our world altogether.

Chögyam Trungpa Rinpoche in simple Zen teaching robes. Photographer Ray Ellis.

When we meet the spiritual friend, we realize that we ourselves can give birth to both absolute and relative bodhichitta by our own effort, but we cannot do this without their example. By means of the spiritual friend's example, we can actually take a step forward—and the first step we take is to develop kindness to ourselves.

ATTITUDES TOWARD THE SPIRITUAL FRIEND

Once you have discovered the spiritual friend, there are several attitudes that you can develop toward him or her. You could view the spiritual friend as a guide or a scout. When you have no idea how to journey on the path, the spiritual friend is the good scout who leads you on.

You could view the spiritual friend as an escort. When you are traveling on a dangerous road and all sorts of obstacles come up, the spiritual friend acts as your protection so that you do not get frightened or fall into any problems.

You could view the spiritual friend as a good ferryman. A ferryman will cross the river with you and for you. If the river is so big that you can't swim across it and you are stuck on one side, it is not very pleasant. You long to cross over to the other side, and you are looking for someone who can take you. The spiritual friend is the best ferryman to take you across the river. The river might be quite turbulent, but this ferryman is willing to sacrifice their life for your benefit, and is willing to share the danger.

LEARNING TO BE GENUINE

By relating with the spiritual friend, you are learning how to work with genuineness. If you hope somebody will give you an easy time so that you can build up your own hypocrisy, then you will have no way to connect with the genuineness and goodness of enlightened mind. But having already been individually salvationed in the hinayana, having already sorted yourself out in your own right, you then can meet with a spiritual friend. That friend will work with you in terms of your own particular genuineness and capability. At the same time, that spiritual friend will never miss an inch of anything that you might miss. They will work with you inch by inch, step-by-step, stitch by stitch.

We have to work to overcome the basic habitual tendencies that we might have developed early on, long before we entered the bodhisattva path. Such habitual tendencies are obstacles to realizing enlightenment. They are what we use to hide ourselves, to cheat ourselves, and to short-circuit our discipline. The problem of habitual tendencies is an ageless problem, a timeless problem. It existed in medieval times and runs right up to the present century. It doesn't matter whether we are talking about the manual world of medieval times or the automatic-machinery world of today: ordinary human beings still use the same excuses and complain in the same way. I'm sure that people in medieval times also used to say, "I feel so sick. Can I excuse myself from sitting practice?" That has been going on for a long time. It is an old story; it is even written about in the sutras. And we are still doing it today, right now, this very minute.

The habitual tendency of short-circuiting your discipline is seemingly done for your own benefit, but strangely it seems that you want to hurt yourself, which is quite shocking. You prefer to remain an invalid and you don't want to be cured. If you look at it from the enlightened point of view, it is utterly shocking. You prefer to be like an Egyptian mummy, with bandages all over your body. You prefer to sleep on like that. You don't want to completely recover from your wounds and be ready and willing to work; instead, you want to go back to your bandages. Isn't that strange? Many of us tend to do that. It is quite shocking and may be quite natural. Sometimes it is surprising and sometimes it is obvious—it is shocking when somebody else does it, and it is obvious when you do it.

Beyond that, when you realize what you have been doing, you become willing to be a truly genuine person. You are genuinely willing to listen to the dharma. You do not just come and listen to the dharma because of your credentials or your connections, but you come in your own right, with your own neuroses and your own problems.

LISTENING TO THE DHARMA

Once you are willing to listen to the dharma, there are instructions on how to listen to, or receive, the dharma. Generally speaking, students are referred to as receivers, or containers, into which the dharma is poured. Such containers may be upright, upside down, leaky, or poisonous.

An Upright Container

A good student is a pure vessel, into which the dharma, the elixir of life, the truth, can be poured. If you are free from the concept of "me" and "mine," you can develop discriminating awareness, or *soso rangrik*. *Soso* means "separateness," *rang* means "self," and *rik* means "perceiving or seeing properly"; so *soso rankrik* means "individually seeing things as they are as separate entities." It is general common sense that allows you to see that red is different from green.

Perceiving things as they are allows you to fully experience the teachings. Your sense of hearing allows you to hear the teachings; your sense of smell allows you to perceive the fragrant scent of discipline; your sense of taste allows you to experience the flavor of dharma. Your meditation practice allows you to experience the soothing quality of the dharma, not as a euphoric state, but as an organic gentleness. An understanding of wisdom arises out of all that. It may be very faint, but it is still quite deep. You see that wisdom is like a crystal, which possesses the property of sending out light, but nonetheless maintains an embryonic brilliance within itself.

An Upside-Down Container

There are other vessels that are not suitable for receiving the dharma. They represent how not to listen to the dharma, and you should try not to be one of those vessels.

Number one is an upside-down container. You cannot pour the dharma, the elixir of life, into such a container. You become an upside-down container when you are completely turned off to the dharma, or so preoccupied with something else that your preoccupation is more important to you than listening to the dharma. If you are thinking about your love affair or your economy or something else at the same time that you are listening to the dharma, you are like a container that is turned upside down.

A Leaky Container

Number two is a container with a hole in the bottom. Because this container is leaky, it cannot hold whatever *amrita,* or elixir of life, is poured into it. You are naive and willing to listen, but you are not willing to memorize what you have heard and to regard it as your own practice. You just let the dharma go by, as if you were a container with a hole in the bottom. The more dharma that is poured in, the more leaks out. What you have heard is completely lost; it just makes a mess on the carpet.

A Poisonous Container

Number three is a container that is unclean, or poisonous. Anything poured into such a container becomes tainted. While you are receiving the dharma, your mind is preoccupied with your own personal egotism. You are trying to make sure that what you hear coincides with what you would like to hear. You would like the dharma to fit in with your own particular point of view, which you would like to continue. Therefore the dharma that is poured into this container turns into poison instead of being medicine.

Those are the three aspects of what to avoid when you listen to the dharma. We don't regard these three as examples of bad students, exactly. Such students are somewhat sweet; they are not quite capable of hearing the dharma, but we would not call them bad. If somebody comes along very sweetly and sits down on a meditation cushion with bad posture, we wouldn't say they were a bad sitter. We would be appreciative that they came to meditate at all. In addition, a container could be upside down one day, and proper the next. It might have a hole in it one day, and poison in it the next. So it is a changeable situation, but it is still problematic.

The way to relate with teaching situations and to listen to the spiritual friend is not to be an upside-down pot, a pot with a hole in the bottom, or a pot with poison in it. Rather, you should be a pure vessel. Instead of being closed off, you could cultivate complete openness. Instead of being a leaky container, you could learn to memorize and be able to comprehend the teachings. Instead of being a poisonous vessel, you could free your mind from kleshas.

You should listen, receive, and understand as much as you can from the spiritual friend and their teachings, as naturally and directly as possible.

You should learn about the mahayana and how to go about it, and you should develop know-how. You should study the techniques of the bodhisattva path, the stages of the path, and everything else about the mahayana. You should learn manually by discussing these teachings with your spiritual friend, and comparing what you hear with your own personal experience and how you feel about what you have been taught.

Working with a teacher is an absolutely necessary prerequisite for journeying on the bodhisattva path. Once you have discovered your enlightened gene, you need something to cause it to grow, and that cause is the spiritual friend. So working with the spiritual friend is like sowing a seed and pouring water over it. In that way the seed will sprout, begin to develop young green shoots, and blossom. Then you can be quite certain that what you have done is right, that it is the best possibility.

As a student, you should begin by being prepared. You should not jump in right away. If you do want to jump in, you should begin by developing a personal practice. That way you are not jumping the gun, so to speak. It is very natural. Before you jump into a swimming pool, you should know the depth of the water. Likewise, as a student, you should know what you are doing, and you should have basic hinayana training. In working with a spiritual friend, personal training is absolutely important.

Part Four

MAKING A COMMITMENT

11

Indestructible Wakefulness

With bodhichitta, your heart is "gentle-awake." You feel very homey about your world. Your world is workable, people are workable, and your senses are workable. Therefore, you feel very tender toward everything. Everything you touch, everything you experience, is tender. Because there is more tenderness, because there is no irritation, you feel very cheerful and very awake.

The Uncompromising Ground
of Ultimate Bodhichitta

It is necessary to realize that there is a basic ground that is not bound by passion, aggression, and ignorance. There is a state of existence that is invincible, tough, and monumental. That state remains very solid and inspired, but it is not regarded as ego, which has a quality of defending and collecting. In this particular monumental state of existence, the ground has become very tough and uncompromising. It could be said to be the black and blueness of wakefulness, which nobody can hamper or interfere with. That state of being is bodhichitta. It is the confidence, pride, and heroism of the bodhisattva path.

Ultimate bodhichitta is very important and powerful. It does not refer to a process but to an experience that is beginningless. As in unconditional buddha nature, the idea is that you are already fully developed; you do not need to be awakened. The idea of relative buddha nature was formulated for those who have lost hope, in order to encourage them. It is like saying that you have George Washington–ness in you, rather than that you yourself could be president. Ultimate bodhichitta is saying that you yourself

89

can become president. You don't have to try to become like George Washington, and you don't have to transplant George Washington–ness into yourself—you could do it on your own. The difference is one of aspiration as opposed to actuality. It is the difference between being a would-be buddha, and having the essence, the heart, and the mind of wakefulness in you already. Ultimate bodhichitta means that you are eternally awake. It means that fundamentally you have never gone to sleep. Whether you are asleep or awake, eating your breakfast, lunch, or dinner, whatever you are doing, you are always awake. That is ultimate bodhichitta, the heart of wakefulness.

Conditional buddha nature is simply an encouragement, whereas ultimate bodhichitta is already there. The only obstacle is that you don't believe it. You prefer to indulge in ignorance, and wallow in samsara. Even those who have heard the teachings still prefer to fall asleep and snore. That is rather shocking, and a big obstacle. We have to learn to cheer up; we are so meek and so poor that we have not yet touched our possibility of pleasure, our possibility of attaining enlightenment, or having even a little taste of what it could be. Although we might have problems with pain, we are more likely to have a problem with pleasure. We haven't actually looked at the good side of things. We don't want to hear about it. We don't want to add an extra spoonful of sugar to our coffee; we prefer to drink it bitter, which is not so good.

You could cheer yourself up very simply. You can make yourself happy by not indulging in the samsaric style of happiness. It is very real; I can assure you that this is not a myth. You can actually aspire to the level of bodhichitta. It takes tremendous guts, which makes the whole thing clean-cut. You can indulge yourself; there is no problem with that. It has been sanctioned by the bodhisattvas and the buddhas of the three times. In order to wake up your bodhichitta, that kind of self-existing celebration is okay.

Not being able to open up is one of the biggest problems human beings have. In our society, we have been too involved with ourselves for a long time, and we do not want to give an inch. After the Industrial Revolution, people began to proclaim themselves. They created commonwealths and democracies, but they still clung to their individuality and would not give up their territory. Even missionaries, who acted with goodwill, did not have enough decency. They were too stiff and righteous, and the people they converted became even stiffer. That has been the situation right up to this very day. Decency means giving up our territory properly and fully, and becoming part of the big mind of bodhichitta. It is opening up to big vision, wakeful vision.

Due to our confidence in buddha nature, we realize that obscurations are temporary, and we are able to appreciate our human birth, free and well-favored. Aided by our spiritual friend, we are inspired to realize and practice the disciplines of mindfulness and awareness. And as a result of mindfulness practice, we begin to develop *pagyö*, which means "bare attention," or "heedfulness," and *tren-she*, or "recollection." We develop decorum and keen attentiveness, and an intrinsic kind of knowing.* These are the prerequisites for arousing absolute bodhichitta.

In the mahayana, in order to arouse absolute bodhichitta, we have to join shamatha and vipashyana together. Having developed the basic precision of shamatha and the total awareness of vipashyana, we put them together so that they cover the whole of our existence—our behavior patterns, our daily life, everything. So both meditation practice and postmeditation practice, mindfulness and awareness, are happening simultaneously all the time. Whether we are sleeping or awake, eating or wandering, precision and awareness are taking place. That is quite a delightful experience.

Bodhisattva heroism is open and genuine, and it cannot be stained by anything because its own existence is so tough. With such openness and gentleness, you do not give in to any kind of aggression. Such heroism is unyielding and does not give away its secrets. Telling your secret to everybody and proclaiming it everywhere does not seem to work. You are making a fool of yourself by just giving it away like that; you are being cheap in telling people everything that you think. You are not only giving away your secret, but you are polluting the world.

GENTLE WAKEFULNESS

The Sanskrit term *bodhi* means "wakefulness," and those who have achieved bodhi are called buddhas. Why are people awake, and why do they search for wakefulness? They are wakeful because they have decided to abandon aggression and its activities, both in themselves and toward

---

* For more on *pagyö* and *tren-she*, see volume 1 of the *Profound Treasury*, chapter 34, "Cutting Thoughts and Short-Circuiting the Kleshas."

others. That is the fundamental definition of *bodhi,* or wakefulness. When you are awake, you are no longer able or willing to cause harm to others. You are gentle, and the more gentle you become, the more wakefulness happens.

The dictionary might say that an enlightened person is somebody who is brilliant, intelligent, learned, and ambidextrous in all kinds of ways. But as the translation of the word *bodhi,* the word *enlightenment* means "gentle," and therefore capable. The more gentle you are, the more capable you become; and the more capable you become, the more you have the power to influence others. Buddhist logic works that way always. For instance, the meaning of dharma is passionlessness. Since passion means trying to assert one's own energy or strength in the service of egohood, passionlessness is egolessness. Similarly, gentleness is wakefulness. That is how Buddhist logic works.

Bodhi is the basis of the word *bodhichitta.* With bodhichitta, your heart is "gentle-awake." You feel very homey about your world. Your world is workable, people are workable, and your senses are workable. Therefore, you feel very tender toward everything. Everything you touch, everything you experience, is tender. Because there is more tenderness, because there is no irritation, you feel very cheerful and very awake.

At the same time, some kind of suffering is necessary. But there are two types of suffering. It is said in the texts that those who have attained the highest level of enlightenment suffer more than ordinary people. Their suffering is like the difference between having a hair in your eye as opposed to feeling a hair touching your palm. You feel much more. In other words, they are more in tune with how other people feel. That kind of discomfort is necessary in order to work for others. Positively speaking, it's like the ache a mother or father would feel if their child cries. But there is another form of discomfort that arises from losing your grip on how to maintain your ego, which is not necessary. That kind of discomfort is an extra burden. So suffering could be very helpful or it could be somewhat of a nuisance.

How can one become an enlightened person? How can you train the mind properly and fully? It is by arousing bodhichitta, the heart or essence of enlightenment. And having aroused bodhichitta, you can continue to practice according to the bodhisattva's example. You can be an active bodhisattva.

THREEFOLD PURITY

The experience of bodhichitta is described in terms of threefold purity, or *khorsum yangdak*. *Khorsum* means "threefold," and *yangdak* is "pure"; so *khorsum yangdak* is "threefold purity." The three purities are the non-existence of the actor, the action, and the object of the action. That is, there is no "you" as actor, there is no action, and there is no one to be acted upon.

The principle of threefold purity applies to both absolute and relative bodhichitta. In terms of relative bodhichitta, your way of behaving toward others contains a lot of strength and warmth. In terms of ultimate bodhichitta, there is very little territorialism. If there is no territory, there is no boundary. Therefore, there is no you, no other, and no project. For example, if I am going to kill you, I don't exist, you don't get murdered, and the act of murder doesn't occur.* In any action, if there is no giver and no receiver, we are one. Therefore, there is no action taking place: you can't take action within yourself alone, because then you become two.

Threefold purity is immediate, on the spot, simultaneous. It is not a practice, but an experience that arises as a result of practice. Throughout the mahayana, all practices are based on threefold purity. Therefore, actions come only from warmth and openness.

With threefold purity, there is less territory, so there is more freedom. Because there is more freedom, there is a greater sense of obstacles because there are fewer obstacles. At the basic vipashyana level, territorialism still arises, but that experience of territoriality brings a greater version of vipashyana awareness, or the shunyata experience. The experience of territoriality reminds you that you are practicing at a primitive level rather than an enlightened level—and that reminder takes place constantly. Even the greater vipashyana, or *mahavipashyana*,† experience of a glimpse of shunyata is territorial from the point of view of a bodhisattva.

---

* Although this example is quite extreme, it does not imply that killing one another is okay. The mahayana teaching of threefold purity is always joined inseparably with that of loving-kindness and compassion. Furthermore, the mahayana path altogether rests upon the strong ethical foundation of the hinayana.

† *Mahavipashyana* is the highest form of vipashyana, or awareness practice, described as "seeing things as they are"; that is to say, as empty of self-nature.

UNCONDITIONAL COMPASSION

Relative bodhichitta is regarded as our starting point, and absolute bodhi-chitta is regarded as a further achievement, but one is not necessarily regarded as better than the other. You have to see the play of the phenom-enal world first, and after that you can begin to see further reality. Ultimate bodhichitta is an exploration of karuna, the noble heart of compassion. In Tibetan, absolute compassion is *yang-dak-pe nying-je*. *Yang* means "per-fect," *dak-pe* means "purity," and *nying-je* means "compassion," or "noble heart"; so *yang-dak-pe nying-je* means "perfectly pure compassion."

Our state of being, our basic nature, contains our capability for com-passion. So compassion is more than a potentiality. We do possess fun-damental softness, which cannot be stained or diluted by aggression or ignorance. This softness is how we are. You could call it love, if you like, but probably the best word would be *gentleness*. Such gentleness possesses intelligence and brilliance.

We might feel terrible, utterly hopeless, but if we look at ourselves fully and thoroughly, we will find fundamental goodness. There is some-thing that makes us look up at the blue sky or the clouds or the sun, something that allows us to polish our shoes and press our clothes. When we wake up in the morning, there is something that allows us to brush our teeth, comb our hair, or use a bar of soap. Such actions may seem rather ordinary, but they come from a very powerful instinct. That sense of workability comes from ultimate bodhichitta.

Ultimate bodhichitta is ultimate because that basic instinct exists in us as our natural state of being, or alaya. Nobody has produced or given us such a state of mind, which has enormous intelligence and capabilities. Alaya is the basis of our intelligence; it is what allows our sense percep-tions to function. Alaya is the starting point of following the breath in meditation; without it, we could not begin. It is the discipline for attaining enlightenment.

The process of developing absolute bodhichitta is dependent on the development of relative bodhichitta. That is to say, we have to begin by developing a quality of gentleness, softness, and kindness that permeates our whole life. We bring this about by developing mindfulness and aware-ness, and being thoroughly processed, or shinjang-ed.

Relative bodhichitta is the basic understanding of how things work, how there is an omnipresent soft heart existing throughout our life.

Out of that, we begin to go deeper into the experience of softness. As we do so, we begin to see beyond ego-centeredness and selfishness. We become loosened up to such an extent that it is very easy to develop absolute bodhichitta, which is free from reference point, free from struggle, and free from goal orientation. And from that experience of absolute bodhichitta, we begin to realize the ultimate meaning of compassion. So compassion does not mean feeling sorry for someone who is trying to sell pencils on the street corner. Compassion is the general willingness to open up and to regard any obstacles that might arise as stepping-stones rather than hindrances. Compassion is also a feeling of faith and trust in the kalyanamitra, or spiritual friend, the person who guides you and shows you the way.

Compassion has the quality of existing in a state of nonreference point. You might wonder how one can understand anything if there is no reference point, but having a reference point does not necessarily help you to understand. Reference points can be helpful when you have lost your way, but by the time you realize you have lost your way, it is too late; you are already trying to find your way back. So reference points bring bad news rather than good news. In fact, any reference point becomes an obstacle to experiencing true reality.

Entering the state without reference points is referred to as going into the state of alaya, the storehouse consciousness. This state does not have any particular hope and fear—it is just basic cognitive mind. Seeing yourself in that basic cognitive state of being brings a sense of relief and freedom, because you do not have to go through the usual bureaucracy of your psychological makeup. Then you can begin to go even further, beyond the cognitive state of being. You can begin to experience something beyond cognition or recognition. Instead of just going deeper, you begin to expand outward. Things perceived by the sense consciousnesses become very vivid, but you do not just store them in a memory bank—you expand beyond that.

At that stage, you naturally begin to develop a sense of warmth and comfort. You experience freedom or liberation. That experience of freedom might be purely a glimpse, not necessarily long-lasting or euphoric. But you can receive that small glimpse of freedom, that glimpse of absolute bodhichitta, by faithfully cultivating relative bodhichitta. That short glimpse of absolute bodhichitta enables you to continue working with others and with yourself.

With relative bodhichitta there is a reference point, and with absolute bodhichitta there is no reference point. Absolute bodhichitta is unconditional softness and gentleness, whereas relative bodhichitta may still be a conditional thing. Relative bodhichitta is like learning the alphabet, and absolute bodhichitta is like learning how to spell words. With relative bodhichitta, there is a question of who is helping whom. But with absolute bodhichitta, there is no such question; generosity simply pours out of your whole being.

12

Planting the Moon of Bodhi in Your Heart

The mahayana teachings are based on communication, openness, and being without expectations. When we begin to realize that the nature of phenomena is free from concept and empty by itself . . . there is nothing in the way. So . . . we could fill the whole of space with affection—love without expectation, without demands, without possession.

IN THE mahayana, there is a lot of room for affection and love, and there is immense openness and daring. As long as you are generating affection toward other beings, there is no time to simply work on yourself or to come out clean. The hinayana path of individual salvation is based on not causing harm to others. You are becoming reasonable, good thinking, and polite. Such training is important, but how can you keep smiling on the basis of individual salvation alone, without doing anything for others?

In the mahayana, by means of relative bodhichitta, and with the help of the four brahmaviharas and the four limitless ones, you finally awaken. Waking up in this way is known as planting the moon of bodhi in your heart. When you commit yourself to the bodhisattva path, you feel as if you have done it before and you have been doing it all along. It is like living up to your inheritance, or taking over your parents' business. You feel that there is something quite natural and right about it.

Relative bodhichitta practice begins with maitri, or loving-kindness. In the mahayana, you are learning to love one another and to love yourself. It is very difficult to learn to love. If an object of fascination or some kind of dream or promise is presented to you, you might fall in love. But it is very hard to love if it means purely giving love without expecting anything in return. It is very difficult to do that. We usually expect a person to fulfill our desires and conform to our hero worship, and we can only fall in love if we think our expectations will be fulfilled. So in most of our love affairs, our love is conditional. It is more of a business deal than actual love.

To learn to love, to learn to open, is one of the hardest things for us, yet we are conditioned by passion all the time. Since we are in the human realm, our main focus is on passion and lust, yet we have no idea how to communicate warmth. When we begin to communicate warmth to somebody, it makes us very uptight, and when the object of our love tries to cheer us up, it becomes an insult. It is a very aggression-oriented approach. So in the mahayana, particularly in the contemplative tradition, love and affection are free and open love, love that does not ask for anything in return. Love is a mutual dance that takes place, and even if you step on each other's toes during the dance, it is not regarded as problematic or an insult.

The mahayana teachings are based on communication, openness, and being without expectations. When we begin to realize that the nature of phenomena is free from concept and empty by itself, that objects such as chairs, tables, rugs, curtains, and walls are no longer in the way, we can expand our notion of love infinitely. There is nothing in the way. So the purpose of discussing shunyata, or emptiness, is so that we could fill the whole of space with affection—love without expectation, without demands, without possession.

13

Cultivating a Mahayana Mentality

What type of personality is suited to the mahayana mentality and approach? It is a personality characterized by four factors: affection for the world, faith in the right situations, compassion for sentient beings, and bravery.

PEOPLE WHO are inspired to take the bodhisattva vow are excited by the possibility of becoming a bodhisattva and working with something other than themselves—the possibility of devoting their lives to sentient beings. Their own involvement and heightened spirituality is not a consideration.

At the time the vow is taken, it is based on, and in a sense caused by, an external agent or spiritual friend. Yet the vow ceremony is purely a reminder, like celebrating your birthday. At a birthday party you need to have a cake and some friends to sing "Happy Birthday." That makes it official that you have become one year older. Likewise, the bodhisattva vow is a kind of landmark.

What type of personality is suited to the mahayana mentality and approach? It is a personality characterized by four factors: affection for the world, faith in the right situations, compassion for sentient beings, and bravery.

FOUR FACTORS OF MAHAYANA MENTALITY

Affection for the World

The first factor is having a genuine affection for the world. It is based on both developing warmth and seeing through your aggression. The problem with aggression is that there is no genuine affection or sympathy for the world. You favor areas of the world that are in keeping with your own philosophy, discipline, or literature—and everything else is regarded as unworthy. So on the metaphysical or conceptual level, a sense of separation exists. But with nonaggression, there is a feeling of openness and discriminating awareness. Along with that, you have an appreciation and respect for bodhichitta as unconditional sympathy, with no reference to ego or to anything in the phenomenal world that will encourage ego. Such softness may seem somewhat naive, but due to discriminating awareness, it is not.

Faith in the Right Situations

The second factor is having faith in the right situations. You do not have faith in that which is subject to decay, and you do not have faith in that which is subject to eternity. Faith in either is equally the same. Neither is regarded as real faith, because both options are based on having allegiance toward certain situations and experiences, which enables you to gather greater confirmation for your ego. Faith in the right situations has nothing to do with the confirmation of your ego. It is just simple, rightful faith.

Right faith is genuine. It is direct warmth, direct sympathy, direct devotion, and direct openness. It is direct worship, sacredness, respect, awe, and inspiration. Right faith comes from having an attitude of unconditionality, and whenever there is unconditionality, your emotions are always wholesome. In the mahayana, there is lots of room for emotions. At the same time, the mahayana is somewhat unreasonable to the ordinary confused ego because you cannot indulge in your worship or your sympathy. But you could indulge in unconditional emotionality, which is connected to the idea of shunyata. Right faith inspires a vision of the Buddha, the dharma, and the *sangha,* or community. It inspires a vision of the bodhisattvas. With right faith you develop trust in all sentient beings, who are worthy to be objects of compassion.

With this factor you are awakening as a bodhisattva or would-be bodhisattva. Based on devotion to the Buddha, you feel that you are on the right track. You know that other people have done it the same way, so there is a feeling of comradeship. There is healthiness in your approach, and healthiness in your involvement with others. As a result, you do not become evangelical or dogmatic, and you do not become angry or thirst after power.

Compassion for Sentient Beings

The third factor is a genuine sense of warmth and compassion for sentient beings. By sentient beings, we mean those forms of existence that have intelligence, that function by using some kind of brain, that have love-and-hate relationships with the world, that possess calculating qualities. Sentient beings do not need constant nutrition from the ground like plants, which have their roots in the earth. Insects, animals, and human beings can be independent of the ground, but plants do not have such independence, so plants are not regarded as sentient beings. A sentient being is one who grows up and leaves the nest or home; the equivalent of the umbilical cord is cut. Sentient beings have intelligence and can function independently.

Compassion is not just feeling sorry for somebody. It is not that you are on a high pedestal looking down on some miserable wretch who couldn't get their life together, and it is not based on trying to bring someone up to your particular standard. True compassion is based on warmth and sympathy, independent of security. You simply work with sentient beings, and by way of that, you work with yourself.

Bravery

The fourth factor is having a brave attitude toward pain, discomfort, and loneliness. There is a quality of bravery and asceticism. You are willing to relate with pain and discomfort for the sake of your practice. At this point in Western society, relating with discomfort is seemingly very difficult. Since everything in the philosophy, psychology, and lifestyle is designed for pleasure, people have problems with that kind of bravery, exertion, and fearlessness. There is an immense attachment to comfort. If you want to take the wax out of your ears, you do not just use an ordinary stick, but you use Q-tips especially designed to make sure that your eardrums do not burst. If you use a walking stick, there will be a rubber tip on the end so that it won't slip. Little expressions of hospitality of that nature build a whole society of immense comfort.

That level of comfort is amazing and very, very efficient. It is impressive that human beings can come up with such hospitality for their own sake. The problem is that you begin to give in to that comfort, until finally it becomes a way of living. You expect that same kind of comfort and security all the time. In working with sentient beings, this approach puts you in a difficult situation. Things do not usually work all that smoothly, and we expect occasional chaos, but the basic concept is that everything has to be smooth from birth until death. If you are flying, when you leave the airplane, you do not even have to go outside and down the stairs to walk to the gate. You have little tunnels so you are always indoors, whether you are fifty thousand miles up in the air or down on the ground. So you never feel fresh air, or heat or cold. When you arrive you have a car waiting outside, conveniently and precisely placed right in front of your doorway so that you can just dash into it. And that car has lights, and central heating or air-conditioning. Everything is programmed in that way. You can live inside and be completely tunneled. And that same approach applies even after you die. Your body is put into a convenient place and beautified so that your relatives and friends will be impressed with how nice, neat, and dressed up you are. So all along there is immense hospitality.

Recognizing that such extreme hospitality is designed for cowardly or spoiled people, you might decide to go out and live in some mountain cabin for a while. But when you come back and begin to get involved in your daily activities, if your coffee is not as good as you expected, you still complain. This does not mean that one should never complain. It is simply an example of the expectations we have and the hospitality we expect from the regular world, which is very strange and somewhat off-key.

In terms of practice, it is very difficult to work with such a situation. We have been softened and corrupted by that point of view. We have been weakened by that hospitality, and as a result we cannot bear pain properly. That does not necessarily mean that we have to go to the other extreme and become martyrs and heroes, and sleep in sackcloth. We do not have to punish ourselves or think that because we are soft, we now have to tighten up. If we do begin to do that, it becomes a way of trying to gain even higher comfort. It becomes a way for us to not suffer at all.

The bodhisattva way of working with sentient beings is based on dignity and openness. You are not too tired to work with any situation, however challenging or demanding. People taking the bodhisattva vow do not look for hospitality. And once you have taken the bodhisattva vow, the teacher is not going to issue you hats and coats and rubber gloves and boots so that you can fight the world outside. The teacher presents you with nothing, and you can present yourself as you are.

14

The Seven Mahayana Exercises

If you are a true mahayanist, you do not gather merit and you do not make money. You are constantly sharing with others.

T HE ATTITUDE of a bodhisattva is one of devotion, reverence, and openness. You are willing to purify yourself and to share with sentient beings. That is the point for all mahayanists, whether you are a bodhisattva or not.

To cultivate such qualities, bodhisattvas as well as lay mahayanists practice what can be called the seven mahayana exercises.* This list provides a set of directions on how to conduct your service, your devotion, and your meditation practice.

Prostrations

You begin with prostrations, with surrendering yourself. This is a well-known practice at the hinayana level as well, such as when we offer prostrations during the refuge vow ceremony. But in this case, the surrendering is greater and more open. You are doing prostrations based on threefold purity, knowing that within the state of shunyata, there is no prostrator, no object of prostrations, and no prostration. At the same time, there is a quality of openness and devotion.

---

* This traditional sevenfold practice is also referred to as the "Seven-Branch Prayer" and as the "Sevenfold Puja."

Offering

The second exercise is offering. You might offer incense or flowers to the shrine, which exists as a reminder of awakened mind. You might out of generosity give things to needy people or pick up a hitchhiker. Anything like that is regarded as an offering or a benevolent act.

Confession / Acknowledging What You Have Done

The third exercise is usually translated as "confession," but actually it is simply acknowledging what you have done. So it is not like the Christian tradition of going to confession. You are simply acknowledging your own weaknesses and proclaiming that understanding.

Adoration / Rejoicing in the Virtues of Others

The fourth exercise is rejoicing in the virtues of others; it is admiration or adoration. You have adoration for the greater vision of the enlightened state of being and for enlightened ones, such as the Buddha and the lineage. People in the past have done a great job and fantastic work; they are very impressive. Keeping that in mind is a very important and powerful thing to do.

Asking Your Teachers to Turn the Wheel of Dharma

The next exercise is asking your teachers to turn the wheel of dharma. Requesting the bodhisattvas and buddhas of the ten directions and the ten stages to teach is an intelligent thing to do. However, you don't just say to somebody, "Turn the wheel for us, please." When you are with a teacher, or even without a teacher, a certain temperature and atmosphere takes place in the present moment. So it is important to ask your teachers to teach subjects appropriate to the understanding of what is taking place in the present.

In the mahayana, bodhisattvas traditionally act as spokespeople for laypeople in the presence of Lord Buddha. They ask him various questions, and in response the Buddha expounds the teaching for the sake of the laypeople as well as the bodhisattvas. In the tantric path, it is the consorts of the various *sambhogakaya* or celestial buddhas who ask questions appropriate to the present situation. In any case, the point is knowing what to ask. You need to know what questions are appropriate in order to give hints or directions about how to elucidate the dharma and clarify confusion. That is really turning the wheel of the dharma.

Requesting Your Teachers to Remain and Not Pass into Nirvana

In this exercise, you express your gratitude, and request your teachers to remain alive in the physical world and not pass away. You request them to remain in samsara and not pass away into nirvana.

Dedicating the Merit for the Benefit of All Beings

Finally, whatever merit you have accumulated is never kept for yourself, but is always shared with others. So you are not really making any profit. If you are a true mahayanist, you do not gather merit and you do not make money. You are constantly sharing with others.

15

Taking the Bodhisattva Vow

When you take the bodhisattva vow, it is very personal and at the same time very public. What you are doing is becoming like one of the objects in a pawnshop: you have pawned yourself. You have sold yourself to others, and you are no longer your own property, but the property of sentient beings.

BODHICHITTA AND THE BODHISATTVA VOW

Bodhichitta has three components: compassion, skillful means, and knowledge, or karuna, upaya, and prajna. However, depending on the context, these three components are usually described in terms of pairs: compassion and knowledge, compassion and skillful means, or knowledge and skillful means. When skillful means are combined with discriminating awareness, you are able to see things very clearly. You know what to do and what not to do. Bodhichitta consists of tremendous gentleness and fearlessness, which enables you to act skillfully and wisely. Bodhichitta is big-mindedness.

On the whole, our mind is made up of basic wakefulness. There is always a level of decency and of wakefulness in humans. That is why the human realm is known as the world of opportunity: it is the only realm in which you are able to practice and attain enlightenment. The other realms are too involved with their own neurosis, so beings in those realms first have to work out their karmic consequences. But all humans possess some kind of decency; they all possess the essence of bodhichitta.

Our level of bodhichitta may be embryonic. We may not yet have awakened our basic genes. We may have been brought up in a ghetto, and become so involved with street fighting that there was no chance to awaken. But even then, we have decency. When we give up our street-fighting mentality and come to terms with our decency, we begin to develop relative bodhichitta. We are actually transplanting bodhichitta in our heart. Taking the bodhisattva vow is part of that process. When we take the bodhisattva vow, we are proclaiming our decency, gentleness, and reasonability. We are offering to serve our fellow sentient beings.

Taking the bodhisattva vow is an expression of commitment to share that decency and big vision. You are willing to give up being petty. You are willing to become a genuinely big person, a person with larger vision and fantastic openness. It is interesting that when you do that, you are not suspended in that bigness, but you begin to get some kind of feedback from the world. The world begins to invite you and welcome you. The tathagatas and bodhisattvas, as well as the people of the samsaric world, begin to see the difference in you. They see the difference between the days when you are tight and the days when you are virtuous. When you actually become a generous person, a vast, large-scale, open person, even cats and dogs and three-month-old babies begin to feel the difference in you. You have become a genuinely soft and compassionate person. The essence of the bodhisattva approach is to become like that.

You could expand yourself without invading anybody else's territory. This vastness, power, and grandeur come from the pre-split level, before the birth of duality. When you take the bodhisattva vow, you are endorsing your pre-split or ultimate level, but it has to manifest at the relative level. On the bodhisattva path, you are not expanding yourself because of your territory, but because you have no territory. Therefore, you are limitless; you are egoless.

Although you may not yet have touched on the further levels of egolessness, you can pretend; you can act that way. When you pretend, you are not pretending something that you are not, but something that you might be, something you already have. For example, you have no problem pretending to be a human being, because you are already a human being. So pretending to be a more decent human being is not a far-fetched idea. Pretending to be a decent human being is not particularly false. In the beginning, you feel that you are pretending because your samsaric emotions are trying to draw you away from any possibility of decency, and make you into a hell-realm or animal-realm person. But you could behave like a lady or a gentleman, which you already are. Even the pretense of sitting like the Buddha is not far-fetched or false. You are just trying to connect to that level, to approach it. So it is not really pretending; it is just pushing yourself slightly further. It is very simple: you could pretend to be Buddha.

As far as we are concerned, the world is a gentle world, an enlightened society. Such a society is not based on just drinking coffee or tea at the right times, or dressing up on the proper occasions. Rather, there is a sense of celebration and basic goodness. It feels good and it feels real, and there is a quality of overall gentleness. Taking the bodhisattva vow is committing yourself to being gentle. You are willing to say that you will give up your personal privacy. Doing so allows you to be a decent person, a good person, and so heroic. The bodhisattva vow is heroic in the fundamental sense that you begin to feel that you can actually do it and that you are actually doing it—and when you do that, you get feedback confirming it.

Taking the bodhisattva vow does not mean that you have solved the problems of the world, and enlightened society does not mean that everybody is going to eat marmalade and sugar all the time. But there could be at least a skeleton of a world that functions in terms of wakefulness. Because of wakefulness, there is a lot of space. There is room to become larger scale. There is a sense of goodness, arrogance, and wakefulness, all at the same time. The heroism of the bodhisattva is beginning to fulfill its role and become very real, because you are not trying to kid yourself or anyone else. You just do it. It is very simple.

JUMPING INTO THE OCEAN OF DHARMA

It is important to realize how precious the teachings are, and how extraordinary it is that out of millions and millions of people, you are able to study the dharma properly and fully. It is an extraordinary experience. Along with an appreciation of the teachings, it is also important to have an appreciation of the teacher. Without the teacher, you would not have the teachings. When you take the bodhisattva vow, it means that from now onward, until the attainment of enlightenment, you will have such an individual to refer back to. You have an unbroken lineage of companionship, and a friend whose example you can follow. You are working with your own buddha nature, with the spiritual friend, and with an unbroken lineage of goodness that has continued without interruption from the time of the Buddha until right now.

When you meet a spiritual friend, you should trust in that situation. But in this case, trust does not refer to conventional trust. It is not like being a landlord and trusting that your tenants will pay the rent. Trusting in the spiritual friend and the teaching of buddhadharma is not a business deal. It is giving your whole being, and jumping into the deep ocean of dharma. Obviously, the first time you jump into the ocean, you need to work with the waves and tides. But as you learn to swim with the tide as it goes out, you can swim across the Atlantic.

As you swim across the ocean of dharma, you do not have any reference points. I have done it myself, so I speak from firsthand experience. The dharma may seem to be full of reference points, but in crossing that ocean, there are no reference points. That contradiction is in itself a noncontradiction. When you find yourself without a reference point, you have the reference point of no reference point—the reference point of being without reference point. You keep going in that way—reference point, without reference point, reference point, without reference point—until you wear yourself out completely. When you become confused and you have completely run out of reference points altogether, you have reference point without reference point. But you have to do it, rather than talk about it, and you have to relax. That is why it has been said that words do not produce the awakened state of mind, only experience does so.

Once you have committed yourself by jumping into the ocean, you can swim across the ocean. In doing so, you don't use any means of getting across other than your own hands and legs. That process seems to be both good and necessary. Samsara may be quite bewildering, and it creates blindness, but at the same time, there are ways to get out of it. First of all, you have to give up trying to find a way to end samsara. You mustn't have any goal orientation or goal-oriented scheme. Whenever there is goal orientation, that puts you back into the familiar cycle of samsara, and you spin around in the whirlpool of samsara again and again. It's like working with a business: if you have too much goal orientation and you just want to become a millionaire, the business fails, whereas if you regard yourself as selling what is necessary and appreciating what you sell, then you might become a millionaire by seeming chance.

ATTAINMENT AND NONATTAINMENT

Your inspiration in the hinayana is to save yourself personally, which is a big jump. To do so, you need to make a relationship with suffering, impermanence, and a crude level of egolessness, and you need to have trust in nirvana. When all that begins to make sense and you begin to understand it completely, then based on that, you begin to develop a different viewpoint and larger thinking. In the hinayana, you transcend one form of goal orientation by understanding that you have to cut through your own personal ambition and aggression, and relate with egolessness and suffering. But having cut through that, you still have the goal of attaining enlightenment. That ambition has not been cut through. So the last ambition of the hinayanist is the desire to watch yourself attaining enlightenment. You would still like to see that. But that ambition is cut through at the mahayana level.

The notion of the nonattainment of enlightenment is not a hinayana one. Hinayana teachers would say, "If you would like more peace and tranquillity, you better come to Buddhism because we know about suffering as well." They would say, "Everybody wants to have happiness, but they have the wrong concept of happiness. If you want to attain better happiness, you better join us." That is what you see in the pamphlets flying around: an emphasis on personal salvation. But even if someone were to attain enlightenment tomorrow, it would be very corny to proclaim themselves as the buddha of the age. That would not be such a good idea, even if it were real. Although you might respect such a person's achievement, that style of proclamation is very crude.

THE INSPIRATION TO GO FURTHER

The basic hinayana attitude is based more on individual discipline than on social service. But when you begin to expand yourself to the mahayana, your shamatha experience begins to increase because you are more sensitized to the rest of the world. Your vipashyana experience also becomes greatly increased, because the particular world that you are working with is a much wider world than you ever imagined in the early stages of your sitting practice of meditation. Because of that, a feeling of inadequacy begins to come up, and you want to go further. Having heard of the bodhisattva path, you begin to be enormously inspired. You feel you are ready for the mahayana because you want to go on, rather than staying with one particular technique, one particular method, or one particular security. You begin to feel that you are willing to jump into the ocean of dharma and swim.

Various signs indicate that you are ready for the bodhisattva path. In the yogic tradition of the practice lineage, two signs in particular appear in students who have been trained by a proper teacher: the mark of learnedness and the mark of meditation. The mark of learnedness is that you are tamed and peaceful rather than a snobbish intellectual or an angry scholar who makes enemies with everybody. The mark of meditation is that you are less distracted and temperamental. You have quick reactions, and you are watchful and aware. Someone possessing those two signs is an ideal person to begin to tread on the bodhisattva path.

At this point you are not concerned with whether you can swim to the shore or not—you just want to do it. There's that kind of heroism, openness, and inspiration. The path may be immense and wide and long, or it may be like an ocean, which is deep and endless. But you still would like to get into it. You don't feel that the path is a threat, and you do not have the anti-bodhisattva attitude that you should preserve yourself as you are because you might not make it or that you might make a fool of yourself. You do not regard the path as a competition, and you are unconcerned with who is the best bodhisattva—you just want to do it. There is a hunger for the teachings.

MAKING A FORMAL COMMITMENT

The question then is how to go about it, how to enter the mahayana. Traditionally, the way you enter the mahayana is by taking the bodhisattva vow. You may feel that taking such a vow is redundant, that you are already following the bodhisattva path, but it is still necessary to have a place and time in which you could make a formal commitment to becoming a bodhisattva. It is also possible to fool yourself by thinking you need to wait until you are really ready. But that is like the play *Waiting for Godot:* nothing ever happens, and the play just ends.

In addition to the bodhisattva vow, there are hundreds of thousands of other ways to enter into the mahayana. There does not have to be only one official way of entering, as long as there is a feeling of being awake and cheerful, and the inspiration to help others.

If you are inquisitive about the bodhisattva path, if you have an interest in it and are not scared by it, it means you are already fertile. You belong to this particular family, and you have the right to join the mahayana. Taking the bodhisattva vow is like buying a ticket and reserving your seat. And once you have taken the vow, it is like stepping into the vehicle and actually taking the journey.

When you take the bodhisattva vow, it is very personal and at the same time very public. What you are doing is becoming like one of the objects in a pawnshop: you have pawned yourself. You have sold yourself to others, and you are no longer your own property, but the property of sentient beings. You are public property, and you no longer have any privacy. That nonexistent privacy seems to be connected with a wider range of awareness. Concentration may need privacy, but awareness does not. In taking the bodhisattva vow, you are dedicating yourself to the benefit of others. You are not involved with first making yourself perfect; instead, you first make things perfect for others. If by chance any possible repercussions occur for you, it seems to be all right. We are not saying, as the Christians would, that charity begins at home—we say that charity begins in the neighborhood.

In the mahayana, you begin to expand yourself, and all kinds of things happen. Finally you begin to realize that no ground exists for you to operate on two levels at once. You have been trying to operate on the public-service level, and at the same time trying to operate on the privacy level—but those both become nothing, and the whole thing begins to dissolve. You have already enlisted as a soldier, so to speak, and there is no way of getting out. You have already jumped out of your airplane, your parachute has opened, and you are suspended in air. You cannot say it is just a rehearsal and you want to go back to the airplane.

There is a festive quality about taking the bodhisattva vow. You are celebrating the fact that you have found tathagatagarbha. It is not just that you are getting into a long-term commitment, which sounds very gray. You are inviting the sugatas and tathagatas to celebrate with you that you are pregnant with buddha nature, with compassion and wisdom. In taking the vow, you are acknowledging that.

One of the very powerful and contagious things about the bodhisattva path is that you cannot waste your time at all. There is no chance of wasting time, or of regressing. In taking the bodhisattva vow, you are relating with somebody who has the bodhisattva lineage. You are relating with a person, teacher, guru, or spiritual friend who has already gone through that particular system.

ASPIRATION AND APPLICATION

The bodhisattva vow is a twofold process: aspiration and application. The first is the wish or aspiration to enter the bodhisattva path, which is called *mön-pe sem-kye*. *Mönpa* means "aspiration" and the inflected form *mön-pe* makes it "of aspiration"; *sem* means mind, and *kye* means "develop"; so *mön-pe sem-kye* means "developing the mind of aspiration." The second is the application, or *juk-pe sem-kye*. *Jukpa* means "entering" and the inflected form *juk-pe* makes it "of entering"; *sem* means "mind," and *kye* means "develop"; so *juk-pe sem-kye* means "developing the mind of entering." Having already developed aspiration, you really want to commit yourself to this path. Mön-pe sem-kye is like desiring to take a journey, and juk-pe sem-kye is actually preparing for and taking that journey. You cannot take a journey before you have the aspiration and inspiration to do so. But as soon as you have the aspiration, you are already practicing. It is like ordering food in a restaurant: having ordered your food, you eat it. You don't say, "I'm sorry, it was a mistake, I don't want to eat anything after all." It is as simple as that.

The inspiration is real identification with the bodhisattva ideal of giving and surrendering. It is like signing up for the army: you are willing to give your name and to go through the physical examination. If your country is at war with another country, you feel that you might get killed or you might come back home, but it is still uncertain. There is a feeling of empty heart. You are leaving your friends and family, your house, your commitments, your hobbies, and everything else behind, and committing yourself to this particular discipline. As soon as you walk into the recruitment office, you see other young men and women like yourself doing the same thing, making the same commitment, so a whole atmosphere is built up. It is almost like walking into heroism, but it is uncertain if you will live through it.

When you commit yourself to the bodhisattva path, there is a tremendous sense of "What have I done?" If a person is taking the bodhisattva vow properly and seriously, not just as a ritual, there is a feeling of empty heart. That sense of empty heart is the first aspect, mön-pe sem-kye. You want to take the journey, and you pick up the vibrations of emptiness, the vibrations of giving and opening, the vibrations of giving yourself for the benefit of all sentient beings.

The second aspect begins as soon as you take the bodhisattva vow. It begins when you say, "I, so-and-so by name, am going to take the vow of a bodhisattva. From today onward, until the attainment of enlightenment, I am going to commit myself to the path of the bodhisattva lineage and practice the bodhisattva path. I am willing to be a bridge, boat, earth, water, or fire. I am willing to be a slave, physician, path, highway, taxi, bus, airplane, whatever is needed. I am willing to commit myself to having people walk on me, sit on me, and use me. I am willing for people to be inside me or outside me. I am willing to be like a big whale that could swallow somebody, swim across the water, and spit them out. Anybody could use any part of me, any part of my physical existence or psychological territory."

The bodhisattva vow is the statement that you are wholly committed to the bodhisattva path. For the first time in your life, you are no longer a nuisance, but a good citizen. That step of taking the bodhisattva vow comes from the inspiration that tathagatagarbha is already in you. That is why you could make such a commitment.

16

Becoming a Bodhisattva

After taking the bodhisattva vow, there are possibilities of slipping or regressing. The bodhichitta that has been transplanted into your heart is at jeopardy, so you need to transcend goal orientation.

HAVING TAKEN the bodhisattva vow and committed yourself to the path, the quality of doubt begins to become more benevolent, compassionate, and kind. That doesn't mean that you develop complete tranquillity, or that you never lose your temper, or that you never think twice, but there is a sense of openness, warmth, and compassion. There are no grudges against anything, no grinding teeth.

After taking the vow, you do not ask for reassurance from anybody. You have direction already; there is no need for reinforcement. Seeking reinforcement is the action of a coward. As Buddha said, liberation means individual liberation. Occasionally, when you are scared or feel limited, you may look for somebody else to save you. The function of the teacher is to encourage you to do it yourself, so the teacher's business goes on.

At this point, you know what you are; you have a sense of definiteness about yourself. You have doubt, and you work your doubt into compassion; you have joy, and you work your joy into wisdom and inspiration. So the whole thing becomes really workable and up-to-date. At that point, surprisingly, your practice of shamatha-vipashyana becomes much more spacious. You are constantly having flashes of awareness and mindfulness. Sudden glimpses, sudden flashes of awareness, come much more often.

Having taken the bodhisattva vow and committed yourself, you may tend to get carried away. You get high and joyful and confident, but in the back of your mind, there is a faint fear that this effect might wear out. That fear seems to be necessary and good. In fact, that fear is the source of discipline. As a layperson, you could become a bodhisattva, as long as you meditate. You do not first have to become a monk or a nun in order to take the bodhisattva vow, nor do you have to be an arhat. You could advance on the hinayana path by sitting a lot and disciplining yourself, and you might find yourself being a bodhisattva before you know where exactly you are on the path. That is highly possible.

Your sitting practice may be hinayana, while your daily living practice is mahayana. Sitting practice provides a guideline for the day-to-day living practice of the six transcendent virtues, or six paramitas: generosity, discipline, patience, exertion, meditation, and prajna, or knowledge.* No matter how advanced your meditation practice, you can still apply the paramitas. And although your everyday actions may be on a small scale, the heroism of the bodhisattva still applies. By joining the choiceless quality of meditation practice with the heroism of paramita practice, you can bring the hinayana and the mahayana very conveniently together. The realization of tathagatagarbha is a combination of choicelessness and something happening, but if you stop sitting, you are wasting your time and you will not get anywhere. It is not dangerous to do so, but it is a waste of energy. It might be better to stand on a street corner and sell ties.

EGOLESSNESS AND LONELINESS

After taking the bodhisattva vow, there are possibilities of slipping or regressing. The bodhichitta that has been transplanted into your heart is at jeopardy, so you need to transcend goal orientation. Doing so brings an understanding of twofold egolessness. The lower yanas still have a quality of ambition and goal orientation: although they have understood the nonexistence of self, and have partly understood the nonexistence of dharmas, their understanding of nonexistence provides them with a feeling of glory or promise. So a kind of achievement orientation continues, which is a problem.

So goallessness is important for the understanding of egolessness. Egolessness is not only realizing your own nonexistence, but also the nonexistence of the reference point. This happens in various degrees from

---

* More information on the paramitas can be found in part 6, "Bodhisattva Activity."

*The bodhisattva Guanyin (above) is the embodiment of compassion in femi-
nine form. Compassion in masculine form is represented by the bodhisattva
Avalokiteshvara. Nelson-Atkins Museum of Art.*

the hinayana to the mahayana. The loneliness of the hinayana notion of
egolessness continues in the mahayana, but at the mahayana level that
loneliness becomes an exciting adventure, which could be a problem or
a promise. In the mahayana, loneliness does not mean that you have to
reduce or shrink yourself into dry meat—you can expand and share the
greater vision of mahayanism. That actually creates a crescendo, immense
drama, and sudden excitement. Up to this point, you have been involved
with a smaller scale of thinking, and now you are exposed to a larger scale

of thinking. You have all kinds of possible ways to relate to the world. Nevertheless, there is still your own loneliness.

In the mahayana, the egoless aspect of loneliness continues in the realization of the nonexistence of your self. But you have to give up the possible excitement of watching yourself attaining enlightenment. You have to go away, to disappear. The ego part has to disappear, and the reference point does not exist. So it is kind of a sweet-and-sour promise and experience. Loneliness becomes heroism because you are fighting this particular war all by yourself. You are not relying on anybody's help to work with sentient beings or to work with yourself. The spiritual friend is just an adviser who tells you how lonely you are, and how such an individual fight is necessary. So you do not get any personal help, and nobody is going to be a copilot on your journey. Nevertheless, there is still a quality of delight, and there is a feeling of comradeship with other people who are doing the same thing. So at the mahayana level, the loneliness begins to dissolve to a certain extent. The restriction of the loneliness dissolves, but the essence of the loneliness becomes egolessness.

FIVE POWERS

Once you have taken the bodhisattva vow, you develop what are known as the five powers: having a spiritual friend, being inspired to work with others, expanding virtue, intellectual study, and identifying what you have learned with your own practice. These powers are not spiritual powers; they are purely confirmations or landmarks.

The first power is having a spiritual friend as a companion who initiates you into the bodhisattva vow. The second power is awakening from your particular family into the mahayana family and behavior patterns, and being inspired to work with others rather than on yourself alone. Working with others is more interesting and more spiritually enlightening. You may tend to work with other people because that is also a way to develop yourself, but that is not particularly important.

The third power is that virtue begins to expand. When there is no reference to your own achievement as being important, you begin to extend your possibilities of attaining enlightenment.

The fourth power is intellectual study. You learn the mechanics and functioning of the bodhisattva path and study how people in the past achieved the goal and awakened so that you can do it in the same way. The fifth power is that you are able to identify whatever you have learned with your own practice. You are able to relate your learning with your own situation.

BINDING YOURSELF TO THE TEACHINGS

When you take a vow, you are binding yourself together with the teachings. You already have a vague idea of the teachings, and now you would like to tighten the whole thing up to make sure that it is actually being practiced and worked on. The term *dompa,* or "binding," applies to all vows: the refuge vow, the bodhisattva vow, as well as the vows of tantrayana. In the dompa of the bodhisattva vow, the discipline is living up to your aspiration to work for others. You would like to work with sentient beings and relate with the rest of the world, to offer your service and have your particular effort be put toward other people's benefit.

You realize that the attainment of enlightenment can only take place for the benefit of others rather than yourself. If you are doing it for yourself, you could become an egomaniac. You might like to be an important person in history, or you might want to be something less significant than that, but still you would like to build yourself up, to create a monument to yourself. But in this case, none of those possibilities are available, because you are not attaining enlightenment for yourself. However, in order to work with others, you need more training. If you want to become a good chauffeur, you first have to learn how to be a good driver.

On a crude level, when you take the bodhisattva vow, you make certain promises and take on certain disciplines because of your surroundings. You commit yourself, not for yourself, but for others' sake. On a more refined level, having done such a thing, there is an immense input into your memory. You realize what you have done, and you realize that you are stuck with that particular process and style of thinking for the rest of this life, as well as the lives to come. You cannot actually shake it off by saying that it was a rehearsal—it becomes a part of your basic existence.

However, simply taking the bodhisattva vow does not make you a bodhisattva. Bodhisattvahood is a spiritual level. After you have taken the bodhisattva vow and gone through a training process, you may then finally begin to tread on the mahayana path and become a bodhisattva.

17

Joining Profundity and Vastness

If you develop depth, at the same time you are developing benevo-
lence. Because of that warmth, you don't have to defend yourself
anymore. When you realize that you don't have to defend yourself,
you realize there is no defender, either, so a big dissolving process
takes place. That seems to be the basic idea of compassion. So com-
passion is not just being loving and emotionally kind; it is actually
compassion that cuts through.

W HEN YOU take the bodhisattva vow, you are not intensely mimicking the Buddha or the bodhisattvas, nor do you feel particularly
belittled by trying to follow their example. You are not reduced to
a helpless little person who just wants to be saved. You simply take on the
twofold attitude of a bodhisattva: profundity and vastness. We inherited
the vastness tradition from the great master Asanga and the profundity
tradition from the logician Nagarjuna,* but as far as the path is concerned,
they happen together.

PROFUNDITY

Profundity refers to the realization of twofold egolessness. With twofold
egolessness, the belief in individuals and the belief in dharmas are both

---

* *Asanga* (ca. 300–370 ce) was an exponent of the *yogachara* school of Buddhist philosophy. *Nagarjuna* (ca. 150–250 CE) was an Indian philosopher and logician who founded the
madhyamaka, or Middle Way, school. For more on Nagarjuna, see chapter 20, "Emptiness
and the Middle Way."

seen to be irrelevant. Prajna cuts through this and that altogether, both "I" and "am." You are cutting completely. It is like a double-edged sword that cuts the experience as well as the experiencer. When you begin to see through the ego of "I," the experience itself is cut at the same time. So with a single stroke of the sword, the ego of "I" and the experiencer of the egolessness of "I" are both cut. Then you also cut through the ego of "am" and the experiencer of the egolessness of "am." In that way, you cut through everything completely.

In this dualistic, manipulative world, you cannot clear up one side of a situation all by itself. If you have a problem, that problem has to be solved by something else. Whatever you do is a twofold situation, even drinking a cup of tea. It is like a diplomatic game in which you are both the initiator and what is being initiated. There is always some kind of split taking place, a very subtle schizophrenia. For instance, when a thought occurs—"There is a pigeon flying"—there is the experience of the pigeon flying, and at the same time there is the experience of somebody experiencing that pigeon flying. The sense of "I" occurs in the first instant, when something is first beginning to evolve, and along with that, there is also the sense of something occurring in your situation. That occurrence and the somebody watching that occurrence are equally fake. So in talking about "am" and "I," "that" and "this," we use the analogy of the sword of Manjushri, the bodhisattva of wisdom. The sword of Manjushri has two blade edges—with one stroke it cuts both the thinker and the thought.

Cutting through ego is not regarded as a process of destroying an enemy. You cannot cut through ego with the blow of a sword, as if you were killing somebody. That approach would be like ordinary suicide or hara-kiri. One of the criticisms of egolessness is that it means having to give yourself up altogether, to kill both "I" and "am," and organize the ideal seppuku. But the idea of the destruction of ego does not have to do with killing anything. The two levels of egohood, "I" and "am," consist of tremendous hunger and thirst, immense wretchedness, and a terribly deprived feeling. When you say, "I am," you feel hungry, thirsty, deprived, and lonely. That wretchedness actually embodies itself when you say, "I am." That very term, that very concept, is filled with fundamental poverty. "I am" is the expression of being personally disturbed. The proclamation of "I am" is so painful, and the only thing that will cheer you up is the verb that follows that proclamation: "I am . . . drinking," "I am . . . happy-ing," "I am . . . this-and-that-ing."

VASTNESS

As your bodhisattva practice begins to evolve, you realize that ego pain can be overcome and destroyed. The source of the destruction is compassion, a benevolent approach to yourself. When you recite the *Heart Sutra,** you chant that there is "no eye, no ear, no nose, no tongue, no body, and no mind." But that actually means, "I love my eyes, I love my ears, I love my nose, I love my tongue, I love my body, and I love my mind. I feel sympathetic to all of that." When you develop that kind of sympathetic attitude, all that ego-pain actually begins to dissolve.

GREAT COMPASSION

By transcending fixation on the phenomenal world and seeing the world as insubstantial, you develop an appreciation of emptiness. From the appreciation of emptiness, compassion or karuna develops: you develop great compassion, or *mahakaruna.* Mahakaruna has four aspects: mahakaruna itself, luminosity, skillfulness, and peace. At this point, you may not have reached the level where you experience these things, but you can aspire to that level.

Mahakaruna

The first aspect of mahakaruna is mahakaruna itself, or *nying-je chenpo* in Tibetan. *Nying-je* is "compassion," and *chenpo* means "great," so *nying-je chenpo* means "great compassion." Mahakaruna, or great compassion, is also big vision. You begin to see that the phenomenal world is an expression of shunyata, so it is no longer problematic. It is marked with emptiness; therefore, there is a quality of freedom. That freedom is absent of aggression and struggle, with no possibility of resentment toward yourself, others, or the situation. Great compassion is a source of great genuineness in the practitioner. Usually we want to cheat, to deceive and twist things for our own sake. We distrust something or other, and feel that the situation is not quite right, so we begin to cheat or become evasive. We try

---

* The *Heart Sutra,* or the *Sutra of the Heart of Transcendent Knowledge,* is a beloved teaching on wisdom and emptiness recited in many schools of Buddhism. See appendix 3, "The Heart Sutra."

to ease out of any pressure, which is another form of deception. We are not willing to face facts, and we are trying to avoid something. But in the case of great compassion, there is no attempt to avoid anything because everything is clear. Everything is completely seen through.

Luminosity

The second aspect of mahakaruna is luminosity, or *öselwa* in Tibetan. *Ösel* means "luminous" and *wa* is "-ness," so *öselwa* means "luminosity." *Luminosity* means "brilliance," or "brightness." At heart, it is an eternally rejoicing, joyful, and delightful situation. Although there might be occasional attacks of neurosis, as a practitioner of great compassion you do not give in to them. You no longer have any obstacles in the way of being completely true. You are like a person with good balance: you might skid on a surface, but you do not fall down.

Skillfulness

The third aspect of great compassion is known as true skillfulness, or *thapla khepa* in Tibetan. *Thap* means "method" or "means," and *la* means "in"; *khepa* means "skilled," so *thapla khepa* means "skilled in means." Because you have no fear of yourself, of the other, or of the situation, you are completely in touch with what is happening. You are no longer bewildered by consequences or by the situation as it is, but you feel that everything is under control and you have nothing to worry about. You act very skillfully, but not in terms of scheming or strategizing. Because you have developed clarity in your perspective, you do not have doubts and you are not unreasonable. You realize that the best way to be skillful is to be reasonable. When you are fully reasonable, actually reasonable—and to a certain extent, painfully reasonable—you begin to experience the genuineness of situations and act accordingly, in a way appropriate to the situation.

Peace

The fourth aspect of great compassion is peace, or *shiwa* in Tibetan. In the state of great compassion, you experience a natural state of peacefulness. This has nothing to do with euphoric pleasure as the absence of hassles.

In this case, peace is a quality of vast space. Wherever you go, you cover vast space. Even though your schedule might be interrupted by occasional upheavals, you are not perturbed and you do not give in to them. You have never given in. Therefore, there is a quality of conquering and an experience of peace, of being at ease.

JOINING DEPTH AND BENEVOLENCE

According to the mahayana, egolessness can happen only if you have a sympathetic, compassionate attitude to your own ego. Only then does it dissolve. That is the boundary between profundity and vastness, between the experience of egolessness, or shunyata, and the practice of compassion. It is impossible to understand the profundity of the destruction of the twofold ego without understanding the vast discipline of compassionate bodhisattva activity. So vastness and profundity work together.

Overcoming twofold ego can only be done by means of sympathy and softness. It requires a compassionate and even emotional attitude. With such sympathy, you are willing to be cut by the prajna sword. You are willing to take the bodhisattva vow, which says, "I don't believe in myself, and I don't believe in others. Nevertheless, I would like to save all sentient beings before I attain my own enlightenment." The moment you take the bodhisattva vow, you are deciding to commit yourself to practicing bodhisattva activities, and at the same time you are committing yourself to realizing and experiencing the nonexistence of ego. So the traditions of vastness and profundity work together simultaneously.

Profundity and vastness are the ground of both mahayana vision and action. If you develop depth, you are developing benevolence at the same time. Because of that warmth, you don't have to defend yourself anymore. When you realize that you don't have to defend yourself, you realize there is no defender either, so a big dissolving process takes place. That seems to be the basic idea of compassion. So compassion is not just being loving and emotionally kind; it is actually compassion that cuts through.

Your attitude toward your own existence is based on aggression, so when you have a loving attitude toward yourself, your aggression dissolves. Therefore, you don't exist. Your attitude toward others is also an expression of aggression, so when you have a loving attitude toward others, they don't exist either. Based on compassion, a mutual dissolving or opening-up process takes place. And when you open up, you don't have to have an opener. From the Buddhist perspective, dwelling on any experience could be regarded as the activity of aggression. This applies even if you are trying to maintain a quality of peace, or *shanti*. When you do not have to maintain anything at all because everything is okay, there is no confusion. That is the epitome of twofold egolessness: there is both the profundity of twofold egolessness and the vastness of compassionate bodhisattva activity.

Part Five

EMPTINESS AND COMPASSION

18

Emptiness

Shunyata is not anti-life; life is infested with shunyata-type experiences. Shunyata is the basic reason that life can happen, because shunyata represents nothingness. If there is nothingness, then there is everything.

IN ORDER to understand the practice of the bodhisattva path, we need to discuss the various experiences of shunyata, or emptiness. Shunyata is one of the key points in studying mahayana. *Shunya* means "not," "nothing," or "empty," *ta* makes it a noun; so *shunyata* means "emptiness." The Tibetan word for shunyata is *tongpanyi*. *Tongpa* means "empty," and *nyi* is "itself," or "-ness"; so *tongpanyi* means "emptiness" as well.

What is shunyata empty of? It is empty of holding back, empty of maintaining oneself. But emptiness is not merely negation, because the bodhisattva path is a positive state of existence with a lot of creativity. However, if you do not give up on the idea of "me" and "mine," you could be in a difficult situation. "Me" and "mine" is a fantasy concept, in the same way that "There is a flying saucer in the sky" is a fantasy concept. There actually isn't any such thing.

Shunyata is not anti-life; life is infested with shunyata-type experiences. Shunyata is the basic reason that life can happen, because shunyata represents nothingness. If there is nothingness, then there is everything. So shunyata is the instigator of life, fundamentally and ecologically. Because of shunyata, you can do your practice and other things as well. But before you go about your business, you should take some time for yourself. You need to keep referring back to the hinayana practices of shamatha and vipashyana, which continue to be extremely important. At the same time, you should be aware that in the mahayana you are transcending the mental-gymnastics aspect of the hinayana path. The mahayana brings a different perspective: it brings together awareness, compassion, and non-reference point.

Mental gymnasticism seems to come from the idea that you have to do something because it is good for you. It's like health-food fanatics who very aggressively try to develop peace of mind by eating the right food, and are very pedantic about what should and should not be eaten. There are many versions of gymnasticism. You could be carried away by an ideology and think: "The hinayana path is the only way," "Vipashyana is the only way," or "Shamatha is the only way." You might think that if you do this push-up called mindfulness, you are sure to have good health. The problem with that approach is not with the practice, but with your attitude. With any practice on the path, how you relate with it makes an enormous difference. If you become dogmatic and snobbish about a practice, thinking it is the higher way, it may become a problem.

NONREFERENCE POINT

Experientially, emptiness is described as complete threefold purity. So in that sense, the practice of shunyata does not exist. There is no reference point: no this, no that, and no this-and-that together. The problem is that you either have allegiance toward *that* or you have allegiance toward *this*—*this* being the notion of "me," and *that* being the rest of the phenomenal world—and you can't play both sides. By breaking down the this-and-that reference point, *this* and *that* become *it*. So in the actual shunyata experience, there is no longer any discrimination. However, you would still distinguish between the disciplined and the undisciplined state of being. When you were disciplined, you would simply be disciplined, and when you were not, you would know it.

Nonreference point comes from openness, friendliness, and warmth. It comes from compassion, which is absolutely necessary, and compassion comes from awareness. So we have to refer back to vipashyana, for if you have not developed awareness, you will not develop friendliness, and you will not develop nonreference point either. It is a natural process. In order to let go and open in all directions—to open to this, that, and the actions taking place between this and that—you have to develop trust or warmth. In order to have warmth, you have to have an awareness of thisness and the nonexistence of thisness, and an awareness of thatness and the nonexistence of thatness.

MEDITATION WITHOUT TECHNIQUE OR GOAL

At the same time, shunyata is a meditative experience that regards neither the awareness nor the achievement of awareness as important. Your mind is not focused on any technique; there are no techniques whatsoever, not even techniques of awareness. Your mind is just open, simply open, simply being—or nonbeing. So the shunyata experience is not awareness as such; it is just being open. Awareness is still a reference point of some kind, in that you are aware of something. With the egolessness of vipashyana, you are more aware of the doctrine, but once you get into shunyata, you are less aware of the doctrine. It is just a question of being.

Nagarjuna quite rightly said that if people viewed shunyata wrongly, if they viewed it with very little prajna, they could be devastated.* If there is little experience of vipashyana awareness or prajna-like wakefulness, then the shunyata experience becomes just a bundle of vague nothingness, which doesn't mean anything. Therefore, it is necessary to know that from awareness comes warmth, and from warmth comes nonreference point. That process is very important to know and appreciate. The point is that you can't begin with nonreference point. If you try to do so, you are simply making it up.

It is very difficult to grasp a principle such as shunyata. It is not something you can do. However, awareness or mindfulness practice *is* something you can do. When awareness is no longer a battle, warmth arises as a natural process. You develop warmth through dissolving the possessiveness of you being aware and the world being strange. Having experienced that warmth, you begin to realize that you don't have to label it as belonging to a certain territory. So warmth brings nonreference point. As it is said in the *Heart Sutra,* there is no path and no goal. Your accustomed reference point has been completely cut through; it is gone forever.

---

* From the *Mulamadhyamakarika:* "Shunyata wrongly conceived destroys the dimly witted. It is like a snake grasped by the head." Quoted in Nancy McCagney, *Nagarjuna and the Philosophy of Openness* (Lanham, Md.: Rowman & Littlefield, 1997).

Nonreference point does not mean just going berserk and getting so confused that you don't know who is who or what is what. Nonreference point is an intelligent perspective in which you begin to see that nothing is its own primary spokesperson. You see that everything is a repetition of something else, so things do not speak for themselves; they are just an echo of themselves. The experience of nonreference point is not a process of collecting reassurances so that you could be nonreferential. It is just simple and straight nonreference point—absolutely open.

Actually, you may find yourself very confused, wondering what to do. But instead of asking, "What does one do in meditation?" you just do it. There is an absence of technique, absence of reference point, absence of any purpose and goal. You just sit like a rock. You can do that; you can just sit there and do it. It is like the Zen *shikantaza* technique of just sitting. The spiritual desire to attain enlightenment accompanies the entire bodhisattva path, and there is also the desire to help other people. But those ideas are based on the perspective of nonreference point, so it is not at all personal. The whole thing is based on impersonality.

Without the background of shamatha and vipashyana, you cannot actually experience the shunyata state of meditation. If you did not have any experience of awareness or mindfulness, you could quite possibly have problems if you tried to jump ahead into the mahayana jargon of shunyata. You might try to imitate the shunyata experience, to make it up without going through it. You might think, "Wow, that's a great idea," and expect some kind of direct confrontation with reality. But somehow it is not all that direct, and it is not warfare. It is a very simple personal experience.

The craving for sudden experience could instead lead to sudden nuttiness. It is like the story of the meditator who was trying to see that everything is empty and nonexistent. He was trying to subjugate his invented perceptions, his perceptual obstacles or demons. One evening when he was in retreat he went out for a walk, and while he was gone his sister brought him a pot of yogurt. She waited and waited, and finally she got tired of waiting so she left the pot of yogurt in his meditation cell. When the meditator came back from his walk and entered the room, he saw the pot of yogurt. It was getting very dark and hazy, and he saw this huge eye staring at him. He said to himself, "I'm going to have combat with this. It is obviously an obstacle to my path, some kind of demon." So he hit the pot of yogurt with his shawl, and the yogurt began to splatter all over the cave. The whole cave became filled with eyes, and the more he hit the pot, the more eyes he produced.

THREE TYPES OF EMPTINESS

The shunyata state of meditation is described as externally empty, internally empty, and absolutely empty.* Externally empty means that the phenomenal world and the sensory perceptions are seen as equally empty, although they may be vivid and colorful. Internally empty means that the internal world of emotions is also seen as empty, vivid maybe, but still empty. Absolutely empty means that there is nothing particularly to do. There is nothing to work on, no one to make a reference point, nothing whatsoever.

---

* Traditionally, eighteen types of shunyata experience have been described based on external, internal, and absolute emptiness. Chandrakirti's *Madhyamakavatara* lists sixteen kinds of emptiness. The first set of four includes inner emptiness, outer emptiness, emptiness of both outer and inner, and emptiness of emptiness. The second group includes emptiness of immensity, emptiness of the ultimate, emptiness of the compounded, and emptiness of the uncompounded. The third set includes emptiness of what is beyond extremes, emptiness of what is endless and beginningless, emptiness of what should not be spurned, and emptiness of essential nature. The fourth group includes emptiness of all phenomena, emptiness of defining characteristics, emptiness of the unobservable, and emptiness of nothings. To that list can be added the emptiness of the nature itself and the emptiness of transcendent quality, to make eighteen in all. See Padmakara Translation Group, trans., *Introduction to the Middle Way: Chandrakirti's Madhyamakavatara with Commentary by Ju Mipham* (Boston: Shambhala Publications, 2005).

19

Discovering a World beyond Ego

You have possessed youthful qualities all along, but your involve-ment with preconceived notions of society, tradition, concepts, and ideas has made you old. So in a sense, the bodhisattva path is a path of regaining your youth.

DEVELOPING EGOLESSNESS: THE HINAYANA FOUNDATION

The mahayana, like the hinayana, is based on the development of ego-lessness. In general, the various levels of the path have to do with your relationship to ego and your understanding of egolessness. The mahayana realization of twofold egolessness is dependent on the hinayana in that you first need to develop the egolessness of individuality as well as the first half of the egolessness of dharmas. You might have the intention of attaining the state of twofold egolessness, and you might aspire to the benevolence and gentleness of the compassionate path, but before such things take place, it is absolutely natural that you first go back and develop individual salvation.

Individual salvation means working with yourself. It is based on the idea of renunciation, and in turn, renouncing the renunciation itself. In the hinayana, you take refuge in the Buddha, dharma, and sangha, and begin to overcome the ego of individuality. Once you have accomplished that, you are on the brink of the ego of dharmas. You begin to question why you are doing all this, and you discover the karmic chain reaction of the twelve nidanas. And as you study the nidanas, or interdependent co-origination, you realize that you have to reverse that process in order to cut through it.

All this helps you to develop the egolessness of dharmas, but there are still little uncertainties left behind. You have managed to work on the gross level of your experience of dharmas, or things as they are, but you still perceive primarily in terms of opinion and attitude. At a gross level, your attitudes, perceptions, and opinions about the ego of dharmas have been cut through by your experience and understanding of the twelve nidanas. In relating with things as they are in their solid form, you have worked with the crude world of the twelve-nidana chain reaction process up through the ignorance level. But at a subtle level, you have not reached a full understanding of where all those things come from. The source is not yet cut through. So you are back to square two: to the source of the ego of dharmas.

The ego of dharmas comes from fixation on the "am" of "I am." As a practitioner on the boundary between hinayana and mahayana, you have liberated the "I," but you still have not completely clarified the level of "am." You are still fixated on "am" and on where the "am" came from. The gross level of "am" has been related with, but the primordial "am" still has not been completely clarified.

The primordial "am" comes from some kind of "I am," but not from the original "I am." That situation has already been overcome at the shravakayana level. But at that level, and even at the pratyekabuddhayana level, the ego has not been completely cut through. In fact, pratyeka-buddhas regard the little ego that's left as useful and necessary in order to go further. They would probably say that if you completely cut through everything, there would be nothing left to practice with. There would be no reason to go on and no purpose to life, which is quite true. In other words, pratyekabuddhas are afraid of the prajna principle; they are both afraid of it and attracted to it.

In entering the mahayana, you are giving up and letting go. You are letting go of your fixation on individual salvation and you are letting go of your righteousness and religiosity. The last hold of the ego of dharmas is cut through. Everything is regarded as attitude, but it is not attitude that is being cut through—attitude has been cut through already. Rather, it is the "attituder" or the experiencer of attitude that is cut through, which is the second half of the ego of dharmas. When the experiencer of mind's creation has been cut through, you realize that everything is understandable

135

and perceivable. You have cut through twofold ego by realizing that the seemingly subtle mental grasp of "am" is really very gross.

When you begin to overcome the fixator, the philosopher, and the conceptualizer, you begin to develop an appreciation for the absence of twofold ego. Although it is not so easy, and may not have happened completely, you still feel that you have overcome something, that you have cut through. At that point, the dawn of mahayana, or the dawn of the absence of twofold ego, occurs in your mind, and you begin to feel that something is worth celebrating. It is quite cheerful; nothing is depressing. The vast action of the bodhisattva begins to develop, and you experience the dawn of mahayana as luminosity and brilliance.

DIFFERENTIATING TECHNIQUES AND EXPERIENCE

The development of egolessness is a progressive process, not a sudden attainment. Shamatha is the basic technique. On the basis of shamatha, vipashyana is the practice that leads to the realization of the first egolessness, which is the egolessness of self, and then to the realization of one-and-a-half-fold egolessness, which is the egolessness of self and the first half of the egolessness of dharmas. Vipashyana practice culminates in prajna, the technique that brings the complete experience of twofold egolessness, or shunyata. So first there is the tool, and then there is the experience. We should be absolutely clear about that, and not confuse technique with experience. You cannot have mahayana without vipashyana—it would be like a tree without a trunk. The whole thing is ancestral. Prajna gives birth to the shunyata experience of the buddhas, and vipashyana is the stone that sharpens the sword of prajna. You could not experience twofold egolessness just with vipashyana, because you could not do it without prajna—but if you abandon vipashyana, you don't get anywhere at all.

Prajna is a technique as much as vipashyana or shamatha: shunyata is what you get, and prajna is what you are going to get it with. Shunyata is like death, and prajna is like a deadly weapon. That may sound rather morbid, but in terms of overcoming ego, I am sure you will understand what I mean. Prajna can be regarded as a microscope, and shunyata as what is on the slide. That is why the *Heart Sutra* places an emphasis on prajna, but little emphasis on shunyata. Shunyata is discovered in the phrase, "No eye, no ear, no nose," and so on, but prajna is actually more important.

Sharpening and cleaning your instrument is more important than what you see with it. You cannot cut with shunyata, as if it were a weapon. That would be absurd, because shunyata happens after the fact. Since prajna is the instrument with which you discover shunyata, shunyata is regarded as the child of *prajnaparamita,* of the perfection of wisdom.*

LOSING YOUR EGO AND REDISCOVERING YOUR YOUTHFULNESS

In the early stages of the path, your journey could be seen as an actual journey—you think that you are getting somewhere. But as soon as your commitment has been made and you have begun to practice and to work on your mind, your journey becomes a nonjourney. Instead of a journey outward or higher, the journey becomes inward and deeper. In the mahayana, that deeper journey takes place by means of compassion. You are willing to give, willing to open and extend yourself. Because of that inward journey, that encouragement within yourself, you can afford to open out to others. You do not constantly have to complain about this and that; instead, you could do something. And the more you are willing to open and to extend yourself to others and the world, that much deeper is your inward journey, and that much more apparent, definite, and real it becomes.

The first step of the journey takes place when you commit yourself to mahayana principles and ideals by taking the bodhisattva vow. The bodhisattva vow brings you much closer to being enlightened. You begin to find that dedicating yourself to others brings you much closer to the idea of basic sanity, enlightenment, tathagatagarbha, buddha nature, or whatever you might call it. You are not concerned with dogma or with reference points. All that is in the background, and your case history has already been dropped. Because of your respect and surrendering, you are no longer trying to hang on to your old hats. What you are getting into—if anything—is a new hat.

---

* Since *prajnaparamita,* or the perfection of wisdom, is said to lead to the realization of emptiness, it is a central focus of many mahayana scriptures. There is an extensive body of prajnaparamita teachings, one example being the *Heart Sutra,* a short text that is chanted, studied, and revered throughout the Buddhist world. Prajnaparamita is regarded as the mother of all the buddhas.

Old preconceptions, old ideas, and old trainings that might encourage you to hold on to your stronghold of ego, such as religion, spirituality, theology, or craftsmanship—all of those have to be abandoned in order to rediscover yourself. Those things from your past have become obstacles. You may have lived with them and wanted to work with them, but you still have not made heads or tails out of anything. You have not begun to realize who you are or what you are. You have not discovered the continual, inexhaustible, exuberant youth you possess within yourself. Such youthfulness has nothing to do with chronological age. You have possessed youthful qualities all along, but your involvement with pre-conceived notions of society, tradition, concepts, and ideas has made you old. So in a sense, the bodhisattva path is a path of regaining your youth. But we need to be very clear that this has nothing to do with looking for eternal life.

The approach of regaining your youthful quality is apparent in both the mahayana and the vajrayana. In the mahayana, rediscovering your youthfulness is based on both inspiration and loneliness. When you have lost the grip of ego, you can no longer entertain and indulge yourself in your usual ways. You begin to discover a new and clearer perspective toward the phenomenal world.

Your phenomenal world is old hat: you have studied it, written stories about it, painted pictures of it. You have fought with it and struggled with it, and it is fighting back. Your own autobiography keeps popping up all the time. You may try to censor it, but when that censorship fails, your old stories keep coming back. In the mahayana, you are not trying to forget the past, as if it were a failure or redundant, but you are including the past. You are including it not as a saving grace, a reference point, or a bank of quotations, but you are looking at that old-hat world with the perception newly gained by jumping out into the open and becoming a bodhisattva. By taking the bodhisattva vow and becoming a potential bodhisattva, you are beginning to find a new approach to that old-hat world.

Coming As You Are

This new-old hat is called shunyata, or emptiness, but what it is called is not important. What is important is the new faculty or new lens you are using to see your old hat as a new hat. When you use a new lens or a new microphone to heighten your visual and auditory perceptions, you see or hear things from an entirely different perspective. But then you are fooled again, and once more you become as inaccurate as you have been in the past. So what the Buddha actually asked is that you do not bring along any new eyeglasses, binoculars, microscopes, lenses, hearing aids, microphones, or anything else, but that instead you come as you are.

You might find that inconvenient, embarrassing, or inadequate, because you want to be masked by all of those things. You might like to hide behind all those gadgets, but you could forget those gadgets altogether. You could come as you are. You could simply present yourself to your teacher and to the Buddha. If you think they are going to be embarrassed by your nakedness or your so-called inadequacy, it is *your* language that says inadequacy. You might bump into a corner, make a mess out of yourself, and knock over a teacup, but they are perfectly happy to accommodate you. It is nice that you have finally decided to make yourself at home, to come as you are.

When the Buddha related with his disciples, some disciples who came to hear him came with what they were not. They came along with their particular cultures, their particular traditions and inheritances, their particular lenses, their particular masks, microphones, and hearing aids. When the Buddha uttered his teaching on shunyata, such people found that they could not use their gadgets to hear him. In fact, their gadgets fell apart and they panicked. They had heart attacks and died on the spot. The reason that happened is because they liked their culture, their habits, and their tradition of individual salvation. They had managed to crack down on one portion of ego, but a certain amount was left behind, and they took shelter and security in that leftover portion of ego. That remaining portion of ego was their security—and with the teachings of shunyata, the rug was pulled from under their feet for the first time. More likely, their *zafus,* or meditation cushions, were pulled from under their bottoms, so they had nowhere to meditate and their security was gone. But the teaching of shunyata is not actually all that outrageous; it is very simple and ordinary.

GAPS OF UNKNOWING

In order to understand the bodhisattva path, we need to refine our understanding of shunyata as much as we can. We need to look at shunyata in terms of absolute and relative truth and in relationship to tathagatagarbha, or buddha nature. Mahayana provides an immense sense of freedom: freedom to think, freedom to react, and freedom to practice. Freedom to think means that we can work with the essence of buddha mind, with prajna and compassion. It means that we are free to use our insight, our basic existence, what we fundamentally are. Freedom to react is that we can go along with the emotionality of the practice of compassion. Freedom to accomplish is that we can practice in accordance with the disciplines of the first two types of freedom. That provides us with the ground to work on our understanding of shunyata.

Freedom is connected with the notion of basic sanity. In order to gain, to achieve, or to understand the meaning of basic sanity, we have to know how it operates. Basic sanity usually comes through when we are going about our everyday life; otherwise, such sanity would be purely theoretical. Basic sanity operates and can be worked with properly and thoroughly in our ordinary world—the world of kitchen sinks, the world of bread and butter, the world of dollars and pounds.

In the ordinary world, we operate in terms of our reactions to things. If we want to make a business deal with somebody, we meet with the person and we talk about business. We talk about what terms we can arrive at, and whether it is lucrative for the other person as well as for ourselves. If we are relating with somebody who needs help, we do it in the same style. We begin by making sure that helping this person does not destroy us, and only then do we begin to help them. Let us straightforwardly face the fact that nobody really sacrifices their own interest in relating with the world. We decide to take part in things when we have more to gain than we have to lose. In general, everybody operates in the world of this and that. We operate in a businesslike fashion all the time, and our terms are that whatever we give, we expect to get back in return. So it's give and get all the time. That world of exchange involves a misunderstanding of reality, definitely and absolutely.

Relating with the current issues in our life raises questions about reality and what that reality is based on. How can we understand this particular reality? How can we actually perceive reality in the proper and fullest sense? How can we make sure that we have understood the basic phenomena of reality? The attempt to understand reality requires a certain attitude of expectation—the expectation to understand things as they are. We are waiting to understand, we are expecting to understand, we are hoping we can understand. That hoping, waiting, and expecting contains a quality of bewilderment. It contains confusion, and quite possibly it also contains a quality of blankness or uncertainty.

If we expected our guests to arrive at our house at five o'clock sharp and they have not turned up, if they are two hours late and usually they are on time, we have all kinds of ideas. Maybe they had an accident on their way or got sick. Quite possibly they did not want to come and visit us. In a more paranoid mood, we might think maybe they are pissed off at us and are making some kind of statement to undermine our existence or our hospitality. But all we really know is that they are late, that they have not arrived when we expected. So between all the flickering of thoughts in regard to that situation and the development of a state of mind regarding the people who haven't arrived, we experience a gap, space, uncertainty.

You could say that there is nothing very profound about that example. It is just ordinary expectations and waiting, a mundane little thing—nothing comparable to a shunyata experience or anything of that nature. That is quite true. But shunyata experience is not far from that. This example may seem terribly domestic and cheap; it may even seem sacrilegious to say that when a guest doesn't arrive, it is a glimpse of emptiness. I'm not quite saying that, but there is a possibility of that being true. Actually, shunyata experience takes place in very simple moments of life. At the point when our expectations are fading out and future possibilities have not yet turned up, there is a faint little gap in which there is the possibility of some unknown factor taking place.

It is not all that fantastic or profound to experience shunyata. Throughout our life, there are possibilities of encountering gaps in our expectations. Usually we think in terms of hope and fear, but something beyond hope and fear is possible: emptiness is also taking place. Whether we call it hope or fear, behind the whole thing there is a feeling of not knowing exactly what to do or what kind of input we can present to the situation. Seemingly, the experience of not knowing what to do is based on confusion and ignorance, but not knowing what to do is not necessarily ignorance. It could be that we have run out of new games, new gimmicks, and new concepts to fill in the gap. We may have run out of ammo, so to speak. Usually we are extraordinarily resourceful in providing convenient ammo of all kinds, but we sometimes run out of possibilities and we are completely unarmed. This not finding—not finding new possibilities, not finding new tactics, not finding new techniques, or not finding new plans—is shunyata. With shunyata, it is not possible to come up with anything.

20

Emptiness and the Middle Way

Shunyata is not regarded as a religious experience, nor is it regarded as a nontheistic mystical experience. Shunyata is neither religious nor secular. It is not particularly sacred; neither is it profane. It is what it is. However, it covers a lot of ground. It is the first clear thinking and conclusion about reality in the history of the human mind.

NAGARJUNA AND THE MIDDLE WAY

We could approach the mahayana in two ways: we could approach it from the viewpoint of the teachings of madhyamaka, or the middle way, or we could approach it from the viewpoint of shunyata, or emptiness. Madhyamaka is the name of the philosophy that developed at the height of the growth of mahayana Buddhism. It is said to have been developed by the great second-century Indian teacher Nagarjuna.

Nagarjuna wasn't just a professor or a scholar, although he knew a lot. Since Nagarjuna was a great practitioner, any arguments Nagarjuna presented could be regarded as the voice of experience. Nagarjuna was somebody who presented his experience very simply and directly to his friends and students. He was not simply a professor or an absentminded scholar. I am sure that he could make a cup of tea very beautifully, cook his own meals, and do his own laundry. Nagarjuna was also one of the tantric *mahasiddhas*. *Maha* means "great," and *siddha* means "power"; so *mahasiddhas* are "realized beings known for their great spiritual powers." So Nagarjuna led an extended life rather than burying himself in books.

Western scholars tend to misinterpret the nature of Buddhist philosophical traditions and logical systems such as madhyamaka and yogachara. But madhyamaka is not a philosophical school in the Western sense, so it is a disservice to say that Nagarjuna was the founder of a particular school, as if he were the Carl Jung or the Karl Marx of the Buddhist era. Buddhist philosophical traditions are not "founded" in the same way Jung and Freud founded their particular schools, and they are not regarded as established institutions or philosophical schools. They are just forms of truth that people happened to discover and present. This is a very important point. I am sure that in the time of Nagarjuna, or even after the time of Nagarjuna, none of the traditional Buddhist universities developed departments specializing in the study of Nagarjuna's thought. In fact, there were no departments of any kind. Learning Buddhism was approached as one organic whole. So it would be good to drop the concept of philosophical schools, and view madhyamaka not as a philosophical school but as a system of thinking.* A philosophical school develops arguments to protect its own concepts and ideas, while a system of thinking is a process of presenting a certain viewpoint very harmoniously and systematically to people's minds.

NEITHER ETERNALISM NOR NIHILISM

The reason madhyamaka was known as the middle way is that madhyamakans were neither eternalists nor nihilists. Eternalists believe that life exists eternally, in spite of birth and death. They think that because our karma continues, we can still hang on to our life, that we can continue to exist and attain everlasting life. Nihilists believe that everything comes and goes in the midst of unconditional space, so there is room to make mistakes, room to correct things. There is also room to indulge, room to expand our ego. We are on our own, whatever we do—and since everything is in our hands, we can do whatever we want. So we should stop hassling with our life; we should forget about chaos, practicality, and

---

* Logical debate and dialogue are often used in teaching students about madhyamaka and shunyata. Appendix 4, "Prajna Dialogues," contains three short exchanges taken from Vajradhatu Seminary question-and-answer periods as illustrations of the use of dialogue to awaken a student's prajna.

earth-boundness. Instead, we should just enjoy and celebrate in this nothingness or emptiness.

According to madhyamaka, neither the eternalistic nor the nihilistic approach is particularly safe or right. Eternalism is as confused as nihilism. The traditional analogy is that as long as you fall off the horse, it doesn't matter whether you fall off the right side or the left side—you just fall off the horse. Similarly, whether you are a nihilist or an eternalist, you are making a wrong judgment about reality. Seemingly, those two traditions do not have any sense of heritage, and if they did, it was lost a long time ago. They both seem to be a kind of free ride, an expressionistic approach to the spiritual journey. The madhyamakans do not follow the concepts of either the eternalists or the nihilists. They incorporate the essence of eternalism or nihilism, but without the neurosis. That is how the middle path, or madhyamaka, came into being.

DISCOVERING SHUNYATA
WITH THE TOOL OF PRAJNA

The idea of shunyata or emptiness is discovered by prajna. Shunyata is not quite the same as the existentialist concept of nothingness, and it is not made into a concept, put into a box, and catalogued. In the *Uttaratantra* of Maitreya, it says that the basic nature is empty of adventitious stains, which are separable, but it is not empty of unsurpassable qualities, which are inseparable.* That makes a lot of sense. The basic nature, which is empty of dualistic fixations, is regarded as the real supreme dharma. Adventitious stains or dualistic fixations are temporary; they do not actually hamper the basic enlightened state of mind at all. So conceptual mind and mental concepts are not regarded as permanent damage. We realize the temporariness of such experiences, and we are not alarmed by dual-

---

* A reference to verse 155 of the *Uttaratantra*, a treasured four-line verse on emptiness and buddha nature. In the English translation by Rosemarie Fuchs this verse is translated as: "The element is empty of the adventitious [stains], / which are featured by their total separateness. / But it is not empty of the matchless properties, / which are featured by their total inseparability." See Rosemarie Fuchs, trans., *Buddha Nature: The Mahayana Uttaratantra Shastra with Commentary by Arya Maitreya* (Ithaca, N.Y.: Snow Lion, 2000). This translation includes a commentary by Jamgön Kongtrül Lodrö Thaye as well as an explanation by Khenpo Tsultrim Gyamtso Rinpoche. For a commentary on this verse by Dzongsar Jamyang Khyentse Rinpoche, see Arya Maitreya, *Buddha-Nature: Mahayana-Uttaratantra-Shastra* (New Delhi: Siddhartha's Intent, 2007).

istic problems. We recognize that they do not have any kind of ground to stay.

Shunyata is not quite the same as the existentialist concept of nothingness. It is not made into a concept and put into a box and catalogued. Shunyata is what you experience, and prajna is what you use to discover shunyata. Prajna is like a cup that you use to drink water; shunyata can only be contained in prajna, in the same way that water can only be contained in a cup or something with a dented shape, like the hollow of a hand. Prajna is a way to see; it is a kind of radar system that is trying to perceive the phenomenal world in the language of shunyata. Prajna is supreme knowledge; but in this case, knowledge does not refer to something you already know, as when somebody knows how to fix cars. It is not that kind of preconceived knowledge. Prajna is the capability of having knowledge. Knowledge of what? Of nothing. Just knowledge.

One of the problems that comes up with linguistics, particularly in the English language, is that you have to qualify things all the time. You cannot simply say "it." You think, "It what?" You cannot just have an unconditional "it," but you have to have somebody or something that is referred to as "it." But in the case of prajna, knowledge is not knowledge of something—it is just knowledge. Prajna is the faculty to know; it is the ability to know in the fullest sense. Although prajna is supreme or best knowledge, it does not have the connotation of computation or comparison, as when one thing is sharper, and something else is duller. In this case, it is sharp without any question; there is none better.

Shunyata is not regarded as a religious experience, nor is it regarded as a nontheistic mystical experience. Shunyata is neither religious nor secular. It is not particularly sacred; neither is it profane. It is what it is. However, it covers a lot of ground. It is the first clear thinking and conclusion about reality in the history of the human mind. In the god realm, people are caught up in their absorption, and in the hell realm, people are trapped in their own suffering. Likewise, people in the other realms are caught in various ways. So technically the only mind that can perceive true shunyata is in the human realm, the world of opportunity.

EXPERIENCING EMPTINESS

Shunyata is a state of realization of our phenomenal world. We might realize the nature of shunyata while we are preparing a meal or drinking a cup of tea. It is an experience, very much so. That is why an emphasis is made on trying to find out what is reality at the levels of absolute and relative truth.

Shunyata could also be considered a practice or discipline. You look into things as you go about your life—how your curly hairs work, how your socks could be cleaned, what the next good meal will be, and who is going to cook. You look into anything of that nature and how it affects your sense of reality. By looking into such things, you are actually working on how to understand basic reality.

With shunyata, you realize that the emptiness of phenomena and the emptiness of yourself is the same emptiness. You realize that everything is bounded by that totality, that otherwise, there is no totality. You might ask, "Then who is it that does the experiencing?" It is the total experience of emptiness that experiences things as they are. When we talk about emptiness, we are not talking about vacancy, but about the absence of clinging. Beyond clinging, a greater freedom can be experienced that is not particularly a vacant or a blank state of being, but a much clearer, unpossessed state of being. It is total spaciousness, which you cannot actually label. Once you begin to label it, you lose it. You become nonspacious immediately.

Space or spaciousness means fullness and claustrophobia at the same time. Those two things can work together on one ground. It is very much like my personal life, actually. I have a lot of time to rest and to sleep late, but my time is still completely filled, including my own dreams. That fullness has a positive quality—not positive in the sense of promises but positive in the sense of sanity. There is a difference between promise and sanity. You cannot really do a complete censoring or weeding out of what you want and what you do not want. Everything bombards you, particularly once you decide to become sane. Once you are sane, you are bombarded all the time by all kinds of possibilities.

When shunyata was introduced to hinayana practitioners, the problem was that they did not want to give up their culture, their hinayana tradition. They were threatened by someone saying that everything is arbitrary. They felt that if you presented that particular case to their students or to themselves, they might violate their monastic rules. Their resistance was based on very simple facts like that. I think it would be very difficult to teach shunyata to its full extent in a place like the ancient

Nalanda University, where people were very uptight about their own discipline. They had a hard enough time keeping their own tradition of discipline already, so if you presented something beyond that, saying that everything is okay, everything is empty, it would be a terrible thing to say.

If there is not such cultural uptightness, not only is shunyata teaching appropriate, but further vajrayana teaching becomes appropriate as well. At the same time, it is still necessary to have some kind of culture or tradition. But as long as you realize that you are not functioning on fixed ground, as long as ego's territory has been eliminated, mahayana practices such as the paramitas do not become new forms of cultural fixation. You realize that you are building those disciplines on an ice block, and that if you have a fixation about generosity or morality or patience, sooner or later it is going to melt away.

BODHISATTVAS, PRAJNA, AND EMPTINESS

Bodhisattvas develop prajna not only by meditation, but by actions, by relationships, by working with the world. They begin to work for sentient beings; they act as laborers. The bodhisattva tradition possesses immense practicality. Bodhisattvas are not just sitting on their meditation cushions, but they are doing something; they are relating with the world and helping people. Bodhisattvas are not stuck in absorption, but they are doing something all the time.

Bodhisattvas do not have to use their own concepts to judge somebody else. Their realization is beyond the conceptual-framework mentality of dealing with reality. What you say might be conceptual or padded with all kinds of ideas, but bodhisattvas can see through you because they do not have to use double vision. Bodhisattvas are just there without anything, without any tools. They can see with the naked eye, which makes things much clearer. In their communication, bodhisattvas can make use of the concepts you are generating, which is very embarrassing. Since they do not have any concepts that you can play back to them, they are just there, very naked, very open, just looking at you. Bodhisattvas do not have any preconceptions or anything of that nature—and you keep building up your little paddings, which keep falling apart. When you communicate with a bodhisattva, that is usually what happens.

A Continual Awakening of Prajna

The confirmation of the spiritual journey at the hinayana level is the experience of awakening from samsara into nirvana. And what runs through the hinayana and gives you hope of continuing on the Buddhist path of non-ego is the continual development of prajna. Prajna is constantly cutting through and providing further inspiration to practice. Prajna occurs right at the beginning and continues through the middle, right up to the end. Prajna brings about further prajna, so you experience a continual awakening of prajna.

In the mahayana, prajna is regarded as a tool, and egolessness or shunyata is regarded as the product uncovered by that particular tool. Egolessness, shunyata, and compassion are what prajna exposes. You take the bodhisattva vow because you realize that continuing on the path of fixation is problematic. You begin to wonder about fixation and what is beyond fixation, and you begin to get an answer to your question. You hear that fixation comes from not believing that you are already impregnated by enlightened power. Because you realize that enlightened power or buddha nature is in you already, you can enter the bodhisattva path. For hinayanists, that realization is frightening because they detect a whiff of tantra and the possibility of something coming up that they cannot handle. That kind of fear and hesitation has always happened; a lot of people have had that combination of arrogance and cowardice.

Prajna, the weapon you have been using all along, is a legitimate weapon, but up to this point you had no idea what was behind that weapon. But when you become a bodhisattva-like person, you begin to realize where that weapon is inherited from, which is bodhichitta or buddha nature. Buddha nature is what makes you a legitimate person to carry the sword of prajna from the beginning of the hinayana path on through the mahayana. You can inherit that sword, but in order for you to do so, you need devotion—and devotion comes from renunciation, which comes from the recognition that you are already impregnated with buddha nature.

21

Realizing the Emptiness of Ordinary Reality

The enlightened ones just experienced it on the spot, but we can experience shunyata only by contrast. When you have powerful emotional threats and extreme messages of all kinds being presented to you, as extreme as such events become, that is how much shunyata could be experienced.

Ground Madhyamaka

There are three levels of madhyamaka: ground, path, and fruition. The study of madhyamaka begins with ground madhyamaka, which has to do with our basic approach to reality. Ground madhyamaka is based on understanding the two truths, the absolute and the relative. In ground madhyamaka, there is not particularly any leap into the realization of shunyata. There is no leap and no flash. It is more a matter of realizing logically and dialectically that what you are doing is useless and senseless. To begin with, you have to see that completely and fully.

In path madhyamaka, there could be lots of leaps. You are taking leaps of generosity, discipline, patience, exertion, meditation, and prajna. You are taking leaps at the pragmatic-action level.*

---

* Trungpa Rinpoche discusses *ground madhyamaka* as an understanding of the two truths, and *path madhyamaka* as paramita practice. He follows Jamgön Kongtrül in approaching fruition madhyamaka in terms of the ten *bhumis*. For a discussion of the bhumis, or stages of the bodhisattva path, see part 8, "The Bodhisattva's Journey." Every teacher will define ground, path, and fruition madhyamaka a bit differently, depending on context. For instance, some teachers say that the fruition of madhyamaka is emptiness, and others say that it is freedom from elaboration.

Ground madhyamaka is based on a contemplative approach. The question is, how much can you hang on to this reality? It is already rotting and it does not make any sense, so it is about time to come to your senses. That is what the *Heart Sutra* is supposed to do to you—to make you come to your senses. The problem is that by now it has become a familiar classic, old language, so when you read the *Heart Sutra,* it does not make the same impact on you as it did for people in the past. The idea is that when you realize the concept of shunyata, when you actually experience it, then what you are already involved in—your ideas, concepts, theories, and philosophy—does not hold up. So with ground madhyamaka, the approach is basically intellectual in nature.

In Buddhism, we have practice first, and then study. We do not discuss the philosophy right at the beginning, beyond the bread-and-butter level. So if you want to become a Buddhist, you have to sit. Buddhism is less apt to impose a philosophy on you than many other traditions, because Buddhists are practitioners. They are monastics and laypeople who have actually renounced their particular environment of entertainment. They lead a complete life of sitting meditation practice, they come to some conclusions, and they begin to pronounce them—and they have handed that down to us.

KÜNDZOP IS ONE GIGANTIC WORLD OF INCEST

There are two levels of perceiving shunyata: superficial prajna perception and transcendental prajna perception. Traditionally, these levels are known as relative truth and ultimate truth. The Tibetan term for the concept of two truths is *denpa nyi. Denpa* means "truth," or "reality," and *nyi* is "two"; so *denpa nyi* means "two truths."

The relative truth comes first, so we will begin our discussion of the two truths with relative truth, and then move on to discuss ultimate truth. "Relative" is a convenient English translation of *kündzop,* but actually *kün* means "all," and *dzop* means "outfit"; so the meaning of the Tibetan term is more like "an outfit that fits everything." It has a quality of superficiality, like ketchup, which goes with any kind of food.

Kündzop is the phenomenal world, which is an outfit, a self-existing show. The phenomenal world is a performance, living theater. As the perceiver, you would like to see things in your own way, in a certain fashion, so the performance shifts around: you could be the audience or you could be the show. If you are a cook, for instance, the people who want to eat could be the show and you the audience, or you could be the show and the people who are going to eat could be the audience.

The idea of kündzop implies that different people would have different perspectives on the world. When we try to discuss reality, we have disagreements. Every one of us has a different attitude about water and a different attitude about food. For instance, in the six realms of being, the perceptions of people in the various realms have been programmed, and these perceptions have slowly degenerated into different forms of neurosis or psychosis. So when people from the hell realm see water, they regard it as extraordinarily threatening, thinking that it is melted iron or something terrible. People from the hungry ghost realm would have an entirely different attitude to water, craving it to quench their thirst, and people in the realm of the gods might see water as the elixir of life.

Every one of us has entirely different ideas, different attitudes, and different approaches at all kinds of levels. People might think that the water in New York is terrible, or that a mountain stream up in the highest world of Everest is fantastically fresh. Some people's visions or concepts might be more accurate, and other people's approaches might be very gross and wrong. We can make that judgment, that division between psychosis and neurosis, but that whole approach is questionable. The edges of neurosis and psychosis begin to dissolve, and they may come so close together that we are not able to distinguish between the two. With kündzop, the distinction between unreasonable and reasonable logic begins to break down into a series of expectations and preconceptions.

Kündzop is a show-off, a bluff. There is no substance, but there are still a lot of things going on. However, kündzop should not be looked down upon. In fact, we have a lot of problems realizing kündzop and relating with the world. The dressed-up world is actually very hard to work with. To realize the truth of kündzop, you need to transcend neurosis and psychosis. When you have become sane through your relationship with the spiritual friend, and when you have experienced twofold egolessness, you see that the real world is actually the real world. You see the world of reality completely and fully without any problems and without any big deal.

Kündzop, the ordinary and popular world's truth, is said to be empty of itself and by itself. Kündzop is empty of its own nature; it is based on constantly filling gaps of all kinds. But whatever we experience at the kündzop level eventually runs out of steam. When there is no new ammunition, we run out of energy, and even seemingly new energies have limitations.

Kündzop is known as relative truth because it is not absolute. Not only that, but it is known as relative truth because it is its own relatives. It is like an amoeba, which does not need a mate to reproduce, but mates with its own self. Relative truth is self-perpetuating. It has intercourse with itself, and produces its own child and eats it up. It is its own relatives: it is its own grandfather, its own grandchild, its own wife and husband. So relative truth is continuous. It is one gigantic world of incest.

Practically, that is why we are in trouble. We are in a world of incest, like old European royalties who had too much interbreeding. In such a world, things begin to get slightly chaotic, but nobody can solve it. We keep having to return back to our own selves, the kündzop world of incest in which things keep reproducing and there is no way out and no way in.

SELF-PERPETUATING MENTAL PIGEONHOLING

The idea of kündzop can seem very complicated and difficult. Trying to understand it solely by means of the madhyamakan approach may be a bit too vague, so I have decided to do something outrageous. I have decided to borrow from the yogachara, or mind-only, tradition. Yogachara is very powerful and insightful. It has had a great influence on the Zen tradition, although some scholars may disagree with that. Yogachara is very accurate, and in fact quite beautiful. It has produced fantastic works of art such as calligraphy, poetry, flower arrangement, and architecture, particularly in Japan and China.

According to yogachara, kündzop is actually your state of mind. It is like the popular liquor ad that says, "Bombay Gin is a state of mind." Yogacharans say that the relative world is made out of your mind. When you see something for the first time, you know how to react to it immediately. Why? Since you have not seen it before, do you have clairvoyance or a premonition that such a thing is going to confront you? No, you don't. But you still know how to handle new situations. You know how to relate with new food, new tastes, new visions, new sounds, new concepts, and new ideas. You automatically put them into your preconceived pigeonholes. You do that all the time; such preconceptions are always there. So when you see something new, it is not really new, because you already have expectations about it. Shapes and sizes are not really new to you, and the five colors are not really new to you. You know about them already. Movements such as fast, slow, and medium are not particularly new to you either. You know all that too. Those basic assumptions are already in your mind; your mind is already programmed. Therefore, you know how to act and how to relate with things. Everything is recorded in your brain system. That is why it is called kündzop.

Why are the things we see perpetuating themselves? Aren't new things happening all the time, every day? It seems that every day is new, not the same old day. Although you might have the same schedule, different things happen every day. So aren't new days and new things happening? It seems that fresh blood is coming in, that it is all relatively fluid. But according to the yogacharan tradition, that is not true. There is no fresh blood coming in at all.

If we look at the kündzop aspect of reality as it is, simply and directly, we realize that kündzop is a manifestation of its own incest. That incestuousness can be overcome by realizing that a trick is being played on us constantly, but that trick doesn't quite work. We see that kündzop perception is just another Disneyland, another area of deception based on entertainment of all kinds.

The whole thing is constantly inbreeding. You might think that you had an idea for the first time. The fantastic idea of sudden enlightenment may have occurred to you by seeing a grasshopper jumping or a dog shitting. The first time you see such a thing, it is a fantastic experience. But you know dog, and you know shit, and you know that a dog shits—and if you put all those things together, there is nothing really new. With combinations that occur unreasonably, beyond your expectations, you know how to put things together very quickly and speedily so that everything fits into its own socket, so to speak, and nothing is missing. We manage to put everything into our mental preconceptions and pigeonholes all the time.

TRUE KÜNDZOP AND FALSE KÜNDZOP

There are two types of kündzop: realistic or true kündzop, and perverted or false kündzop. Realistic kündzop is what you see, and perverted kündzop is what you imagine. If you see that your dog is a dog, that is true kündzop. However, if you think your pet dog is a lion, and you perceive it in that way, that is false kündzop. It is not true. False kündzop is the psychosis level, and true kundzöp is the neurotic or relatively true level. It is the level of practicality, the fact that it is good to vacuum your floor and wash your dishes, little things like that.

False Kündzop

False kündzop includes the psychotic dimension of building up mental images, such as thinking the CIA keeps following you and trying to kill you. It is the way the world really looks to a psychotic, or to a person under the influence of a drug, a dream, strain, or tiredness. If a psychotic comes up to you saying, "Are you drinking blood?" you reply, "No, I'm drinking coffee." It is very simple. In psychosis there is an immense exaggeration of reality, but even though the psychotic thinks you are drinking blood, you actually are drinking coffee. That is the reality, the simple truth.

The traditional analogy for perverted kündzop is seeing a rope as a snake. Whether it is caused by bad eyesight or bad lighting or by some other condition, you see the rope as a snake. As far as your mind is concerned, it is true, but it is still perverted. That is what we mean by saying the psychotic world is a kind of kündzop, or truth. Although it is not all that true, it cannot be denied as false because, after all, it *is* what you are experiencing on the spot. So even though it is a lie, it is a true lie, because it is experienced as the truth. It is true false reality.

Pure Kündzop as Ordinary Sanity

With the first level of pure kündzop, you are not suffering any kind of hallucination, you are not under the influence of drugs, and you are not involved in metaphysical or religious fantasies. You just see blue as blue, and white as white, very simply. You see a snake as a snake, and a rope as a rope. Real things are seen as they are. This kind of kündzop is a so-called sane person's attitude to reality. It is ordinary sanity. Ordinary sanity means seeing things very directly, seeing things as they are. You no longer have visions of elephants in your cup of tea. Black is seen as black, and white as white. It is absolutely direct and simple.

Seeing pure kündzop is what we mean by being grounded or earthy. There is no superstition. You just see water as water, and fire as fire. Pure kündzop is like acquiring a new pair of eyeglasses that makes it completely clear how to relate with regular, ordinary life. You might think that this is not all that profound, that anybody can do it. But usually it is impossible to experience real kündzop. Most people cannot see things as they are properly and directly at all. Although true kündzop is still considered to be neurotic, there has to be that kind of simple truth, otherwise we could not do anything in our life. We need to take care of our physical world, to have a sense of what is reality and what is not reality. It is quite simple and basic.

Pure Kündzop as Enlightened Sanity

The second level of pure kündzop, or enlightened sanity, is slightly different. It is how you see once you have started on the bodhisattva path and are able to develop twofold egolessness. Only someone who has been able to cut through twofold ego is able to see things as they are in their fullest and most real sense. People possessing twofold ego, random people in the street are all wrapped up in their preconceptions, memories, dreams, and fantasies. Because of that, their attitudes toward water, fire, black, blue, and white are distorted.

People are usually very nervous about experiencing the bright and colorful world, although the degree of nervousness varies. People either love the world or hate it, or lukewarmly love it or hate it. But nobody can see this level of true kündzop without having cut through twofold ego, because there is still a little attachment. People may see blue as blue, but at the same time, they use that to reinforce their idea of how blue affects their state of mind. Whether they regard things as powerful, good, nice, or threatening, there are always psychological implications behind the colors, forms, noises, and physical sensations they perceive. There is always some implication behind the whole thing. True kündzop is very difficult to experience, although it is very ordinary. But once you have attained the second level of pure kündzop, it is no longer possible to relapse to the first level of kündzop. Once a person has experienced smallpox, they never have a recurrence.*

Relating with kundzöp is an expression of prajna, but it is not particularly an experience of shunyata. Here, the prajna is in seeing kündzop as it is. Any perception that clarifies things is a form of prajna. If you are able

---

* In discussing *true kündzop,* Trungpa Rinpoche seems to be referring at times to the view of true kündzop as simply correct relative truth, and at other times to the view of kündzop as a highly accomplished and more ultimate view of the phenomenal world.

to see kündzop, you know that if the kettle is whistling, you have to turn down the heat. If you are going to the supermarket, you know how to buy proper things at proper times and get a good bargain. You may not be working toward enlightenment, but you are keeping track of reality. You are relating with reality step-by-step. And if you go further with prajna, you can see how you are coloring reality. You can begin to see through kündzop.

KÜNDZOP AND EMPTINESS

The shunyata experience of the bodhisattva path comes from shamatha, vipashyana, and egolessness. The shamatha possibility of shunyata comes from kündzop experiences presenting themselves colorfully, but without any personal, emotional attachment being made. There is no clinging to the phenomenal world, although the phenomenal world continues to be colorful and vivid. That lack of fixation brings in the element of absolute truth as well. It brings about harmony and gentleness, because we do not have to fight for anything. That is the first point, the shamatha experience of shunyata.

With vipashyana, you begin to understand how to see things as they are in a very simple, nonaggressive way. You begin to see things as an illusion. This does not mean that you are being fooled or seeing a mirage, but that you are seeing things as a self-existing game that does not apply individually or personally to you or others. You are beginning to realize the mirage-ness of the situation in a very simple way; you see that things are not all that good, not all that bad, not all that entertaining, and not all that nonentertaining. Things are being seen as they are on a very basic and fundamental level.

On the whole, there is no substance, although there is seeming substance. If somebody is not helping you to pay your phone bills, or if somebody doesn't give you your dinner, or the dinner is badly cooked, such things may be touchy situations for you. But at the same time, it is because you are so touchy and intensely emotional that new possibilities begin to occur to you. When you have powerful emotional threats and extreme messages of all kinds being presented to you, as extreme as such events become, that is how much shunyata could be experienced. Because things are so extraordinarily intense; therefore, they are so ordinarily a mirage because of the intensity. In other words, human beings are unable to experience shunyata as the enlightened ones experienced it a long time ago. The enlightened ones just experienced it on the spot, but we can experience shunyata only by contrast.

You might have thought that shunyata would be purely a meditative experience, but that is not quite the case. Actually, according to the traditional Kagyü-Nyingma teaching of our lineage, it is said that shunyata is also a postmeditation experience. Extreme situations happen all the time. Somebody steals your last dollar, and you can't do anything about it. Somebody runs away with your girlfriend or boyfriend, and you are left so despairing, so lonely. For that matter, somebody scoops out a huge spoonful of ice cream from your dish, so you don't have much left to eat. But what is there to do about it? How much can you blame the phenomenal world for playing tricks on you? Because you have fixated so very powerfully on one thing or another, and then somebody comes along and takes that thing away from you, that tends to bring about some kind of flash between two contrasting situations. That experience of contrast actually makes a lot of difference.

The contrast between immense grasping and immense loss of that grasping brings about a feeling of loss and gain at the same time. So when you begin to realize shunyata, there's a twist in that realization. You feel that you have lost, but at the same time you feel that you have gained. It is simultaneously absolute loss and absolute gain, simultaneously hot and cold. At that point, you can no longer tell the difference. It is not just on the cheap or simpleminded level that you can't tell the difference between good and bad, and it is not because you are so freaked-out. Rather, it is because there is an intelligence that experiences the departing situation and the coming situation as one experience. That experience cuts through the birth of crude and subtle fixations altogether by allowing you to realize the truth of the dharma.

Usually this experience comes in a sequence. First there is loss; then when you realize that you have lost, it becomes gain; and finally there is both loss and gain at the same time. It takes three steps: one, two, three. This is an ongoing process, and the stopping point is not experienced except at the vajrayana level. At the mahayana level, this process is said to develop genuine devotion and sympathy, so that you finally manage to fall in love with all sentient beings through your dedication.

In looking at how to bring about or click into shunyata, we could refer back to the hinayana and the experience of the blind grandmother.

You realize that you cannot teach your blind grandmother the dharma, and you cannot talk her out of her opinions. Whatever you try with her doesn't help. She's blind, she's on her way to being deaf, and she loves you a lot. She not only loves you a lot, but she possesses you. She regards you, her grandchild, as her possession completely. So how can you let go of that blind grandmother? By feeling good, feeling happy, or any way at all? There is no way. The only way is to abandon your blind grandmother, to let her go by not feeding her any further food of neurosis. The absence of that blind grandmother is the shunyata experience.

22

Experiencing Reality in Its Fullest Sense

Töndam exists by itself, a cosmic orphan. That is why töndam is said to be empty of other. Töndam does not need to refer to other to make itself empty—töndam is empty of any reference point; therefore, it is empty. But at the same time, töndam is somewhat full. It is full by itself, and completely unique.

THE GROUNDLESSNESS OF ABSOLUTE TRUTH

The second of the two truths is absolute or ultimate truth, or töndam. *Tön* means "meaning," and *dam* means "superior," or "ultimate"; so *töndam* means "absolute truth." It is the real truth as opposed to the relative truth, and quite difficult to explain. One of the definitions of töndam is that it is experiencing reality in its fullest sense, without regarding any individual style as tangible from the ego-clinging point of view.

In discussing absolute truth, I have decided to drop the yogachara viewpoint and approach it from the point of view of the madhyamakans. The yogacharans are very good at relative truth. If you want to understand relative truth, you cannot help but see it from the yogacharan point of view that everything is about your mind, how your mind boggles and how your mind bucks and kicks. However, I don't think you can experience absolute truth properly from the yogachara point of view.

Absolute truth is that we have no truth. In talking about absolute truth, I do not want to discuss hypothetical theories about absolute truth, but to build some kind of ground for experiencing the groundlessness of absolute truth. Just knowing about absolute truth does not help you, particularly. The question is, how do you know it is absolute truth?

Shunyata and Buddha Nature

Fundamentally, the meaning of *shunyata* is "emptiness," and the nature of shunyata is being able to see the phenomenal world in the absence of dualistic fixation. The function of shunyata is to see that dualistic fixations are not particularly appropriate and valid. By realizing the negativity of its own nature, we could see further positivity. The awareness of shunyata could act as memory, in the sense that its presence is never lost. It is a present memory rather than a past record. From shunyata's point of view, everything is present.

Questioning whether we really know what things are, whether we really know what blue is or what green is, is a way of trying to cut through conceptual mind. We discover that we cannot actually find any permanent, fundamental, satisfying ground on which to stick our concepts or to nail them down. Things seem to be arbitrary, but we see that our perceptions also are arbitrary. Because such dualistic fixations are just temporary, they do not play a very important part in our understanding.

On the whole, we can say that shunyata is emptiness. The reason shunyata is emptiness is because our perceptions of the phenomenal world have no characteristics of any substantial nature. They are arbitrary, and dependent on our particular state of mind. Therefore, they are detachable; they are a lie.

How does the shunyata experience function? What does it do to us? By realizing such a thing, by seeing through such lies and falsity, we begin to understand groundlessness, or the egolessness of totality. That could be called a glimpse of vajra-like *samadhi,** or the true experience of buddha nature.

We could say that even the realization of the wakeful quality of enlightenment is empty. The definition of buddha nature, or tathagatagarbha, is that it is free from preconceptions. The quality of buddha nature is that we contain enlightened wakeful qualities in us that are free from dualistic obstacles. The function of buddha nature is to awaken us to the actual buddha nature itself, so that we can realize greater wakefulness, or buddhahood.

---

* Vajra-like *samadhi* is an indestructible meditative state of complete awakeness or enlightenment.

If there were any concept attached to buddha nature, then it would no longer be the realization of enlightenment. So things are fundamentally empty, basically empty. If you have a sudden flash of emptiness, it may be temporary, particularly if you are trying to possess that experience as a great flash of insight. But if you actually make a link with the wakeful quality of buddha nature, the realization of emptiness could be said to be permanent, although the concept of permanence does not really arise. Buddha nature is self-existing; it is your own nature. Realizing your buddha nature is like realizing for the first time that you are a Jew or an Arab. It is like realizing something that is part of your makeup and that you cannot get rid of.

FREEDOM FROM NAMES AND CONCEPTS

There is not very much you can say about ultimate or absolute truth. It is freedom from fixation, and freedom from fixation means being free of names and concepts. But if you take out name and concept, what is left? There is the shadow of name and concept, but is that real? It is not real, but pure shadow. Is the name real or the concept real? You could give someone a name—you could decide to call your son "George." Is he actually "George"? Maybe he is not just "George," he is "George Smith." Is he actually "Smith"? That is just a name you decided to call him for lack of an alternative. You have to call him something; you have to put him in school, and you have to get him a passport if he is going to travel in foreign countries—and he should know who he is, so if somebody asks, "Who are you?" he can answer, "My name is George." Everybody has done that to us for generations and generations and generations. So we have begun to regard giving our children names as a very ordinary thing to do. But where did that come from? It came from all kinds of misunderstandings that took place over a long period of time, from the time we grunted and wore animal skins and carried stone weapons. From then onward, our human society developed. We began to be smart enough to call somebody "George" or "Tim."

"My son, George Smith" is a concept. "I am George Smith" is a concept too. Where did that come from? How did we do that? We call this "bread," and we call that "pot." So "bread" is always connected with something you can eat, and "pot" with something you can cook in. The concept of

Chögyam Trungpa next to one of his brush calligraphies, an art form that combines into a single gesture emptiness, compassion, and awareness. Photograph © Andrea Roth.

"bread" does not have any background as such. Do we actually have a real feeling of the word *bread* in our mind before we have been told that something is bread, before we have decided to call something "bread"? We call something "bread," and it actually performs its function as bread properly, fully, and completely. But we never think about those things, we just think, "I had bread." It has gone down and out to the sewage system by the time we think about it.

There is something very empty about the whole thing. It is actually very hollow, full of all kinds of hoaxes. We think very cleverly; we even think up all kinds of philosophical terms, beyond bread-and-butter language. We think of all kinds of fantastic words, which we call our beliefs: "I believe in the blah-blah. I believe in this. I don't believe in that." But what do we really mean by those things? Do we really know the language completely? And what is language, anyway? Sometimes we get panicky about that. We decide to call language something deeper, such as a mantra, or an utterance that comes from above us. But then again, what do we mean by "above us"? What do we mean by "deeper"? The hollowness still goes on; it goes on all the time. Whatever we do, whatever we say, there is always something fishy happening. Something really stinks.

Some kind of rumor has been built up for centuries and centuries, and we decided to believe that fantastic rumor—we decided to call it reality. But who created the rumor? It is said that somebody who has jaundice will see a white conch shell as yellow. So if a whole people or a whole nation were subject to jaundice, with generations and generations of jaundice cases, everyone would see anything white as yellow. That is actually what has been happening to us, although maybe not at such a gross level. Seeing white things as yellow goes against relative logic; it is confused kündzop. How do we know that we are not doing that at the ultimate level, the real level? What do we mean by "red," what do we mean by "green" or "yellow"? How do we know that we share the same experience? Somebody has conveniently put these things together, and we have been programmed since our childhood so that we believe in certain things. But how do we know that we are all not color-blind? Your red could quite possibly not be my red at all. I may see an entirely different red than yours, although we appreciate redness mutually because we have been programmed that way from childhood. That makes things very scary.

Our perception, our approach to reality, could be entirely different than someone else's. On the whole, there is kind of a hole there; there is some kind of leak. Something does not hold together in how we experience our life. We say, "I love you" or "I'm your friend," but what do we really mean by that? What is behind the whole thing? Do we actually say it, or is it just kind of a facade—not even kind of a facade, but an all-around facade? A big hole or big leak is taking place. Things do not seem to be as solid as we think, and it is not really fixable. Things are actually very shaky underneath.

Due to our lack of sanity, we have no idea what we are doing at this point. Maybe everybody is mad; that is possible. You might say, "Of course I'm not mad." But maybe you are mad. Because you said you are not mad, it is possible that you are one of the maddest of all. How do we know? There is complete hollowness.

Shunyata is very real; I am not particularly talking about sixth-grade-level shunyata at this point, although it may sound that way. The question is still, how do we really know about our part of reality? Can we really trust in that if we are fixed in our perceptions? These are very simple questions.

We are not talking about philosophy necessarily, although it entails that as well, naturally. But when we perceive things, we label things: "This is a jar, this is a table, this is a house, this is a room, this is a door, this is a drink, this is food." We seemingly share those things together. We even come to agreements together; for instance, we agree as to whether the food we ate was good or not. But still, how do we know that we are saying the same thing? Or do we?

One of Nagarjuna's ideas in connection with shunyata is the realization that there is nothing we can hang on to that is actually a common idea. Everybody believes blue is blue, yellow is yellow, and red is red, but nobody really knows because we have no way of talking with one another except in terms of our own conceptual language. We could actually tune ourselves in to a kind of make-believe. How much does the lingo we are learning make us think we share the world together, and how much are we actually sharing the world together? That is what it really boils down to. It is a very suspicious world. We do not know who we actually are, from that point of view; we have absolutely no idea. What do we mean by "me" or "I"? What do we mean by "that"? If we do not know what we mean by "red" or "blue," we could also ask, what do we mean by "me"? When your mother says "you," somebody else might think "me."

It is very tricky, but very simple logic. It is extremely simple logic, actually. That is one of the interesting points about shunyata. As a contemplative practice and a way to study shunyata, you could think about all this. Do we really know who we are? Do we really know what is yellow, what is blue, what is green, or what is red? Do we really know what is up and what is down, what is water and what is fire? Well, do we?

The shunyata principle is connected with the nidanas. The nidanas are coincidences, which make things seem real and solid, and shunyata is something that kind of deflates itself. Supposedly, by understanding the deflatableness of shunyata, we can begin to realize the coincidence of the nidanas, or *tendrel*. That is to say, certain things coincide; coincidence takes place in our life. For instance, although my students and I might have a gross misunderstanding of each other and what we are talking about, something has brought us together in a very strange way. We may have entirely different ideas about the whole world, but we are still connected. That is an example of the nidana principle, which brings things together. But at the same time, there is deflatable shunyata, which is all-pervasive.

ULTIMATE TRUTH AS COSMIC ORPHAN

Ultimate truth implies that there is something behind the reality of kündzop. It is fine to begin to see reality, or things as they are, as empty, but töndam is not just emptiness—töndam is absolutely full. It is full of all kinds of things and possibilities, but it is empty of other. Since ultimate truth does not have any relatives, it could be called an orphan. Töndam is an orphan in that it has no reference point for itself. Who are the parents? Who are the brothers and sisters? Töndam exists by itself, a cosmic orphan. That is why töndam is said to be empty of other. Töndam does not need to refer to other to make itself empty—töndam is empty of any reference point; therefore, it is empty. But at the same time, töndam is somewhat full. It is full by itself, and completely unique.

Since töndam has no need to refer to other to make itself empty, you could say that "Form is emptiness" without having to say that "Emptiness is form." Instead of saying, "Emptiness is form," emptiness just is. Particularly in the Zen tradition, the idea that emptiness is form is a very important reference point, but in true madhyamaka, you don't actually have to say that. It is what it is. Some logical traditions would say that a vase is empty of its own nature because a vase does not exist with preconceptions. Other logical schools would say that the vase is empty because the vase is empty of fixation and clinging. The problem is that when you say the vase is empty of fixation, you might knock out the fixation, but you still have the vase. You have not destroyed the vase itself, so subtle fixations still exist. When we say that the vase is empty by itself, it does not mean that we have to break the vase in order to take out the fixation. The vase is what is; therefore, it is not.

When we say that the vase is empty, we are not judging from concept. In fact, we cannot actually say the vase is empty. We say the vase is not; therefore, it is. Madhyamakans talk about the idea of two negations, that there is an immense difference between saying "no" and "not." When you say "not," you are substituting something else, but when you say "no," it is a complete negation—which is also a complete affirmation of its existence. "Not" is a view. Because this is not a cow, therefore it is something else. Saying "not a cow" is different than saying "no cow." So it is better to say "no." It is like *mu* in the Japanese tradition. Mu means "no"; it doesn't mean "not." In saying that the vase is empty, the idea is not simply that it is no vase from our point of view; therefore, it is a vase as it is. It is not even that it is no vase insofar as we have a concept of vase; therefore, it is a vase just as it is, without our concept added. In both statements, there is still a shadow of us. Instead you could say, "The vase is utterly no; therefore, simply yes."

TWO TYPES OF TÖNDAM

There are two types of töndam: countable or categorized töndam, and uncountable or uncategorized töndam.

Countable Töndam

Countable töndam is *nam-drang-pe töndam*. Nam means "all," *drang-pe* means "countable," and *töndam* means "absolute truth"; so *nam-drang-pe töndam* means "countable töndam." Countable töndam refers to what occurs when we begin to experience certain portions of our life with less fixation. When we have less problem with the reality of töndam, we begin to realize and experience the simplicity, ordinariness, transparency, and nonexistence of certain issues. Therefore, it is countable. It is not yet vast, but it is workable, touchable, able to be experienced.

At this level, we might have no problem transcending our fixation on a cup of tea, but we still have a problem with our grandmother. We might have transcended our conceptualization of chopsticks, but we still have a fixation about our Chinese cook. We may have transcended our fixation on our mother, but we are still not letting go of our mother's nipple. It is a partial letting go.

Uncountable Töndam

The second type of töndam is *namdrang ma-yin-pe töndam*. *Namdrang*, again, means "all count," *ma-yin-pe* in this context means "not having," and *töndam* is "absolute truth"; so *namdrang ma-yin-pe töndam* means "not having countable töndam," or "no longer having countable fixations." At this level, a person's experiences of both the chopsticks and the Chinese cook are transcended, and the mother's nipple is transcended. Everything is completely vast experience. This type of töndam is the madhyamaka level. The truth of pure kündzop is the yogacharan level, which is also very profound.

The uncountable level of töndam is connected with the experience of shunyata. The countable level is a lesser experience. In the *Heart Sutra*, when things are broken into pieces by saying "no eye, no ear, no nose," and so forth, that is purely on the level of countable töndam. When it says that all dharmas are marked with emptiness, this is the uncountable töndam level. At that point, an actual glimpse of shunyata has begun to occur. But even the countable töndam level is more adult than pure kündzop. There is the emptiness of recognizing that kündzop does not make any sense. You see that kündzop is helpful, but that it does not produce any progress reports.

CUTTING THROUGH NEUROTIC RESIDUES

Countable töndam transcends pure kündzop, but only partially. With the clarity of pure kündzop, you see that the sky is blue, but you still have not let go completely. Seeing without any delusions that the sky is blue is fine, but that just means you have become sane in the conventional sense.

But there is more insanity beyond that, which namdrangpe töndam cuts through. You discover that seeing blue as blue is not all that you thought. It is not the last result, but there is more to come. There are further psychological fixations and subtleties. You may no longer have psychoses or see pink elephants in front of you, and twofold ego may seem to be completely cut through, but you still have neuroses. Those neuroses are cut through by the two töndam experiences.

The ego of dharmas is extensive and very hard to cut through. At the level of pure kündzop, the gross level of the ego of dharmas may have been cut through by committing yourself to bodhichitta and becoming a bodhisattva-like person, but at a subtle level it is still happening. Although you seem to have become grown-up, your teenager-ness and infant-ness are still continuing. So you still have a journey to make; it's not a clean-cut job. The ego of dharmas is hard to cut through because you still have some idea of the path and the teachings, and some idea of the person who is making the journey. All those connections make up a big bundle. You still have a sense of direction; although you experience many flashes of directionlessness, they do not last very long. They are just temporary. There is still the continuity of "me" taking a certain direction, "me" making a journey.

There is another residue in addition to that. You have learned a lot and cut through a lot, but in the meantime you have inherited a lot of things to replace what has been cut through. It has been said that until you get to the highest tantric level, or *ati*, each one of your achievements is also your way of messing up. Although you learn many new things, you leave deposits behind. It is like a worm in the middle of a piece of wood: it eats what's in front of it, and excretes something back out behind it. You leave deposits behind, and they have to be cleared out as well.

In the hinayana, pratyekabuddhas feel that their ability to cut the karmic chain reactions is an achievement. But in fact, although they have managed to cut through the chain reactions of karma, in the process they have created further chain reactions. So their achievements and accomplishments are good for them, and at the same time they are bad for them. In the mahayana, bodhisattvas engage in the world, but they are unable to immerse themselves in their world actually and fully because they are still fixated on being religious. So it is as though they were walking on ice instead of walking on rock.

FOURFOLD DEFINITION OF ULTIMATE TRUTH

The definition of töndam, or ultimate truth that does not need any reference point, is fourfold: joy, purity, permanence, and being. This list may seem to be a complete contradiction to the rest of the buddhadharma, but somehow it is true.

Joy

Ultimate truth is joyous or pleasurable. Ordinary pleasure comes from drawing entertainment from the other. We generally cannot just have a good time simply by ourselves, but our enjoyment has to be opposed to something else. For instance, we might experience joy if we were being hassled by somebody, and we managed to get away from that person once in a while and just be alone. Beautiful people or celebrities face that problem of being hassled by photographers and admirers, so they appreciate being alone. But the joy of ultimate truth is a quite different kind of pleasure or joy. It is joy without any reference point. There is not even the reference point of pain or pleasure, or pain and pleasure together. The experience of joy is direct and precise.

Purity

Ultimate truth is pure because the quality of shunyata experience is beyond indulgence. We do not have to create extra garbage in order to exist, but we exist in our own way. That way becomes very personal, very definite, and very direct. It does not need any feedback or further excitement.

Permanence

Ultimate truth is permanent. Permanence is quite a tough notion to handle, because the whole teaching of buddhadharma is based on the idea of impermanence or transitoriness. But in this case, permanence does not mean longevity or eternity. It has a greater imprint in our present existence than on the future. The idea is that present existence is permanent. It is a complete mark, or *lakshana,* a complete imprint. Every moment of experience is full and complete in its own basic sanity or emptiness.

So this notion of permanence has nothing to do with longevity or eternity.

Being

Ultimate truth is being. Being may seem to have a quality of ego, something that has to be gotten rid of. But in this case, it is just being. It is the existence of a fundamental reference point. That fundamental reference point could become a resource for encouragement or confirmation, but in this case it is simply self-existing being. When you are there, you are there; if you are not there, you are not there. There is a quality of actually being there properly and fully. You exist in your own way—there is no other way to exist. Since you exist as you are, you do not need any reassurance or the territoriality of egohood.

These four definitions of töndam—joy, purity, permanence, and being—are the basic reference points of ultimate shunyata experience, which is equal to tathagatagarbha, which is another name for ultimate truth. However, not all ordinary madhyamakans talk about ultimate truth and tathagatagarbha in such an easy way. They feel guilty because they have not realized the ultimate meaning of emptiness. Therefore, they think they are violating the true teachings of Buddhism by re-creating ego of some kind. But the Madhyamaka school of our tradition says that tathagatagarbha does exist, and we do not feel the existence of tathagatagarbha creates any problem for the teaching of the nonexistence of ego. In fact, when we negate the ego, that affirms the existence of tathagatagarbha at the same time.

23

Contemplating Emptiness

You and your wakefulness have different opinions altogether. It is very important to understand how the whole thing goes wrong at the very beginning. If you understand that, then you understand the whole thing. And that split is not a "once upon a time" story—it happens all the time in your everyday life.

DROPPING CONCEPTUAL FIXATIONS

At the true shunyata level, having experienced kündzop completely and properly, we realize that kündzop is problematic. We realize that clinging to relative reality is not particularly workable, wise, or inspiring. Kündzop becomes altogether meaningless. In fact, there is no kündzop as such. Everything that we experience, such as tables or chairs or whatever, is based on fixation, and that fixation is already empty by itself. It is empty because there is no substantial ground to be fixated on, so nothing actually happens.

When we experience fixation, that fixation seems dramatic and realistic from the ordinary point of view. But if we view that again and again from the logic of who and what and where such fixation takes place, we find that we need fixation itself to encourage us to do that. But if we are working purely according to the logic of the fixation, we do not need ourselves to work with it. In other words, the subject is not particularly basic—the subject needs an object to relate with it. Anything might seem tangible, but nothing becomes particularly tangible. If we have an idea of something, the subject of the idea, the object of the idea, and the concept of the idea are all divided into so many sections that finally we could ask who actually had such an idea. Where did the idea come from? Where are the final conclusions taking place? It is questionable.

Due to fixation, we would like to hang on to something extremely vague and uncertain, but the vagueness remains vague. How the vagueness came about is uncertain, and where the vagueness is to end is uncertain, so we really have no working basis. If we were able to go beyond the fixation of who possesses what, then we might understand that there is no possessor of such a situation. There is just complete openness, complete spaciousness and nonexistence. So the vagueness is not vagueness in the sense of uncertainty, but vagueness as a panoramic quality. It is the ideal perception of vipashyana that hinayanists dream of attaining. It is ultimate, all-pervasive awareness. If you have a panoramic vision of a city, a bird's-eye view, you see everything very precisely, but at the same time it is vague, because you are seeing everything in too much detail. It is vague because of the abundance of detail rather than because you do not see the details. The vagueness is the precision.

The basic notion of shunyata at this point is "that which is empty of its own conceptualizations." When we see a vase, a chair, or a table, we have a sense of it. But that sense is not the actual vaseness, chairness, or tableness at all. It is just an attachment, something we just plopped onto it. Things are as they are. There is nothing really we can tell about the extent to which they exist. We might say, "Because I decided to call this a table, therefore it is really a table," but we actually have no reference point that allows us to say that, experience that, or realize that. A table is a piece of furniture that has a top and four legs. If we think that anything that has four legs is a table, we might find a cow to be a table, since a cow also has four legs. But a cow is not flat on top, and a table is. If there were a flat-topped cow, then it would absolutely be a table. An armchair is something you sit on that has legs and arms. But if that is the case, your parent's lap could be called an armchair.

If we begin to figure out those little details of our confusion, we see that it is quite likely that tables could become cows, or chairs could become parents. Such confusion is a possibility; it is all based on our fixation. We do not actually realize or experience the chairness or tableness in anything. We simply randomly give our names, concepts, and ideas to things. We have no idea why things are as they are, or how things are as they are.

We realize that we cannot grasp onto anything properly and fully, so the only thing we can do is to take off our fixation on things as they are. Doing so begins to plant a seed in our mind, known as buddha nature. Without fixation, things are seen as they are, and there is some kind of basic intelligence taking place. Things are seen to be both colorful and empty of conceptualization.

AVOIDING RED TAPE

Ultimately, anything that you use to perceive shunyata, any way you try to understand shunyata by means of something else, does not work. The idea is to try to avoid such red tape; the whole thing has to be direct. The study of shunyata takes place in your mind, but what is your mind? Who made your mind? Who is your mind? What is your mind? Where is it coming from, and where is it going? Why do you want to study shunyata at all? What's going on in your mind? Where is the background of your mind? What is your mind doing there? It may seem like a vicious circle, but if you spin enough, if you get dizzy enough, you might come to some kind of sense. That is the trick used by the madhyamakans, and it is still used in the Zen tradition of koans. The idea is that the vicious circle has to break down sometime. If you put enough discipline into it, finally you are spinning completely, so you lose track of trying to get hold of something workable, and you give up the whole project.

CONNECTING KÜNDZOP AND TÖNDAM

Töndam, or absolute truth, is connected with the perception of shunyata, and with shunyata, you are relating with reality. We are not talking about absorption into the highest spiritual level or any kind of gift of God, but about a very simple, straightforward, and direct rediscovering of yourself through the inspiration of buddha nature.

Töndam is a higher level than kündzop. But you cannot be born as a full adult all at once. You first have to be a baby and a teenager, and then you can become an adult. So placing a higher value on töndam does not mean that it is something you can reach directly. It may have higher value as far as the progression is concerned, but nobody can reach that level without first going through the earlier yanas.

Kündzop is actually very powerful. Kündzop is the thread or continuity that runs through both the yogacharan and the madhyamakan approach. The activities of the bodhisattva are based on skillful means and wisdom working side by side, like the two wings of a bird: skillful means is kündzop, and wisdom is töndam. So you have to be a good baby, a good teenager, and then a good adult. You have to do all three properly: you can't be a bad baby, a good teenager, and then a bad adult. Töndam is madhyamakan style, and kündzop is yogacharan style. It is Zen style, the appreciation of things as they are. Quite possibly the yogachara teacher Asanga was a greater artist than Nagarjuna.

Although we say that the mahayanists experience the twofold truth completely, it is not necessarily true. Each experience of truth leaves a footprint, which still must be shed. As we go along the path, there are constant footprints, which become lighter and lighter until the attainment of vajra-like samadhi. So even at this level, there is still a footprint of the ego of dharmas. The ego of dharmas is very hard to overcome completely, and the egolessness of dharmas is very hard to go along with. It is necessary to realize that all this does not happen in one sudden flash, but it is a slow thinning-out process.

The *Samadhiraja Sutra* says that dharma does not have letters or language. But if there are no letters and no words, it might seem that there is nothing worthy of discussion. Since everything is nonexistent, what is listening and what is teaching? Why do we teach and why do we study? We can listen and we can teach because that unchanging nature has been exaggerated. In order to teach the absolute truth, we can create a kind of "tripless trip." In other words, we have to exaggerate. In Tibetan it is said that we have to attach more feathers to the unchanging truth so that people can listen and be taught. The *Heart Sutra* builds up concepts such as no eye, no ear, no nose, and the rest in order to show how shunyata is absent of concepts. It is like the old remedy that goes: if you have water caught in your ears, you can get it out by putting in more water.

The connection between kundzöp and töndam is compassion. No matter how much people confuse things, there is a quality of compassion and the desire to work together. That seems to be the link. In terms of kündzop, or relative truth, as long as we breathe the same air, inbreeding is happening. We may regard each other as being individually born and not particularly brothers and sisters under one heading, but that inbreeding is pretty intense. It is like tons of maggots crawling all over one another.

Sitting practice is the only way to get away from such inbreeding. You cannot actually get rid of that process unless you stop. In terms of töndam, or ultimate truth, having already experienced your closed and inbreeding world, you try to inject new blood all the time. Ground madhyamaka is based on the fact that the only working bases we have are relative reality and ultimate truth, which can work together. That is the starting point: relative and absolute truth can work together.

SAMSARIC PERCEPTION
AND RANDOM LABELING

We approach the world the same way all the time. There is a whole spectrum of possibilities—there are big issues and small issues of all kinds, such as making love, taking a shower, brushing our clothes, or combing our hair—but whatever goes on in our life has the quality of stupidity and aggression. However, we cannot say that drinking a cup of tea is bad. That is not a problem, and it is not particularly anti-dharma—it is simply relative truth, or kündzop. So if we have a cup of tea to drink, we should go ahead and drink it. But interestingly, the way that we do so is a samsaric version of drinking tea.

The term for the samsaric style of going about our business is *küntak,* which means "random labeling." *Kün* means "all," but in this context it has the sense of "random," and *tak* means "labeling," or "pigeonholing"; so *küntak* means "random labeling." Küntak is random because it is opportunistic. We don't really know what we are doing, so we are always trying to latch onto situations. Küntak covers both the ego of dharmas and the ego of individuals. It is that which makes us hang on to things, to ourselves or to the world. That is what we do in the samsaric world. We apply küntak in the confused, neurotic, and mercenary way that we try to make friends with somebody, in the way we try to con them. We apply küntak by attaching ourselves to a certain idea, and then trying to perpetuate it so that the world will appear the way we want it. Politically, that seems to be the approach of capitalism as well as communism. Küntak is mercenary and opportunistic, and it is a form of fixation. Fixation may seem to be the opposite of randomness, but before you become fixated, you randomly choose what you will become fixated on. You scan the room, and you zero in on one particular area. So you randomly pick something, and then you fixate.

The idea of küntak is that when you react, there is no basis for your reaction. Things are just a fabrication of reality, a fabrication of so-called reality, rather than actual reality. The point is that anything that goes on within the level of küntak is not really going on at all. It is pure fabrication, just a big scheme to try to occupy ourselves for no reason. It is a big deception. We deceive ourselves so that we could have a very cozy world in which things overlap. We want to have a so-called great time, which is actually *duhkha,* or suffering. Sometimes you see one thing and you react to many things, and sometimes you see many things and you react to just one thing. All such situations are not founded on anything solid; they are fabrications. Shunyata does not just mean emptiness, it means being free from fabrications. If you have no eyes, you can see without fabrication. Having no eyes does not mean that you go blind. In fact, you can see better because your eyes are not clogged up with fabrications.

When we remember something that happened and see that none of it was real, we see how we made the whole thing up. That is why we put so much emphasis on how you get confused right at the beginning, how you split off from your tathagatagarbha, your buddha nature, how you separate yourself from others. You and your wakefulness have different opinions altogether. It is very important to understand how the whole thing goes wrong at the very beginning. If you understand that, then you understand the whole thing. And that split is not a "once upon a time" story—it happens all the time in your everyday life.

In whatever we do, we have lots of küntak. At the level of küntak, having a cup of tea is a big deal. You are very particular about the whole thing. But while you are drinking your cup of tea, ignorance and passion are happening along with it. If you were free from küntak, having a cup of tea could be very simple, no big deal. You could simply have your tea, made out of water and tea leaves. So when you drink your cup of tea, you could do it badly and aggressively, or you could do it gently. When you remove stupidity and aggression, softness and gentleness remain. That softness is known as shunyata and compassion. Gentleness always exists; it goes on all the time.

The shunyata doctrine tells us to disbelieve in küntak, to go beyond it. This does not mean that if you have a fixation on your piano, you should burn it in order to transcend küntak. It is much more subtle than that. You only need to discover your küntak and to understand how it works in order to see that it is no longer real. When you understand küntak, you realize that territory and aggression are not real.

I would like to make one theme quite clear: when you perceive situations samsarically, you do not perceive them properly. You may think that if you transcend all your samsaric desires, you will not be able to make your own cup of tea, or cash your check at the bank. But in fact, it is because of your samsaric desires that you are unable to cash your check properly or make your cup of tea. If you get beyond samsara, you can cash your check much better. You can make your monthly payments on time and make a great cup of tea as well. The idea that giving up samsara means leaving behind the pragmatic world is absolutely ludicrous, and does not correspond in the least to the buddhadharma. In the madhyamaka approach, practicality is not regarded as worldliness. If you have to evict your tenant because they didn't pay the rent, you just do it. It is not regarded as a samsaric act, particularly; you are just responding to the situation. It is not evil; you are just doing what needs to be done.

The Buddhist way of working with our perceptions, with our bodies and minds, is not to annihilate them or to regard them as a curse. We have our bodies, we have our perceptions, we have our mental attitudes, and we have to refine them. We have to work with them properly. That is why it has been said that true kündzop should be respected. We are not talking about running away from the world. We should actually keep up with what is going on in the world, but we should do that purely and properly.

Overcoming Küntak

Traditional madhyamaka logic talks about four ways of overcoming küntak: examining the cause, examining the effect, examining both the cause and effect, and examining the nature of the whole thing. These contemplations can be applied to both psychological states and factual states. They are dialectical, direct thinking.

Examining the Cause

The first contemplation is looking at how küntak arises. Looking at the cause is called the vajra clamp, or diamond clamp. For example, in terms of yourself and others, when küntak arises, what causes it to arise? Does it come from your self or from others? If it appears that it came from you, you ask yourself the straightforward question: "Where in my self does it come from?" When you do so, usually you will not find any background or place of origin. Therefore, you think that it must be the fault of others. You try to pigeonhole it as coming from someone else. But who are those "others" anyway? They also come from you; they come from your view of others. And finally, if the cause of küntak comes from neither of the two, if it is not initiated by you or others, then nothing is actually happening. So a cause does not seem to exist, particularly; it does not seem to happen.

The point of examining the cause is that the root of küntak cannot be found. Küntak does not come from anywhere. You did not really provide the ignorance at the root of the whole situation; you did not create such strong ignorance in yourself. Ignorance is like snowfall; it is not particularly solid. The samsaric fixation of küntak is neither your fault nor the fault of others. In fact, it doesn't really exist.

Examining the Effect

The second means of overcoming küntak is looking at the effect or the fruition. For instance, a fruit comes from a seed. But if a seed is a seed, how can it be a fruit? And if the fruit is a fruit, how can it be a seed? In other words, if the seed is constantly being a seed, it cannot bear any fruit. And if the fruit is constantly being a fruit, then it cannot be a seed. A seed is different from a fruit. So what is the continuity? What is the solid connection between the two?

We usually look forward to the fruit or product of situations. For instance, when we want to go to sleep, we would like to go ahead and fall asleep rather than talk about how to do it. We think that the fruition, falling asleep, will already be there if we desire or yearn for it. From our küntak perspective, we look forward so much to fruition that the fruition has no means of becoming actual. We become so vague and so numb by expecting fruition that the fruition never happens. We are constantly covering things up, but there is nothing underneath, so we are making a big deal out of nothing.

Examining Both the Cause and Effect

The third means of overcoming küntak is looking at both the cause and the effect, the seed and the fruit. You see that one concept can create many products. Does the one expand by itself? If it does so, then one becomes many. But how can one be many? If one is one, how can one become two?

When you examine things in this way, you are unable to conjure up or seize your confusion on the spot. You may be able to do so theoretically, or cook up a few ideas about it, but on an actual experiential level, you cannot grasp it. When "Aah!" has occurred in you as you are looking at the phenomenal world, as you are relating with both here and there, that "Aah!" does not mean anything. You might make a big deal out of feeling that "Aah!" but nothing has actually happened; it is panic without any root. That "Aah!" does not produce any result or solidification. Both the cause and effect of your panic are insubstantial; they do not exist. You have just made them up.

Examining the Nature of the Whole Thing

The fourth means of overcoming küntak is looking at the nature of the whole thing. When you don't find something to blame, your usual trick is to conjure something up. But if you look fully and thoroughly into your magic tricks, your devious tricks, none of them have any real, solid logic. You could write a whole book about how solid your tricks are, but if you genuinely look at where all these tricks come from, you see how you build your castles on ice. If you look at how you go about your business, you begin to find that your so-called talent, your professional acting out of the role of samsaric gentleman, samsaric lady, or samsaric powerful person, doesn't quite make it. It is fundamentally full of holes.

We could call these four topics the four exposés of küntak.

24

Awakening Unfabricated Perception

By virtue of having developed maitri for ourselves and karuna for others, the ground of our existence begins to thaw and the samsaric world begins to flake. We realize that there is no reason for us to hold a grudge against others, or for that matter, ourselves. . . . So we begin to let go, to open further. This quality of openness and gentleness is not a naive or love-and-light approach because it is combined with prajna, or discriminating awareness. . . . When both letting go and prajna take place at the same time, we experience fundamental softness in our view of ourselves and the world.

VIEWING THE WORLD WITH LOVING-KINDNESS AND COMPASSION

When we begin to perceive the phenomenal world from the viewpoint of bodhichitta, we find something quite different from what we are samsarically accustomed to: we begin to have an understanding of things as they are. When we perceive the world according to shunyata and madhyamaka logic, it is necessary to understand that our whole being, our basic essence, is connected with wakefulness. At this point, we may have already practiced and come to that realization, but we still have to shed a lot of obstacles and uncover a lot of things on our journey—and we begin to ask questions as to how we can go about that.

By virtue of having developed maitri for ourselves and karuna for others, the ground of our existence begins to thaw and the samsaric world begins to flake. We realize that there is no reason for us to hold a grudge against others, or for that matter, ourselves. We have no grudge against our world. So we begin to let go, to open further. This quality of open-ness and gentleness is not a naive or love-and-light approach because it is combined with prajna, or discriminating awareness. So our perception is based on a very interesting balance between letting go and prajna, or intelligence. When both letting go and prajna are taking place at the same time, we experience fundamental softness in our view of ourselves and the world.

Prajna is of absolute, utmost importance in Buddhism. As you are pro-gressing on the path, even if you are not yet enlightened, there are always glimpses of prajna. Prajna discriminates between entities very clearly. It distinguishes between what is and what is not, but it does not promote or reject anything. If you are either rejecting or wanting to propagate some-thing, you no longer have prajna. You have allied yourself with that and this, with liking and disliking, with good and bad. With prajna, everything is even and equal. It is almost a gray world. Prajna cuts things into pieces; it distinguishes what is appropriate in order to see the vision of shunyata.

In talking about our perception of the phenomenal world, the term *phenomena* refers to whatever you hear, see, or feel. It refers to whatever you relate with: your lover, your husband, your wife, your in-laws, your book, your table, your food, your sheets, your toilet—all those things. According to the *Heart Sutra,* all phenomena are empty. What does empti-ness mean? We should look into that.

When we see a cup of tea or some food, emptiness does not mean that we do not see the cup, tea, table, or food. If it did, we would starve to death. Emptiness does not mean being above the whole thing so that we don't need to eat. It refers purely to our perception of the phenomenal world. When we look at a cup of tea, we see the cup of tea as a cup of tea, but on top of that, there is tremendous seriousness. That seriousness is based on the absence of karuna and maitri, and it is stupefying. Some people take pleasure in a great cup of tea, regarding their cup of tea as real. But if we look closely and precisely, we realize that seeing our cup of tea from the samsaric point of view is stupid and aggressive. There are all sorts of levels of drinking one cup of tea. Some people like the idea of drinking a cup of tea as a social norm. For others, the appeal is in the smell or taste. Some people enjoy the sensation of drinking the tea for the aftereffect and satisfaction they get. They enjoy their preoccupation with tea. We may jumble all the levels together and say, "Let's just have a cup of tea."

But somehow it is not that simple. If we examine the process of drinking a cup of tea precisely and thoroughly from prajna's point of view, we see how our mind perceives the act of drinking a cup of tea from the very beginning. We see how we order it, how we first perceive it, how we go through the process of waiting for it, sipping it, and finishing it, whether it comes with milk or with lemon.

APPLYING THE TEACHINGS OF SHUNYATA

Shunyata is the perspective that arises when we relate to the phenomenal world purely on the level of perception—when we see table as table, vase as vase, book as book, without anything imposed on them other than what is absolutely the bare minimum necessary. Shunyata is not some great understanding or revelation; it is seeing things as they are, which also means seeing things as they are not. If we do not see things as they are, they become powerfully overwhelming. A vase has more implications than a vase actually has; a table has more implications than a table actually has. Because of that, we extend ourselves unnecessarily. We make a big deal out of our vase, our table, our television set, our tape recorder, our penknife, or our new gun. Everything becomes a big deal.

That big-deal quality of our perception is considered to be a veil that prevents us from relating with reality properly, fully, and thoroughly. That big dealness makes us numb and unable to relate with the phenomenal world in its own right. Ordinarily, a word such as *tableness* has a quality of holding on or fixation, but if we take away that veil, we begin to see things truly and precisely as they are. We see them without their "-ness" quality—without their table-ness, vase-ness, all kinds of "-nesses." The term for that is *isness.* It is also called *tathata,* or "truth." It is "dharma-ness," or dharmata.

Isness in this sense is empty. We begin to see reality at a very direct and personal level. Table is table; therefore, there is no table. Table is table because it is table. It has four legs and a top, it is square, and it is made out of a certain kind of wood, plastic, or metal. Table is table, but there is nothing beyond that. Basically, table is empty. It is quite straightforward. Table is table—so what? It does not have much more to say than that. It might have its history, its value, its previous occupants and owners, but it is still just a simple table.

Carrying that understanding to a larger cosmic level, every phenomenon that we experience has a quality of emptiness. With an understanding of emptiness, the absence of thingness, we begin to see things very clearly, precisely, and fantastically vividly, because we no longer lay conceptual interpretations on them. We begin to see people and things as they are, directly and simply. This is called the discovery of unconditional truth. Such truth is not a matter of beliefs or theories—it is self-existent truth.

With an understanding of spaciousness and precision, developed through the realization of things as they are in their own way, we begin to develop real heart and a sense of appreciation. The experience of shunyata does not mean that we are completely disillusioned with this world and couldn't care less—we are simply seeing that things have no substance. At the same time, we realize that the reason we can see this is because we seem to have some kind of strength continuing in our system all the time. That strength or inquisitiveness is known as tathagatagarbha, or buddha nature. We begin to appreciate things much more because we are not using concepts. Using concepts is like putting price tags on things as they are. When we look at things without such barriers and blockages, we begin to be more inquisitive and clear. More critical judgment begins to take place.

In spite of having taken away our fixation on things, there is still a gut-level journey taking place at this point. We become more eager to realize things as they are. That eagerness brings us to a certain required or prescribed lifestyle. It brings the attitude that we need to relate with the phenomenal world simply and as no big deal, but with a sense of ongoing softness or warmth.

Discipline is important on the bodhisattva path because we still have not quite seen the emptiness of the vase or the emptiness of the table properly and completely. In order to realize the phenomenal world in its fullest aspect, we have to see things as they are more clearly. We also begin to realize that the more aspiration there is, the more a feeling of inadequacy takes place. Our understanding of emptiness leads us to feel the need for some kind of direction or practice: we realize that it is necessary to begin to work.

MINGLING YOUR WHOLE BEING WITH DHARMA

The point of applying the teachings of emptiness and compassion to your everyday life is to make the dharma real, as opposed to fantasy. It is to make the dharma as individual and personal as possible. You might feel that it is becoming too personal and begin to panic, but I am afraid that this is necessary in order to experience who you are and what you are. It is like letting a doctor draw blood from your body in order to study it and tell you what kind of sickness you have. It is very personal for somebody to take blood from your body, even insulting, if you look at it that way—but you still let them do it. You could do the same thing at the dharmic or psychological level. You could let yourself go a little. You could open a bit more so that you could understand who and what you are.

You need to give in to the teachings. If you don't understand a topic, you should not regard yourself as stupid, but rather see that you are not letting go or giving up enough. If you begin to give in and let the dharma understand you, you in turn begin to understand the dharma. That seems to be the secret trick. There has to be a mingling of your whole being with the dharma, otherwise the dharma becomes an alien entity. Gampopa's instructions that your mind should be one with the dharma and that dharma should progress along the path would be lost to you.*

The difficulty is not that the dharma is too technical; it is that you are being too technical. If you stop being technical, you can still sharpen the sword of prajna. If you give an inch to the dharma, you gain a mile of enlightenment. That has been done in the past, and it has worked. So the vision of dharma is very generous, and we can actually do something about it.

We can do something about shunyata as well. Shunyata is not just theorizing about how real or unreal your eye or your nose may be. It is not theorizing at all. Shunyata is based on personal experience, on how we experience things. When you have run out of all your tricks, all possibilities of deviousness, you are actually affected by the shunyata principle, and you realize that you cannot con anything, including your own world. You realize that it is useless, so you begin to relax. At that point, you become extremely open and raw. At the same time, you have no desire to do anything. You may have some kind of nostalgia for the early days, when you used to cover things up and thought you were on top of the world, when you used to do your little tricks and get away with all sorts of things. And now you feel nostalgia, which is painful. You realize that you can no longer do that, that it doesn't even excite you

---

* A reference to the Four Dharmas of Gampopa, a four-line chant composed by the great Kagyü master Gampopa (1079–1153). See volume 1 of the *Profound Treasury*, chapter 6, "Achieving Sanity Here on Earth."

anymore. So there you are: you have become a one-hundred-percent genuine person.

Living in this way is very simple. You feel that your stronghold is useless and futile, that there is no reason to hold on to it anymore, so you begin to give in to yourself. It is a less mercenary approach than just thinking that the dharma is worthwhile. You begin to realize the shakiness and the unreasonability of your existence, and you give in to the dharma. When you do so, you begin to go much faster along the path. It is a question of personal surrendering rather than aspiring to the dharma in a theistic way, or thinking how great the whole thing is. It is not like saying that "God is great" or "Allah is great"—or whoever or whatever is great—and knowing that you will be saved if you give in. In this case, you just realize that you are wasting your time by not giving in to the simple truth.

You might have nostalgia for more romantic days, but this could be romantic as well. Usually our romanticism or nostalgia is for the past. But you can conjure up nostalgia for the present and rejoice in the realization of shunyata. Nostalgia can become not a memory of the past but a way of being where you are right now. There is a twist between now and what was, which turns your mind around. If you feel that you are in the past, the present begins to beckon to you on the spot. This is an interesting twist that could develop.

If we can actually exert ourselves and discipline ourselves, we will begin to see shunyata. Shunyata is extremely personal. We might feel that our territory, our privacy, is being invaded. When we begin to feel that way, that's great. It means we are getting somewhere. We should go beyond that and let our privacy be further invaded. We should let our personality be condemned so that we could dissolve into the sea of shunyata. It is quite delightful and peaceful, quite natural and ordinary. It is much more ordinary than being operated on under general or local anesthetic. Sooner or later we have to experience, or at least learn to experience, our stomach being opened without any anesthesia. The first slit is painful, but the rest is quite simple.

The experience of shunyata is very natural. It is like the personal experience I had after my car crash in England.* My lips were completely cut

---

* This accident took place in 1968, shortly after Trungpa Rinpoche returned from a pivotal retreat in Bhutan. For an account of this period and of Trungpa Rinpoche's early life in Tibet, see Chögyam Trungpa, *Born in Tibet* (Boston: Shambhala Publications, 1977).

through, and the doctors refused to give me local anesthesia because it would slow down the healing process. When the doctor came with needle and thread, the nurse was very kind and said, "Everything's okay. Just look at me." Then the doctor made stitch after stitch, saying, "It's fine. It's no problem." So my lips were sewn up. That is a celebration of life—to be in a car crash and have your lips sewn up. There are lots of people around you and you are unable to move. You can't do much of anything, but you still could feel great; you still could make some kind of breakthrough. This is the idea of the shunyata principle. We could carry out our whole life in that way.

Shunyata means that you do not need the reference point of some solid entity in relating with your friends, your food, your clothing, your world, or your accommodations. You can actually open yourself up. You have no personal territory, no personal game, no actual personal entity that provokes your existence or the notion of your existence. You still are what you are, but "you" is not what you are. "You" is not. That is the shunyata approach: "you" is not. You are not even a grain of sand, not even dust. You don't exist. Therefore, you exist so much. You are brilliant, luminous, skillful, and at peace. Because you have given so much territory away, you actually can work with others. You have not vanished into thin air.

SEVEN RICHES OF SUPREME BEINGS

The practice of shunyata meditation is accompanied by what are known as the seven riches of supreme beings, or the seven noble riches: not being distracted by the sense experiences, diligent practice, joy, generosity, composure, reasonableness, and knowledge or prajna. These riches are related with the postmeditation experience.

Number one is not being distracted by the sense experiences.

Number two is diligent practice. You keep up with your regularly scheduled meditation practice. A proper approach to food is an aspect of diligent practice because food is often used as a break from discipline. For example, when you are doing hard work, you take a coffee break or a tea break, which you could build up with embellishments such as biscuits, sandwiches, and oysters. You need to eat, but food can become an obstacle to diligence. Since food is good for you, you think that what you are doing is okay, but you are beginning to use eating as an excuse to be other than diligent. It is more than simply entertainment; it is an excuse, which is worse. So you need to keep up your meditation schedule as well as your awareness of food and eating.

Number three is joy, or faith. You know what should be done and what should not be done. In terms of neurosis, you know what lead you should follow and what lead you should not follow. You are not intimidated by acts of virtue and you do not review your actions, thinking, "Am I in the right?" but you just do the right thing very simply and directly. Virtue, in this case, is healthiness. It is psychological and physical wholesomeness. There is a feeling of joy that what you are doing is a worthy cause. You are remaining in the faith, and your discipline is clean, because neurotic interruptions do not take too much control over you.

Number four is generosity. It is your habit to be generous. You also have an appreciation of the learning process, and you have gathered a lot of both intellectual and experiential knowledge.

Number five is composure, or modesty. Instead of constantly being bold, there is a quality of shyness or restraint. Here, shyness does not mean that you are intimidated, but that you keep your composure.

Number six is reasonableness. You do not upset other people because of your outrageous behavior, but you are friendly and reasonable. If you are a guest, quite possibly you offer to wash up the family's dishes, not purely as a dutiful thing, but as an expression of your generosity and helpfulness.*

Number seven is knowledge, or prajna. It includes both intellectual and experiential knowledge.

Those categories may seem extremely mundane and ordinary, like the dietary laws of the Jewish, Christian, or Muslim schools. But a student of the mahayana has to be reasonable. You need dedication, openness, and kindness. The point is not to be "good" in the popular sense of doing everything right, and saying "Please" first and "Thank you" afterward. But you also do not upset people. The point is to be reasonable.

---

* The categories here translated as *composure* and *reasonableness* are often translated as "shame" and "embarrassment." The idea is that one refrains from negative actions either due to one's internal conscience (shame) or to avoid the disapproval of others (embarrassment).

You might ask how these mundane details are connected with such
high principles as shunyata, nonduality, and so forth. There seems to be
a big hiatus, but that is absolutely not so. In fact, there is an enormous
link between the two, because the more you begin to see nonexistence,
the more chance you have to relate with existence. For instance, Zen
practitioners who actually see the nonexistence of the self, who see that
everything is empty, tend to wash their cups and their bowls well and to
make a neat room. So in practice, working with both high principles and
mundane details is not at all contradictory.

Shunyata has a haunting quality, which comes from a sense that nothing is outside, nothing is inside, and profoundly there is nothing. The most
haunting of all is that there is no one to haunt you. The seven riches are the
binding factor that connects the haunted world of shunyata with our own
highly claustrophobic world. In other words, the seven riches of supreme
beings are about how to bring a gem into a nonexistent population.

The basic principle of mahayana is that bodhisattvas are supposed
to save sentient beings from samsara rather than making a nuisance of
themselves. The seven riches are jewels of conduct, showing you how to
handle yourself in whatever activity you do. They show you how to deal
with the world in general. As an elaborated form of compassion, they are
very important, very personal and powerful.

The seven riches of supreme beings are based on awareness and the
nonexistence of awareness at the same time. Nothing is particularly calculated, like trying to be a good housekeeper or a good sociable person.
There is room for everything in the mahayana approach. The bodhisattva
path not only tells you how to meditate, but also how to handle society, because the biggest work of the bodhisattva is dealing with society.
Whether that society is an enlightened society or an unenlightened one
doesn't make much difference.

The seven treasures are applicable right now. They are things we
could do ourselves, right away. At this point, we are talking about the lay
bodhisattva approach, the beginner's level. Before we discuss the various
levels of the bodhisattva path, we need to make a very concrete connection with how all this could be done. Otherwise, you probably would be
dreaming up all kinds of things. It would be a kind of sales pitch to hear
about the various achievements and experiences of the bodhisattvas, and
how beautifully and smoothly they can be done. You would want very

much to buy, but you would not have enough money to do so, which would be frustrating. But with shunyata, there is a connection, and the experience of shunyata matures as you go along. Everything matures on the path, because you are moving forward. There is no stepping back and there is no reverse.

Part Six

BODHISATTVA ACTIVITY

25

Paramitas:
Techniques of Nongrasping

Paramita practice is based on human decency, and how to be in the world and help others who are suffering. . . . Paramita practice is the essence of how to be a bodhisattva. A bodhisattva is someone who is brave, and utterly and thoroughly involved in the discipline taught by the Buddha. Bodhisattvas are ideally soaked in the water of helping others in every way.

THE MAHAYANA path, or the bodhisattva path, is regarded as an intermediary process in the development of enlightenment. That is to say, enlightenment is the final result, and hinayana is the starting point. We start from the viewpoint of individual salvation, and go beyond that into an understanding of reality as shunyata and compassion. The mahayana is the way to develop or cultivate shunyata, and paramita practice is how we can apply those teachings very personally and directly.

EXERCISING GOODNESS

When you realize a spark of goodness in yourself, real basic goodness, you may experience an attack of negativity. You may suddenly feel angry, anxious, or depressed. But that kind of attack serves as a reference point for you to recognize your basic goodness, so it is no longer destructive. You are seeing things as they are, so all of it is fine. Basically, if you don't see white, you don't see black. That's how it goes.

If you don't have basic goodness, you don't have anything. But you don't just *have* goodness or *feel* goodness—you have to *exercise* goodness. Goodness has to be worked with. You do not have goodness for your own sake, but for the sake of others. So the bodhisattva ideal is to share your goodness with others. Otherwise, why do you have goodness at all? But the actual application of basic goodness is very demanding. You have to develop the ground to help others, but you can't help anybody while you are sitting by yourself and meditating. You actually have to go out and help them.

Before taking the bodhisattva vow, you need to have the conviction that it is necessary to do so. You need to have genuine interest, gentleness, and a sense of egolessness. And after you have already taken the vow, there is a feeling of continuing further along the path and beginning to understand what the bodhisattva path is all about.

The Work of a Bodhisattva

The technique for becoming a good practitioner, a decent person, a good warrior, and a good bodhisattva is to follow the six transcendent disciplines. With generosity you open yourself and give away everything, including yourself.

Out of that naturally grows transcendent discipline. With discipline, you do not get tied up in your generosity. You don't have any hangover from giving away too much, and you don't develop any heroism from giving so much away.

Out of discipline comes patience. You control your aggression by means of shamatha and vipashyana and by means of realizing absolute and relative bodhichitta. You develop nonaggression.

Out of patience grows exertion, which is having a sense of joy in, and appreciation of, your livelihood and your practice.

After exertion comes meditation. Meditation does not mean purely sitting on your meditation cushion, or *gomden*. Meditation means that the cushion is sewn to your pants, so your gomden goes with you everywhere. Instead of wearing a crucifix, you might sew a gomden onto your skirt or your pants, so that you always have an awareness of meditation. It's as literal as that.

From the paramita of meditation, an extraordinary intelligence begins to open up, known as *prajna* paramita. From the extraordinary intelligence of prajna, you develop an understanding of mindfulness and awareness, as well as an understanding of all five previous paramitas. Prajna is also like the horse that pulls the chariot, or the rest of the paramitas. Prajna knows where to go and how to go. Therefore, prajna is a very important part of bodhisattva discipline: everything begins to spark. It has also been said in the texts that all rivers go to the south and that all rivers flow into the ocean. That ocean is prajna.

Prajna is the wakefulness that occurs to everybody at the moment of panic. At the moment of panic, at the moment of pleasure, at the moment of doubt, at the moment of comprehension, there is a gap—and before you realize what it is, prajna happens. It is like coughing or sneezing: while you are coughing or sneezing, your mind stops, and then you resume your previous situation all over again. So there is a gap, and then, "Gesundheit!"

The paramitas of generosity, discipline, patience, exertion, meditation, and prajna are the natural habitual patterns of a bodhisattva's work. But there needs to be a total involvement in the bodhisattva path, so that your approach does not become purely charitable work inspired by an emotional surrendering to the world. You are not just trying to do a good job or trying to perform a good deed every minute. Bodhisattva activity is not quite the same as that of the Red Cross or UNICEF. The bodhisattva's work is much more organic and somewhat less organized. The organization is within the bodhisattvas themselves, rather than being based on any external setup or projects, such as collecting a penny a minute. You are not looking for any reward, not looking for achievement, and not looking for any personal complement to your own existence. Your approach is based on something other than that.

People who work in the Red Cross are serious and dedicated to their global vision of charity, or aid to children, or other causes. But the bodhisattva's approach has to be much more deep-rooted than that. Such dedication can only come about when you have an understanding of yourself and your particular attitude and involvement in such an endeavor. Having taken the bodhisattva vow, your approach may at first be quite vague. You may think, "Now that I am on the way to becoming a bodhisattva and am a member of the family of Buddha, maybe I can do something great. But what can I do? How can I render my service?" That question might be the first impact on your mind, but initially it is not so important to know what you should be doing; it is more important to find out where you are and what kind of world you are in. The question is, what is your state of mind? Your state of mind is ordinarily a confused one. You do not know what to do, and you hope that you could do something. But the more you think that you have to do something to fulfill your bodhisattva activity, the more confused you feel.

When you first take the bodhisattva vow, you have some understanding of the nature of the commitment you have made, and you have some kind of faith in the transplanting of bodhichitta into your heart. But you still need something beyond that—you need an understanding of egolessness. You need to understand that you can only be a bodhisattva if you give up the idea of attaining enlightenment for yourself. The ideal bodhisattva, or ideal student of the bodhisattva path, is the person who actually gives up the idea of personally attaining such a thing as enlightenment. Instead, you simply enjoy working with the paramitas, with the basic energy inspired by taking the vow.

From a Western viewpoint, that approach may seem to be very impractical. You might ask, "Why do I have to slave to death if I have no idea what I am going to get out of this?" You may be quite familiar with that approach. It is like parents telling their children, "You should get your life together. If you have greater responsibilities, you should get higher pay. At least you should have some security, a house, and a car. How much are they paying you?" That kind of approach comes from animal instinct, and that instinct continues, which seems to be a problem. Anything other than bodhisattva activity, in fact, could be regarded as animal instinct. Whether it is the highest culturally evolved society or a more simple society, it is basically the same. Whether your money is in the form of gold or paper, you think you should get your money's worth. But the bodhisattva approach is not that you should get your money's worth or that you should get your practice's worth. That kind of business approach to practice or to the bodhisattva path does not work. In fact, the more you regard the whole thing as purely a business deal, the more you cut your own throat in a non-bodhisattva-like way.

UNDERSTANDING THE SUBTLETIES OF PARAMITAS

The key point of the mahayana approach is the commitment to dedicate yourself to helping other sentient beings. Building yourself up or perpetuating your own existence is regarded as neurosis. Instead of building yourself up, you should continue with your pursuit of helping others. Instead of being selfish, you should empty yourself. The basic definition of ego is holding on to one's existence—and paramita practices are techniques that allow you not to grasp onto or propagate the notion of me-ness, or "I am." Experiencing egolessness is a process of letting go. But you do not regard the ego as an enemy or obstacle, you regard it as a brussels sprout that you cook and eat.

Paramita is a Sanskrit word that means "going beyond." *Para* means the "other shore of the river," *mita* means "arriving"; so *paramita* means "arriving at the other shore." The Tibetan word for paramita is *pharöl tu chinpa. Pharöl* means "other shore," *tu* is "to," and *chinpa* means "arrived"; so *pharöl tu chinpa* means "arrived to the other shore." It means crossing the turbulent river of mental gossip and continuous passion, aggression, and ignorance. As you go across that river, the captain of the boat is the spiritual friend. You go across with the captain, who has experience, and you get to the other shore by practicing the six paramitas, beginning with *dana* paramita, or generosity. Paramitas are based on not holding on to your personal territory. When you become a bodhisattva, you are going beyond habitual patterns altogether.

Although we have been discussing the six primary paramitas—generosity, discipline, patience, exertion, meditation, and prajna, or knowledge—there are ten paramitas altogether, according to the Buddhist tradition.*

A natural sense of appreciation of things as they are without poverty mentality of any kind is referred to as *skillful means,* which is the seventh paramita. Having made that discovery, you wish to share your discovery with others. That is the eighth paramita, *aspiration.* Beyond that, you begin to experience *strength,* the ninth paramita. You are not subject to or enslaved by some other entity, but a natural quality of strength takes place. Ordinarily, when you experience something special, it drains the energy out of you and diminishes your strength. But in this case, your strength is not based on struggle. Therefore, it becomes a natural food in itself.

The last paramita is *wisdom.* I would like to make quite clear that wisdom does not come from reading read many books and or collecting a

---

* The *ten paramitas* are: (1) generosity, (2) discipline, (3) patience, (4) exertion, (5) meditation, (6) prajna, (7) skillful means, (8) aspiration, (9) power, and (10) wisdom. In Tibetan they are: (1) dana, (2) tsültrim, (3) söpa, (4) tsöndrü, (5) samten, (6) prajna, (7) thap, (8) mönlam, (9) bala, and (10) yeshe.

lot of material. Wisdom means that you have naturally settled into the situation. Wisdom is self-contained. Adding these four to the initial six paramitas makes ten paramitas altogether. On one hand, it might be hard to achieve all that or go that far step-by-step; but on the other hand, minute by minute, you can actually achieve the ten paramitas right away.

Sometimes it is said that there are thirty-six paramitas, which is a way of showing the subtleties of the development of the paramitas. For instance, with the paramita of generosity, you could have the generosity of discipline, the generosity of patience, the generosity of exertion, the generosity of meditation, and the generosity of prajna. Dividing each of the six paramitas into six different aspects in that way makes thirty-six paramitas altogether. Such hairsplitting is necessary and important—particularly if you are actually going to practice the paramitas, rather than theorize the whole thing, write your book, and take off on the next airplane to Mexico. If you are going to stick with the practice, it is important to realize the subtleties of the paramitas. You may think you are working purely on prajna paramita or on the paramita of meditation, but maybe at the same time you are still working on the basic generosity level. So understanding the subtleties of the paramitas is very important and necessary.

The idea of the paramitas is that they all should happen at once. But we cannot talk about them all at once; that would be impossible. So we have to speak about them one after another.

Some of the teachings are linear, and some are more environmental. But in either case, there is a process of growth. There is the way you eat your food as an infant, the way you eat your food as a teenager, the way you eat your food as an adult, the way you eat your food as a middle-aged person, the way you eat your food as a very old person, and the way you eat your food as a dead person. That is linear, and at the same time it is equally environmental. We cannot dissect the path by saying this belongs to that, and that belongs to this. But we can say that the development taking place in your own state of mind can be applied to a further evolution.

The Delight and Workability of Paramita Practice

Paramita practice transcends both the simple, ordinary pain of samsara, and the hinayana notion of peaceful attainment, or nirvana. The traditional phrase for this is: "Not wandering in samsara, not dwelling in nirvana." It transcends both worldly views and shravaka and pratyekabuddha notions of virtue. Paramitas do not refer to ordinary ethics, such as the ethics of bank loans or the world of business, nor are we practicing the paramitas in order to achieve spiritual tranquillity or equilibrium. Not at all! Paramita practice is based on the realization that there is no individual here seeking individual little goals. There is no "you." In fact, at this point, your existence and the existence of others are both questionable. The only thing guiding you on this particular journey is a sense of delightfulness, warmth, and sympathy. At the same time, there is also the realization that sentient beings do exist, and that they wander around in their own little world and suffer a lot—and you try to help them. The approach is not that you too are bogged down in the world of sentient beings and trying to struggle out. You are not a worm wandering around in a sewage system; you have greater vision than that.

Paramita practice is the essence of how to be a bodhisattva. A bodhisattva is someone who is brave, and utterly and thoroughly involved in the discipline taught by the Buddha. Bodhisattvas are ideally soaked in the water of helping others in every way. However, paramita practice is not particularly a religious practice. It is different than the missionary approach of trying to convert people into your faith. It is more like teaching people how to be. Paramita practice is based on human decency, and how to be in the world and help others who are suffering.*

As you gallop along the mahayana highway, it is important to have a good understanding of paramita principles. Some Buddhist traditions say that only when you have already gained some spiritual attainment can you practice the paramitas or even take the bodhisattva vow. But according to my tradition, you do not have to attain a high state of realization in order to enter the mahayana. There is always a place for you: there is always a stirrup for you to put your foot into, and there is always an empty chair for you to jump into as you ride up the ski slope.

According to the practicing lineages of Kagyü and Nyingma, there is always a way for very ordinary and basic laypeople like ourselves to enter the path and experience the teachings. What has been described in the teachings can actually be achieved and worked with. There is always

---

* One way to learn more about paramita practice is by looking at the many ways in which a person's actions fail to reflect these transcendent virtues. For a listing of contradictions to paramita practice, see appendix 5, "Forty-Six Ways in Which a Bodhisattva Fails."

the great possibility that you could attain some level of realization. Your realization may be crude; nonetheless, it is workable. So although some traditions say that if you want to be a dharmic person, you have to become worthy first, we say that if you want to become a dharmic person, you are worthy of it in any case. That is the difference between the two approaches.

Some people might say, "If you can't afford to buy underpants, why are you dressed up in a suit and tie?" But somehow or other, we have managed to have a suit and a tie as well as decent underpants. That is how we do it. Otherwise, there would be no way to begin. If we said that you had to be a millionaire in order to become a king, this would make it impossible for you. Instead, we say that you simply begin as a king—and in the process, you could also become a millionaire. The point is that you don't abuse your opportunity, but you use it. Whether we are talking about the hinayana, the mahayana, or the vajrayana, you should realize that we are always talking in terms of something that is reachable.

Characteristics of Paramita Practice

Paramita practice has four characteristics. The first characteristic is that paramita practice overcomes neurotic hang-ups and defilements.

The second characteristic is that paramita practice develops an understanding of threefold purity. You understand the relationship of actor, action, and object. You realize the relationship of you as the doer, your act as the doing, and the object of the action as the other. The emptiness of those three principles has to be very clear: there is no "you," there is no action to perform, and there is no "other," or object. There is no "you" because you are dependent on yourself, which in turn is dependent on the other, which is purely the working of conceptual mind. There is no "other," because "other" would be your projection; therefore, no other actually exists. There is no "activity" to relate you with the other, because if everything is open and free from conception, there is no activity taking place. No conceptual world of "you," "other," and "activity" actually exists. So bodhisattva activity is free from all debts.

The third characteristic of paramita practice is that your actions are completed. You understand that the paramita practices are necessary not simply as reference points or feedback, but are needed in order to fulfill actions very precisely.

The fourth characteristic of paramita practice is that your actions have benefited others. Through your actions, you have created a proper relationship with others.

INTENTIONAL ACTION IN PARAMITA PRACTICE

In paramita practice, the notion of trying is a problem; it's like trying to climb up the Empire State Building from the outside. But with paramita practice, you don't actually try; you just do it. There will be obstacles and problems, but you keep doing it. You do it on the spot. Then there are more obstacles, and you do it again. So you keep on doing it, rather than trying to do it, and at some point it becomes real. When you look back on your past and see how much you have been doing it, you realize that you have done it. Then you keep on doing it, until doing it becomes more real than trying to do it. You have a realistic attitude to the whole practice rather than a dreamy attitude. You are not just listening to a tale.

You should practice the paramitas in spite of your subconscious gossip, such as thoughts about what you are supposed to be doing or feeling, as opposed to what you really are doing or feeling. Such activity is important, because it stops the nidana flow. Your intention is secondary. When you have actually done something, you may feel that your intention was dubious, but your intention has followed your action. When you realize what you have done, you may wonder whether you can undo it. But you cannot undo the past, and since you have done it already, you resign yourself. As you go on in that way, the whole thing becomes genuine.

You have to teach your mind. In order to do so, sometimes action is best, because when you are performing an action, your mind follows. At other times, you have a good intention, and your body follows. At the mahayana level, those two approaches are complementary, but when you get to the vajrayana level, action is always the first breakthrough. Action means that you just do it. As an example, many people have difficulty saying "Yes." If you have that difficulty, you could practice saying "Yes." When you say "Yes" verbally, your mind says, "I said it halfway, but I didn't really mean it." You keep a little corner. But the more you say "Yes," the more you mean it. That is the whole idea behind reciting aloud. For example, when you take the bodhisattva vow, you say that you aspire to become a bodhisattva even though you don't really mean it all the way. Having said it, you have to think about it. You follow the words with your mind, and you actually begin to get it.

Sometimes a physical message is the most direct. It is the best way to deal with a situation like sitting practice. You sit, although you don't really want to sit; you just assume the posture of the Buddha and do it. Then your mind begins to curve toward it and actually do it. It is that way all along, in all three yanas. The first way to bend your mind is to work with what is there.

26

Applying Emptiness to Everyday Life

*When dharma is theorized, you have no hope of doing anything
with it. It becomes merely a decoration, a cosmetic of your ego. But
if you apply mahakaruna, if you apply luminosity and skillfulness,
you finally begin to know the meaning of peace.*

IF YOU are not shown how to apply shunyata, you will not be able to
practice good generosity, good discipline, good patience, and all the
other paramitas. In terms of the two madhyamaka traditions of vastness
and profundity, the vastness school puts more emphasis on practicality
and on how you can apply shunyata, and the profundity school is largely
based on theory and on how far you can go metaphysically.

In the profundity approach, you try to expose and explode your mind
by using the dialectic system of questioning yourself and by sitting practice. Profundity is a philosophy that accepts everything. That might be
attractive at the beginning, but with such an approach you will not know
how to behave as a Buddhist, as opposed to being a good Christian missionary or Red Cross worker. Here we are discussing shunyata according
to the vastness tradition. The reason we are discussing shunyata from
the point of view of practicality is so that we can actually apply it to our
everyday life.

THREE SUPREME DISCIPLINES

Traditionally, the way to apply shunyata is by means of the three disciplines of *shila,* samadhi, and prajna, discussed previously at the hinayana

level.* In the mahayana, the three disciplines are known as the three supreme disciplines. To indicate this, the Tibetan terms *tsültrim*, *tingdzin*, and *sherap* are qualified by the prefix *lhagpa*, which means "supreme." This distinction is similar to the difference between the four brahmaviharas and the four limitless ones.

Shila / Discipline

The first supreme discipline is shila. It is comprised of generosity, discipline, and patience, the first three paramitas.† Because you have great compassion, luminosity, skillful means, and peace, you could practice the supreme discipline of shila. To begin with, by giving up ego and territoriality, you develop the generosity to let go. Then, having let go, you develop morality. You begin to let go as part of your daily practice, and you do not give in to the kleshas. Once you have morality, you then learn patience. You learn how to forbear and how to deal with your impatience. When temptations happen, by practicing patience you can quell them. Patience is the absence of aggression, so you do not get pissed off at little obstacles, but you go on with your discipline. With the supreme discipline of shila, you work on all three of these qualities, back and forth.

Samadhi / Meditation

The second supreme discipline is samadhi. It contains the fifth paramita, the paramita of meditation. In this case, meditation refers to the careful consideration of situations. You understand the nature of temptations and the fickleness of your state of mind, and you do not give in to them. You work with peace and skillful means, so everything functions harmoniously. You are able to work properly in your world and in your particular state of being. You develop good control over your mind, over your mental events, and over the products of those mental events. Everything

---

* 1. See volume 1 of the *Profound Treasury*: part 2, "Discipline / Shila"; part 3, "Meditation / Samadhi"; and part 6, "Knowledge / Prajna."

† The term *shila* is used in two ways: as the second paramita (discipline or morality), and as one of the three supreme disciplines, in which case it includes the first three paramitas of generosity, discipline, and patience.

is meditatively controlled through mindfulness and awareness practice, through both shamatha and vipashyana.

Prajna / Knowledge

The third supreme discipline is prajna, which contains the sixth paramita, the paramita of knowledge. You use luminosity and great compassion, to the point where you are able to discriminate dharmas and perform awakened activities. Acting in accordance with prajna is an act of great compassion, so learning is important. You should be literate and a good grammarian, and you should know how to speak properly and behave properly. Bodhisattvas performing bodhisattva activity in the confused world should not be clumsy, stupid, or uneducated. A quality of intelligence should permeate to your fellow sentient beings, those for whom you are working, whomever they are.

The fourth paramita, exertion, is missing from these three categories. But it is not quite missing, because it applies to all three supreme disciplines. Throughout the whole process, you take pleasure in work and in exerting yourself. A sense of joy and delight takes place in working with the six paramitas together with the three supreme disciplines.

By using shila, samadhi, and prajna to practice the teachings of shunyata, you can avoid the problem of theorizing the dharma. It is always a problem when you try to theorize a situation—and theorizing the dharma is the worst of all. When dharma is theorized, you have no hope of doing anything with it. It becomes merely a decoration, a cosmetic of your ego. But if you apply mahakaruna, if you apply luminosity and skillfulness, you finally begin to know the meaning of peace. You actually can get into the nitty-gritty of it. If you understand the brass-tacks level of shila and samadhi, you can act in full accordance with prajna as well.

27

Generosity

You can afford to open yourself and join the rest of the world with a sense of tremendous generosity, goodness, and richness. The more you give, the more you gain. But that should not be your reason for giving. Rather, the more you give, the more you are constantly inspired to give—and the gaining process happens naturally and automatically.

PARAMITA PRACTICE begins with generosity. The paramita of generosity, or dana paramita, is described as a treasury of wealth.* Generosity is the starting point of the bodhisattva path, and it is also said to reach to the highest levels of realization. The paramita of generosity only arises when you are trained in shamatha and vipashyana, and you have made a relationship with absolute and relative bodhichitta. At the same time, you should not be dependent on your own practice or discipline alone. You need to be aware of your immediate surroundings, as well as the once-removed surroundings, of whatever situation you might find yourself in.

In Sanskrit, generosity is *dana,* which is connected with words like *donation* in Indo-European languages. The idea of dana is one of giving, donating, opening yourself up. It is the strength to work with others and

---

* The notion of a *treasury of wealth* is one of twenty-two traditional similes for stages of a bodhisattva's development. See chart, page 396, "Stages of a Bodhisattva's Development and Corresponding Similes."

to relate with other people's energy as well as with your own. Generosity is free from desire, which means free from desiring for oneself. In Tibetan, generosity is *jinpa,* which means "letting go," or "giving away." *Jin* means "to open one's hand," "to give," or "to let go," and *pa* makes it a noun; so *jinpa* means "generosity." It is letting others have joy, and not being stubborn or holding back. With jinpa you are removing stinginess and not hanging on to psychological possessiveness. Generosity takes place in stages. There are domestic, cultural, linguistic, and educational barriers, so it takes some time to give in to generosity.

In Buddhism, the idea of generosity is giving without expectation. That is the paramita, or transcendental, aspect. When you give something, you transcend the gift and you do not expect anything in return. You are giving away your wealth, giving away your wisdom and understanding of dharma, giving away with daring—and when you give, you feel richer. Jinpa opens up the journey toward wakefulness.

GENEROSITY AND NONATTACHMENT

The nature of generosity is nonattachment. It is based on having the personal intelligence and vision that everything is not constantly dependent on what you want. So a key point is that in your activities or in your work, the first message should never be, "I want. Therefore, we should try to work things around me." There should be other considerations. How about the rest of the world? That seems to be more important. In some cases, "I" should come last—in most cases, in fact! In Buddhism, we make sure that everything else is all right first. We are willing to be the last person, the full stop, the period. That is fine. We do not have to cut ourselves out completely, but we are willing to be the period at the end of the sentence.

This may be painful because we are used to putting ourselves first. Ever since you were a child, you have been building up your ego. But the Buddhist approach is completely the opposite, so it might hurt. At the same time, you might feel tremendous relief that you do not always have to bring along the "I," which is like a sore thumb and always embarrassing and painful. If you don't have to start with that, you can come out into the crisp, clear air. You can speak for the rest of the universe. That is what is meant by egolessness, or individual salvation: "you" don't have to be there.* There is tremendous freedom to move around without "you" being there. It feels very good.

OVERCOMING POVERTY MENTALITY

In the paramita of generosity, giving is not based on the idea that you have so much to give, and therefore you should give it. For that matter, it is not based on the idea that you have so little to give, and therefore you should give whatever you have. It is being willing to part with anything precious, anything that you want to hold on to. You are learning how to part with whatever you have. Whether you are a beggar or a millionaire, you could still have a mentality of poverty and not want to part with anything. Even if you have nothing material or physical to part with, your basic state of mind is that you should keep what you have, including your aggression or passion. Whatever you might have, you think, "Just keep it, I might need it later on."

With dana paramita, you are learning to part with the resources and ammunition you might need to attack the next problem that comes up for you. You might have a brilliance for losing your temper, and you may have had success with it in the past; therefore you feel you should keep your short temper. You might have a way with words, a way with seduction, or a way with salesmanship—and you want to keep that with you. There are all kinds of things you would like to keep to yourself so that you do not feel absolutely resourceless. We all have our usual ways of going about things when we want to get something out of somebody. We do quite well tapping our resources by acting out crying, acting out being jovial, acting out being all kinds of ways, even pretending to be worthless or neurotic. You may be able to dig out such resources pretty well when you need to, but those resources have to be parted with, given up, expended, done away with.

Generosity is based on both parting with and giving: you are parting with what is precious, and giving what is precious. The nature of generosity is one of not wanting to possess anything for yourself. There is a sense of togetherness, in that you do not have to borrow anything from the phenomenal world or your mind's phenomenal world, which is wild

---

* Trungpa Rinpoche has taken the hinayana term *individual salvation* and interpreted it in mahayana style to mean salvation from your self, or egolessness.

and confused. You can stick with your own resources completely. You are giving up miserliness and stinginess, and developing a mentality of plentifulness and opulence. What do you have to offer? You have everything that you have learned up to this very minute, everything good that you have ever received. You could share all that and give it away. By letting go, you could transmute the heat of aggression into the cooling quality of bodhichitta.

By giving, you are giving your basic state of being, or wakefulness. Once you are awake, you are no longer concerned with yourself alone; you would rather contribute something to others. Being wakeful comes from properly carrying out shamatha and vipashyana disciplines at their best, by being completely comfortable with your in-breath and your out-breath and the practice of meditation. With dana paramita, by being wakeful, you can actually convert people who are mindless into mindfulness.

The best donation you can make is to extend your beauty, smiles, and loving-kindness to others. Generosity is not based on despising others or looking down on them. If you do not respect others, you cannot offer generosity to them. Generosity is conceived out of compassion, tenderness, and benevolence, so respecting others is a very important point. Even though a person might not seem to be worthy of respect, if you can come up with even one respect-worthy quality, you can use that as the ground to work with such a person. People should not be left under the influence of the *maras*, the evil ones.*

Generosity is considered to be unshakable. When you possess great generosity, your mind cannot be changed. Your mind is not based on withdrawing help from others, but on exchanging yourself for others, which is one of the first and best attributes of the bodhisattva path. When you extend a sense of generosity, you do not do so in order to gain some kind of relief or to take time off, and it is not based on false comfort or being left alone. You maintain yourself and you are always predictable, like the sun. The sun always rises from the east, it never rises from the west. That pattern is immovable.

Generosity is based on feeling yourself to be wealthy and rich. You feel that since you are so rich and wealthy, you have enough to give away.

---

* *Mara* refers to the tempter who appeared to the Buddha as he approached enlightenment. More generally, the term applies to the evil influences and difficulties a person encounters on the path.

But generosity does not mean losing everything and becoming a slave of others. You are not giving away your shareholdings, but your profits. Generosity means becoming a master of the situation so that you can give more and gain more at the same time.

THREE LEVELS OF GENEROSITY

There are three levels of generosity: the gift of material generosity, the gift of fearlessness, and the gift of dharma.

Material Generosity

The first level is material generosity. Material generosity is straightforward. If people do not have food, you bring them food. If they do not have housing, you put them in a house. You give them clothing and everything they need. To begin with, it is a welfare situation. In expressing your generosity to somebody physically, there is a quality of opulence. Instead of giving a rag, you give good clothes; instead of giving a broken cup, you give good china. Material generosity is an expression of your nonpassion. It is a way of working with others and expressing your richness.

The process of giving is extremely subtle. First you have to find out about the receiver. You need to study that receiver and not just act on your impulse to give. You need to know whether they are ready for your gift or not. And sometimes, if they are overready, you have to become powerful and be willing to give them what they need in order to shock them.

Since the nature of generosity is dispassionate and nonattached, the material gift you give to somebody should be good. If you cannot afford a Cadillac, at least you could give a well-made tricycle. By giving in such a way, a dignified attitude is communicated. The point is not to expand yourself by thinking that what you are giving is the best and the most expensive—it is to assume an attitude of richness and generosity. You might give a notepad that is in extremely good taste; you don't have to give a gold fountain pen. But whatever you do, it had better be good. You could buy a good birthday card or you could make it yourself. It is as simple as that. You give something decent; you do not need to feel that you are so poor that you have to give any old junk. You could experience real taste, even at the plastic level.

When panic arises and you have no bank account and no money, you can still adopt the psychology of richness and nonattachment. The magic of generosity is that even though you do not have a full bank account, even though you don't have abundant wealth, you do not proclaim your poverty, and you can still inspire other people. You can help them to see how they can fill their own bank accounts with their own skillful means; you can inspire them to build richness in themselves. You can help them to see that they too could relate with generosity. It is not a question of buying a cow in the autumn, when it has abundant milk. It is like buying a cow in the spring, when it is lame and has gone through the hardships of winter. You plan to raise the cow throughout the summer so that when autumn comes, the cow will give lots of milk and you can make lots of cheese and butter.

The Gift of Fearlessness

Once they have received material generosity, people want more. They are still terrified, therefore you give them the second kind of generosity, the gift of fearlessness. People have to learn how to develop fearlessness so that they can help themselves, rather than coming back to you all the time saying that they need more food. With fearlessness, they become respectable; they are no longer welfare cases. You give people fearlessness so that they, in turn, can give it to others.

The gift of fearlessness is not purely psychological. It does not just mean saying nice things to people in order to make them feel better; rather, you make them work. By doing so, people begin to understand that they can actually survive and maintain themselves. So they begin to feel good about themselves and to have dignity. They realize that they do not have to constantly be beggars or poor people, but they could develop their own capital.

When you have developed dedication to others and passionlessness, you are no longer afraid. Therefore, you can afford to be arrogant in the positive sense. If people need security, you can give the gift of fearlessness. You can reassure others and teach them that they do not have to feel completely tormented and fearful about their existence. You can help them to see that there is basic goodness and spiritual practice, that there is a way for them to sustain their lives. To those who feel afraid of the dharma, afraid of their teacher, afraid of their sangha, afraid of their food, or afraid of their companions, you can give the gift of fearlessness. You let them know that fearlessness can be proclaimed, and you show them how to develop it. Your fearlessness can comfort their fearfulness.

The Gift of Dharma

The third level of generosity is the gift of dharma. You could present the dharma at a very basic, ordinary, and reasonable level so that it does not panic anybody. You could teach people about discipline, meditation, and knowledge. Dharma makes people's minds grounded so they do not experience instability. Having heard the dharma properly and fully, they begin to trust in themselves, as well as in the dharma. It is said that in order to engage in bodhisattva action, first you have to have good conversations with people, then you should charm them and make a connection, and finally you might present the dharma. You should take time with people.

As long as you are following the bodhisattva path, you should be practicing all three types of generosity at once. It is quite a lot of work. Through all three types of generosity, you can open up people's minds so that their closedness, wretchedness, and small thinking can be turned into larger vision. That is the idea of mahayana altogether: to let people think bigger, think greater. At the first stage of the bodhisattva path, you begin to become generous and genuine. You become somewhat opulent by giving expensive gifts; you become somewhat arrogant by giving the gift of fearlessness; and you become somewhat righteous by giving the gift of dharma as basic sanity.

REHEARSING BEING GENEROUS

In the paramita of generosity, giving comes first, and from that a sense of vision and richness arises. According to the bodhisattva manuals, you can actually rehearse being generous. For instance, you can hold a precious object in your hand, and practice giving it away by extending your arm. Then you pull your arm back, and give it away again. You can learn to stretch your arm and give. The word for extending your arms is *tong-phö*, which means "daring to let go." *Tong* means "letting go," and *phö* means "daring"; so *tongphö* is "daring to let go." It is a challenge as well as a delight.

Many people do not want to extend at all. They want to bring everything back to themselves. It is a very simple psychological practice to extend your arms and give, but in many cases you do not want to do that. You get frightened, particularly of giving to strangers. You do not know exactly who is going to receive what. You think that somebody might take everything you have, that a stranger might do anything! But the attitude of this practice is precisely the opposite: you invite *all* strangers. If they do anything strange, that is their problem. But as far as you are concerned, you have to extend yourself and invite them. You have to extend yourself as much as you can.

You can also rehearse your generosity by literally handing something over to somebody. When you are eating a delicious meal, in the middle of enjoying the good food, you could take a piece out of your mouth and give it to your pet. You could give some of your food to a beggar. You shouldn't always consume the whole meal and take it all into your system.

The richness of generosity is not smug. It is not the experience of self-snugness; it is going from here to there all the time. Although you may not feel generous, you just have to do it. That is what is meant by rehearsal. But you also have to be very careful about the object of your generosity. You should not be generous to the wrong cause. For instance, you should not be generous to somebody who is producing an atom bomb to kill all human beings.

To begin with, everything is a rehearsal. However, as long as you willing to go along with the practice, such manufactured generosity seems to be okay. If you are purely trying to find out whether the dharma works or not, if you do not have faith in the dharma, you might give up the whole thing. But you need to keep working with people. That is the whole point: you keep trying to work with people all the time. You can be inspired by mahayana vision. You can afford to open yourself and join the rest of the world with a sense of tremendous generosity, goodness, and richness. The more you give, the more you gain. But that should not be your reason for giving. Rather, the more you give, the more you are constantly inspired to give—and the gaining process happens naturally and automatically.

28

Discipline

The basis of discipline is the behavior pattern or psychological state of not thinking of yourself as the star of the world. You do not come first. In the mahayana tradition, in any case, you do not come first. A noncentralized existence brings proper conduct.

T HE SECOND paramita is discipline, or shila paramita. The paramita of discipline is described as a perfume infusing good discipline all over, and as being free from passion. It is connected with vipashyana. If generosity is not met with discipline, it can become sloppy. Discipline in Sanskrit is *shila*. In the Tibetan translation it is *tsültrim*. *Tsül* means "proper behavior," and *trim* means "rules," "norm," or "way"; so *tsültrim* means the "proper way to behave," or "proper conduct."

The difference between the hinayana and the mahayana approach to shila is that on the mahayana level, you are working much more for others. At the hinayana level, individual salvation is being emphasized. The idea is that in order to save others, first you must save yourself. Even the airlines use that logic: when you fly in an airplane, the flight attendant announces that in case the cabin pressure changes, you should put on your mask first, and then do it for your children.

It has been said in the *Madhyamakavatara* that even if you have an excellent practice of dana paramita, if you do not practice shila paramita as well, it is as if you have no eyes and cannot see, as if you have no legs and cannot walk. The paramita of generosity is like gathering seeds to sow, and the paramita of discipline is like plowing the field in order to be able to sow the seeds. If the field is not properly cultivated, no good fruit or good harvest can come about. So the paramita of discipline is very important.

Discipline in the ordinary sense of the word has a quality of tightening up. You are supposed to behave in a certain way, and you either go along with it or you do not. But in this case, discipline is slightly different than conventional morality. In the Buddhist tradition, discipline is said to be like possessing a pair of eyes: when you don't have eyes, you don't see anything. Similarly, if you do not have the eyes of tsültrim, you do not see dharmas properly. If you are exceedingly speedy or absentminded, you do not see clearly. When you are driving, if you have no awareness of what you are doing, you just keep speeding along, and you experience what is known as an accident. Much of the confusion you experience in your life is due to your being unable to see dharmas properly. So tsültrim does not mean simply obeying the rules of the party or the church. Tsültrim is definitely intelligent discipline. When you begin to see dharmas very simply and clearly, you realize that you can actually perform your discipline properly and fully, without any contradictions.

MAINTAINING SIMPLICITY

Dharmic discipline does not necessarily mean saying mantras all the time; it could mean washing your kitchen floor. Shila paramita is regarded as a way of making yourself available to the practice or discipline of whatever you are doing, rather than punishing yourself because you have been a bad boy or girl, or trying to correct yourself. This kind of discipline is much more pleasurable and much more rewarding in the long run. You should enjoy having discipline. You can enjoy making a good cup of tea, pouring it into your cup without spilling it, drinking the tea, and then finishing up properly and nicely, so that there are no mishaps. Discipline is very much a question of properness. Usually the word *properness* implies some sort of stuffiness, but in this case "being proper" means being in accordance with the laws of nature. You are simply being where you are, with things as they are.

The analogy for discipline is that of the wish-fulfilling jewel. According to Indian mythology, if you place a wish-fulfilling jewel on the top of a banner and pray, it brings many more jewels. Tsültrim is like a wish-fulfilling jewel because it is the basis of all kinds of virtues. So discipline is seen as a general sense of richness, rather than as a tightening up.*

In the beginning, however, discipline is not always very pleasant. It is embarrassing and awkward and tight. You begin by gritting your teeth; that is how you have to start, and that is how I was brought up myself. But once you get used to it and begin to give in, you make your home in it. You find comfort in the discomfort. Eventually, you may find a little bit of the elixir of life between your teeth, which gives you strength. At that point, discipline is no longer effort oriented—it is effortless.

The practice of discipline is like spending time in a cave. Obviously, the first time you stay in a cave, it is very harsh, particularly when there is lots of snow and cold air coming in. But after a while, you begin to settle down in your cave. It is your home, your practice place, and you begin to take pride in it and praise it. The great yogi Milarepa spent many years living in caves. Toward the end of his practice, a gang of local demons came along to tempt him, but that just inspired him to praise the place where he was meditating. He sang a song in praise of his cave, the mountains, and the whole environment around him. He began to appreciate the whole thing, including the climate. It began to feel good and natural. So nothing is all that comfortable and ideal at the beginning. You should not approach discipline as if you were getting new teeth from the dentist, where you get put to sleep and then wake up with new teeth. That is a twentieth-century approach.

Discipline is based on awareness, which brings appreciation and a proper relationship with the phenomenal world. Proper conduct is to maintain what you have, to stick to the bare minimum. Its nature is simplicity. The link between generosity and discipline is that having given up your usual flashy, exhibitionistic, and colorful attachments, you end up with the bare minimum and you stick with that. You do not borrow anything unnecessary, and you do not need to buy anything unnecessary. Discipline means constantly continuing with simplicity.

An important point about discipline is that you are not looking for signs of improvement. You do not expect that you have paid your penalty by being simple, so now your rank should be changed and you should be put on a higher level. Discipline is said to be the counterweight for happiness

---

* The traditional simile for *discipline* is that it is like a jewel mine, because it is the basis for the arising of precious qualities.

and the terminator of suffering. If you are dancing in happiness, discipline brings you down; if you are rotting away with suffering, discipline lifts you up. Both suffering and happiness keep you company—and discipline keeps you from both extremes with a big hammer, up and down. Finally there is no chance to get carried away with anything, either happiness or sadness. You are basically stuck with what you are, which is very hard discipline.

Having already stripped off attachments, you end up as a simple, straightforward, naked child without companions. Discipline makes you a lonely person. You cannot cry to anybody because nobody will come to get you, and you cannot ask for milk because there are no nipples. So discipline is a real appreciation of loneliness. You have an appreciation of your own discipline, but you do not make a big deal out of it or use it as company.

STEPPING BEYOND PREOCCUPATIONS AND BUSYNESS

Without discipline, your preoccupations become much more intense. You are much more involved, more frustrated and busy with the complexities of your own neuroses. Even though you are in the human realm, you could become enslaved in the hell realm, the hungry ghost realm, the animal realm, the jealous god realm, or the god realm. You could re-create these realms and manifest them in all sorts of ways. Without discipline, it is difficult to free yourself from such preoccupations.

When you are busy and preoccupied, you feel hassled by your own existence. You torment, torture, and busybody yourself. You are so busy that you think that you do not have any time to spare for your practice. Such torment and busyness seem to be monumental or historic, but that is not the case. As far as we are concerned, that kind of torment is absolutely ordinary. As you begin to work on that, you realize that the inconvenience, discomfort, and anguish that you experience is no more than anybody else experiences. So your experience is no longer regarded as monumental—no more than if you step on a cat's tail, and the cat cries out, "Wooaaaoow!" However, it is still a problematic situation. Therefore you need to practice the paramita of discipline, which overcomes that type of preoccupation altogether. You begin to realize that preoccupations are garbage; they are worth flushing out so that something real could come up. Then paramita activity begins to make sense, and you begin to act in a more genuine way.

Basically we are trying to put a stop to frivolity of any kind. *Frivolity* is an interesting word. It can mean being crazy and indulging unnecessarily in a very crude fashion, but it could also mean indulging in something in the name of humor and overdoing it slightly. If you are embarrassed to deal with a particular subject, you find another subject to discuss. If you are tired of drinking vodka, you switch to sake. If you are bored with talking to one person, you switch to somebody else. Frivolity is anything that creates further confusion, or the longing for further confusion. Confusion may seem luxurious: when you no longer have it, you begin to miss that confusion, and you would like to re-create it. It is like going back to an adult bookshop and getting more magazines. But with discipline, you control any form of potential escape from reality.

The paramita of discipline undermines the attempts to make small things big, and it allows big things to be made quite small. Our habitual tendency is to exaggerate small things into large things, so that the small neuroses grow into larger neuroses. But with discipline, you begin to see that whenever neurosis arises, it can be regarded as workable. If you have a little ache on the bottom of your spine as you begin to sit on your gomden, it doesn't necessarily mean that you have cancer of the spine! It may seem funny, but those kinds of thoughts come up and are very real. The idea is to overcome the busybodyness of excuses, no matter what comes up, and to concentrate on your discipline. Even if you have a disability, you could still practice meditation. The reason we practice discipline is to train ourselves fully and properly, so that eventually we will be in a position to exchange ourselves for others' misery and pain, as best we can.

By engaging in unnecessary preoccupations, we have become enslaved to ourselves—and by overcoming such unnecessary preoccupations and complaints, we begin to liberate ourselves. The paramita of discipline is said to be the ground of all the virtues taught by the Buddha. It is said in the sutras that shila paramita is the ground of life, the basis on which animate beings and inanimate objects can survive. It is very fundamental and important: without discipline, we do not have any basis for practice at all.

Freedom means that you are free from being belabored and enslaved by your own mind. You are free from preoccupations, free from that kind of imagination. Being free from unnecessary preconceptions is the basis of all virtues. It means constructively organizing your life as creatively as possible. Creativity is regarded as a virtue: you are not destroying and you are not on the side of death, but you are working toward healthiness. You are not obsessed with death, thinking that you might die or catch some terrible disease anytime you sneeze or chew the wrong kind of rice. All sorts of things could happen, but in this case nothing happens, which is the basis of virtue.

Virtue means healthiness and wholesomeness. You do not give in to paranoia of any kind, particularly paranoia as to your own survival. That begins to cut down the possibilities of passion, aggression, ignorance, jealousy, arrogance, and all the rest. You begin to attain what is known as jnana, or wisdom, which is the essence of the practice and the source of the attainment of enlightenment. Wisdom seems to be the source of the discipline that leads us into enlightened reality.

Being disciplined is quite a cheerful situation, but sometimes we might find that it is not so cheerful, because we do not have any chance to play games with ourselves or to plead for sympathy from our friends. Being disciplined is how to remain a happy, healthy person. The paramita of discipline does not mean you grind your teeth and work yourself to death, or meditate yourself to death, or find at the end of aeons that you are a dried-up little meditator. Instead, you discover that you are a reasonable person, able to exchange yourself for others. You are completely connected with the dharma. You possess two legs; therefore, you can walk on the path. You can step beyond busyness, preoccupations, claustrophobia, and paranoia about potential attacks on your survival. Finally, you can relax.

BASIC GOODNESS AND SELF-CONTROL

Shila paramita is geared to the notion that you have something to offer. Once you begin to control your lack of discipline, you discover basic goodness. You do not find candy right away; first you have to find the vending machine and put your money in. Likewise, with discipline, first you practice and refine your discipline, then you find the goodness.

When you do the tonglen practice of exchanging yourself for others, you can begin by thinking of basic goodness. You have lots of good things to breathe out to others; you have lots of goodness, lots of sanity, and lots of healthiness to give out. And all of that comes straight from the basic awakened and enlightened attitude, which is alive and strong and powerful. So what you give out is no longer purely imagination, or something that you have to crank up. You realize that you actually have something good to give out to others. In turn, you can breathe in what is painful and negative. The suffering that other people are experiencing can be brought in because, in contrast to their pain, you have basic healthiness and wakefulness, which can certainly absorb anything that comes to it. You can absorb suffering because you have a lot more goodness to give.

That seems to be the basic point of paramita practice altogether, to build up that sense that you have something to offer. You have something absolutely good and wonderful to give out to others. You can do it! You have it! The only question is, do you *know* that you have it? In this discussion of the mahayana, we have not talked about anything that you do not already have, or that you have to crank up. You do not have to imagine that you have it. Not at all. We have been discussing qualities that you have; you just have to realize that you have them. You do have to dispel problems, but beyond dispelling the problems, you don't have to crank up anything. You have it already, so you don't need to create anything artificially. This particular approach is not a manufactured one. It is very real and very definite. We all agree that we can be this way.

The notion of tsültrim includes such things as good table manners and basic decency in the very ordinary and simple sense. The analogy of the wish-fulfilling jewel means that everything could happen when you begin to behave properly. So discipline is a question of learning to behave properly and to appreciate yourself. You are learning to appreciate the way your hair is arranged, the way your clothes are tailored, the way your shoes are shined, the way you eat your food, the way you hold your knife and fork, the way you say hello, the way you shake hands, and the way you look at somebody.

Such forms may seem to be very trivial and ordinary. They are not often introduced by the leading North American spiritual disciplines. In Zen, there are Oriental forms that tell students how to eat, how to sit, and so forth. But Zen does not work in the same way with Occidental forms such as table manners or dress. Beyond dressing up in their robes, American Zen students are left to find their own way. However, we do not make any distinction between the traditions of Occident and Orient. We are working toward a blanket policy, an umbrella policy. With that blanket approach, we can demonstrate our discipline, our bodhisattvahood, and the awakening of tathagatagarbha. In terms of discipline, some behavior patterns make more sense than others. They actually work. They might be regarded as outdated, according to our nuclear, plastic world, but certain medieval styles of dealing with the world are always up-to-date.

When you become a generous person and develop your dignity and wealth, if you do not have control over your existence, generosity goes down the drain. Control means that the way you relate with your sense perceptions and the world of pleasure has to be modified. A purely generous person might say to you, "This is an excellent pastry. I have tried it myself, and it is very good. Why don't you have some?" If you kept accepting what people offered you and ate all that pastry, you would begin to gain weight and feel slightly heavy and sloppy. The logic of control is that when you are offered pastries, you have to learn to control your desire to eat them. At the same time, you can appreciate the generosity of the person who offered you the pastry. You have to learn when to give a sign that you appreciate someone's generosity, and when to say, "No, thank you." The same principle applies when you are the offerer of the pastry. In that case, it becomes a question of how much you should control yourself in offering pastry to your guests. The discipline of controlling the sense perceptions is the basis of all virtues. It is like the earth: if there were no earth, there would be nothing for us to walk on.

The basis of discipline is the behavior pattern or psychological state of not thinking of yourself as the star of the world. You do not come first. In the mahayana tradition, in any case, you do not come first. A noncentralized existence brings proper conduct. When your life is centered on yourself as a central theme, you are usually telling a white lie of some kind in order to avoid something. The idea of discipline is that you cannot do that and you should not do that. Physically, unless your health has really broken down, you cannot use your body as an excuse. Discipline means controlling the faculties of your body as well as your mind.

Discipline is said to be the basis of all virtues because of the evenness of temper, the evenness of existence, and the trustworthiness of experience that it produces. When your temper and your existence become predictable, then you become a basis of virtue. You do not organize your life purely according to your moods. Your senses are controlled, and you create predictability for yourself and for others.

INTENTIONS AND ACTIONS

At the mahayana stage, discipline gets somewhat more complicated, more psychologically oriented. In terms of threefold logic, the ground is your individual commitment to a practice, the path is actually working with a practice, the fruition is that you continue with that practice until it is fulfilled properly and completely.* Hinayana practice is mainly a matter of ceasing to cause problems for yourself, but in the mahayana, your practice includes both yourself and others. The mahayana is a two-dimensional situation of yourself and the world around you. The mahayana view of the precepts differs from that of the hinayana: in the mahayana, discipline is formed around your intention, together with how you follow up on that intention. With the precept against killing, for example, the thought of rejecting somebody else, ignoring their existence, or trying to get rid of them, is breaking the precept as much as actually killing them. A similar logic applies to drinking alcoholic beverages: if your intention in drinking alcohol is to change the environment of your life by substituting one thing for another, it is breaking the precepts. With that intention, you are failing to relate with alcohol or with your existence altogether. You are rejecting the possibility or potentiality of things that could happen.

It is said that keeping the hinayana precepts is like dusting off your mirror: while you are dusting, more dust might be landing on it. But keeping the mahayana precepts is like keeping dust away from the mirror in the first place. In the mahayana, you reach the phase in which the slightest intention of breaking a precept destroys the purpose of your life and of living as a human being. But you could be without such an intention—and if an intention arises, you could label it "thinking." When you notice a thought of breaking a precept arising, you could cut that thought.

THREE TYPES OF DISCIPLINE

Traditionally, tsültrim is divided into three types: binding yourself, gathering virtuous dharmas, and benefiting sentient beings.

---

* For more on the practice of *threefold logic,* see volume 1 of the *Profound Treasury,* appendix 2, "Working with Threefold Logic."

Binding Yourself

The first type of discipline is the discipline of binding yourself. In Tibetan, it is *dom-pe tsültrim*. *Dom* means "binding," and *pe* makes it a noun, *tsültrim* of course is "discipline"; so *dom-pe tsültrim* is the "binding factor of discipline." You are binding yourself to the discipline and to the dharma. This does not mean punishing oneself and being a hermit, or running away from the world, but rather that you are not indulging the neurotic aspect of sense pleasures. Dom-pe tsültrim cuts the nervousness of mind; it cuts discursive thoughts and unnecessary preoccupations. It allows your mind to dwell in one particular place, which puts your mind at ease. You are bound by your authentic, genuine commitment.

Traditionally speaking, dom-pe tsültrim is practiced by becoming a monk or nun, but the basic point of the binding factor of discipline is taming the mind. It is related to the refuge and bodhisattva vows that you take. You are bound together with your particular world, with your immediate family and friends, as well as with the vaster world. With dom-pe tsültrim, you keep the discipline of not being a nuisance to yourself, and beyond that, the discipline of not being a nuisance to others. The aspirations you had when you took the bodhisattva vow are actually taking place. So with dom-pe tsültrim, you become a decent person. When you respond to and fulfill the needs of others, you begin to fulfill your own needs as well. In relating to yourself, you learn to give up ego-centeredness and relate much more to the notion of maitri, or loving-kindness. In relating to others, you develop the notion of karuna, or compassion—and beyond that, mahakaruna, or great compassion.

One of the qualities of dom-pe tsültrim is that it brings stillness of mind. You are controlling your mind whether you are prone to agitation or to laziness. Both laziness and excitement are controlled by dom-pe tsültrim. Through discipline, you are controlling your system altogether.

Dom-pe tsültrim is similar, in a sense, to the popular and very ordinary concept of social graces. If you are having an elegant cocktail party, for instance, you don't yell at the top of your voice. Maybe that is a rather low-level example, but the idea is that it is possible to be constantly even all the time. In that way, you are bound by basic, good behavior throughout your life. Through breakfast, lunch, and dinner, from the time you get up, as you go through the day, until you retire in the evening—throughout the

whole day—you maintain basic uprightness all the time. You are free from
laziness and free from too much excitement, frivolity, and emotionalism.
That allows your mind to settle down.

At the beginning, the discipline of dom-pe tsültrim could be a tremendous strain. You feel that you have to behave like a zombie, the same from
morning to evening, and you cannot even express yourself. Particularly in
modern culture, people are supposed to scream and shout. So you might
think that disciplining yourself not to do that would be absurd and terrible, that you would not have any chance to show your characteristics
or your particular color and beauty. But if you think about it further, you
will see that your basic goodness is showing throughout the whole thing.
Your good aspects are being cultivated, and your wicked aspects are being
subjugated. In turn, you will find that being in your company becomes
pleasurable to yourself and to others. You become a decent person twenty-
four hours a day. Through dom-pe tsültrim, you have bound your frivolity,
which is usually allowed so much room.

Gathering Virtuous Dharmas

The second type of discipline is known as gathering virtuous dharmas, or
gathering goodness. In Tibetan it is *ge-we chödü*. *Ge-we* means "goodness,"
or "virtue." To express this from a negative point of view, ge-wa is nonaggression, and from a positive point of view, ge-wa is a sense of expansion,
relaxation, sympathy, and benevolence. That is the definition of virtue
in Buddhism altogether, and it also applies here. *Chö* is "dharma," and *dü*
means "gathering"; so *ge-we chödü* is the "way to gather in the goodness of
dharma." It is the discipline of ripening and developing oneself.

With ge-we chödü, there is an emphasis on the idea of intellectual
study: hearing, contemplating, and meditating. There is also an emphasis
on realizing the value of your teacher, which comes from hearing, contemplating, and meditating on what the teacher has said. Ge-we chödü is
also connected with mindfulness. You become a very tamed person, as
well as a heroic, bodhisattva-like person.

Gathering virtuous dharmas, or the discipline of ripening or developing yourself, is the only way for dharma to mix with your mind and your
existence so that your mind and dharma are one. With this view, you begin
to listen to the dharma, to think about it, and to practice it. Furthermore,
you respect your teacher, who only exists because of the teachings. Rec-

ognizing the value of the teachings through the practice of ge-we chödu allows you to realize how to appreciate dharma twenty-four hours a day, and how to put your dharma practice into effect. You are interested in understanding the meaning of dharma, and you are also interested in how the world functions. The way the world functions becomes a message of dharma each time, so whether you are in Grand Central Station or an airport in Tokyo, you are inspired. You are never off guard. You understand that everything that happens in your life, whether your rice burns or your milk boils over, is an expression of dharma. Seeing that whatever happens in your life is dharma takes enormous discipline.

The meaning of gathering dharmas is that you are making your whole being ripe for the dharma. You are trying to become a completely dharmic person, as opposed to someone who is purely learned. You may know the terms and ideas, but if you do not apply the dharma to yourself personally, it remains foreign to you. By means of ge-we chödü, you become thoroughly soaked in the dharma—in passionlessness and egolessness. You are soaked in the softness, gentleness, and reasonableness of the dharma. When you become a dharmic person, your whole being is completely ripened with dharmic capability, like a fully ripened fruit.

We can actually see the differences between a dharmic person and a non-dharmic person. A dharmic person speaks with awareness, mindfulness, and softness, whereas a non-dharmic person shouts, or jumps up and down, and is always nervous. It is quite literal. It is obvious in the way people walk, in the way they conduct themselves, and in the way they talk to others. Becoming a dharmic person through ge-we chödü is not just a tale or myth; it actually takes place.

Benefiting Sentient Beings

The third type of discipline is the discipline of benefiting sentient beings. It is called *semchen tön-che*. *Semchen* means "sentient beings"; *sem* means "mind," and *chen* makes it "those who have a mind." *Tön* means "benefit," or "purpose," and *che* means "doing it"; so *semchen tön-che* is "fulfilling the purpose of those who have a mind," which simply means benefiting others. Semchen tön-che also means making others worthy, preparing them for the dharma. It includes bodhisattva actions such as relating with relatives and friends, business partners, bosses or subordinates, people who may not have any connection with the dharma.

Benefiting sentient beings means that you are willing to spend time working for someone else, whether it is your own child, your parents, or, for that matter, a stranger or someone you do not particularly like. There is always work that needs to be done. Discipline is not moralistic; you do not work with others because it is good for you to do. You do it automatically because of your interest. Working for others means propagating the message of gentleness, which seems to be the core of the Buddhist approach altogether.

The basic idea of semchen tön-che is that you bring together your mind and the dharma, so there is no conflict in performing the actions of both absolute and relative bodhichitta. Both bodhichittas come along right at the beginning, and then continue through all the paramitas. Relative bodhichitta is like a flashlight with a beam of light coming out of it: in order to use the light, you have to hold the flashlight properly. Holding it properly and making it work for you so that the light will shine wherever you need it is absolute bodhichitta.

With semchen tön-che, you are able to produce psychological harmony for others. When you are practicing this particular shila, you do not create a disturbance when you walk into a room. Instead, when you enter a room—whether you are working at Western Union, or the post office, or in a factory—there is a feeling of harmony. When you enter a particular situation, there is a good feeling about the whole thing. That is what is known in the texts as organizing the discipline of harmony.

With semchen tön-che, you can create harmony, and beyond that, because of your virtue, you are also able to cut through other people's neurosis. You can benefit people by your good presence in any situation. For example, if a person is creating chaos, you should have enough power and strength, wisdom and control, to say or do what is needed to cut through that person's confusion and destroy their neurosis. When you see that someone is doing something neurotic, the first thing to do is stop them, and not even bother to tell them why you are stopping them. Later that person may realize that it made sense for you to stop them. They may have a second take on the whole thing. At that point, if they are interested, you can tell them why you stopped them. That is our Kagyü style. We stop people first—we don't talk it over with them through our lawyer.

If you want to reach people, you have to take positive action. People in samsara always do harmful things. Quite literally, they hang themselves up and kill themselves. So there is no room to philosophize. It is a very immediate situation, like walking into the emergency room of a hospital. You see that same kind of craziness everywhere. From a bodhisattva's point of view, the whole world is a giant emergency room. You have to stop people from harming themselves. As a would-be bodhisattva, that is what you have to do. You cannot just leave, and hope somebody else will come along and do the job for you. You have to be the person who does the job, who actually saves somebody. The responsibility is on you. You should be willing to use the corrective mechanism of telling the truth; from the minute you wake up, you should be willing to speak up if there is a problem. The discipline of working for others applies to everything you do.

Through the practice of the three principles of shila paramita, you are able to let go of your ego. Paramita means going beyond. You are going beyond your preconceptions, your neurotic habit patterns, and your guilt (guilt being an addition from the Western world). Paramita means having arrived at the other shore. Starting out from an ego-structured situation, going to the other shore is like traveling to a foreign land. It takes adaptation, some getting used to. With paramita practice, you are learning how to go to a foreign country, as opposed to staying securely at home.

It has been said that until you reach prajna paramita, everything that you do involving the first five paramitas is mindfulness practice. It is upaya, or skillful means. Shamatha and vipashyana continue throughout all the paramitas. With the help of shamatha, you learn how to be settled in your own spot; you are able to settle down and make yourself at home in this universe. Paramita practice begins with being: being patient, being exertive, and being meditative. It is a question of how to be a full-fledged buddhadharma person. And when you finally reach the level of prajna paramita, you know how to apply the paramitas in the world. So first of all, you have to be, and then you can act out what you are. It is be and being.

The paramita of discipline is somewhat a matter of repression. There is repression, but it works, and quite rightly so. The repression of mahayana is inherited from the careful precision of hinayana discipline—and when you get to vajrayana, which is greater and more dangerous, you have to control yourself even further. By comparison, the quality of repression in mahayana is very small. You have to be careful here and there, but you could still take delight in working with others. In general, the wider the highway, the more you want to speed along it—but you have to control yourself. You have to slow down. That is why the paramita that follows discipline is patience.

In the mahayana, what you are developing is heart, or compassion, and what you are trying to get rid of is conducting your life in an ego-centered and unmethodical way. That may get a little messy. The more aware you are, the more outstanding the obstacles seem to be. But you have to work with them—and I can assure you that there is such a thing as attainment at the end. You are controlling yourself, because whatever you do affects you, and not only you alone but everybody else as well. If you make one little mistake, you mess up hundreds of other people. It is like building a highway: if you build a highway badly, all the travelers are bound to have more accidents and more pain. So in the mahayana, you have greater responsibility—and that is good news.

29

Patience

Patience has the quality of balance and equilibrium. But we need to add to the notion of equilibrium a quality of emotionality, and a desire and longing for the dharma. Some kind of spice has to be added. When that spice has been added, you begin to fully develop the real meaning of patience. Ordinarily, patience means to hold off or to hold on, but in this case it means that you give in and feel the flavor. You might bite your tongue, but that is good. You could taste the blood, swallow it, and use it as nourishment.

THE THIRD paramita is patience. In the Buddhist tradition, the paramita of patience, or *kshanti* paramita, means that you are not perturbed by any samsaric conditions. According to the *Oxford English Dictionary*, patience means being willing to wait a long time for something to happen, but in this case it means that you bear your existence. You hold it as it is, stay where you are. Whether you are wearing green, yellow, red, or gray clothing, whether your stature is tall, short, or distorted, whether you have short arms or long arms, whether you are wearing blue shoes, green shoes, or purple shoes, whether you have short hair or long hair, you remain as you are, on the spot. You maintain your existence and bearing uninterruptedly. The analogy for patience is the ocean: whatever happens, the ocean cannot be disturbed. It remains the same all the time.

The Tibetan term for patience is *söpa*, which means "forbearance." *Sö* means "bearing any problems," and *pa* is "doing so"; therefore *söpa* means "willing to bear any problems." The Sanskrit term for patience is *kshanti*, which means "having equilibrium." It is a kind of indifference in the sense of not giving in to the discursiveness or chaos of whatever has arisen in you. With kshanti, you are able to practice your shamatha-vipashyana discipline in the middle of Grand Central Station. You are willing to wait for the harmoniousness of a situation to arise by not correcting the disharmony. It is like waiting for good weather to happen.

OVERCOMING AGGRESSION

The Buddhist meaning of patience is freedom from aggression, and the main obstacle to patience is anger. According to the sutras, there is no greater evil than aggression, and there is no greater practice than patience. You may have attained a level of generosity and discipline, but if you cannot be without aggression, you have not achieved the paramita of patience. Aggression is the most dangerous emotion, because it does not allow any form of gentleness. One instant of aggression can destroy your connection with the world, including your dedication to the relative and absolute bodhichitta principles. If you want to kill your dharmic connection, a moment's aggression is your best weapon. It has been said in the scriptures that one moment of aggression will destroy aeons and aeons of virtue.

Aggression is absolutely terrible; it is anti-mahayana. Passion, lust, and desire may have qualities of neurosis, and they may destroy your mindfulness and awareness, but at the same time they have the nature of acceptance. However, aggression is based on total rejection, whether it is aggression toward yourself or aggression toward other sentient beings.

When you recognize your ego-orientation or your indulgence in aggression, there is a tendency to punish yourself. However, patience is not based on punishing yourself. Patience means that you wait a minute; you wait and see what happens. It means not coming to conclusions too quickly. Just because you have indulged, you should not panic. Just wait. Be patient.

The paramita of patience continues the pattern of alternating shamatha and vipashyana through the paramitas. That is, the first paramita, generosity, is connected with shamatha; the second paramita, discipline, is connected with vipashyana; and with the third paramita, we are back to shamatha. Patience is the way to quell the heat of aggression by following the way of shamatha tranquillity and peacefulness—but it is a highly advanced level of shamatha discipline. As we go on to higher and higher levels of paramitas, the standard of shamatha and vipashyana escalates, so the paramita of patience involves a higher level of shamatha than the paramita of generosity.

The sequence of the paramitas is significant. Generosity is the stripping-off process, and discipline is remaining in the loneliness. Having gone through those two processes, we find our situation unbearable, as if we were being beaten by hundreds of people. All kinds of pain come up in our life, not as the result of punishment but as the result of being generous and disciplined. We actually invite pain by being alone and keeping our discipline. We are like an owl in the daylight, physically and psychically attacked from all directions by visible and invisible forces. The paramita of patience means not getting resentful about that.

When you have anger and resentment, however disciplined or generous you might be, you are not actually that enlightened. When you have a burst of aggression, it makes everything dry and terribly unproductive. You may have cultivated the soil, sowed the seeds, and watered the ground beautifully, but aggression destroys the whole thing. When you are angry, you reject both other people and yourself. At that point, you have no connection with the dharma at all. When you lose your temper, you are so furious that you couldn't care less about the sacredness of anything. You couldn't care less about yourself, or the other person, or your teacher, or your path. But if you reverse the logic, when somebody is angry with you and you are patient with that person, you are creating a thousand *kalpas** of merit on the spot. When somebody is angry, that is your chance to be patient. You could breathe in the anger, and not only that, you could project goodness. But if you get angry in turn, you lose it.

One of the best things about patience is that it is very sharp and clear. It speaks for itself. Anger is anger, and patience is patience. They are very sharply divided, and that distinction should be properly understood. However, patience is not based on suppressing anger. At times aggression may be legitimate, such as when others are doing something wrong and you lose your temper in order to stop them. At other times aggression is not legitimate, such as when you are simply unable to cope with a situation and become impatient. But basically, it is not appropriate to apply anger unless you are in the role of teacher. When you are teaching somebody

* A *kalpa* (Skt.) is an endlessly long period or time, a world cycle.

how to behave or you are helping others, some form of anger may be necessary.

Anger may be obvious or subtle, but whether you are expressing anger in subtle or obvious ways, the point is to get rid of the anger at the first possibility. Any method that quells aggression is valid. You might even need to manifest your anger first, if that helps, and develop patience afterward. You don't have to be genteel about the whole thing.

Overcoming aggression is not simply based on the moralistic approach of saying that you have been bad, so you had better be good. You develop patience and forbearance in order to maintain a quality of continual virtue. Such virtue is based on the idea of basic goodness and the sense that you are a worthy person, a healthy person. You are able to develop basic goodness, and you have the potential to attain enlightenment and eventually be a buddha.

Freedom from the Maras

It has been said that when there is no patience, we invite more maras, or more temptations. Basically, there are four types of mara. The first mara is the *mara of seduction* (Skt.: *devaputra-mara*). This mara is based on attachment to pleasure and richness. It has a kind of softness or candy-bar approach, based on calculated aggression against discipline and patience, which could be called the setting-sun approach.

The second mara is the *mara of kleshas* (Skt.: *klesha-mara*). It is based on the kleshas, or the confused emotions, accompanied by a sense of aggression.

The third mara is the *mara of skandhas* (Skt.: *skandha-mara*). The skandhas, which are experiences giving rise to a false sense of self, are a more subtle manifestation of aggression, whereas the kleshas are more direct and obvious.

The fourth mara is the *mara of the god of death* (Skt.: *yama-mara* or *mrityumara*). It is the fear of death, and the attempt to overcome our death and not get old. Patience consists of being free from all such maras.

Three Categories of Patience

There are three categories of patience: overcoming other people's destructiveness, realizing the nature of other people's aggression, and individually examining. The first two categories are regarded as the kundzöp, or relative truth, level of patience, and the third category is connected with töndam, or ultimate truth.

Overcoming Other People's Destructiveness

The first category is the patience of overcoming other people's destructiveness. It is related with relative truth. The Tibetan term for this kind of patience is *shengyi nöpa la söpa*. *Shen* means "other," *gyi* means "of," *nöpa* means "harm" or " harming," *la* means "toward," and *söpa* means "patience"; so *shengyi nöpa la söpa* means "patience with other people's destructiveness." In this category, the point of patience is to control other people's aggression.

If you react aggressively to those who harm you, you will only encourage their aggression further. But if you do not respond to others' aggression with your own aggression, you will stop encouraging them and no longer be under attack. With patience, those who cause harm to you are not regarded as a threat, so you do not have to retaliate. It is quite straightforward. You might have a bad relationship with somebody, but if you give in to that person, they no longer have any reference point for their aggression. If they think they are punching solid rock, they become more aggressive. But if they find that the rock is a pile of balloons, then there is nothing to fight, and they begin to feel that their anger is absurd.

Realizing the Nature of Other People's Aggression

The second category is also related with relative truth: it is the patience of realizing the nature of other people's aggression. You realize that it is caused by their pain. In Tibetan, it is *dug-ngal kyi ngowo söpa*. *Dug-ngal* means "pain," *kyi* means "of," *ngowo* means "nature," and *söpa* means "patience"; so *dug-ngal kyi ngowo söpa* is "patience with the nature of suffering."

People have aggression because they can't help themselves. So you should not regard their aggression as an attack, but you should develop patience with them. People have no control over their minds, and their impatience is based on ignorance. They may not realize that you are trying to help them, and because of that they attack you without any reason.

Such ignorance is the result of preconceived aggression and preconceived reference points. It is the result of people pigeonholing you according to their particular concept of who you are.

Aggression coming from others could be overcome by analyzing the nature of that aggression. By such analysis, you realize that both your own and others' aggression is insignificant and can be overcome. There has to be a reasonable, analytical way of cutting aggression and becoming patient. Otherwise, you would have no reason not to lose your temper with your husband or wife, you would have no reason to discuss things— you would just yell all the time. In situations where you are challenged, where something arises that makes you impatient, you could step back and examine the nature of suffering. When you understand that suffering is created by you, by others, or by the situation, you do not react unreasonably. When you have studied and practiced, when you have understood suffering and its origin and the nature of the aggression, you become much more reasonable than those who never heard of such things. The analytical approach is important. You are learning strategies of negotiation and how to talk someone out of their aggression. In turn, you find that you yourself are becoming more patient.

By realizing the nature of pain, you are also developing patience in relating to personal discomfort. You do not tire of the various practices that are required in the discipline of the path. You are willing to experience discomfort, such as a pain in your back during sitting practice or the pain in your legs. You don't cop out suddenly, halfway through, but you realize that temporary inconveniences and discomforts are necessary. You are also patient with the discomfort that arises in postmeditation, such as the pain of talking to an irritating person.

At the kundzöp level, you understand what people are saying to you, who they are, and what they are. You do not want to cause pain to anybody, and you learn to understand other people's distress. You understand that if you get in a shouting match with someone, it doesn't help to say that you are sorry or that you made a mistake. It is better to ask where the obstacle or blockage is coming from, to ask who is experiencing the pain, and how that person feels. The analytical approach can usually solve the problem, but it has to be very skillful. You cannot just read a Buddhist text on how to deal with anger, and then try to deal with people in that way. That doesn't quite work.

Individually Examining

The third category of patience is known as *sosor tok-pe söpa*, "individually examining." This category is connected with *töndam*, or ultimate truth. The word *soso* means "individual." If you add an *r* to the end, you have *sosor*, which makes it "individually." *Tokpa* means "examining," the suffix *-pe* makes it "of examining," and *söpa* means "patience"; therefore *sosor tok-pe söpa* is the "patience of individually examining."

Whenever there are any irritations in your life, you examine them individually. When you look at them individually, you find that they are empty by nature, they have softness in them, and they can provide mindfulness. Whenever irritations or aggressions are encountered, they are reminders of your existence. Therefore, you should constantly examine and understand the nature of irritation.

In postmeditation practice, you do not neglect any small details. If you see that there is a speck of dirt on your well-polished spoon, you could look at that speck of dirt with sosor tok-pe. Gradually you begin to realize that the irritations occurring in your life do not have to be regarded as an attack. Those little irritations do not mean that you have a bad life or that you are being punished by the world. You can still appreciate the basic goodness of your life, that you possess sugatagarbha. Instead of regarding all those little things that happen to you as bad, you could include irritations within your practice of patience. In that way your perceptions and the journey you are making can become very real.

Experiences of irritation are a kind of message. Sometimes the message is disruptive and messy, but it is a true, good message being presented to you. Maybe one of your chopsticks falls on the floor before you eat your food, or you find that the cracks between the prongs of your fork are filled with dirt. You begin to realize that such situations are messages of patience. They are not regarded as a bad deal.

A lot of irritation may come from the practice of meditation itself. This is partly because you are not used to being still for a long period of time, and partly because you have never faced your own state of mind for very long. Irritations also may arise with tonglen practice when you do not want to give away your goodness or to bring in the badness. But irritation that comes up in practice could be met with forbearance. You could apply tonglen when you are irritated, even if only for a fraction of a second. Just remembering that you have that possibility is helpful. It means you are reflecting on the dharma, and once you are reflecting on the dharma, you are liberated to a greater or lesser extent.

By individually analyzing, you develop devotion to the dharma. You understand that dharmas are not, on the whole, problematic. You do not feel the need for a change of theme or subject matter. You accept with patience teachings such as impermanence and egolessness. The dharma demands certain things from you, and you meet those demands with patience. When you have an understanding of shunyata, egolessness, or spiritual materialism, you might get tired of so many ideas coming into your head, since you are soaked in the teachings already. With patience, you do not block out those ideas, but continuously explore your understanding. Discursive thoughts on the dharma should be encouraged.

On the whole, patience means working with any tiresomeness or discomfort brought about by being a Buddhist. By holding a dharmic attitude, you develop patience, and you practice your discipline at its best. You realize that patience is the only means that will carry you through. You could handle all dharmas in that way, as part of your practice of patience. You could act with relaxation, humor, and fundamental nonaggression.

If you tried to practice patience on the spot, without the previous paramitas, it would not work. But if you already have given up territory as an aspect of your practice of the paramita of generosity, and you already have become softer through the experience of the paramita of discipline, there is no problem when you come to the third level, the paramita of patience. It is one continuous process. The tendency toward suppression has already been undermined by maitri and by generosity, which is why the whole thing works. In paramita practice, there are checks and balances, and the way to go about it is all perfectly worked out. It is very amazing.

Patience has the quality of balance and equilibrium. But we need to add to the notion of equilibrium a quality of emotionality, and a desire and longing for the dharma. Some kind of spice has to be added. When that spice has been added, you begin to fully develop the real meaning of patience. Ordinarily, patience means to hold off or to hold on, but in this case it means that you give in and feel the flavor. You might bite your tongue, but that is good. You could taste the blood, swallow it, and use it as nourishment.

Patience and the following two paramitas, of exertion and meditation, always work together. They are like the legs of a tripod: each one carries its own weight. The fruition of patience, or forbearance, is the development of extraordinary protection. The practitioner cannot be harmed by any obstacles. Why? You are not putting out any aggression; therefore, you are not inviting any aggression. Quite the opposite; you are beginning to generate peace and kindness.

The main point of all this teaching is that we should not be overwhelmed by aggression, and just act out and go crazy. There is a pattern to things. Every inch, every moment, every second of samsaric mind has been measured by the Buddha, so we have a complete map. In the dharma, every fraction of a second of a person's thinking is divided and prescribed and catalogued, so to speak. We are learning to understand samsara altogether, so that we have a comprehensive idea about how things work. But even more important than cataloguing every samsaric situation is how you work with it: what happens before, what happens after, and what happens in the process. That interchange could be based on natural indifference rather than making the situation into a personal attack.

Each situation, each coincidence, has its own peculiarities, but on the whole you should remain patient. You do not remain patient because you are a coward or because you feel that you can get away with it. But when everybody is up in arms, you should sink into patience. That is the message of the paramita of patience. You could be a very basic human being and not join in with the bandits of the occasion, the bandits of life. Somehow, you could just sink; you could just *be*. You could remain as a seated buddha.

30

Exertion

Exertion means being consistent, continuous, and faithful to the practice. Being consistent allows you to have a sense of joy, rather than seeing practice as a duty that you have to perform. The practice of dharma is getting into your blood. . . . You begin to regard exertion as a part of your basic, natural activity, rather than as something that is imposed on you.

T HE FOURTH parameter is exertion. It has been said in the texts that without exertion, all the previous paramitas are hopeless. Exertion is the most important paramita for you to practice in order to achieve the bodhisattva ideal, and awaken absolute and relative bodhichitta. Exertion is regarded as one of the best ways to speed up the journey to enlightenment. The paramita of exertion is *tsöndrü* in Tibetan, and *virya* in Sanskrit. *Tsön* means "hard work," or "persistence," and *drü* means "getting used to," or "becoming comfortable with"; so the basic idea of *tsöndrü* is becoming familiar with, or getting used to hard work.

The paramita of exertion, or *virya* paramita, is described as a good horse, joyful and free from laziness. Exertion is connected with the idea of how to organize our lives as practitioners on the path. The definition of exertion is not giving up, and the nature of exertion is being delighted in the practice. The analogy for exertion is a diamond, which is indestructible. This indestructibility, this hard-coreness, is what allows you to proceed on your path.

According to Shantideva and others, exertion is a way of developing an attitude of delight toward the path. When you feel delighted with what you are doing, working hard evolves effortlessly. At the same time, you still have to encourage yourself further. It is like falling in love: when you fall in love, you have to maintain your love affair, no matter what obstacles come to you. Likewise, when the first splash of delight comes along, you don't just sit and gaze at it and hope for the best, but you maintain it and develop it.

Although you might have generosity, discipline, and patience, without exertion you do not achieve anything. Without exertion, you lapse into laziness, stupor, and slothfulness. Exertion helps you to destroy the whole range of egohood, of viewing solidity as a big deal. It helps you to transcend, or go beyond, all of that. Exertion is joyful and enthusiastic. It is large-scale enthusiasm rather than small splashes, such as when good ideas come up and you get excited about them.

Exertion is continuing what has happened already in the previous three paramitas and taking delight in continuing. If you put together generosity, discipline, and patience, they amount to exertion. As you go along, you are constantly building on previous paramitas, and collecting new ones in the process. The paramitas begin to pile up in that way. The idea is to remember to practice one of the paramitas, or all of them at once, during your daily life. As long as you remember to handle yourself in that way, then you are practicing properly, and you are completely steeped in Buddhism. If you begin to make a separation between dharmic practice and regular, ordinary life, there is a problem.

One way to look at the paramitas is in terms of what each of them overcomes. Discipline overcomes passion, and exertion overcomes laziness. That is the difference between discipline and exertion. With generosity, you are trying to overcome stinginess and selfishness, and with patience, you are trying to overcome aggression. That is how it works. So each of the paramitas has its counterpart.

Another way to look at the paramitas is in terms of how a paramita is paired up with either shamatha or vipashyana. In the development of the paramitas, shamatha and vipashyana alternate six times. So it is shamatha (generosity), vipashyana (discipline), shamatha (patience), vipashyana (exertion), shamatha (meditation), and vipashyana (prajna). In this process, the residues of shamatha and vipashyana from the previous paramitas are not rejected, but the underlying, heightened point of each of the previous paramitas continues. At the level of exertion, we have a lot of residues piled up already, but at the same time we are working on a particular, very powerful point.

The paramitas are mostly postmeditation practices. You cannot practice generosity in the meditation hall; you have to go out and be generous to somebody. You cannot just visualize being generous; that does not really fulfill anything. So paramita practice is postmeditation experience. With paramita practice, the actual sitting-meditation technique does not really change very much. It is more a question of how you deal with the feedback coming to you from the world outside. Your growing sophistication might take the form of shamatha or vipashyana. With shamatha meditation, you have a level of steadiness, and in postmeditation, it is a question of how much you can maintain that steadiness. Shamatha is first thought, and vipashyana is second thought. Shamatha is usually the instigator; it is how well you have been trained, and it is your education. With shamatha, you come across as a good, educated person.

SMILING AT OBSTACLES

The ultimate meaning of tsöndrü is joy in practice. Exertion means appreciating virtue, rather than just working hard. Holding on to seriousness can be a form of self-protection. You do not want to face facts, whatever the situation may be. But when you accept the pain, or obstacle, it is like tonglen: there is the possibility of joy. With exertion, you appreciate virtue because you begin to feel that what you are doing is right and best, and it feels good to do it. For instance, you never get tired of taking showers, seeing the sunlight, or eating breakfast, lunch, and dinner. You feel that those things are an integral part of your life; therefore, you accept them.

In a lot of situations, there seem to be obstacles trying to push us backward. Nonetheless, with exertion, we do not give up, and we do not expect others to support us as an automatic response. It is quite the contrary. We try to keep going and to become completely fearless, so that our fear becomes fearlessness. We never lose heart and never look for alternatives unless our situation is really, absolutely, fundamentally, totally, utterly unworkable. Otherwise we do not give in or give up.

You cannot expect an easy journey, an easy situation, or easy circumstances. For instance, Milarepa had a lot of problems and difficulties in his life. His teacher would not give him teachings, and when he returned to his home, everything was devastated. There was no easy journey for Milarepa, but he still managed to be a happy person, a happy yogi. In the Kagyü tradition, as well as in the general Buddhist tradition, we try to rejoice whenever there is an obstacle. We try to regard an obstacle as something that makes us smile, and each setback creates a further smile. We keep going in that way, and we never give up.

For instance, I myself had a lot of hard times getting out of my country, and obstacles such as sickness happen to me all the time. But I do not regard those obstacles as a sign of anything—I just keep going. In life, you always have ups and downs. It is like riding on a roller coaster: the more you go up and the more you go down, the more you smile each time.

The more you develop, the more laziness and contentment could cause problems. If you have heard the dharma many times before and have practiced quite a lot, you might feel that dharma is old hat. You think, "I have studied such things before. Why should I go over them again?" With such an attitude, you begin to lose all that you have accumulated, and you begin to lose your joy in the practice. The essence of tsöndrü is to delight in the practice you are doing and the teaching you are hearing, as if it were fresh, as if you had never heard it before. Even though you might have heard a teaching two thousand times before, you still never tire of hearing the same thing again and again. Experiencing the dharma is more of a privilege each time.

The paramita of exertion is free from regarding ordinary activity as just boring. No matter what you do, you do not regard it merely as a replay of something that you have done many times before. The notion that things become boring when you do them again and again is just in your mind. If you look thoroughly and fully into situations, you will see that each situation is unique. It happens on a different date and time, and you are in a different stage of your life, so everything is entirely different each moment. You do not repeat anything. I wish you could do everything twice, but you cannot repeat anything and you cannot go back. So the ordinariness of experience is completely conceptual. Whatever happens is new.

By bringing together patience and exertion, you are working with both the shamatha and vipashyana disciplines. You are always taking a fresh approach to life, and you are not trying to look for new occupations or new entertainments. Although the occurrences of life may be entirely repetitious, your perception or awareness could be fresh and extraordinary. That gives you a sense of joy and cheerfulness.

LAZINESS: THE MAIN OBSTACLE TO EXERTION

The main obstacle to exertion is laziness. In Tibetan, laziness is *lelo,* which sounds like "lay low." Laziness feels quite deep-rooted when you are in it, but it is much easier to work with than passion or aggression. Laziness is like sleepiness; somebody can wake you up. But when you are dealing with aggression, you have to apply patience again and again and again and again, which is why aggression is considered to be one of the three root kleshas. Aggression and passion go very deep, whereas laziness is somewhat superficial.

There are three categories of laziness: casualness or slothfulness, losing heart, and degraded laziness. These categories are very simple and ordinary because that is the nature of laziness.

Casualness / Slothfulness

The first category of laziness is *nyom-le kyi lelo,* or "casualness." *Nyom-le* means "common," "together," or "even," *kyi* is "of," and *lelo* is "laziness"; so *nyom-le kyi lelo* is trying to make everything even or the same. You are too concerned with and attached to comfort. You are tremendously attached to leisure; you do not want to raise a finger. Sitting on a rock or washing your face in a running stream is regarded as inconvenient. You always want to have running water in your bathroom, and you would like to have your seats stuffed so that you always have a soft cushion under you. You fight against a simple rural existence, and regard urban delicacy as the only way to treat yourself well.

Nyom-le kyi lelo includes ordinary laziness or slothfulness. You keep falling asleep and are unable to get yourself together. You have not organized your life properly. Therefore, you begin to feel that you are a victim of your life situation. Students say, "I have this thing to do or that thing to do, and I don't have a chance to practice." It is as if they were victims of their lives rather than of their own laziness. Laziness is the problem, although nobody seems willing to admit that.

Tsöndrü is the proper way of relating with your life. It is good scheduling. When it is time to wake up, you wake up; when it is time to eat, you eat. You find time to practice, to work with others, to study the dharma, and to do your business. So exertion is the good scheduling and good organization of your life. In that way, there is time for everything. But most importantly, there is time and space for practice. So the laziness of being casual is an obstacle to the practice of meditation as well as to the practice of exertion. You have an aversion to sitting practice; there are no French settees and no armchairs for you to lean back on. You have to learn to support yourself, like a stalk of corn growing in a field.

Losing Heart

The second category of laziness is called *gyi-luk-pe lelo*. *Gyi-luk* means "losing heart," *pe* means "of," *lelo* means "laziness; since *gyi* means "weight," this expression literally means "losing weight." It is being disheartened; you lose heart because you like samsara so much. You like your old-fashioned games and your good old days, and you do not really want to leave this world. Therefore you say, "How is it possible for someone like me to attain enlightenment? It is impossible. I should never even try. I have been this way for many years, and I will be this way for many years to come. What is the point of trying to attain enlightenment? What is the point of trying to do anything at all?"

Interestingly, the fact that you say this means that you are beginning to have a faint fever of what enlightenment would be like: you realize that the attainment of enlightenment means that you can no longer indulge in your samsaric world. Therefore, you begin to feel panicked, and you say, "I cannot do it. How could I ever do it?" You disguise that as losing heart, but in your heart of hearts, you want to stay in your samsara. You are afraid of losing any of your reference points in the samsaric world because you are very attached to samsara.

Degraded Laziness

The third category of laziness is degraded laziness: *mepa lelo*. *Mepa* means "base" or "degraded," and *lelo* means "laziness"; so *mepa lelo* means "degraded laziness." Degraded laziness is the laziness of being preoccupied. You are preoccupied with dealing with enemies, collecting wealth, and other activities. You are busy with activities other than dharmic ones, and exert yourself in those situations instead of devoting yourself to dharma practice. You couldn't care less about the dharma. Sometimes you think about practice, but that does not bring up a great deal of exertion. Your effort is spent on other things. Degraded laziness is caused by a feeling of depression: you feel down, you are not cheered up, and you don't realize the value of the teachings. You do not think the dharma is worthwhile. So me-pe lelo implies depression and laziness combined.

This third type of laziness is the most dangerous one. You are taking advantage of your life in order to avoid practice. You feel extraordinarily energetic when you exert yourself in doing other things, but when it comes to sitting practice and working with dharmic situations, you are very lazy. For instance, you prefer to vacuum the floor rather than sit; you prefer to go out and mail your letter rather than sit; you prefer to take a shower rather than sit; you prefer to make a pie first and sit later. Such situations in your life are known as insulting the dharma.

These three types of laziness are not the only list that we could come up with. I'm sure we could come up with hundreds of thousands of ways and levels of cheating and indulging ourselves.

The three forms of laziness are very simple. More complicated or sophisticated kinds of laziness might come up on top of that, but basically any form of laziness is simple: you do not want to work with the harsh core of being awake. You would like to avoid that direct contrast. You do not want to feel awake; you prefer to take another nap, rest just a few minutes more. You would like to have lots of padding around you so that you don't actually have to experience the sharpness of reality, which could be either extremely painful or extremely pleasant. When you are getting close to an experience of wakefulness, you could actually delight in that, but instead you shy away from it. You would rather go back to your stable, which is full of shit and very smelly.

On the whole, all three types of laziness should be overcome by having a sense of urgency and directness. Traditionally, exertion is referred to as joy in practice, and at the same time, a feeling of immediacy. I wouldn't exactly call it panic, but it is a panic-like situation. According to the texts, if you are truly practicing exertion, you should behave as if a snake had landed on your lap, or as if your hair had caught on fire. It is very immediate and very direct. That is precisely what is meant by the absence of laziness. The point of the analogy is not the snake, or your hair on fire, but your reaction to it. You cannot just relax, lie back, have a good time, and philosophize about Buddhism. You have samsara on your lap and madness in your brain, so you have to do something about it.

If you stay too long in samsara, you are going to fall apart very soon. You have to do something to prevent that from happening. It's like the concept of vaccination: you have to do something before you actually get hit with sickness. You have to save yourself sooner or later—and the sooner the better, because you will still be young, and you won't yet have been eaten up by the cancer of samsara. You will still have some strength, and you won't be exhausted all the time. So the earlier the better. That is the importance of exertion.

THREE QUALITIES OF EXERTION

Laziness is overcome by three qualities of exertion: exertion like a suit of armor, exertion of action, and exertion of never being satisfied.

Suit of Armor

The first quality is that exertion is like a suit of armor. You never let go of your desire to attain enlightenment, just as you would never go onto the battlefield without wearing your armor. You literally never take off your armor until your attainment of enlightenment. You vow to practice and become accomplished in your practice until the attainment of enlightenment. That kind of definite commitment is quite different from ordinary ambition, because it is based on a sense of joy.

The armor of exertion is connected with the joy and the longing to attain enlightenment. It is a question of realizing that whatever you experience is not all that solid and substantial, but there is an illusory quality to things. It is like driving through very thick, solid-looking fog: although it looks solid, you know the fog is not a wall, so you can just drive through. If you keep driving, at some point you can get beyond the fog and see the road.

Action

The second quality of exertion is action. The action of exertion is three-fold: (1) making an effort to overcome the kleshas, (2) making an effort to develop virtue, which comes from basic goodness, and (3) making an exceedingly great effort to work with others.

OVERCOMING THE KLESHAS. Action is necessary to accomplish what needs to be done on the path. It takes action to overcome the kleshas of passion, aggression, and ignorance. With the exertion of action you do not wallow in your own neurosis, but have joy in practicing virtue. A quality of gentleness goes along with your exertion, so things do not become too speedy.

DEVELOPING VIRTUE. The action of developing virtue can be divided into five subcategories: perseverance, joy, immovability, not changing your mind, and nonarrogance.

With perseverance, you are willing to see through yourself completely, and not stop halfway through. You are marked with exertion, and you will never give up.

Joy is based on recognizing that what you are doing deserves respect from others, and also self-respect because your action is dharmic. You enjoy yourself because you have the feeling that your world is sacred. Whatever you do in the name of exertion, whether you drink a cup of coffee or wash the dishes or change the tires on your car, there is a sense of sacredness, which is joyful.

With immovability, although all sorts of upheavals, kleshas, and suffering happen to you, you just continue with your exertion.

Because you are not changing your mind, although you might see all sorts of things that ordinarily would put you off, you do not give in to those things. You continue with your practice, and you do not just drop out because you have had an unpleasant conversation with someone. Not only can your mind not be changed, but you overcome your timidity in working with others. You could stay in New York, and not be put off by the New Yorkness of it. You could work with it.

You also develop nonarrogance. Because exertion could be a showcase, or a way of glamorizing yourself, it is important to overcome arrogance and pride. Although your exertion might be inspiring to others, even though you have done something quite good and your exertion has been fantastic, you do not become bloated by your achievement.

WORKING WITH OTHERS. The action of working with others is not easy. It takes real diligence.

Never Being Satisfied

The third quality of exertion is that you are never satisfied with your exertion. You never relax and say, "Now I have exerted myself enough." According to Gampopa, exertion is connected with the sense of being one with the dharma. You avoid obstacles to the dharma, and you do not come up with unnecessary excuses to avoid practice. However, overcoming laziness has nothing to do with being speedy, or with being quick and fast in the contemporary Western sense. Rather, exertion means being consistent, continuous, and faithful to the practice. Being consistent allows you to have a sense of joy, rather than seeing practice as a duty that you have to perform. The practice of dharma is getting into your blood.

When you have accomplished the three kinds of exertion, and have mindfulness and awareness in your everyday experiences and activities, you begin to regard exertion as a part of your basic, natural activity, rather than as something that is imposed on you. You don't say, "Now it is time to practice, and now it is time to switch off practice and do something else." Instead, exertion becomes part of your makeup, part of your being in whatever you do. You realize that you are not fundamentally stuck in the mud. You can pull up your anchor and sail away.

SPARK OF HUMOR

Between the levels of patience and exertion, there is a point at which you can spark some kind of flash on the spot. You can understand that in your ordinary life, you are very extremely heavy-handed without any genuine humor. In order to invite a sense of humor, you do not need to go back to the root of the problem and you should not go forward, thinking that you can solve it. There is something in between those two, a little lump, so to speak.

You can actually feel it on the spot, right now, this very fraction of a second. You have a lump in your mind. Look at it. When you look, it begins to become rather ridiculous that you are holding on to that particular lump. You begin to feel that it is very funny, but at the same time it is worth celebrating.

You can work with that lump; it could be a very chewy situation. It is pleasurable and worth celebrating that you can get the substance of your life between your teeth. You can chew it and work with it. It becomes food for your mind, food that is not bad or poisonous, and not particularly pleasurable either. It is much better than chewing gum; you can chew that lump very beautifully. It is nourishing, as long as you pay attention to what you are doing, as long as you work with your lump, as long as you stay with it long enough.

You find that the lump in your jaw, the lump between your past and future states of mind, is very chewy, but it is also quite good. It is quite real. Don't try to get rid of it; don't take it out of your mouth and throw it in the garbage pile. Chew it and swallow it. It is the juice of your life. You are swallowing your kleshas, your *ayatanas,* your *dhatus,** and your skandhas. All those things contain pretty good chewing gum. It is very basic. You do not need too many metaphysical interpretations—just feel it. You are chewing right now, on the spot. Look at it, chew it, and swallow it. You will feel that you have done something at last, this very day. Such chewing is connected with shamatha and vipashyana practice and everything within them. It is very simple and delightful.

---

* The six triads of sense organ, sense object, and sense consciousness are called the eighteen *dhatus* in Sanskrit, or *kham* in Tibetan. The six pairs of sense organs and sense objects are called the twelve *ayatanas,* or *kye-che* in Tibetan. See volume 1 of the *Profound Treasury,* chapter 37, "Rediscovering Your Own Mind."

31

Meditation

With samten, or meditation, you cannot be moved by wandering thoughts. Your attention is good, and your desire to do things becomes very real. Exertion encourages some sort of feistiness, and the practice of samten establishes that feistiness as grounded and real. . . . Working for sentient beings is finally becoming fully and thoroughly established as the ground of your whole being. Your state of mind is completely and fully soaked in it.

T HE FIFTH paramita is meditation. The paramita of meditation, or *dhyana* paramita, is described as a good rider. You ride on the horse of exertion with complete mindfulness and skill. You develop constant steadiness, which is like maintaining a good seat as you ride your horse.

The Sanskrit term *dhyana* is similar to the word *Zen* in Japanese, or *Ch'an* in Chinese. At the paramita level, *dhyana* means "subdued thinking," or "mindfulness." The Tibetan word for dhyana is *samten. Sam* means "thought process," or "steadiness of mind," and *ten* means "stabilized"; so *samten* means "stabilized thought process." Dhyana or samten is like the king of the mountains. You are never moved or challenged. You always stay very still. Samten is a further elaboration on the notion of patience, but it is much more insightful than patience. By learning how to extend your attention further and to stay on one spot for a long period of time, you can cultivate the dharma and the notion of enlightenment.

The nature of samten is to cut distractions, and its function is to develop groundedness. Samten consists of watching your thoughts and whatever goes on in your mind as a flowing river or a mountain range. Meditation is one of the key ways to attain enlightenment, because it allows us to cut through preoccupations and desires. We see how we attempt to fill up our space, how we divert ourselves, and how we preoccupy ourselves with family, money, food, and entertainment.

The meditation paramita is a step beyond the paramitas of generosity, discipline, patience, and exertion. At this point there is a quality of immense solidity, which derives from the previous four paramitas and an awareness of everything that is taking place. At the same time, there is a little irritation coming from the awareness, which reminds you that you have to go back to your state of being, that you have to be precise and solid. This is reflected on the faces of the *lohans,* the original accomplished disciples of the Buddha.* There is seemingly a sense of serenity, a superficial calmness—but underneath, turmoil takes place. It is interesting that lohans are not really demonstrations of a perfect state of being, as a lot of people have made them out to be. There is a superficial diplomacy, dignity, and confidence, but underneath is uncertainty. The reason for that uncertainty is that there is not yet prajna, which is the next paramita. When prajna strikes, that uncertainty is transformed into knowledge. Then you could be a full, solid individual without any problems.

On the level of dhyana paramita, shamatha is not so much taming—we have pretty much tamed everything at this point—it is rather getting used to being tamed. The shamatha experience is more a matter of synchronizing body, speech, and mind. If you are unable to control your body, speech, and mind, you will constantly be led into heedlessness, in spite of all the other paramitas you may have attained. You will be subject to passion, which is based on fickleness, wandering mind, and the inability to pay heed to what happens in your life. If you are not able to attain ideal steadiness of mind, you may not be able to attain the ultimate awakened state, which is free from passion.

Dhyana paramita includes postmeditation experience as well as meditation experience. The quality of postmeditation is a sense of composure in which body, speech, and mind are well-coordinated. You are able to be where you are, in a state of ease and relaxation, with less anxiety and frivolity. You are able to cut through your passion, longing, desire, or looking for further feedback. Because your body, speech, and mind are fully

---

* *Lohan* is the Chinese translation of the Sanskrit *arhat,* or "worthy one," a term applied to a level of realization that many disciples of the Buddha attained.

occupied and at their best, you experience complete satisfaction. That is the definition of shamatha practice on the meditation paramita level.

The practice of dhyana paramita allows you to concentrate on the virtues of nonaggression and contentment. Once you realize that your state of mind is already content, and that your body, speech, and mind are synchronized and at ease, you begin to find yourself relaxed and at your best. Because of that, you are able to attain the ultimate seclusion, the ultimate hermitage. You do not have to look for a means of escape, or physically run away from the city and take a rest in the countryside, but you can find your hermitage within yourself.

You might find that inner hermitage very lonely. Usually when you go to a lonely place, you know that you can always go back to your busy life. You know that you can cut your loneliness and entertain yourself all over again. But in this case, you are carrying your loneliness with you all the time, so you might find it very difficult to shake off. You might find it somewhat hauntingly lonely. However, although I am warning you that you might have that kind of difficulty, it should be all right, because we all feel that way. Even though you might feel somewhat lonely, you still could feel extremely relieved and joyful. You no longer have a need for unnecessary toys and babysitters and playmates. You are completely coordinated, and you are in one piece. Your mind is one, and your concentration and actions are at their best. That is the real idea of dhyana.

From the bodhisattva's point of view, if you do not have good concentration, you will not achieve intuitive appreciation or intuitive insight; and if you don't have intuitive insight, you will not be able to work with other sentient beings. The term *intuitive insight* has often been mistakenly translated as "clairvoyance," which is slightly hokey. The idea of intuitive insight is that you have a way of seeing and experiencing how other people's minds actually work.

Two Categories of Samten

Samten is divided into two categories: common samten, or shamatha, and special samten, or vipashyana. Common samten is based on developing concentration and mindfulness, in the basic and ordinary sense of paying heed to everything. Special samten is the development of awareness. This awareness is present throughout your everyday life. It is constant awareness, which brings the possibility of combining shamatha and vipashyana together. Doing so allows you to be fully steady, and free from preoccupation with the world of desire.

THREE LEVELS OF SAMTEN

In addition to two categories of samten, there are three levels: dwelling in the dharma of seeing, accumulating goodness, and enthusiasm in working for others.

Dwelling in the Dharma of Seeing

The first level of samten is dwelling in the dharma of seeing. It is the practice of shamatha. Your perception and your state of mind are working along with the ayatanas and dhatus, so you are constantly projecting outward. You are not trying to contradict the ayatanas, but you are maintaining yourself within the ayatanas, so you are able to remain in the state of shamatha quite leisurely. Your mind becomes peaceful and your body relaxed. That seems to be the essence of shamatha practice.

The relaxation that comes with shamatha is called shinjang. You are thoroughly processed. Your mind is processed by the peace and one-pointedness of mindfulness practice, and your body is processed by assuming certain postures. Eventually the posture of sitting meditation practice becomes a soothing and natural exercise; it is natural relaxation. It is as if both mind and body were put into a washing machine and then into a dryer. But it is a dry-cleaning process rather than a wet-cleaning process. You do not have to go through the wetness of passion, just the dryness of prajna. So shinjang is the Buddhist version of dry-cleaning our whole being. It is achieved through shamatha practice, which is the first level of samten.

Accumulating Goodness

The second level of samten is accumulating goodness or virtue. Having fully and thoroughly achieved shamatha mindfulness, you begin to develop vipashyana awareness. Mindfulness is a very localized situation, but with awareness, you actually can discriminate dharmas. At the same time, you develop a further appreciation of concentration. In the state of awareness, you can appreciate the possibility of seeing the world properly and fully. You can see how your ayatanas and dhatus function or operate, and you can see how the world works. This is what is known as vipashyana.

252

According to the Buddhist tradition, virtue can be defined as clear perception. Clear perception is not involved with ego. If you have ego, you cannot have clear perception; your perceptions will still be clouded. When you no longer have any obstacles or cloudiness, you experience clarity, and you are able to practice immaculately. Because you are able to practice immaculately and purely, you can also help others beautifully—and because you can help others, you yourself become trained at the same time. And because of that, you can attain enlightenment and help others attain enlightenment.

Enthusiasm in Working for Others

The third level of samten is enthusiasm in working for others. You are not purely interested in peace and insight, or shamatha and vipashyana alone, but you develop agitation in your state of mind. That agitation is to work for sentient beings. From the mahayana point of view, when you develop shamatha, you are developing shunyata, and when you develop vipashyana, you are developing compassion. So you have a sense of compassion and shunyata already.

At the third level of samten, you gain further energy to combine shamatha and vipashyana, to join emptiness with compassion. So the discipline of working for sentient beings begins to evolve. But nobody is going to get an award for saving all sentient beings, that's for sure, because nobody can keep up with it. That is the saving grace. It is like working as a doctor: if you are a doctor, how many people are you going to cure? Are you going to cure the whole world, or are you going to cure people one by one? You just keep working every day. Do you expect that everybody is going to be healthy, that one day the whole world will just say, "I'm healthy"? You wouldn't expect that—but you still keep working.

With samten, or meditation, you cannot be moved by wandering thoughts. Your attention is good, and your desire to do things becomes very real. Exertion encourages some sort of feistiness, and the practice of samten establishes that feistiness as grounded and real. "We mean business," so to speak. Working for sentient beings is finally becoming fully and thoroughly established as the ground of your whole being. Your state of mind is completely and fully soaked in it. At this level, working for sentient beings becomes the activity of shunyata and compassion.

The other paramitas are very good in their own way, but they could be very jumpy. With dhyana, because your span of attention becomes much more vast and definite, you do not have to be constantly jumpy. You have learned how to concentrate, how to attend to one theme for a long time, and that affects how you can practice compassion and how you can work for others. If you want to help someone, you spend lots of time with them, you cultivate them, and you never get frustrated. Your span of attention becomes so vast, so good, and so willing, that this person can shit on you, piss on you, kick you, try all sorts of ways to provoke you, but you are never moved. You are just like a mountain. Since your span of attention cannot be interrupted, you can listen to someone and work with them for many years. You do not look for shortcuts. Your real commitment to that person is an act of compassion—and because you are also practicing exertion, you enjoy what you are doing.

EIGHT MAIN OBSTACLES TO SAMTEN

There are eight main obstacles to samten, to stabilizing one's mind. (1) When the body is not controlled, you have physical chaos; (2) when the speech is not controlled, you have chaos in your discursive, habitual thought patterns; (3) when the mind is not controlled, you have the problems of mindlessness, random thoughts, and casualness. (4) When there is too much indulgence in your kleshas, or your emotions, and you make a big deal of them, you have the problem of emotional upheavals. (5) When you engage in mindless talking, chatter, and gossip, it is a problem not just for yourself, but also for your neighbors, because it allows them to re-create their memories and gives them a chance to reconnect with their own subconscious gossip. (6) When you let go and relax too much, or in the wrong way, you allow yourself to be attacked by evil forces: you get influenza, you run into all sorts of accidents, and you become subject to the obstacles of Mara. The remaining two obstacles are (7) heedlessness and (8) regressing in your practice of shamatha and vipashyana.

Once you are able to overcome those obstacles, you begin to attain some kind of relaxation. This approach is quite similar to the hinayana description of the obstacles to shamatha and their antidotes.* But going

---

* For more on the *obstacles to shamatha and their antidotes,* refer to volume 1 of the *Profound Treasury,* chapter 32, "Identifying Obstacles to Shamatha," and chapter 33, "Antidotes to the Obstacles to Shamatha."

further, you begin to realize that what you experience in your daily life is not particularly a threat or a source of discomfort. You begin to quite happily snuggle yourself, so to speak, into samten. Because of your exertion in shamatha-vipashyana discipline, you begin to find that both mind and body are shinjang-ed. However, you do not exactly fall asleep in your snuggly bed. Instead, you become industrious, full of delight, and active. You might even discover the possibility of creating discriminating awareness, or prajna. You become very industrious in helping others. You have given birth to ultimate and relative bodhichitta, and you are able to generate compassion, properly and fully.

IMPLEMENTING SAMTEN

The meditative state of samten can be divided into four types of practice, which correspond to the four limitless ones we discussed earlier. With the first limitless one, loving-kindness, or maitri, you develop intellectual and theoretical reasons for why you should practice meditation, and you begin to cut through discursive mind. You realize that your thought patterns are not such a big deal. Therefore, you develop a sense of gentleness and lovingness to yourself.

With the second limitless one, compassion, or karuna, you begin to feel compassion toward others very naturally and toward yourself as well. Therefore, you have a sense of delight.

With the third limitless one, joy, or *mudita,* you are delighted because what you are doing is perfectly legitimate and excellent. You don't have second thoughts about whether you are doing the right thing or the wrong thing, because what you are doing is very satisfactory, delightful, and good.

With the fourth limitless one, equanimity, or *upeksha,* you are beginning to lose the notion of taking sides, of friend and enemy, and so forth. There is a sense of equality about everything.

Altogether, the four limitless ones are about pragmatic implementation. They are about how practically to cultivate the ideal meditative state, based on egolessness and compassion.

32

Prajna

[With prajna] you cut methodically, one situation after another. When you cut through your primitive beliefs about reality and your conflicting emotions, there is compassion. Emotions are very aggressive, so in order to cut through them, you need some kind of cool moon, fresh water, iceberg. So prajna is automatically linked with compassion. The freshness of a cool mountain stream and the tenderness of a pigeon's heart are always connected.

THE SIXTH paramita is prajna. Prajna paramita is described as a sword; it is the clear perception of the phenomenal world. The closest word we have come up with to define *prajna* is "knowledge." *Pra* means "superior" or "higher," and *jna* means "knowing," "knowledge," or "comprehending."; so *prajna* means "superior knowledge." Prajna transcends purely technical knowledge alone, or the kinds of learning you go to school to cultivate. The hinayana approach to prajna is based on *soso tharpa,* or individual salvation, but in the mahayana you are helping others, so it is an altogether different level of prajna. It is like the difference between going to nursing school to learn medical theory, and practicing that theory by actually working with others.

The Tibetan word for prajna is *sherap. She* means "knowing," and *rap* means "the best"; so *sherap* means the "best knowledge," or "supreme knowing." It is the "best of cognitive mind," the "best of cognition," and the "best of knowledge," all put together. The emphasis of sherap is on both the knowledge itself and the state of mind of the knower. But we need to clarify what we mean by knowledge. Ordinarily knowledge refers to being knowledgeable *about* something or other. You collect information and try to understand that information, and then store it in your memory bank. But in the case of sherap, we do not qualify or give credentials to the knowledge. It is simply knowledge. Sherap, or prajna, means being able to discriminate black from white, light from dark, purple from yellow, green from red. It is being able to discriminate sharp from dull, awake from asleep, happy from sad. Sherap is unconditional knowledge, where knowingness can take place at a very high level. It is not knowing this or that, but simply knowing, which connects with the quality of wakefulness. Sherap is not described in terms of technicalities or information, but in terms of simply being there with knowledge. Sherap is the state of knowingness, the state of wakefulness.

Sherap refers to the subject and the object together. You possess sherap when you have the state of mind that is capable of learning, but the various subjects that you learn are also known as sherap. So sherap can refer to both subject and object. It includes both knowledge and the person who looks at the knowledge. It is like the lute and the hearing consciousness: the sense object and the sense consciousness are put together, and you hear music between the two. Sherap is very fresh and very much on the spot. You could even say it is very much on the surface, although it is not superficial.

In describing sherap as the best of cognitive mind, cognition means being able to see, rather than being able to perceive. The word *perceive* might have the sense of banking things in the memory, but cognition has the quality of simply seeing without storing. The senses do not have to be captured and re-stored. Fundamentally, the sense processes could come and go, like anything else in our state of being. Capturing is what our parents told us to do. and it is how we have been educated, but it is a bad habit. That is what is called samsara: we just take in and churn out, take in and churn out. The problem with samsara is that it is like pissing on the ground: when you piss on the ground, it goes out into the rivers, and from the rivers it goes back into the reservoirs, so we drink our urine again and again. But the experience of prajna is fresh. It occurs, and it has happened, and that's it. It is like the vajrayana concept of nowness. Nowness is like getting fresh banknotes and spending them on the spot—there is a quality of freshness.

Cognition goes beyond the level of the alayavijnana, or alaya consciousness; it does not stay on the level of resting in alaya—it is just seeing.* Such seeing is not necessarily visual; it is any first beam that projects out, be it vision, hearing, touch, or whatever else. Cognition could accommodate anything. It is somewhat related with re-cognition, as if you have seen your own nature before. Cognition is the subject, and knowledge is the object.

The basis of prajna is that you are fully trained in the practice of sitting meditation. Because you are inspired by shamatha-vipashyana discipline, you are able to develop the wonderful paramitas of generosity, discipline, patience, exertion, and meditation—and with prajna you are actually able to put them into effect. Prajna shows you how to develop ideal compassion, true compassion that is sharp and precise. Without prajna, when you try to help somebody, you might do it in the wrong way and actually cause harm instead.

Prajna is said to be the medicine that will free us from the sickness of the two veils that prevent us from going beyond samsaric bondage: conflicting emotions and primitive beliefs about reality. The interesting thing about the analogy of prajna as medicine is that there is the implication that originally we were well and then suddenly we became sick. This is slightly different from the usual idea of bondage or obstacles. With prajna, the way to relate with the world and with ourselves when we experience obstacles is to view them as a temporary fever or flu.

SKILLFUL MEANS AND WISDOM

Prajna cannot develop without the rest of the paramitas; they work together. The first five paramitas are known as upaya, or skillful means. But skillful means also need wisdom, or prajna.† This combination of skillful means and wisdom makes mahayana special and unusual. We could even go so far as to say that by joining skillful means and wisdom, mahayana is superior to hinayana. Prajna is connected with the feminine principle, and upaya with the masculine principle. Prajna is sharpness; it

---

* The practice of resting in alaya is an aspect of mind training described in chapter 36, "Point Two: Resting in Ultimate Bodhichitta."

† Chögyam Trungpa referred to *prajna* as "knowledge," or "transcendent knowledge," and the related term *jnana* as "wisdom." However, at times he also used the term *wisdom* to refer to prajna, particularly in the context of upaya and prajna, or skillful means and wisdom. In the vajrayana teachings, many forms of jnana, or enlightened wisdom, are described. Prajna, or transcendent knowledge, is a key teaching of the mahayana.

is said to be very precise and clear. Prajna has passion and directness, and upaya has the resources to work with the prajna.

Upaya without prajna would be ineffective. It would be like the sun without rays. The first five paramitas can free you from the samsaric world, but they can never enable you to go beyond the transcendent world. The mahayana concept is not to dwell in either the samsaric or the transcendent world. You have to go beyond both nirvana and samsara in order to be of benefit to others. As all the rivers flow south to join the ocean, likewise all the other paramitas flow toward the ocean of prajna. Therefore prajna is a very important factor in mahayana Buddhism altogether. Without prajna it is impossible to attain enlightenment, because you have no way of viewing your journey, no way of looking at your path. It would be as if you were a blind person trying to enter a big city, not knowing where it was or how to get there.

In the mahayana, you start with skillful means, and you become a good bodhisattva. You begin with generosity, and go on to discipline, patience, exertion, and meditation. You practice all those paramitas as they are given to you, and then you begin a big reviewing process. You question what you are doing with all of these. In doing so, you are developing prajna, which allows you to look back at the whole thing properly. So you practice first, and you figure out what you are doing afterward.

PRAJNA AND SHUNYATA

The nature of prajna is that it has allegiance to shunyata. Without that connection with shunyata, it would be completely overwhelming if there were too many clear perceptions. But clear perception qualified by emptiness is stable. So shunyata is solid as much as it is empty. If you want to buy a poodle, you have to know what it eats and how it should be groomed. In the same way, if you want to know prajna paramita, you need to understand shunyata.

In understanding shunyata, intellectual learning is not applicable. Nonetheless, you could try to understand shunyata logically and come to the conclusion that everything is nonexistent. You could definitely do that. But having understood this, you should not dwell on that understanding, but try to absorb that understanding into your whole being, if there is any being left at that point. Loneliness might be a beacon that points in this direction. From there, you can explore further. You ask basic questions, such as "Who am I?" or "Does this have any substance?" You begin to look for real substance, not just something imaginative, and not just what your mother and father told you.

Shunyata opens up all kinds of questions. The teachings only go so far, then it is up to you to figure it out. You need to question yourself. For instance, if you know about shamatha-vipashyana, but you continue to choose fixation, you could ask yourself why. This is what is called the study of Buddhism. Somebody gives you a clue: "This is the case. This is the world, and this is you. This is what not to do, and this is what to do. Now I leave it up to you." But then you need to do it and find out for yourself. If you do, you will come to a conclusion no different than what the Buddha found. Strangely enough, everybody comes to the same conclusion, but from different directions and in different ways. So the question is the answer.

You might ordinarily think that finding yourself nonexistent is a source of panic. But in this case, it is a source of joy. Egolessness is the source of great joy, the greatest joy, because you do not have to maintain yourself anymore. So from a practical point of view, there is great joy because there is less struggle and less hardship. In terms of personal experience, it is also joyful, because there is no need to keep this and that going simultaneously. Nobody has to synchronize the two worlds of this and that, which is what we usually tend to do. So shunyata is an open world. It is empty, yet joyful.

At a certain stage, nonreference point is the reference point. That is why we call it brilliance or luminosity. But it is not so solid, which is why you have to go through training and do practices. It would be too easy to say that once you understood nonreference point fully, you would be enlightened right away. In our tradition, we do not actually believe in sudden realization. Nobody can be enlightened all that suddenly. Sudden realization is more like a password or initial behavior pattern, and after that you go on a journey; you keep going with nonreference point. That is why prajna is known as discriminating-awareness wisdom. There are more subtleties than just becoming enlightened in one go.

DISCRIMINATING-AWARENESS WISDOM

Discriminating awareness means that you are able to separate dharmas. The opposite of prajna is being unable to see or experience precision; it is being ignorant and wallowing in confusion. Discriminating does not mean taking sides. It is not that you like something and you accept it, or that you dislike something and you reject it. In this case, discriminating refers to having tremendous precision, and being able to see the sharp edges of situations. Everything is very bright and beautiful. Although you do not take sides, you still have a sense of what is what, which is which, when is when, how is how, and why is why.

When you begin to work with your body and mind with proper posture in the sitting practice of meditation, you actually begin to act like a prajna person. You begin to distinguish between confusion and direct precision. In meditation practice, you begin with the first and closest thing to work with, which is the breath. You notice that you do breathe, and you notice that you do think. You learn that certain things could be accepted and included as part of the practice, and that certain things could be rejected. Through that kind of precision and directness, you are developing prajna as a contemplative technique.

As you practice meditation, your prajna begins to be sharpened. You are beginning to develop discriminating knowledge, and you are able to distinguish one dharma from another. It is like growing a baby in your body: as a fetus grows, it begins to react to what is other than itself. Your prajna begins to react that way too, distinguishing prajna from non-prajna. You find that when you develop mindfulness fully and properly, looking at the sun is much brighter, and food is much more tasty. It is not that your food tastes good or bad particularly, it is just more tasty. Walking, wearing clothes, and conducting yourself in ordinary life, you begin to realize that things have sharpened as a result of mindfulness practice.

At the same time, you begin to feel free from forgetfulness, because in dealing with the present, you experience the past as vivid and the future as clear. Because of that, the present situation has no fear. You have a perfect idea of how your future is going to be. For instance, you know that in the future your house is going to fall apart and all the systems are going to break down. You know it is either going to be sold or become a part of the landscape. It is quite simple, not particularly magical.

THE SWORD OF PRAJNA

Prajna enables you to cut through your early kleshas, which are known in the *abhidharma*, or teachings on Buddhist psychology, as mental events.

With a tremendous sense of mindfulness, you begin to develop awareness as well. You acquire a sword at the shamatha level, quite a sharp one. At the vipashyana level, you acquire further knowledge so that in case that sword is corrupted, you know how to sharpen it again. The blade of this particular sword has two edges: it cuts both yourself and other. You begin to realize that you can actually cut the frigidity and fickleness of your own existence, the sense of individuality that you hold so dear and cherish so lovingly. You have been accustomed to it for so long that you would like to hold on to that "I," or ego. I was quite amused to see the New Hampshire license plate, which says Live Free or Die. We have been looking for freedom by proclaiming our imprisonment, by wallowing in a state of existence rather than a state of freedom.

That which we cling to, hang on to, that very core, is what is cut by the double-edged blade of the sword of prajna. It is cut not in suicidal terms, but from the point of view of delight. There is delight in the sense that impurity has been purified. There is a gooeyness or dirtiness that we usually have in our attitude toward ourselves as "me." We feel that we have to put up with ourselves, try to get along with ourselves, although there will be occasional embarrassing corners and deep pools of all kinds. Sometimes we are decorated with jewels, perfume, silk, or satin; nevertheless, we basically have a cheap notion of ourselves. That problematic view of ourselves is cut through by one side of the blade. And having cut through that, having destroyed it, we begin to develop an appreciation of ourselves. We replace that sense of cheapness with delight. Prajna, elegant and arrogant, begins to happen.

Having struck with one side of the blade, we then strike our sword in the other direction. We begin to realize that the outside world we are creating is precisely the same as that which we are creating in ourselves. So we begin to strike the other side and cut the outer world, or the relative situation, as well. This happens very naturally.

Having cut with both sides of the blade, we experience shunyata. We begin to realize the absence of fixations and clinging, the absence of random labeling and samsaric perception, or küntak. We find that we are without küntak, or false conceptions, all along. No küntak here, no küntak there, no küntak everywhere.*

---

* For a discussion of *küntak*, or random labeling, see chapter 23, "Contemplating Emptiness."

THREE PRAJNAS

Prajna is divided into three sections: mundane prajna, prajna that transcends worldliness, and prajna that transcends dharmas.

Mundane Prajna

The first prajna is called mundane prajna, or common prajna. Common prajna is shared by theists and nontheists alike. According to tradition, you are supposed to learn how to read and write and how to think properly. You are supposed to learn mathematics and science and how to conduct yourself in the ordinary world. Having that kind of sophistication seems to be a requirement from the point of view of prajna. In other words, you cannot say, "I am just a simple yogi, practicing my own way. I do not have to learn how to put a stamp on my mail or how to put the zip code on somebody's address." If you shrink to that level, there is no prajna and there is no upaya either. Conducting yourself with some kind of intelligence and sophistication in your state of mind is necessary and important. You might have an idea that this kind of learning is a dead end, but it is not. On the nontheistic path, you realize that if you know how to go about your business in ordinary situations, it inspires further inquisitiveness. You want to learn more, to find out more. You are not intimidated by your world, so you can go beyond it and explore further.

Fundamentally speaking, mundane prajna is just an ordinary education. You learn to appreciate the arts, medicine, philology, and philosophy. That kind of education is very important, particularly if you are going to be a spokesperson for the buddhadharma in the future. If you are going to help people, you yourself have to be somewhat educated and learned. The point is not just to become qualified for your own sake, but also for the sake of liberating others. You do not have to be learned in everything, but at least you should be familiar with one area of learning. The Buddha was brought up as Prince Siddhartha, and he had to study and learn all kinds of technical and secular knowledge before he set out to become the Buddha.

Even your table manners are important. You learn how to eat properly and how to dress nicely, in accordance with social norms. You learn how to speak properly, and how to write and behave properly. You learn how to be good at doing things, purely by paying attention to reality. Mundane prajna deals with the basics: you learn how to be a good person, an art-ful person.

Prajna That Transcends Worldliness

The second level of prajna is prajna that transcends worldliness. This type of prajna is related with your understanding of the dharma. You are learn-ing, you are contemplating what you have learned, and you are trying to practice what you have learned. Prajna is able to transcend worldli-ness by seeing through the ego of self. You understand the beginning, the middle, and the end of the teachings of dharma. The whole thing is understood.*

Prajna That Transcends Dharmas

The third type of prajna, superior prajna, is the prajna that transcends dharmas. At this level of prajna, you realize that all the dharmas you expe-rience are unborn and unoriginated. Dharmas are free from dualism and free from theistic concepts. They have no origin, they just arise. Therefore you begin to see that there is no point in hanging on to them. Through superior prajna, you begin to realize that there is nothing to dwell on. You are not lost in nowhere, but you are unable to dwell or to label yourself. If you say, "I am Joe Schmidt," where is this Joe Schmidt? Is he the name of the form, the feeling, the concept—the name of any of the skandhas? What was Joe Schmidt in the past? Who is he in the present? Who will he be in the future? When you examine and dissect the existence of Joe Schmidt, you find that there is no Joe Schmidt at all. You begin to wonder whether you exist or not. That is the state of egolessness.

There is nothing that you, personally, can actually pinpoint as "I am," yet a general sense of cognition occurs. Cognition is like clear light; it is brilliant light shining through. Beyond that cognition, or basic conscious-ness, there is nothing at all. This is not a negation of existence, and it is certainly not an attitude of eternalism either. Instead, there is a sense that

---

* In *The Jewel Ornament of Liberation,* this level of prajna is connected with the hinayana level of realization. The next level of prajna, which is the prajna that transcends dharmas, is connected with the mahayana level of realization. See *The Wish-Fulfilling Gem of the Noble Teachings,* translated by Khenpo Konchog Gyaltsen Rinpoche (Ithaca, N.Y.: Snow Lion, 1998).

when you sit and meditate and follow your breath, you find that there is actually no one doing that, yet there is a process taking place.

Basically speaking, when you say "I am," you begin to ask yourself the question, "Who said that?" You might say, "I said that." But then you ask, "Who are you?" And when you look, you find it is very difficult to find out who that actually is. You might timidly come back to saying your name, thinking that this is who is speaking, but beyond the name that was given to you, nothing really exists. You may think that you exist because your name is so-and-so, or because your driver's license says so-and-so. But if you look beyond such things, and beyond beyond, you find that there is no substance. That is ultimate prajna: it is the discovery of egolessness, which frees you from fixation.

Ultimate prajna allows you to examine other things in the same way. You can look at people, or you can look at the phenomenal world. When you look at the phenomenal world, you see that although the phenomenal world does exist, it is a composite of many things. Therefore it does not exist as a single entity, as one thing. If you look closely and thoroughly, by means of the steadiness of mind of the meditation paramita, together with the wisdom of the prajna paramita, you see that the soul that theistic traditions talk about does not exist. By examining yourself again and again in that way, you find that there is no substantial "me."

This particular message of the Buddha is supposed to have caused tremendous fear among the arhats and students of the time. It is said that many of the great arhats had heart attacks and died on the spot when the Buddha began to teach things like the *Heart Sutra*, shunyata, and egolessness. Obviously, the egolessness seen by prajna paramita was a breakthrough of some kind in the teachings of the Buddha. It is essential to understand.

SUPERIOR PRAJNA AND TWOFOLD EGOLESSNESS. This type of prajna is based on the experience of the twofold egolessness of self and of other, and on the understanding of the two veils of conflicting emotions and primitive beliefs about reality. It begins by realizing the egolessness of self. Finally, your prajna begins to see through that game. You begin to realize that ego is a nuisance, and you see that the ego of self is sophistry, a big joke.

You have developed twofold ego purely by assuming that there is *this*; therefore there should be *that* as well. And ironically, when you realize the existence of *that*, you use that to further confirm *this*. By throwing yourself back and forth in that way, and by means of neurosis and wishful thinking, you have developed the ego of self. Prajna cuts through that ego of self. You realize that the game you have been playing is absurd. You are lonely, you want company, so you recruit something—the other, the world—and you have been doing that for a long time. Once you have convinced yourself that you exist, you begin to recruit the other. You develop a system of reference points: *that* is good because *this* feels bad; or *this* feels bad, therefore *that* is good; or *this* feels good, therefore *that* is good as well.

You begin to develop numerous systems of stabilizing your fixation and holding on to things by re-creating reference points. It is like setting up an echo chamber. But soon it is no longer purely an echo chamber, because you begin to stabilize your reference points. You tape-record them, and you make photographs of them: stills, slides, and movies. You begin to make your world into a monument, create a "real" record of the whole thing. You take so much pride in it. You try to hang on to your reference points so much that sometimes the whole thing becomes revolting to you, and you begin to think that maybe it isn't a good idea. But what else can you do? It might not be a good idea, but it is comfortable and predictable. You have been fixated on such reference points—and prajna begins to see through all of that.

At the first level, ego of self, you have both yourself and the other already. At the second level of ego, ego of dharmas, you and the other are in cahoots. You and the other begin to make up schemes: "Since we are here together, what shall we do now?" You and the other begin to develop policies, rather than just discovering *that*. You have discovered *that* already. You cannot discover the ego of self without having *that*, otherwise it doesn't work. You have to have a reference point in order to have "me." When you cut one-and-a-half-fold ego, there is no ego of *this* or ego of *that*, but there is still the ego of *this* and *that* together. There is still the scheme.*

Schemes are more solid than *this* and *that*. Schemes are our defense mechanism. That is why bodhisattvas of the highest level still have to overcome that scheming, which is the last stain of ego. It is like a bottle that once contained musk: you can still smell the musk although there

---

* For more on the ego of self and the ego of dharmas or phenomena, see chapter 8, "Cutting Ego Fixation."

is none left. In the same way, the smell of ego-schemes hangs on for a long time.

The original logic of "I" and "other" is not all that solid, but together the two create this world, which becomes more and more solid. That solidity is more like having a thick skin than having an actual, solid body. The outer layer is much more solid than the constituents of what is inside. You begin to see that you are not anything tangible, and that there is no substantiality to anything. Having realized the egolessness of self, you begin to realize the egolessness of dharmas.

First, prajna sees through the ego of self, which does not actually exist. Beyond that, the ego of self tries to find its mythical mate, known as the "other." Then you and your mate go on to the ego of dharmas. You and your mate begin to name everything, one thing after another. You are confident in your own confusion and frivolity. That is how you build the whole world. And it is prajna that actually cuts through that particular situation.

Prajna sees things clearly. You have no room to dwell on anything. Prajna actually makes you homeless. The previous paramitas might still leave some reference point, but prajna cuts through the whole thing. With prajna, the idea of you practicing the dharma and gaining results is seen as hocus-pocus. Prajna says, "No. You cannot attain anything or gain anything because you do not have 'it' or 'you' at all." This makes you see things in an entirely new light.

APPLYING THE BIGGER MIND OF PRAJNA. The egolessness of prajna is good background for practicing the rest of the paramitas. If you practice generosity with a sense of nonexistence, your generosity has no giver and no receiver; therefore, your gift is a pure gift. The same is true for discipline: since there is nothing or no one to discipline, discipline just dawns in you, so you are naturally disciplined. In the practice of patience, there is nothing to be angry about, so anger goes away naturally. With exertion, the joy of action and practice becomes natural because there is no one to pull you down and no one to be depressed. In the paramita of meditation, or shamatha-vipashyana discipline, there is nobody trying to accomplish or achieve anything, so meditation is effortless.

From the point of view of ego, the practices of the hinayana and mahayana may seem to be a form of imprisonment. If you are simply practicing the first five paramitas, you might feel that you are imprisoning yourself in little pigeonholes. If you do not cultivate the bigger mind of prajna, you may be imprisoning yourself by trying to be good at exertion, good at patience, good at generosity, good at discipline, and so forth. But with prajna paramita, nothing in these practices imprisons you. In the competitive world, you try to achieve, but through prajna paramita you begin to experience a larger world. In that larger space, nobody really needs to struggle. Struggles become just little ripples in the water. In fact, they go away completely.

Superior prajna is one of the most important aspects of practice. It is an eye-opener. Because of it, you can also practice mundane prajna. You can learn such things as art, poetry, drama, grammar, and philosophy, because there is no mental blockage; there is nothing but pure open space. You realize that all dharmas, all existence, and all the things that you examine in your mind are fundamentally insubstantial. They are not just insubstantial simply in the sense of being impermanent, but they are *always* insubstantial. Whether or not they go away, whether they die or live, they are insubstantial. Right at this very moment there is clarity and a wide view. That is why this is known as the mahayana, the greater vehicle. It is greater because it does not try to cling to any primitive beliefs in solidity.

TRANSFORMATION AND COMPASSION

With prajna paramita, you are getting somewhere. You are not just going to stay here as good old Joe Schmidt for the rest of your life. Instead, you are going to transform yourself, change yourself, go a little bit beyond. Going beyond is delightful, although there may not be anyone to congratulate you, or receive you, or take care of you on the journey. It is your own journey, a journey of your state of being, rather than one in which you are trying to go somewhere else. Therefore, egolessness, or shunyata experience, is very important.

Prajna can discriminate every detail and particle of the world's existence, because the process and processor are never stuck in a biased state of existence. Because there is no doer and nothing is being done, you are able to examine the entire world. Therefore, you can do the best research of all. Otherwise, if you get stuck in a particular philosophical bias or logic, if you believe in a particular axiom, and then conduct yourself according to that particular metaphor, you try to bring everything in line with your beliefs and ideas. When you do that, you lose that bigger reference point. You keep so much under your feet that you begin to lose the many other things that you haven't even examined. You just look down, rather than looking at everything altogether, inside and out, everywhere, all over the place. When there is no looker or no searcher, everything is fluid. Everything is seen, experienced, understood, and realized. That is a basic and very primitive explanation of prajna paramita.

It is important to understand that Buddhism altogether, particularly mahayana Buddhism, is based on this theory of egolessness. We should not even call it a theory. It is nonexistence, nonlogic; therefore, it transcends all logic. According to Nagarjuna and to madhyamaka logic, if you do not claim anything, you are victorious. As soon as you begin to make a claim, you are making yourself into a target. Therefore, you could get hurt or be left behind. That seems to be the basic point of prajna, which is quite a mindful.

Prajna cuts the random choices and methodical logic of küntak. You cut methodically, one situation after another. When you cut through your primitive beliefs about reality and your conflicting emotions, there is compassion. Emotions are very aggressive, so in order to cut through them, you need some kind of cool moon, fresh water, iceberg. So prajna is automatically linked with compassion. The freshness of a cool mountain stream and the tenderness of a pigeon's heart are always connected.

Part Seven

MIND TRAINING AND
SLOGAN PRACTICE

33

Introduction to Mind Training

The lojong, or mind-training, slogans are very simple, and not particularly philosophical. They are purely what one of the great Kagyü teachers referred to as a "grandmother's finger pointing." When a grandmother says, "This is the place where I used to go and pick corn or collect wild vegetables," she uses her finger rather than writing on paper or using a map.

S O F A R , our approach to the mahayana has been a philosophical one. But to experience reality properly, we very much need an application or working basis. We need to change to a slightly more contemplative approach. This comes in very handy. We may have begun to understand the shunyata principle or the teachings on relative and absolute truth, but what are we going to do then? What are we going to do with those two truths? It is like we have eaten an immense amount of birthday cake: we are completely bloated and do not know what to do next. So at this point we need to shift our emphasis from the theory of the bodhisattva path to the practice and experience of it.

What is the difference between theory and practice? Theory is an understanding of the possibility of egolessness, and practice is actually shedding your ego. The effect is relating with reality according to the bodhisattva path. At the theoretical level, you can understand how the realization of the egolessness of individuality and the egolessness of dharmas can be achieved simultaneously and properly. And at the practical level, how you are going to do that is largely based on your practice and personal discipline.

In the mahayana, our main concern is how to awaken ourselves. The mahayana takes quite a lot of effort because it is a big job. That is why it is called the mahayana, the great vehicle: it is a big deal. The mahayana is no joke, and you had better not fall asleep at the wheel when you are driving on such a big highway. But you can't go wrong with mahayana heavy-handedness; it is the best kind.

With mahayana practice, there is no cultivation—you just do it. It's like taking medication: the pills you take might taste terribly bitter, but you take them anyway. The mahayana is very harsh, but it is also very gentle. The intention is gentle, but the practice is harsh. By combining the intention and the practice, you are being both "harshed" and "gentled." That process turns you into a bodhisattva. It is like jumping into a blender: you begin to feel that you are swimming in the blender, and you might even enjoy it a little bit after you have been processed.

The technique of shamatha-vipashyana does not change very much in the mahayana; it is pretty standard. The only difference is the idea of an enlightened attitude, or bodhichitta. When you take the bodhisattva vow, you are actually transplanting bodhichitta in yourself. So bodhichitta is not purely conceptual; it is pragmatic. Out of bodhichitta comes the idea of working with a spiritual friend, or kalyanamitra, as the guide for your practice. You begin to be willing to commit yourself to working with all sentient beings. But before you launch yourself into such a project, you first need lots of training. In that way, the mahayana approach is similar to the hinayana logic of soso tharpa, or self-liberation.

Atisha and the Transmission of the Lojong Teachings

Lojong is one of the mahayana contemplative practices taught in Tibet by Atisha Dipankara. Lo means "intelligence," or "mind"; it is that which can perceive things. Jong means "training" or "processing"; so lojong means "mind training." It is similar to the concept of shinjang, which means "thoroughly processed."

Atisha Dipankara visited Tibet at the beginning of the eleventh century, during the second revival of Buddhism in Tibet, after the time of Padmasambhava and after the period of persecution of Buddhists. When Atisha came to Tibet, he presented teachings in what was to become known as the Kadam school. Ka means "command," or "teaching." It is like the word *Logos,* or "Word," in the Christian tradition, as in "In the beginning was the Word." Ka is a fundamental sacred command. It refers both to absolute truth and to a quality of practicality or workability from the individual's point of view. *Dam* means "instruction." It is oral teaching, personal teaching, a manual on how to handle your life properly. So *Kadam* means "sacred command teaching." The Kadam tradition developed around the time of Marpa and Milarepa, when Tibetan monasticism was beginning to take place and become deeply rooted. The Kagyü teacher Gampopa also belonged to the Kadam order, and incorporated this practice into the Kagyü tradition.

Within the Kadam tradition, there is a contemplative school and an intellectual school. In the contemplative school, the teachings are seen as instructions for practice rather than as an intellectual system. All the commands and messages are regarded as practical and workable for students, and there is an emphasis on contemplative and meditative disciplines. Since the Kagyüpas received instructions on the proper practice of mahayana through Gampopa, who studied with Kadam teachers as well as with Milarepa, we practice lojong based on the contemplative school of the Kadam tradition.

The Geluk tradition developed from the intellectual, or *pandita,* school of the Kadam tradition. *Ge* means "virtue," and *luk* means "system"; so the *Geluk* tradition is the "study of virtue." Gelukpas take a dialectical approach to understanding the mahayana and are philosophically oriented. They study logic, and analyze and intellectualize the teachings, whereas the Kagyü and Nyingma schools, which are my traditions, are referred to as practice lineages.

Atisha's lojong teachings were later summarized in a text by Geshe Chekawa Yeshe Dorje entitled *The Root Text of the Seven Points of Training the Mind.* My discussion of lojong is based on this text and on Jamgön Kongtrül's commentary, called *Changchup Shunglam,* which means "the main path to enlightenment."* *Changchup* means "enlightenment," *shung* means "main," and *lam* is "path"; so *Changchup Shunglam* means "main path to enlightenment." *Shung* is also the word used for "government." For instance, we could call the Tibetan government *pö shung: pö* meaning

---

* Geshe Chekawa's text, along with Jamgön Kongtrül's commentary, were translated by Ken McLeod and published as *The Great Path of Awakening: A Commentary on the Mahayana Teachings of the Seven Points of Mind Training* (Boston: Shambhala Publications, 1987).

Tibet, and *shung* meaning government. The government running the country is supposed to be a wide administration rather than a narrow one. It takes care of the psychology of the country as well as the economics, politics, and domestic situations. *Shunglam* can also mean "highway," or "boulevard," like a road in the middle of a city. It is extraordinarily wide and open, the main path on which everybody travels, the way any good old Buddhist should travel.

In the *Changchup Shunglam,* Atisha Dipankara's teachings on lojong are presented as a sevenfold cleaning or processing of one's mind, based on fifty-nine slogans designed to teach people how to become good mahayanists. These instructions were given to very simple people as well as to educated people. When the mahayana was first presented in Tibet, people were quite savage. So basic teachings, such as trying to be kind to your neighbors instead of destroying them, were revolutionary. In Tibet—or India for that matter—there was not much law and order, and so at first the mahayana teachers were simply trying to establish basic social norms. It took a long time for them to convince people that they could actually trust their next-door neighbors.

We may have gone a bit beyond teachings such as trying to be kind or not gossiping about people we dislike. Social norms about those types of things already exist. In modern society, we have been bombarded with all kinds of moralities and behavioral norms. We also have the police to protect us from doing terrible things to one another. We are told to try to be good citizens, and if we are not, we will get in trouble and end up in jail. But on the way toward trying to be good and kind, our approach has somewhat degenerated. It does not have enough psychological depth or real gut-level compassion. So at this point, although we may be more civilized, we constantly miss the point of *why* we are civilized. We miss the heart of the matter. Apart from being kind and good and keeping out of trouble, there is no greater vision. So it is important to emphasize the psychological aspect of lojong.

THE POWER AND PRACTICALITY OF LOJONG

Lojong is a way of switching allegiance from your ego to buddha nature. It is a process of indoctrination in which your previous preconceptions are wiped out. Quite simply, you indoctrinate yourself into the bodhisattva path and the bodhisattva's way of thinking by realizing that you have in your mind this monolithic principle called buddha nature, bodhichitta, or tathagatagarbha. You indoctrinate yourself so that you cannot get away from that.

The lojong, or mind-training, slogans are very simple, and not particularly philosophical. They are purely what one of the great Kagyü teachers referred to as a "grandmother's finger pointing." When a grandmother says, "This is the place where I used to go and pick corn or collect wild vegetables," she uses her finger rather than writing on paper or using a map. In earlier times, quite possibly students were illiterate or not particularly versed in philosophy, so slogans were used. Jamgon Kongtrul's writing on this practice also very much reflects that approach.

In my own training, I studied a lot of philosophy. So when Jamgön Kongtrül first suggested that I study the seven points of mind training, I was relieved to discover that Buddhism was so simple and practical. You can actually practice it; you can just follow the book and do as it says, which is extraordinarily powerful and such a relief. In my childhood, I enjoyed immensely reading and memorizing the slogans. The simplicity of this text and Jamgön Kongtrül's commentary on it is so precious and direct; it is almost as if it were written for peasants. One of the characteristics of Jamgön Kongtrül's writing is that he can change his tone completely, depending on the subject, as if he were a different author altogether—and in doing so, his relationship with the audience becomes entirely different.

The *Changchup Shunglam* is one of the best books I studied in the early stages of my monastic life. Each time I read this book, I get benefit from it. It is somewhat rugged, but at the same time it is soothing. I was planning to become a simple monk. I was going to study these things and become a good Buddhist, a contemplative person—and such a thread still holds throughout my life. In spite of the complications in my life, I still feel that I am basically a simple, romantic Buddhist who has immense feeling toward the teachers and the teaching.

Lojong teachings are very powerful, particularly when you are facing difficulties. You should realize the importance of these slogans, understand as much as you can, and memorize them. What has been said is like a drop of golden liquid. There is a hard-edged quality of cutting down preconceptions and other ego battles, but at the same time, there is always a soft spot of devotion and simplicity that you can never forget. I am not particularly trying to be dramatic, but I really do feel extraordinarily positive about Jamgön Kongtrül and his approach to this teaching.

The lojong teachings include several points of mahayana discipline, but the foremost discipline is to develop ultimate bodhichitta. Compassion comes from the level of ultimate bodhichitta, an unconditioned state where you begin to realize that you and others do not exist. Therefore, you are able to extend yourself, which gives you joy and further joy. It makes you smile and appreciate the world. But it is important to begin at the beginning, almost at the kitchen-sink level. It may not be all that entertaining, but once you understand the basics, you could play and dance and appreciate the phenomenal world.

In order to practice lojong, you need hinayana training, and you also need to develop compassion and gentleness. At the hinayana level, you disown your arrogance and competitiveness. Beyond that, the mahayana touch is acknowledging your basic goodness, so you don't feel you are completely cut off and hopeless. In the mahayana, you are developing an attitude of strength and energy. You are beginning to trust yourself. You trust that your mind is always workable, that you can actually train yourself. You trust that you are not as bad as you thought, but you can apply yourself by means of discipline and meditation. By witnessing the spiritual friend and their relationship to the lineage, you see that you too can do it. So an overall feeling of positive atmosphere and positive logic is created. Because you have developed such gentleness and sympathy for yourself, you begin to feel frustrated with those who cannot click into this possibility. You feel sorry for them, and out of that frustration you develop compassion.

GETTING A FEEL FOR THE SLOGANS

It is important to understand the structure of the Atisha slogans. Each of them fits into a certain section of your practice. That is why we have seven different groups of slogans, or seven points of mind training. Some slogans apply to your sitting practice on the cushion, and others apply to what happens before, during, and after that. The first slogan is about preliminaries to mind training. The second set of slogans is about bodhichitta, beginning with ultimate bodhichitta and followed by relative bodhichitta. These slogans have to do with simplifying your practice into the ultimate bodhichitta level, and then applying bodhichitta and making it workable, starting with very simple things. Then there are the postmeditation slogans, which are connected with cultivating bodhichitta in your everyday life. These slogans are guidelines for transforming difficulties, working with both living and dying, evaluating your mind training, and developing discipline. They are general rules for how to conduct yourself.

The teaching on the seven points of mind training is like being presented with a fish. You have the head of the fish, the body of the fish, and the tail of the fish—and you need to know which part you should cook, which one you should throw away, and which one you should debone, so that you can have a good meal.

Slogan practice is based on the six paramitas: generosity, discipline, patience, exertion, meditation, and prajna. Bodhisattvas, or would-be bodhisattvas, are like the knights of the medieval tradition. They are wealthy with generosity and they wear excellent perfumes, so they feel good. Then they put on their armor, get on their horses, and ride: and as they do so, they have their weapons around them, their swords and so forth. That seems to be the basic point of the six paramitas—to become a really good warrior.

In order to practice the slogans, your mind has to mix much more with the dharma. Rather than studying these teachings as a scholarly exercise, you have to learn how to listen to the dharma—how to study properly and apply what you have learned. It does not matter if you can come up with a bright idea. What counts is actually knowing how to apply the teachings. If you keep working with the slogans, you will begin to understand the geography of the whole thing. It is like driving into a town: once you understand the layout, you have no problem knowing which way to turn. You will know when to turn left and when to turn right. You begin to get a feeling for the town. If you had just memorized the names of the streets, you probably wouldn't get very far. But once you learn the geography of the town, you even know how to take backstreets to avoid traffic.

You can practice the slogans with the people you work with at your job, the clerk at the shop where you buy your groceries or your clothes, the driver who cuts in front of you—anyone you relate with. The slogans are always applicable, so you have lots of opportunities. People might have mistaken beliefs about what is true. They might disagree about whether human beings came about from karmic formations or were created by God, but that doesn't matter. What matters is the personal level, how we relate with people. What matters is whether we complain or we don't complain. When we cash our check at the bank, how do we relate with that situation? When we eat in a restaurant, how do we relate with that?

Slogan practice is universal. The idea is to use the slogans in dealing with anybody who is around us, anybody within our radius, anybody who has some connection with us.

You can actually sharpen your prajna by relating with people in this way, and they begin to respond to it. They begin to feel that something very precious is taking place. From a practical point of view, if you adopt these principles, things actually work out much more efficiently for you. Waitresses become more friendly, taxicab drivers become joyful, and shopkeepers more accommodating. If you are projecting something that is good and decent, people always pick up on that. It's great!

You can practice the slogans on the spot, whenever a situation presents itself to you. But you don't just say, "Now I'm going to practice slogan number four." That would be absurd, because the situation may not exist to do number four. The idea is that slogans arise in response to a particular situation. The actual words of these slogans bounce in my mind always, even in my dreams. They are very powerful and significant to me. Likewise, they could bounce around in your mind—in your dreams, before dreams, and in relationships with people. They should always be in the back of your mind. When your mind is tuned in to such simple and beautiful words, these slogans arise naturally. It happens that way, rather than actually having to recall them like the Declaration of Independence. They are so innocent and absurd, in a sense, but their absurdity is so insightful.

Slogan practice is delightful. It is very direct and personal, and everything is spelled out. It is much better than the moralistic approach of thinking that you need to stop doing something wrong. The slogans are not particularly traffic signs, they are reminders. And each time a certain slogan occurs to you, the slogans as a whole become more meaningful.

CAUSE, EFFECT, AND ESSENCE

It is worthwhile to realize and understand these slogans, to study and memorize them. They are direct and simple, no big deal, and at the same time they are quite insightful. If I give you too many details, it is not going to help; your mind is going to be further crumpled and crippled. It is better to exercise your own intelligence and understanding of the depth of these slogans. In discussing the slogans and presenting the dharma altogether, I would like to provide you with possibilities of playing with your own intelligence, rather than giving everything to you and having you repeat it back like an idiot.

One way to work with the slogans is to look at them in terms of cause, effect, and essence. It is very simple, once you know how to do it. You could apply this approach to anything. For instance, if you are drinking a cup of coffee, you could ask, what is the cause of drinking a cup of coffee, what is the effect, and what happens in essence? You could also begin with the essence, and work your way back. According to this logic, in looking at a statement, first you determine the basic nature of what it is conveying. For instance, you could say that the basic nature or essence of water is wetness. You could then say that providing water to people or to plants is the cause that gives rise to the effect of quenching thirst or irrigating the land to make things grow. And as a totality, you could say that water provides fundamental wetness, so that plants can grow and people can survive. That is how the whole thing works, and that is how I was trained in my own discipline. I was never told what a particular subject actually does—for instance, what nirvana does. But I was told exactly what water does and what fire does, and I was taught how to work with the logic of cause, effect, and essence.

34

Undermining Aggression

When you begin to realize aggression as it is, there is a sudden flash of spaciousness, and the aggression is completely cleared out. It is like living in a stuffy room, and suddenly the window is wide open and fresh air is coming in. You are crammed in with the aggression and the resentment, but then you begin to see an entirely different approach, a completely new sense of things, a flash.

I N T H E style of the practicing lineage, we are viewing the bodhisattva path in terms of meditation instruction, with a meditative approach rather than a purely theoretical one. We have already discussed the inspiration that comes from tathagatagarbha, or buddha nature, and how ordinary states can be transformed into tathagatagarbha. Realizing that you possess buddha nature gives you a sense of gratification and honor, but at the same time it is like a poor person finding a diamond: you are uncertain how to handle it or approach it. That uncertainty and bewilderment become encouragement to seek further discipline on the bodhisattva path. The bodhisattva path is by no means theoretical; it is experiential.

Once you have taken the bodhisattva vow and committed yourself to the bodhisattva's way, you have the idea that you should be compassionate to all sentient beings, but where to begin is uncertain. Surprisingly, the way to start on the bodhisattva path is not by meditating on shunyata alone, but by training the mind, or lojong. There are various ways of training the mind, but the starting point is developing an absence of aggression. In lojong practice, you adopt an attitude of seeing yourself and your aggression clearly and properly. In order to see your own aggression, you have to become open to yourself and be willing to face your self-conceit and self-deception. You have to be willing to see through it. Nobody is as close to you as you yourself are, so you have to become your own teacher—with the help of a spiritual friend, of course.

THREE TYPES OF AGGRESSION

In the hinayana, the emphasis is on nonpassion, and in the mahayana, the emphasis is on nonaggression. There are various types of aggression. Deep-rooted aggression is constant. Whenever there is a gap, there is always aggression shining through. With deep-rooted aggression, you are perpetually hungry and fundamentally unhappy. Deep-rooted aggression is an underlying and ongoing experience. It is basic negativity.

Analytical aggression is developing your own logic in order to prove that your particular aggression or anger is valid. Because such and such a situation happened and you don't like that, you would like to reshape your opponent, your friend, or your environment. You are trying to create reinforcement for your aggression. Analytical aggression is also referred to as negative negativity.

Then there is the sudden wind of aggression, which is totally illogical. It is aggression without logic. You don't know where it came from, it just hits you, and you become a ball of cast-iron. Sometimes you can't even talk. The sudden wind of aggression jumps between the other two, taking advantage of the deep-rooted aggression or the analytical one.

All types of aggression are predominantly based on not giving. They are related with a sense of meanness and an ungenerous attitude that goes directly against the idea of karuna, or compassion. Aggression is based on shifting and moving. It is like the analogy of the moon reflecting on moving water: the water is disturbed, so when the moon shines on it, the picture of the moon is broken up into fragmented patterns. You do see some fragments of the moon, but you have no clear and undistorted picture of the moon as a whole.

Aggression covers a large area; it is more than anger alone. Sometimes it has the element of duty, of trying to live up to what you are supposed to be. It can manifest as a combination of guilt and righteousness. It may manifest as the fear of losing your ground, or the fear that you might have made a mistake but you still have to be righteous. Aggression may show in people's cowardly little smiles in the midst of arguments, which are not genuine smiles, but signs of hesitation or guilt. When such people reassert themselves, their faces become red.

Aggression seems to be related with the realm of hell. At this point, the bodhisattva has not yet transcended that realm. You have begun to prevent the cause, to shake up the possibility of it, but you still have to wipe it out completely. You may discover that you have the potential of buddha nature, but if you use that discovery to strengthen your ego, you are re-sowing the seeds of the hell realm. This does not mean that you are going to be literally thrown into hell, but rather that you are creating hell on the spot. Because the hell realm is the manifestation of aggression, you could create the hell realm anywhere. It has been said that the bodhisattva exterminates the realm of hell completely. In fact, all six realms should be completely wiped out.

LOJONG PRACTICE: DELIBERATE COMPASSION

With lojong, you are developing what is called *mik-che kyi nying-je*. *Nying-je* is "compassion," *kyi* is "of," *mik* is "deliberateness," *che* is "with"; so *mik-che kyi nying-je* is "deliberate compassion." It is the manual practice of deliberately manufacturing compassion. In order to develop compassion, you have to go beyond aggression, to be without anger. It seems to be absolutely necessary to tame oneself and train oneself.

Often people do not want to do contemplative practice when they are really enraged. When you are resentful about everything, it is very difficult to practice. It feels like a tremendous insult. But it is particularly at such times that the bodhisattva path begins to dawn on you. These times are highly opportune moments to practice the bodhisattva's type of awareness of breathing.*

Deliberate compassion is the first development of compassion: you are developing compassion by means of the awareness of your breathing. On the bodhisattva path, you are not so much trying to suppress aggression, but rather to get over the hypocrisy of failing to see the aggression. The practice of training one's mind, or lojong, consists of various mental exercises in which you recognize and deliberately let go of the tenseness of the aggression in your sitting meditation practice. To do so, you work

---

* A reference to sending and taking practice, or tonglen. See chapter 37, "Point Two: Training in Relative Bodhichitta."

with the awareness of breathing as in shamatha-vipashyana, but as you breathe out, you give away whatever desire you have, and as you breathe in, you take in anything you do not want or that you try to avoid. That is the deliberate technique of the lojong method, which is a type of *anapana-sati,* or mindfulness-of-breath practice.

When you practice lojong, there is a general awareness of your total being, as in vipashyana practice, but there is more to it than that: there is a quality of deliberateness. For example, if you want to borrow something from somebody and that person refuses to lend it to you, you may get rather angry and upset about that. The subject of your practice of contemplation in that case would be to feel the pleasure and gratification you would have gotten out of that object, and also to feel your immense irritation because the person would not lend it to you. You breathe in that which you did not want, and you breathe out that which you did want. A person has to have a real understanding of what aggression is before doing such a practice, but it is a very powerful exercise and very necessary.

You should have already developed shamatha and vipashyana before practicing any new techniques. Once you are able to deal with basic sitting practice, you will also be able to do the bodhisattva type of breathing practice. If you were to begin with lojong practice immediately, without the grounding of shamatha and vipashyana, it might feel like punishment, so it is important to first work with the basic meditation technique and develop some discipline and patience. The sitting practice begins to do something to your psychological state. Whether you become more and more neurotic, or less and less neurotic, something is still beginning to work.

It may seem hypocritical to deliberately cultivate compassion, but there is the possibility of hypocrisy with everything you do. So it is recommended that no matter what you feel, even if you feel hypocritical at the beginning, you continue to cultivate compassion. You particularly do that in situations in your life where aggression is very vivid, for then you will have some kind of experience. When Atisha Dipankara, a well-known teacher of lojong, was invited to Tibet, he had heard that the Tibetans were very kind and gentle people, so he thought he should bring somebody along to remind him of his compassion practice. He brought a very short-tempered Bengali tea-boy with him. Later, he said that he need not have brought the Bengali boy because there were enough Tibetans who were equally as bad. So you need constant reminders in your life, not only on the bodhisattva path, but in Buddhism in general.

The path consists in taking advantage of whatever is happening to you at the moment. You take advantage of aggression, or passion, or whatever occurs in your life, and work with it. If you apply compassion practice when you are in a really bad mood, if you sit and do it, you will have a very real experience of it. This does not mean that when you get angry, you have to dash out to your meditation cushion and practice compassion, but you can recall that instant or something like it and work with that. You will definitely have enough memories to work with—they can last for weeks, if not years.

NONDELIBERATE COMPASSION

The next development of compassion is *mikme nying-je*. *Mik* is "deliberate," *me* is "not"; so *mikme nying-je* is "compassion without deliberate practice." It is the second stage of compassion, which follows the first stage, like meditation and postmeditation. In meditation, you sit and practice the awareness of breathing; in postmeditation, the experience of awareness comes to you in daily life situations. First you sit, then you get up and do other things, but the impression of the meditation, or the awareness, flashes on you. Likewise, the second stage of compassion is unformed, not manufactured.

At first, you need some kind of deliberate practice or direction. If there is no direction, there is no way to proceed along the path. There is just hypothetical shunyata, which does not lead you anywhere. You need effort, but that effort has a watcher-less quality. You just practice, rather than watching yourself practice. You work with what comes up in your life. Life presents you with things, and you just work with them as you go along. That is the very idea of taking refuge in the dharma as path.

REMOVING RESENTMENT

With lojong, you are acknowledging and facing that which is rather insulting to you. You let yourself be the lowest of the low. Later, you begin to realize that aggression is somewhat workable, that it does not seem to be as painful as before. It is not so much that you are destroying the aggression itself, but you are removing the resentment caused by that aggression.

Resentment has the quality of a spoiled infant's angry cry. You resent that you didn't get what you wanted, and underlying that is the basic resentment that you have been trapped and you feel helpless. Resentment ties you inward, and there is no communication, no openness.

Aggression causes tremendous resentment and tightness, but just getting angry is not particularly problematic. With lojong, you are not giving in to the aggression, but you are accentuating the reality of the aggression. You are being accommodating to the aggression. If you can get used to aggression, that is a tremendous achievement. You have solved the rest of the world's problems as well as your own. Through vipashyana practice, you notice when the mind is filled with resentment, and because you notice it, it evaporates. Lojong is an extension of that approach.

Basically, in order to become spontaneous, you have to be deliberate. Since you are in the samsaric world already, you cannot start from the top. The attainment of enlightenment is not sudden; it is always gradual. It is like exercise: if your body is very stiff, getting more exercise might be very painful in the beginning, but you need to exercise in order to move more smoothly. In this case, you are training to loosen up your psychological body, to loosen that very stiff aggression through the practice of the six paramitas.

There is a certain true-believer quality in the teachings. Practice-lineage people are not scholarly or analytical; they just do what they are told. You are given certain things to do that sound very simpleminded. Such practices are designed to manufacture something, to twist your mind a certain way, to steer you in a certain direction. You can't believe it will work, but once you begin to do it and to actually get into it, it does work.

You might think lojong practice is a very benevolent and somewhat love-and-light approach of trying to be good to everybody and remain pure and humble, but that is not the case. In fact, it is one of the bravest practices you can ever do, if you can actually let go. It is not so much that when you give, you lose. The problem is the resistance. With lojong, your aggression becomes workable; a spacious and a refreshing quality begins to arise. As you become more advanced, the anger itself begins to produce spaciousness. But even if you are not so advanced, the afterthought of looking back on your aggression and resentment can bring a sense of spaciousness.

Spaciousness is totally free of logic, totally free of reasoning mind. It is threefold purity. At the hinayana level, sudden, abstract, nonverbal, nonconceptualized flashes begin to dawn on you, so that the meditation comes to you. Similarly, at the mahayana level, when you begin to realize aggression as it is, there is a sudden flash of spaciousness, and the aggression is completely cleared out. It is like living in a stuffy room, and suddenly the window is wide open and fresh air is coming in. You are crammed in with the aggression and the resentment, but then you begin to see an entirely different approach, a completely new sense of things, a flash.

With threefold purity, there is automatically a letting-go process. When aggression comes up, you begin to realize that aggression has no root; it is just a phantom. When you, your actions, and the object of your actions have become open, almost nonexistent, the second type of compassion, nondeliberate compassion, begins to develop. You may begin to feel relief that, after all, you are on the right path and something is happening to you. That sense of gratification and appreciation is not a problem.

Compassion at this point is infant compassion, on the level of trying to crawl. It is not the full warmth and love of a bodhisattva's compassion, but the state of nonaggression as the result of a consciously developed process. Such compassion becomes very personal. You are building compassion within yourself in order to remove your own pain and aggression, so it is more like relief or medicine than acting out of compassion for others. Having done that, the shifting reflections finally begin to settle down, and you can see the clear moon on the water without any distortion.

35

Point One: The Preliminaries, Which Are a Basis for Dharma Practice

This slogan establishes the contrast between samsara, which is the epitome of pain, imprisonment, and insanity, and the teacher, who is the embodiment of openness, freedom, and sanity as the fundamental basis for all practice.

I

First, train in the preliminaries.

Point one includes just one slogan. The idea of first training in the preliminaries is that when you are practicing the slogans as well as when you are going about your daily life, you should always maintain an awareness of the four reminders.

The first reminder is the *preciousness of human life* and the particular good fortune of living in an environment in which you can hear the teachings of buddhadharma.

The second reminder is the *reality of death,* which comes up suddenly and without warning.

The third reminder is the *entrapment of karma.* It is the realization that whatever you do, whether virtuous or unvirtuous, only further entraps you in the chain of cause and effect.

The fourth reminder is the *intensity and inevitability of suffering* for yourself and all sentient beings.

With that attitude as a base, you should call upon your teacher with devotion, inviting into yourself the atmosphere of sanity inspired by their example, and vowing to cut the roots of further ignorance and suffering. In the mahayana, you relate to the teacher as someone who cheers you up from depression and brings you down from excitement, a kind of moderator principle. The teacher is regarded as important from that point of view.

Furthermore, in terms of the spiritual path, it is traditionally considered that the only pure loving object is somebody who can show you the path. You could have a loving relationship with your parents, relatives, and so forth, but there are still problems with that: your neurosis goes along with it. A pure love affair can only take place with one's teacher. Your connection with that ideal sympathetic object is used as a starting point, a way of developing a relationship beyond your own neurosis. So the relationship with the teacher is tied in very closely with the development of maitri, or loving-kindness.

This slogan establishes the contrast between samsara, which is the epitome of pain, imprisonment, and insanity, and the teacher, who is the embodiment of openness, freedom, and sanity as the fundamental basis for all practice. As such, it is heavily influenced by the vajrayana tradition.

36

Point Two: Resting in Ultimate Bodhichitta

An understanding of ultimate bodhichitta can only come about through compassion. A purely logical, professional, or scientific approach does not bring you to that understanding. . . . But to realize how to be compassionate, you first have to know how to be. . . . So ultimate bodhichitta is preparation for relative bodhichitta. That is why the slogans are presented in that order.

P OINT TWO includes five ultimate, or absolute, bodhichitta slogans, and four relative bodhichitta slogans. It begins with the ultimate bodhichitta slogans. These five slogans are very simple, actually, just another perspective on the practice of meditation. They provide reference points for familiarizing yourself with ultimate bodhichitta and are connected with the paramita of generosity. In fact, generosity is the foundation of both ultimate and relative bodhichitta. The paramita of generosity is based on not holding back, but giving constantly. It is self-existing, complete openness—and the best way to open yourself up is to make friends with yourself and others. The opposite of generosity is stinginess. It is holding back and having a poverty mentality. With generosity, you go beyond your poverty attitude and develop a sense of richness and self-sufficiency.

An understanding of ultimate bodhichitta can only come about through compassion. A purely logical, professional, or scientific approach does not bring you to that understanding. A lot of us, seemingly, and very shockingly, are not particularly compassionate. Therefore, we have to develop compassion. But to realize how to be compassionate, you first have to know how to *be*. Learning how to love your grandma, or to love your flea or mosquito, comes later. So ultimate bodhichitta is preparation for relative bodhichitta. That is why the slogans are presented in that order.

In ultimate, or absolute, bodhichitta practice, you are not trying to tell yourself why things are as they are, but you are simply coming back to a basic state of existence. It is like coming back to the breath in shamatha. The ultimate bodhichitta slogans are purely confirmations or ways of recognizing experience. According to Jamgön Kongtrül, slogan practice is known as an analytical approach to practice, but it is also a yogic practice. The slogans are experiential as well as analytical.

Absolute bodhichitta is similar to absolute shunyata. And whenever there is absolute shunyata, you need an understanding of absolute compassion at the same time. Shunyata is basically the realization of nonexistence or emptiness. The more we realize nonexistence, the more we can afford to be compassionate and giving. Usually we would like to hold on to our territory and fixate on that particular ground, and once we begin to fixate, we have no way to give. But when we begin to realize that there is no ground, that we are ultimately free, nonaggressive, and open—and when we realize that we are actually nonexistent ourselves—we can give. We have lots to gain and nothing to lose at that point. We are *not*—we are *no*, rather.*

The experience of shunyata is also related to devotion. You begin to feel loneliness and aloneness at the same time. With shunyata, what you have heard and what you have experienced become part of your conviction.

THE OPEN WOUND OF COMPASSION

Slogan practice is a way of training the mind toward compassion. It is based on a feeling of softness or sore spot. Compassion is said to be like having a pimple on your body that is very sore, so sore that you do not want to rub it because it hurts. Why? Because even in the midst of immense aggression, insensitivity, or laziness in your life, you always have a sore spot. You always have some point you can cultivate, or at least not bruise. Every human being and every animal has that kind of basic sore spot. It is always in you, whether you are crazy, dull, aggressive, or egotistical.

---

* The word *not* implies an object, whereas the word *no* stands alone, and thus *no* is free of any dualistic implications.

That such an open wound is always there is very inconvenient and problematic. We don't like it; we would like to be tough. We would like to fight, to defeat our enemies on the spot and come out strong so that no one attacks us and we do not have to defend any aspect of ourselves. In that way, even if somebody decides to hit us back, we are not wounded—and hopefully nobody will hit us on that sore spot. But without exception, there always will be a sore spot.

That sore spot has nothing to do with Buddhism or with Christianity. It is just an open wound, a very simple open wound. With such a wound, at least we are accessible somewhere. We are not completely covered with a suit of armor all the time. Such a relief! Thank earth! Because of that particular sore spot, even cosmic monsters such as Mussolini, Mao Tse-tung, or Hitler can still fall in love. Because of that sore spot, we could appreciate beauty, art, poetry, or music. We could be covered with cast-iron, but there is still that sore spot in us, which is fantastic. That sense of sore spot is known as embryonic compassion. We have some kind of gap, some discrepancy in our state of being that allows basic sanity to shine through. Our level of sanity could be very primitive. Our sore spot could be purely the love of tortillas or the love of curries, but that is good enough. It is an opening. It does not matter what we love, as long as there is a sore spot of some kind. That sore spot is good. It is where germs could get in and begin to take possession of us and influence our system. It is precisely how the compassionate attitude begins to take place.

Not only do we have an external wound, but there is also an inner wound, which is called tathagatagarbha, or buddha nature. Tathagatagarbha is like having immeasurable slits in our heart. Our heart is wounded; it is being sliced and bruised by wisdom and compassion. When the external wound and the internal wound begin to meet and to communicate, we realize that our whole being is made out of one complete sore spot, which is called bodhisattva fever. At that point, we no longer have any way to defend ourselves. That cosmic wound is gigantic—it is both an inner wound and an external wound.

That feeling of vulnerability is compassion. It is the living flame of love, if you would like to call it that. But we should be very careful what we say about love. Before puberty, one cannot understand sexual love affairs. Likewise, since we have not broken through to an understanding of what our soft spot is all about, we cannot really talk about compassion, we can only talk about passion. It may sound grandiose to talk about compassion, but actually the word *compassion* does not say as much as *love*. Love is very heavy, whereas compassion is a kind of passion, which is easy to work with. Compassion is like a slit in our skin; it is like a wound.

ULTIMATE BODHICHITTA

2

Regard all dharmas as dreams.

Regarding all dharmas as dreams is an expression of compassion and openness. The reason you can regard all dharmas as dreams is because of your training in shamatha and vipashyana. You can do this because you have experienced that your basic existence is questionable as an ego entity. According to this slogan, love and hate, pain and pleasure, aggression and passion—whatever comes and goes in your life—could be regarded as dreams. Nothing ever happens. But because nothing happens, everything happens. When you want to be entertained, nothing seems to happen. But in this case, although everything is just a thought in your mind, a lot of underlying percolation takes place. That "nothing happening" is the experience of openness, and that percolation is the experience of compassion.

Basically, everything we experience is a dream. We have been sleep-walking; we have been sleeping and dreaming for a long time, and are doing so right now. According to the abhidharma, nothing going on in the mind is registered properly and fully. Our mind has been working haphazardly, so we are really not good thinkers. According to this slogan, everything should simply be regarded as not real. We realize that thoughts of love and hate are just profiles of the things we see, and do not in themselves provide any benefit or harm.

The practice of this ultimate bodhichitta slogan seems to be primarily oriented toward the mind-only philosophical school of yogachara. According to yogachara, the phenomenal world is not to be regarded as solid, but as a dream. You can experience that dreamlike quality in sitting practice. When you are focusing on your breath, suddenly discursive thoughts begin to arise. You begin to see things, to hear things, and to feel things. But all those perceptions are none other than your own mental creation. In the same way, you can see that your hate for your enemy, your love for your friends, and your attitudes to money, food, and wealth, are all discursive thoughts. If you did not have a mind, you would not be able to perceive anything, but since you do have a mind, you perceive things. Therefore, what you perceive is a product of your mind, which uses your sense organs as channels for the sense perceptions.

Regarding dharmas as dreams does not mean that you become fuzzy and woolly, or that everything has an edge of sleepiness about it. You might actually have a good dream, vivid and graphic. Regarding dharmas as dreams means that, although you might think that things are very solid, the way you perceive them is soft and dreamlike. You realize that whatever you experience in your life—pain, pleasure, happiness, sadness, grossness, refinement, sophistication, crudeness, hot, cold, or whatever—is just memories. Your memories may be very vivid, but they are not regarded as invincible. Everything is shifty. So things have a dreamlike quality, but at the same time the productions of your mind are quite vivid.

3

Examine the nature of unborn awareness.

Because you could get caught up in the fascination of regarding all dharmas as dreams and perpetuate unnecessary visions and fantasies, it is important to contemplate the nature of unborn insight. The reason insight is known as "unborn" is because we have no idea of its history. We have no idea where this mind, our crazy mind, began. It has no shape, no color, no particular portrait or characteristics. It flickers on and off, off and on, all the time. Sometimes it is hibernating, sometimes it is active and all over the place.

When you look at your own mind beyond the perceptual level alone— which you can't actually do, but you pretend to do—you find that there is nothing there, and you realize that there is nothing to hold on to. So your mind is unborn. At the same time, your mind is insightful because you still perceive things. You should contemplate these things by looking into who is actually perceiving dharmas as dreams.

In mindfulness practice, you are mindful of something: you are mindful of yourself, you are mindful of your atmosphere, and you are mindful of your breath. But if you look at *why* you are mindful—beyond *what* you are mindful of—you begin to find that there is no root. If you look further, you will find that your mind has no color and no shape. Your mind is, basically speaking, somewhat blank. There is nothing to it. When you try to find out why you see things, why you hear sounds, why you feel, and why you smell, you find a kind of blankness, and everything begins to dissolve. By looking in this way, you are cultivating the possibility of shunyata.

In examining the nature of unborn insight, you look at your own mind, just basic simple mind, the thinking process that exists in you. Just look at that! See that! Contemplating does not mean analyzing or dividing things into sections; it is just viewing things as they are in the ordinary sense. Looking at your mind in this way goes along quite well with hinayana mindfulness training. When you sit, your mind fluctuates constantly. Look at that. Just look at that!

Insight is unborn because you have not manufactured it, which is a relief. And you are further relieved, because you can contemplate it. Insight is crystal clear; nobody has made it up, nobody has manufactured it. It is not the product of any philosopher's thinking—it is right here. First thought is best thought, precisely on the spot. Unborn insight is pure consciousness with no defilements and no anger. It has an element of buddha nature because it is so pure, so basic, and so ordinary.

Realizing the nature of unborn insight is the first discovery of *künshi ngangluk kyi gewa,* the "natural virtue of alaya." Sometimes it is timid; therefore, it is good. With such timidity, you might begin to meet your own mind. That quality of timidity is fine; it makes you very sweet and gentle. Then you rise up a little bit. You begin to get into *künshi ngangluk kyi gewa,* which is slightly less timid, and finally you get to bodhichitta. You are still timid and meek, but you are also slightly perky. You are meek and perky put together, which is excellent. It is so pure, genuine, and real.

4

Self-liberate even the antidote.

The antidote referred to in this slogan is the realization of emptiness. By examining the nature of unborn insight, you see that your mind is colored by phenomenal experiences, that it has no root. Realizing that your discursive thoughts have no origin is an antidote or helpful suggestion. But you may begin to develop a twist of logic, thinking that if nothing has any root, why bother? What is the point? So you need to go beyond that antidote. You should not hang on to that so-whatness or naiveté of it.

Because of the nature of shunyata experience, and the occasional glimpse in your mind of nothing being existent, you may think nothing great or small really matters very much. It is all a kind of backslapping joke: ha-ha, yuk, yuk, yuk. Nothing matters, so let it go. All is shunyata, so who cares? Since everything is empty, you may think you can murder, you can meditate, you can perform your art, you can do all kinds of things.

You may think that you can do whatever you want, that as long as you are meditative, everything is going to be fine. But there is something very tricky about that approach. In meditation, we are not particularly seeking enlightenment or tranquillity—we are trying to get over our deception.

Some people view meditation as the simple experience of tranquillity. They may regard going to the movies every evening as their meditation, or watching television, grooming their horse, feeding their dog, or taking a long walk in the woods. They may even regard hunting as their meditation. Other people claim that they do not have to sit because they have always "understood." I do not trust such people.

Dwelling on emptiness in that way is a misinterpretation called the poison of shunyata. You have to work with that antidote, but not dwell on it. However, thinking that the point is *not* to dwell on it could also be problematic. In fact, the idea of this slogan is that antidotes of any kind are not regarded as appropriate.

5

Rest in the nature of alaya, the essence.

According to Buddhist psychology, there are eight types of consciousness. This slogan is about transcending the first seven consciousnesses and resting in the eighth, or alaya consciousness. The first six consciousnesses are connected with sensory perception, or the meeting of a sense organ, a sense object, and a corresponding sense consciousness. The six sense consciousnesses are sight, smell, hearing, touch, taste, and mind consciousness, which is the basic coordinating factor governing the other five. The mind consciousness uses those particular instruments to perceive mental objects, or thoughts. Beyond all that is the intention of doing so, which is the seventh consciousness, or nuisance mind. The seventh consciousness puts energy into all those perceptions and brings the whole thing together. It has a quality of fascination or inquisitiveness. Going further, beyond all that, you find a level of experience known as the alaya consciousness. There is a resting place, which could be called primitive shamatha.

Resting in alaya means that you do not follow your discursive thoughts, but you try to treat yourself well. Basically, you do not follow fixed logic, discursive thoughts, or conceptual ideas of any kind. Generally when you look out at someone or something, you tend to check back on yourself, but you could look further, beyond yourself. When you do so, you are brought back to that resting place, where the orders and information are coming from.

Starting from basic alaya, you develop alaya consciousness, which makes distinctions. You begin to create a separation between this and that, who and whom, what and what. That is the notion of consciousness, or self-consciousness. You begin to distinguish who is on your side and who is on their side, so to speak. But basic alaya does not have any bias. That is why it is called natural virtue. It is neutral, neither male nor female; therefore, it is not on either side, and there is no question of courting.

Basic wakefulness, or sugatagarbha, is beyond alaya. It is pre-alaya, but at the same time encompasses alaya. Alaya has basic goodness, but sugatagarbha has greater goodness—it is wakefulness itself. From that point of view, even basic alaya could be said to be a consciousness of some kind. Although it is not an official category of consciousness, it is a kind of awareness, and maybe even a form of samsaric mind. Sugatagarbha is beyond that. It is indestructible; it is the ancestor or parent of alaya.

We could describe the process of perception with the analogy of a film projector. First you have the screen, the phenomenal world. Then you project yourself onto that phenomenal world. You have the film—the fickleness of mind, which constantly changes frames—so you have a moving object projected onto the screen by the machinery of the projector. There are lots of teeth to catch the film, and mechanisms to make sure that the projection is continuous. This is precisely the same situation as the sense organs: you look and you listen, and as you listen, you look. You connect things together, although they are shifting completely every moment by means of time.

Behind the whole setup is a bulb, which projects everything onto the screen. That bulb is the cause of the whole thing. Resting in the nature of alaya is like resting in the nature of that bulb. Alaya is brilliant and shining; it does not give in to the fickleness of the rest of the machine.

That bulb has no concern with the screen or how the image is coming through. Resting in alaya is the actual practice of ultimate bodhichitta. It is what happens during sitting practice. Ultimate bodhichitta is the realization that phenomena cannot be regarded as solid, but at the same time, phenomena have a self-luminous quality. So alaya refers to experience, not simply to the structural, mechanical process of projection.

In the analogy of the film projector, the bulb can be taken out and put into a flashlight. If you have a flashlight with a beam of light coming out of it, you have to hold it properly in order to use the light. The flashlight is like relative bodhichitta; holding it properly and making it work for you is absolute bodhichitta. You need absolute bodhichitta so that the light will shine everywhere, wherever you need it. Resting your mind in alaya produces absolute bodhichitta constantly.

By resting your mind in the alaya consciousness, in clear and nondiscriminating mind, you are trying to free yourself from sevenfold mind, or the first seven consciousnesses. But before you can transcend sevenfold mind, you have to work with the bulb. Instead of monkeying with the projector, you could just take the bulb out of your projector, screw it into your regular old-fashioned lamp, and look at it. So there is just the bare minimum of you and your mind, very simply. That is the self-liberating alaya. That good old bulb is the real thing. You have your light or you don't—you switch off or you switch on.

Even in ordinary situations, if you actually trace back to find out where everything comes from, you will find a primitive resting level. You could rest in that quality of basic existence, or alaya. However, you should not cultivate alaya as an end in itself, which would be dangerous, but you should use it as a stepping-stone. In this case, we are talking about alaya as a clear mind—as simplicity, clarity, and nondiscursive thought—as alaya consciousness. We have to be very clear on this. We are not trying to grasp the buddha nature immediately, but we are trying to work on our basic premises. For the first time, we are learning to slow down.

Alaya is described in the text as naturally good, as basic goodness. That quality of basic goodness applies to personal wholesomeness as well as to dedication to others. It is like saying you are a good person who can take care of your family and friends. Basic goodness is related to both alaya and bodhichitta. However, bodhichitta is more active and illuminating, while alaya is a resting quality with no grudge against anything, just satisfaction.

With the third slogan, "Examine the nature of unborn awareness," you look at your mind and trace back where your perceptions are coming from. With the fifth slogan, "Rest in the nature of alaya, the essence," instead of getting caught up in your visual and auditory perceptions, you come back home. You return to "home sweet home," which is your alaya. The alaya is where everything began, so you are returning to central headquarters. You see that all your activities—sight, smell, sound, and everything else that happens—are a production of that home ground. Having recognized that, you come back to where they began to manifest, and you rest in the needlessness of those productions. Alaya is a starting point and a returning point. It is internalizing. Resting in the nature of alaya takes for granted that you trust yourself already. It assumes that you don't have to run away from yourself all the time in order to get something from outside. You can just come home and relax.

6

In postmeditation, be a child of illusion.

Becoming a child of illusion means that you continue in postmeditation what you have experienced in your sitting practice. During postmeditation, you take the bulb out of your projector. You might not have the screen or the film at this point, but you still carry a flashlight. You transfer the bulb into your flashlight, and you carry it with you all the time.

Illusion does not mean haziness, confusion, or mirage. You realize that after you finish sitting practice, you do not have to solidify phenomena, but you can continue your practice. If things become heavy and solid, you can flash mindfulness and awareness into them. In that way, you begin to see that everything is workable. Your attitude is that the phenomenal world is not evil—that "they" are not going to attack you, or destroy you, or kill you. Everything is workable and soothing. You swim along in your phenomenal world. You can't just float; you have to use your limbs and swim with the basic stroke of mindfulness-awareness. So you are swimming constantly in postmeditation—and during meditation, you just sit and realize the nature of your alaya very simply.

In the postmeditation experience, you sense that everything you perceive is a creation of your own preconceptions. If you cut through that and interject awareness, you begin to see that the games going on are not big games, but simply illusory games. It requires a lot of mindfulness and awareness working together to realize that—a lot of meditation in action.

Being a child of illusion means that you look at the phenomenal world and see its padded-wall quality. That's the illusion: padded walls everywhere. You think you are just about to strike against something very sharp, and you find that things bounce back on you. There is not much sharp contrast, but everything is part of your mindfulness and awareness. Everything bounces back, like a ball in a video game. When that ball returns, you might hit it back again, but it comes back again with a beep. So once again, you become a child of illusion. When you look at things, you find that they are soft, that they bounce back at you all the time. It's not particularly intellectual. It is first thought, best thought. You can actually experience that things are workable, that there is room. The basic idea of a child of illusion is that you do not feel claustrophobic. There is lots of space.

After your sitting practice, you might think, "Oh no, now I have to do postmeditation practice." But you don't have to feel so closed in. Instead, you can feel that as a child of illusion, you are dancing and clicking with those little beeps all the time. It is fresh and simple and very effective. The point, once again, is to treat yourself better. If you want to take a vacation from your practice, you can do so and still remain a child of illusion. Things just keep beeping at you all the time. It is very lucid, almost whimsical. Being a child of illusion is being willing to realize the simplicity of the phenomenal play, and to use that simplicity as part of your awareness and mindfulness practice.

37

Point Two: Training in Relative Bodhichitta

Relative bodhichitta practice is very action oriented. We give as
much as we can give, and we expand as much as we can expand.
We have a lot to offer because we have basic goodness, which is an
inexhaustible treasure—and because of that, we can receive more
as well. We can be shock absorbers of other people's pain.

T HE DEVELOPMENT of relative bodhichitta is connected with the
paramita of discipline. It has been said that if you do not have
discipline, it is like trying to walk on a road without any legs. Without
discipline, you cannot attain liberation. The process of discipline begins
by realizing that you have a soft spot and that you can work with it. You
can project it out and work with other sentient beings. The idea of relative bodhichitta may seem primitive, but it is also very enlightening, as
bodhichitta should be.

The starting point of relative bodhichitta practice is realizing that others could actually be more important than yourself. You should feel that
you are less important, and that others—*any* others—are more important.
When you do so, you begin to feel as though a tremendous burden has
been taken off your shoulders. You realize that there is room to give love
and affection to more than just this thing called "me" all the time. Even
though other people might provide you with constant problems, you
could still be kind to them. In the same way that a mother cares for her
child, you could put others before yourself. You could be patient enough
to develop selfless service to others.

In order to develop the essence of buddha or enlightenment in your-self, you begin by developing basic decency. Your practice should be very straightforward, based on the principle of not deceiving yourself or oth-ers. You might have all sorts of ego-centered notions of what you would like to be—a great guru, great psychiatrist, great leader, great business-person, great family person, and so on—but you do not need to go along with such worldly or mundane visions. Instead, you could discipline yourself thoroughly, and you could practice in accordance with the clas-sical methods that have been transmitted through the lineage, from gen-eration to generation. You could keep your discipline as pure and ideal as possible.

Pure discipline does not reflect a particular cultural or philosophical view. It does not speak for or against capitalism or communism, democ-racy or dictatorship. It is based simply on human existence. Such disci-pline has been handed down from the time of the Buddha himself, and in spite of the social changes that have taken place since then, it is still being carried on today. We too could maintain such pure, clean discipline.

Bodhichitta is based on prajna and on compassion for others. Instead of simply trying to be comfortable and thinking of yourself alone, you think of the suffering of other sentient beings. You think of someone who is in pain, and you use them as a catalyst or ignition point to light things up, to sharpen your prajna. Basically, the further you go toward the mahayana and vajrayana, the more compassion and benevolence you have. In fact, the level of your compassion determines how far you can go.

Relative bodhichitta practice is quite simple and ordinary; it is an extension of shamatha discipline. In shamatha, we do not dwell on any-thing. We are not only trying to hold our mind completely steady, but we are working with the fickleness of our mental process by following our breath and looking at our subconscious thought process. In bodhichitta practice, instead of simply working with the movement of subconscious mind or discursive thoughts, we include the content of our thoughts, which are based on anger, lust, or stupidity. By including the content of our thoughts, we are going slightly beyond the shamatha technique. Hav-ing realized that we are not as dangerous as we had thought, we return to the most practical level. We develop loving-kindness—and having devel-oped loving-kindness, we begin to switch into compassion.

SENDING AND TAKING

The first relative bodhichitta slogan is related to the central mahayana contemplative practice of tonglen, or sending and taking.

7

Sending and taking should be practiced alternately. These two should ride the breath.

Exchanging oneself for others is one of the leading mahayana disciplines, and a very important one indeed. It is central to the mahayana outlook on reality. Without it, you cannot understand Buddhism at all. You can find the basis of tonglen practice in the realization of relative and absolute bodhichitta and in the understanding of alaya.

In the practice of exchange, you take on the pain and misery of others, and you give away your own pleasure and luxury. In Tibetan this practice is known as *tonglen: tong* means "let go" and *len* means "take on," so *tonglen* means "sending and taking." Sending and taking is the main practice in the development of relative bodhichitta. Tonglen is the actual act of giving and receiving; it is a very specific practice. The more general term *lojong* refers to the approach of mind training altogether.

Exchanging oneself for others means that you become the other and the other becomes you. But in order to exchange yourself for others, you first have to understand shamatha and vipashyana and the notions of maitri and karuna. With that juxtaposition, you begin to have a taste of your own innate goodness. You realize that you possess enlightened genes. In slogan practice, you communicate to the rest of the world with your softness, not on the basis of aggression. So with all of these practices, you have to begin by liking yourself. Then you can do things for others.

Tonglen is not a religious practice; you are simply training yourself to be a decent human being. It is a form of maitri practice, based on the principle of warmth or loving-kindness. While shamatha-vipashyana is considered to be a meditative practice, tonglen is referred to as a contemplative practice because it is not blank mindfulness, but mindfulness with contents.

Prior to practicing tonglen, you need to establish your awareness and

would not be here as an adult. So you could still try to work with that medieval idea of the mother principle.

If you cannot think of such a person, you may be in trouble. You may begin to hate the world, but there is a measure for that: you could breathe in that hatred and resentment. If you do not have a good mother or good person to think of, you could think of yourself.

You might be a completely angry person and have a grudge against the entire universe, or you might be a completely frustrated person, but in spite of that, you could still reflect back on your childhood and think of how nice your mother was to you. You could remember that there was a time when somebody sacrificed her life for your life and brought you up to be the person you are now.

You could appreciate your mother's way of sacrificing her own comfort for you. You could remember how she used to wake up in the middle of the night if you cried, how she used to feed you and change your diapers. You could remember how you acted as the ruler in your little household and how your mother became your slave. Whenever you cried, she would jump up, whether she liked it or not, in order to see what was going on with you. And when you were older, she was very concerned about your security, your education, and so forth.

When you reflect on your life, you realize that throughout your life there have been people who have gone out of their way for you and made sacrifices for your benefit. You should think of those situations and work them into your practice. There have been times when people came along out of the blue to help you, and then went away without even leaving an address or a phone number. You may never have thanked any of those people, but you should. We all have stories about how badly we have treated our parents and other people who helped us. It is very important for you to think of such occasions, not in order to develop guilt, but to realize how mean-spirited you have been.

The development of that quality of gratitude, kindness, gentleness, and appreciation of your world is the realization of basic goodness. You develop a feeling of positiveness. At that point, you can begin to relate to the main practice of relative bodhichitta, or sending and taking.

EXTENDING YOUR PRACTICE. Reflecting on your own mother is the preparation for relative bodhichitta practice. With that understanding, you can begin to extend your sense of nonaggression, nonfrustration, nonanger, and nonresentment beyond your own mother to your friends and to more neutral acquaintances. Eventually you could even try to feel better toward your enemies and the people you do not like. Step by step, you could extend that sense of gentleness, softness, and gratitude toward your own mother to include the rest of the world. Through tonglen practice you are making yourself so soft and reasonable that finally you even begin to feel sympathy toward your bedbugs and mosquitoes.

In the practice of exchange or tonglen you are taking on the pain and misery of others, and you are giving away your own pleasure and luxury. You are training yourself in giving away your own pleasure and taking on others' pain naturally. As your breath goes out, you should give those people the best of what is yours, in order to repay their kindness. In order to promote goodness in the world, you should breathe out everything good, the best that you have. And as you breathe in, you should breathe in those people's problems, misery, and torment. You should take in their pain on their behalf.

APPLYING TONGLEN IN ORDINARY LIFE. Tonglen is usually done in the context of sitting meditation, but you also can join it with any action. But how are you going to apply tonglen in ordinary life? Should you just run up to somebody in the street and say, "Hey, take my candy and give me the dirty Kleenex in your pocket"? You can do that, if you like, and if you are versatile enough, you can probably do it without offending anybody. But that way of experimenting with others is very crude. The actual application of tonglen is more subtle.

You can react to whatever circumstance or situation comes to you by practicing tonglen or applying lojong slogans. In sitting meditation you use your breath as a medium, and in postmeditation you use the fickleness of your mind. When you are speaking, for instance, you do not use your breath in the traditional style of sending and taking. Instead, since your mind is tuned in to your speech, you use that: you work with conversation, with how you project your voice and listen for feedback.

So tonglen is not just about doing your basic breath practice or breathing out the good and breathing in the bad. In any circumstance, you can exchange pleasure for pain. Tonglen is quite demanding, but it can be done, it has been done, and it will be done.

Removing Territoriality

When you practice tonglen, you are letting go of yourself; you are practicing egolessness. As you go out there is less thinking about "I am." You do not hold on to what you are doing, but you keep letting go of *this,* so *this* becomes more diffused. You keep going out and expanding more and more, and at some point, you will find that your own problems and pain are no longer a big deal. That is when you begin to realize the benevolence of the bodhisattva ideal: when there is no big deal about *this.*

The point is to remove territoriality altogether. The usual samsaric approach is that you would like to hold on to your goodness. You would like to make a fence around yourself and put everything bad outside of your fence, such as foreigners, neighbors, or what have you. You don't want them to come in. You do not even want your neighbors to walk their dogs on your property because their dogs might make a mess on your lawn.

So in ordinary life, you do not send and receive, at all. Instead, you try as much as possible to guard those pleasant little situations you have created for yourself. You try to put them in a vacuum, like fruit in a tin, and keep them completely pure and clean. You hold on to as much as you can. Anything outside of your territory is regarded as problematic; you do not want to catch the local influenza. You may not have enough money to build a moat around your house, but you keep your front door locked and are constantly trying to ward off as much as you can. The mahayana path is trying to show us that we do not have to try to secure ourselves. We can afford to extend out a little bit—in fact, quite a bit.

For a long time we have wanted to inflict pain on others and cultivate pleasure for ourselves. That has been the problem; that is what we have been doing wrong. With tonglen, you are reversing that logic altogether. Instead of inflicting pain on others, you take on the pain yourselves. Instead of sucking in others' pleasure, you give your pleasure to them. You are trying to reverse samsaric logic to see what happens—and what usually happens is that you become a gentle person.

It is important to experience and to understand your own unreasonability. Since you have been unreasonable all along, you have to slightly overdo the whole thing in order to make yourself a reasonable person. By doing so, you begin to realize how to be a decent person. That is what tonglen is all about.

Stages of Tonglen

Tonglen makes you grow up and become the ultimate adult. Although there are a lot of obstacles to practicing tonglen, particularly in modern industrial society, you can practice it step by step. When you first practice sending and taking, it is almost like a rehearsal. You would like to experience it fully and thoroughly, but at this stage tonglen is mainly a psychological practice. You are developing the psychological attitude of exchanging yourself with others. Instead of being John Doe, you practice becoming Joe Schmidt.

From that stage of mentally or psychologically sending and taking, tonglen practice progresses very slowly until, in the end, you might actually be able to do such a thing. It has been said in the scriptures that you can even begin to practice tonglen by taking a piece of fruit in one hand and giving it to the other hand. However, if everybody literally began to give things away to one other, there would be tremendous chaos and conflict. But if you develop the attitude of being willing to part with your precious things and to give them to others, that can begin to create a good reality. So it is essential to practice tonglen with conviction and certainty.

You cannot practice tonglen while thinking that it is just imaginary and that it is not going to affect you. When you actually do it, practicing tonglen *will* affect you. The proof is in the pudding. On one hand, after a few days of tonglen, you probably will not get a kind letter from your grandmother with whom you have been at war for the past five years. On the other hand, sending and taking will definitely have a good effect quite naturally. It takes time, but it works.

Depending on your level of development, in tonglen practice you could be really suffering for others or just having that aspiration. It could be either or both. But we mean it literally. It is said that one of the great Kadampa teachers could actually take the pain of another onto himself. When somebody was stoning a dog outside of his house, he was actually bruised. Such a thing could happen to you; you might actually be able to alleviate someone else's suffering. However, the point is not to wait for an effect. You should not look for results, but just do it and drop it, do it and drop it. If it does not work, you take that in; if it works, you give that out. The whole idea is that you do not possess anything.

Genuineness and Hypocrisy

When you feel that you are doing genuine, honest work, you may not only want to give out your pleasure and bring in others' pain, but you may also want to give out your genuineness and invite in their hypocrisy. When you go out driving or shopping, you could practice tonglen in this way. This is the greatest way of exchanging yourself for others; it is needed in the world very, very badly. So exchanging yourself for others can be more than simply exchanging pain for pleasure. It can also be jumping into each other's hypocrisy, which is more interesting.

By sharing your genuineness and bringing in other people's deception, you do not particularly lose your own genuineness, but you develop joy, because you are doing something very useful, workable, and wonderful. You are not only teaching yourself how to be unselfish in the conventional sense, but you are also teaching the world how to overcome its hypocrisy, which is becoming thicker and thicker as the world gets more and more sophisticated—more and more into the dark age, in other words.*

An Inexhaustible Treasure of Goodness

Meditation in action is the saving grace of the mahayana. It is not exertion or higher insight that distinguishes mahayanists from hinayanists, but their skillfulness in practicing within day-to-day life. It is in knowing how to live life through the paramitas and by applying the slogans. The slogans and the paramitas go hand in hand.

Relative bodhichitta practice is very action oriented. We give as much as we can give and we expand as much as we can expand. We have a lot to offer because we have basic goodness, which is an inexhaustible treasure—and because of that we can receive more, as well. We can be shock absorbers of other people's pain. Tonglen is a very moving practice: the more we give our best, the more we are able to receive other people's worst. Isn't that great?

---

* Trungpa Rinpoche referred to the current period of history as a dark age (Skt.: Kali Yuga): a time of spiritual degeneration when wisdom and compassion are in short supply, life is difficult, and there are many obstacles to dharma practice.

Tonglen practice is extremely powerful and helpful, so you should take it seriously. Tonglen could be one of the best measures for solving our ecological problems. It could have the physical effect of cleaning up pollution in big cities and maybe even in the entire world. We might have difficulty taking in pollution, but we should take it in wholeheartedly and completely. We should feel that our lungs are filled with bad air. We should feel that we have actually cleaned out the world and taken that pollution into ourselves. Then a switch takes place, and as we breathe out, we find that we still have an enormous treasure of good breath going out all the time.

Proceeding with tonglen requires courage, humor, and gallantry. However, sending and taking is not regarded as proof of one's personal bravery or virtue, but as a natural course of exchange. It just takes place. Bad and good are always there, neurosis and sanity are always there. The problem with most people is that they are always trying to give out the bad and take in the good. That has been the problem of society in general and the world altogether. But on the mahayana path, the logic is reversed, which is fantastic, extraordinary. You are actually getting the inner scoop on Buddha's mind directly and at its best.

Although tonglen is a mahayana discipline, it is also very important in terms of both hinayana and vajrayana practice. In the hinayana, without tonglen you are just dressing up in monks' robes and shaving your head. In the vajrayana, without tonglen, you are just dressing up as a deity. So it is the mahayana tradition and discipline that holds the hinayana and vajrayana together.

Without tonglen practice, both the hinayana and the vajrayana become like a lion's corpse. As king of the beasts, a dead lion is not attacked by other animals, but it is left to be eaten from within. Likewise, the Buddha said that his teaching will not be destroyed by outsiders, but by insiders who do not practice true dharma, the bodhisattva path. Remember that.

Tonglen is like skydiving or parachuting. Fear is involved, and so is personal possessiveness. You may not want to give away your personal possessions. You may be afraid, but you could extend yourself and fly. I don't think you are going to get into any trouble or crash into the rocks. You could fly like an eagle, fly like a skylark, and enjoy the space. You could breathe out goodness and take in the pain of others. You could be brave. If you are brave, in the end you will begin to enjoy tonglen. You could be a warrior and parachute with a smile.

8

Three objects, three poisons, and three seeds of virtue.

The three objects are the objects of love, hate, and indifference. The three poisons are passion, aggression, and ignorance. The three virtuous seeds are the absence of passion, the absence of aggression, and the absence of ignorance. With passion, you want to magnetize or possess. With aggression, you want to reject, attack, or cast out. With ignorance, you couldn't be bothered; you are disinterested and indifferent. It is a kind of anti-prajna energy.

Whenever any of the three poisons happen in your life, you should do the sending and taking practice. You should look at your passion, aggression, and ignorance, but not regard them as a problem or as a promise. Instead, when you are in a state of aggression, you should think, "May this aggression be a working base for me. May I learn to keep my aggression to myself, and may all sentient beings thereby attain freedom from this kind of aggression." For passion and ignorance, you should do the same: "May this passion or ignorance be mine. By virtue of keeping it to myself, may others be free of passion or ignorance."

When we reflect on our enemy, we have already inspired aggression. We should let that aggression be ours so that our enemy may be free from aggression. With passion inspired by our friends, we should take that neurosis into ourselves so that our friends may be free from passion. And with those who are neither enemies or friends, who are indifferent, unconcerned, ignorant, or noncaring, we should bring their neurosis into ourselves so that such people may be free from ignorance.

Interestingly enough, when you begin to possess any of the three poisons completely, when you take charge of them, you will find that the logic is reversed. By holding the anger as your own, you let go of the object, or intent, of your anger. But without an object, you can no longer hold on to that aggression, so the aggression falls apart. It is impossible to have an object of anger, because the anger belongs to you. Likewise, if you have no object of passion or ignorance, you cannot hold on to that passion or ignorance.

In this slogan, the interesting twist is that you can cut the root of passion, aggression, and ignorance by dealing with others rather than by dealing with yourself. If you give your compassion to the object so that it does not provoke your anger, then what are you angry with? You find yourself just hanging out there with no one to project onto. If the projection is freed from those problems, the projector has nothing to project onto.

9

In all activities, train with slogans.

The idea of this particular teaching is to give our blood and flesh to others. That is a very powerful thing to do. It is like saying, "If you want me, take me, possess me, kidnap me, control me. Go ahead, do it. Take me. I'm at your service. You could cut me into pieces or anything you want. Without your help I would not have any way to work with my journey at all." Langri Tangpa, who was one of the Kadampa teachers, had a saying: "May I receive all evils, may my virtues go to others." He said, "I realize that all mistakes belong to me and all virtues belong to others, so I cannot really blame anybody except myself." Such an idea sounds terribly self-flagellating, if you look at it the wrong way. The popular idea of blaming everything on oneself has in it an ultimate guilt concept. But this slogan is not based on guilt or on the feeling that we did something terribly wrong. It is based on seeing things as they are.

Another saying goes: "Profit and victory to others; loss and defeat to myself." It would be good to put that little phrase up on the wall and memorize it. In Tibet, we used to stick phrases like that on our door handles. In the Vajradhatu community,* when we create a dharmic environment such as a practice center, we post the slogans on a wall in order to remind ourselves of them. The point is to catch the first thought—and in catching the first thought, that first thought should have words. By "profit and victory," we mean anything that encourages us to walk on the path of the dharma, which is created by the world. At the same time, we are filled

---

* *Vajradhatu* International was the name of the Buddhist spiritual community founded by Chögyam Trungpa Rinpoche. He also founded the Nalanda Foundation, which focused on education, social service, and the arts. The Nalanda Foundation included such programs as the Naropa Institute (now Naropa University) and Shambhala Training. Under the leadership of Trungpa Rinpoche's son and successor Sakyong Mipham Rinpoche, Vajradhatu and Nalanda were combined into one entity called Shambhala International. Naropa University is separately incorporated.

with loss and defeat, which is ours. We are not supposed to sulk about that, but to take pride in it.

Whenever you feel the quality of me-ness, you should think of these sayings. Whenever you feel disgust, you make it your property, and whenever you experience vision or upliftedness, you give it to others. So there is a sort of black-white contrast. There is a flip of black and white, nausea and relaxation, feeling ugly and feeling pretty. That flip takes place very simply. When there is "I," you take it, and when there is "am," you give it.

The phrase "loss and defeat" does not refer to fundamental pain. It is just that you did not get what you wanted, so you feel somewhat irritated. It is about relating with the little things that go wrong in your life, like losing your money or crashing into a car. When we do not get what we want, we are always frustrated. We are resentful of something or somebody, or even resent ourselves. That is not really pain, it is just hassles. So in the mahayana, we are dealing with all kinds of hassles and transmuting them. We are working with them as a journey toward enlightenment.

It is a fantastic idea, that we are actually, finally, fearless people, that profit goes to others, and loss goes to ourselves. That is great! Fantastic! We may not always find it to be so, but it is actually true that a lot of things that we tend to blame others for are our own doing. We can employ a lawyer to prove that we are right and somebody else is wrong, but that is a lot of trouble to go through. And hiring a lawyer to attain enlightenment is not possible. Buddha did not have a lawyer himself.

In the mahayana, the opening process is not necessarily painful. One of the problems of the Occidental mentality is that we make a big deal of everything and unnecessarily complicate things. But the process of opening is not a big deal. It is an exchange; it is like a game. You are finally putting your name on the dotted line, which is a lighthearted situation, including death. You could keep that in mind; you could even make a slogan out of it: "Whatever takes place, do not take it all that seriously." You should not regard any problem as the ultimate, final problem, but as just a temporary flare that comes and goes. If you regard something as a big deal, it will become that way, but if you regard it as purely a dance that you are responding to, it will be okay.

To work with slogans such as this, you obviously need a lot of understanding and training. You cannot just practice it without having planned the journey and worked with your state of mind. There is also a need for an understanding of the shunyata experience, because when there is no ground, anything that takes place in the groundlessness becomes workable.

10

Begin the sequence of sending and taking with yourself.

In this slogan, the idea of "first thought" continues. The way we often express this is by the phrase "First thought, best thought." Usually we have the feeling that *this* happens first, then *other* happens. So the idea of this slogan is to start with *this*. Whenever anything happens, the first thing to do is to take on the pain yourself, and afterward you give away anything left, anything pleasurable. By "pleasurable" we do not necessarily mean feeling extraordinarily good, but anything other than pain. So anything other than pain is given away. You do not hold on to any way of entertaining yourself or giving yourself good treatment.

This slogan has to do with giving up passion, as it is passion that makes you demand pleasure for yourself. Therefore this slogan is connected with the paramita of discipline very vividly and closely. You begin to realize that the demands of wanting and not wanting are based on the desire to possess and to not give out. This slogan is not based on masochism or self-destruction, but on opening your territory completely, letting go of everything. If you suddenly discover that a hundred hippies want to camp in your living room, you let them do so—but then those hippies also have to practice.

The practice of this slogan is actually very joyful. It is wonderful that human beings can do such a fantastic exchange. It is wonderful that people are willing to let go of even little corners of secrecy and privacy, so that their holding on to anything is gone completely. People's willingness to invite undesirable situations into their world is very brave. We could certainly say that it is the world of the warrior from the bodhisattva's point of view.

Point Three: Transformation
of Bad Circumstances
into the Path of Enlightenment

Without this world, we could not attain enlightenment. There would be no journey. If we rejected the world, we would be rejecting the ground and the path. . . . All our experiences are based on others. . . . Without them we could not attain anything. We would have no feedback, absolutely nothing to work with. So the irritations and problems in our world are crucial.

THE SIX slogans of the third point of mind training are about carrying whatever occurs in your life onto the path. In Tibetan, this is known as *lamkhyer*. *Lam* means "path," and *khyer* means "carrying"; so *lamkhyer* means that whatever happens in your life should be included as part of your journey. This group of slogans is connected with the paramita of patience. Patience doesn't mean biding your time and trying to slow down—it means that whatever happens, you don't overreact. The obstacle to patience is aggression. When you are too sensitive and don't have any way to deal with your environment, you become very touchy and impatient. Patience is described as being like a suit of armor: there is a quality of dignity and forbearance, and you are not easily disturbed by the world's aggression.

11

When the world is filled with evil,
transform all mishaps into the path of bodhi.

This slogan presents the basic approach of this section of mind training, which is that all problems—environmental problems, political problems, psychological problems, or any other problems in your life—should be transformed into wakefulness. In other words, you do not blame the environment or the world political situation, and you do not use any mishaps that take place in your life as sources of resentment. Instead, all mishaps and problems are transformed into a wakeful state of mind. That wakefulness results from the practice of shamatha-vipashyana and from your understanding of soft spot, or bodhichitta.

Some people react to what is happening in the world by writing poetry or sacrificing their lives for a social cause. The Vietnam War era produced a lot of such poets and philosophers who were purely reacting against the evil in the world, regarding that evil as material for their writing. But they were not able to transform mishaps into the path of bodhi, so their work was not in keeping with the mahayana. Transforming mishaps comes from your sitting practice and your general awareness. Whether or not the world is filled with evil, such mishaps should be transformed into the path of bodhi, or wakefulness.

In our ordinary life, our environment is not necessarily hospitable. You might feel that you are inadequate because you have a sick father and a crazy mother and you have to take care of them, or you may have money problems. Even if you have a successful life and everything is going all right, you might still feel inadequate because you have to work constantly to maintain your business. There are always problems and difficulties, even for those who feel that their lives are successful. You may have become the president of the country, a millionaire, a famous poet, or a movie star, but even if your life goes according to your expectations, you will still have difficulties and obstacles. That is something everybody experiences. You could regard such obstacles as expressions of your own timidity, cowardice, poverty mentality, fixation on loss and gain, or competitiveness. But according to the slogan, any obstacles or mishaps that occur should be transformed into the path of bodhi.

Besides being connected to the paramita of patience, this slogan also has a lot to say about the practice of generosity. The very powerful and direct message of the paramita of generosity is that you do not need to feel poverty-stricken all the time. Having experienced the possibility of absolute and relative bodhichitta and having practiced sending and taking, you should begin to build confidence and joy in your own richness and resourcefulness. You should feel that you can deal with whatever is available around you. For instance, if you are abandoned in the middle of a desert and want to lie down, you can find a moss-covered rock to use as a pillow and have a good sleep. That quality of resourcefulness and richness seems to be the essence of generosity.

Many people relate with everything in their lives purely on the level of pennies, tiny stitches, drops of water, or grains of rice—but you do not have to do that. You can expand your vision. You can give something to others without always having to receive something back. You do not need to "make it" first in order to give something away. You can let go of anything. You can develop a feeling of wealth, free from desire and attachment.

I2

Drive all blames into one.

This slogan, as well as the next one, "Be grateful to everyone," has to do with the relative bodhichitta level. It is also connected with the traditional guide for bodhisattvas, known as "The Forty-Six Ways in Which a Bodhisattva Fails."* It deals with relative truth, with our ordinary experience. No matter what appears in your experience, however interesting or powerful, you should not have any expectations. When you are kind to somebody, you should not expect any reward. The problems and the complications that exist in your practice, realization, and understanding are not somebody else's fault. Although you might try to come out clean, the blame always starts with you.

We prefer to blame our problems on somebody else, whether those problems are political, environmental, psychological, domestic, or spiritual. You may not have a particular individual to blame, but you still come

---

* See appendix 5, "Forty-Six Ways in Which a Bodhisattva Fails."

up with the logic that something is wrong and somebody else is at fault. You might complain to the authorities, your political leaders, or your friends, and demand that the situation be changed. Or your complaint might be purely individual: if your spouse falls in love with somebody else, you might ask him or her to give up their lover. But you yourself feel completely pure, good, and blameless; you never let any blame touch you. Your spouse may be brave enough to challenge you and say, "Isn't there some blame on your side as well? Mightn't you also have something to do with it?" But if you are told that it is your problem and it is you who has to change, you do not like it at all.

A lot of people seem to get along in this world and make quite a comfortable life by being compassionate and open, or seemingly compassionate and open. Yet although we share the same world, we ourselves get hit constantly with problems and troubles of all kinds. So we become resentful. It may feel that somebody is playing tricks on us, but actually we ourselves are provoking such things, so all the blame is on us. We might have entirely the same lifestyle as somebody else; we might be sharing an apartment, eating the same food, and sharing a similar schedule. However, although we have exactly the same situation, our friend manages to handle everything okay, while we are stuck with obstacles and resentment. But who did that to us? We could say that everybody hates us. But why do they hate us? That is a very interesting question. Every blame, every mishap that happens to us, is our own doing.

We could blame the organization, we could blame the government, we could blame the police force, we could blame the weather, we could blame the food, we could blame the highways, we could blame our cars or our clothes. We could blame an infinite variety of things, and we could build up all kinds of philosophies to back up our complaints, but it is we who are not letting go, we who are not developing enough warmth and sympathy. We cannot blame anybody else.

This practice goes very far. Driving all blames into oneself applies whenever we complain about anything, even that our coffee is cold or the bathroom is dirty. We may think that we are the voice of the world, that we are speaking on behalf of others, but we are simply speaking on behalf of ourselves. According to this slogan, everything is due to our own ego fixation, which makes us very vulnerable. Consequently, we provide an ideal target. We get hit, but nobody meant to hit us—we are actually inviting the bullets.

The reason you have to drive all blames into yourself is because you have been cherishing yourself so much, even at the cost of somebody else's life. You have been holding yourself so dearly, and although you might say that you don't like yourself, you are just paying lip service. In your heart of hearts, you know that you like yourself so much that you are willing to throw everybody else into the gutter. You are really willing to do that. And who are you, anyway?

Driving all blames into one is the essence of the bodhisattva path. Even if somebody else has made a terrible mistake and blamed it on you, you should take the blame yourself. In terms of power, it is a much simpler and more direct way of controlling the situation. In addition, it is the most direct way of simplifying complicated neurosis into one point. If you look for volunteers around you to take the blame, there will be no other volunteers but yourself. So by taking the blame on yourself, you reduce the neurosis happening around you. You also reduce people's paranoia so that they might have clearer vision. You can actually say, "I take the blame. It's my fault that such and such a thing happened and that such and such took place as a result." It is easier to talk to somebody when you have already accepted the blame because that person is not in a defensive mood. Then you can clarify the situation, and quite possibly that person, who might be the cause of the problem, will recognize their own wrongdoing. It helps that the blame, which is now just a paper tiger, has been taken on by you.

In organizations, individuals and particularly leaders can take the blame themselves and let their friends off the hook so they can continue their work. That will help the whole organization to function much better. When you say, "No, I didn't do such a thing, it was you who did it," the whole thing gets very complicated. You begin to find this little plop of dirt bouncing around in the bureaucracy. Each person says, "That's not my creation—it's your creation," so it becomes like a football flying back and forth. And if you fight over it too much, you will have tremendous difficulty resolving that problem. So the earlier you take the blame, the better. And although it may not fundamentally be your fault at all, you should take it as if it is yours.

In international politics also, somebody is always trying to put the blame on somebody else. The communists say it belongs to the capitalists, and the capitalists say it belongs to the communists. But throwing the blame back and forth doesn't help anyone. So even from the point of

view of political theory, it is important for individuals to absorb unjusti-
fied blame and to work with that.

Your original intention in driving all blames into one may be based
on wanting to enter into the bodhisattva path. But later, at the level of
vipashyana, you do so based on experiencing the real, visible, logical result
of doing otherwise. You see how aggression and neurosis are expanded if
you drive all blames into somebody else. That seems to be the point where
aspiring and entering come together.*

If you don't allow a little bit of blame and injustice to come to you,
nothing is going to work. Everybody is looking for someone to blame,
and they would like to blame you, not because you have done anything,
but because they think you have a soft spot in your heart. They think that
if they put their jam or honey on you, you actually might buy it and say,
"Okay, the blame is mine." But once you begin to take the blame, it is the
highest and most powerful incantation you can make. You can actually
make the whole thing functional. If you can absorb the poison, the rest of
the situation becomes medicine.

This slogan does not mean that you should not speak up. However,
in confronting political, environmental, or social issues, you could speak
out in the form of driving all blames into yourself. Obviously, there are
social problems, but the way to approach them is not as "I, a rightful
political entity," or as "Me, one of the important people in society." When
you speak to the authorities, usually you come at them in an aggressive
way, but that approach only solidifies the authorities even more. There
could be a better and more intelligent way of approaching things. For
instance, you could say, "Maybe it's my problem, but personally I find that
this water doesn't taste so good." You might gather your friends and the
people in your neighborhood who agree with that, and together speak out
very simply, straightforwardly, and gently.

In a more extreme example, if somebody was about to press the but-
ton on the atomic bomb and "poof" the planet, I would kill them without
any hesitation in order to save millions of people's lives. If there were no
choice, and somebody were about to do something that bad, I would kill
them and take the blame. I would take delight in it! However, it would be

---

* *Aspiring* is a reference to the bodhisattva vow as the initial entry into the mahayana
path; *entering* is a reference to following that up with actual practice, specifically paramita
practice.

too dangerous for most of us to go that far. As long as we know what we are doing, it may be okay. But often, that sort of approach only tends to escalate the warfare.

13

Be grateful to everyone.

Once we drive all blames into ourselves, we begin to realize that if other people didn't exist to hassle us, we would not be able to drive all blames into ourselves. Without others, we would have no chance to develop beyond ego. So being grateful to everyone follows automatically. We feel grateful that others are presenting us with obstacles, challenges, even threats. Without them, we could not follow the path.

The idea of being grateful to everyone is founded on real situations. If someone punches you in the mouth and says, "You are terrible," you should be grateful that such a person has actually acknowledged you and said so. You could respond with tremendous dignity by saying, "Thank you, I appreciate your concern." In that way their neurosis has been taken over by you, taken into you, much as you do in tonglen practice. There is an immense sacrifice taking place. If you think this is ridiculously far-fetched, you are right—in some sense it is. But if somebody does not begin to provide some kind of harmony and sanity, we will not develop sanity in this world at all. Somebody has to plant the seed so that sanity can happen on this earth—and that person is you. As an inspired Buddhist, you have the truth, the conviction, and the power to transplant the root of compassion into the land where you belong, the land where you were born.

Being grateful to those who harm you does not mean that you have to expose yourself to being hurt. That would be martyrdom. But when you come up with such a situation, you could apply this slogan. It is not that you have to stage the whole thing. You do not have to avoid painful situations and you do not have to cultivate them. You just lead your life, being very sane and not hurting anybody else. But if someone happens to hurt you, you know what to do. It is very simple. We are not talking about deliberately jumping on a sword; that would be a misunderstanding. Instead, you are making a close relationship to the person who is hurting you.

Without this world, we could not attain enlightenment. There would be no journey. If we rejected the world, we would be rejecting the ground and the path. All our past history, all our neurosis, is related with others. All our experiences are based on others. As soon as, or as long as, we have a sense of practice and the realization that we are treading on the path, every one of those seeming obstacles becomes an essential part of the path. Without them, we could not attain anything. We would have no feedback, absolutely nothing to work with. So the irritations and problems in our world are crucial.

Without others, we cannot attain enlightenment. In fact, we cannot even tread on the path. If there is no noise outside during our sitting meditation, we cannot develop mindfulness. If we do not have aches and pains in our body, we cannot meditate. If everything were lovey-dovey and jellyfish-like, there would be nothing to work with. Everything would be completely blank. Because of these textures around us, we are enriched. We are so enriched by all these things that we can actually sit and meditate. We have a reference point; we have both encouragement and discouragement.

14

Seeing confusion as the four kayas is unsurpassable shunyata protection.

This slogan is about how to carry everything onto the path at the absolute bodhichitta level. It is based on understanding your mind by studying and watching yourself, and by practicing shamatha and vipashyana. By practicing those disciplines, you begin to realize that the essence of your mind is empty, that the nature of your mind is light and clear, and that the expression or manifestation of your mind is active. That realization can only come about when you have developed mindfulness and awareness. Only on the meditation cushion can you see that your mind has no origin. You see that there is no place from which thoughts arise, and you have no idea where your thoughts go. Furthermore, you have no idea where your thoughts actually dwell. Thoughts just arise and vanish; they disappear.

As you continue to practice mindfulness and awareness, the seeming confusion and chaos in your mind begins to seem absurd. You see that your thoughts have no real birthplace; they just pop up. You see that your thoughts don't go anywhere; they are unceasing. You also see that no activities are really happening in your mind. So the notion that your mind can dwell on anything begins to seem absurd, because there is nothing to dwell on. The point of practice is not to make your mind a blank. Instead, as a result of super-mindfulness and super-awareness, you begin to see that nothing is actually happening—although, at the same time, you think that lots of things are happening. Therefore, realizing that the confusion and the chaos in your mind have no origin, no cessation, and nowhere to dwell is the best protection.

According to this slogan, perception has four stages. First, there is waiting or openness. There may be uncertainty as to how to perceive things, and you do not know how to make a particular situation graspable. Second, you develop a clear idea of the situation and how to organize things. Third, you begin to make a relationship between those two. Finally, you have a total experience of the whole. Those are four states of mind or four mental processes we go through. Those four processes are related with what are called the four *kayas: dharmakaya, nirmanakaya, sambhogakaya,* and *svabhavikakaya.*

The dharmakaya aspect is basic openness. Our reaction to the world is uncertain and bewildered, and strategies and planning have not yet formed. In the nirmanakaya aspect, the second stage of this process, there is some clarity. We have a general grasp of the situation. In order to make a link between the openness and clarity, we have the third aspect, or sambhogakaya. The sambhogakaya bridges the gap between the dharmakaya and the nirmanakaya, and joins them together. According to my tradition, that is the realistic way of looking at things. The more common way of categorizing the three kayas is to start with dharmakaya, followed by the sambhogakaya and the nirmanakaya.

The fourth kaya, svabhavikakaya, is the whole thing, the total panoramic experience. When we begin to flash our mind to an object, when we have a grasp of it, when we realize the link between the three kayas, that totality is known as svabhavikakaya. The svabhavikakaya is a state of mind that is known as transcending birth, cessation, and dwelling. Transcending birth means that the thought process does not come up. There is no such thing as the birth of a mind or the birth of a thought taking place in our state of being at all—there is simply existing and opening. Transcending cessation means that thoughts do not actually subside, unless they are replaced or overlapped by something else. Nondwelling means that thoughts do not actually dwell anywhere, although there is a kind of temporary halt or occasional something. So the idea is to see beyond the birth, subsiding, and dwelling of the thought process.

The reason the four kayas become a great protection is that we begin to realize the way our mind functions. Thoughts do not really come up as such; they just emerge. You cannot watch their birth—they are just there. In other words, everything is nowness nature. Thoughts die; they just [*snaps fingers*]. They don't dwell, they just [*snaps fingers again*]. It is a natural process. We realize that whatever comes up in our mind is always subject to that flow, that particular case history, that nature. Sudden pain, sudden anger, sudden aggression, sudden passion—whatever might arise always follows the same procedure, the same process. So everything is always in accordance with the four kayas. Although we might not regard our own mind as all that transcendent, awake, or enlightened, the pattern is still that of the four-kaya principle.

This protection is called shunyata protection, because it cuts the solidness of our beliefs. We have all sorts of solid thoughts. We think, "This is my grand thought" or "My thought is so cute." We might think, "The star men came down and talked to me," or "Genghis Khan is present in my mind," or "Jesus Christ himself appeared." Or we may think, "I have thought of a tremendous scheme for how to build a city, how to write a musical comedy, how to create a gigantic movie project, or how to conquer the world." Our thinking goes from that level down to "How am I going to earn my living?" or "What is the best way for me to sharpen my personality so that I will be visible in the world?" or "How I hate my problems!" But you realize that you are not the greatest artist and you are not any of your big ideas—you are just authoring absurd, nonexistent things.

All of those schemes, thoughts, and ideas are empty. If you look behind them, it is like looking behind a mask and seeing that it is hollow. There may be holes for the nostrils and the mouth, but if you look behind the mask, it no longer looks like a face—it is just junk with holes in it. Realizing that is the best protection for cutting confusion. With shunyata protection, you no longer have anywhere to dwell—you are suspended in shunyata.

This slogan is a very clever way of approaching egolessness. Instead of approaching egolessness directly, you are trying to work out your protection—and finally you might find yourself being egoless, and realize that there is nothing actually to protect. The protection is groundlessness. This is a very clinical approach, in a sense, for if you have no ground to collect germs, there will be not be any.

The idea of the four kayas in this slogan is not particularly tantric; it is mahayanist high thinking. But the kayas also appear in the *Uttaratantra* of Maitreya and in the *Diamond Sutra*,* so at the same time, they are tantric. Although slogan practice is based on mahayana principles, there is an undercurrent throughout of techniques borrowed from the vajrayana.

15

Four practices are the best of methods.

This slogan is about engaging in special activities and practices in order to transform bad circumstances onto the path of enlightenment. It includes four practices: accumulating merit, laying down evil deeds, offering to the *döns,* and offering to the *dharmapalas.*

Accumulating Merit

The first practice is accumulating merit. Merit does not mean collecting something for your ego. It has to do with the basic twist of how to punish your ego. The logic is that you always want pleasure, but what you always get is pain. Why does that happen? It happens because the very act of seeking pleasure brings pain. So you always get a bad deal because you started at the wrong end of the stick.

The point of this application is that you have to sacrifice something, rather than purely yearning for pleasure. You have to start at the right end of the stick from the very beginning. In order to do so, you have to refrain from evil actions, and cultivate virtuous ones. And in order to do that, you have to block out hope and fear altogether. You do not hope to gain anything from your practice, and you are not fearful of bad results.

This slogan is based on having complete trust in what are called the three types of encouragement, or three reminders. Since the slogans themselves are reminders, these sayings are reminders for the reminders. The three lines of encouragement are:

---

* *The Uttara Tantra: A Treatise on Buddha Nature,* translated and with commentary by Khenchen Thrangu Rinpoche, Asanga, and Ken Holmes (New Delhi: Sri Satguru, 1989). *The Diamond Sutra and the Sutra of Hui-neng,* translated by Wong Mou-Lam and A. F. Price (Boston: Shambhala Publications, 2005).

> Grant your blessing so if it is better for me to be sick, let me
>   be sick.
> Grant your blessing so if it is better for me to survive, let me
>   survive.
> Grant your blessing so if it is better for me to be dead, let me die.

That is the ultimate idea of creating merit. Before you beg, your begging bowl has to be empty, otherwise nobody will give you anything. Similarly, in order to receive merit, there has to be a quality of openness, giving, and surrendering. Who are you asking to grant those blessings? Not any cosmic entity—you are talking to yourself. But reciting those lines and invoking the possibility that such things could happen to you helps you to realize the path. You are talking to yourself, but you are inspired by the lineage, which has also done that. There is such accuracy and genuineness in saying, "If it is right for me to be either dead, sick, or recovered, let it be so." And it will happen if you have directness in your approach. You could apply this to anything that is tricky and sticky. By doing so, you actually begin to cheer yourself up by giving in and jumping into the ocean of mud. It works very well. You could do that instead of taking aspirin and occasional shots of coffee.

When you say, "Grant your blessing so if it is better for me to be sick," basically you are saying, "Just let it happen." You are not talking to anybody. It is more like saying, "Let the rain fall" or "Let the earth shake." It is like reciting magical words. Something actually might happen when you do that, but you are not talking to anybody in particular. You are simply letting things be. And whatever comes up, you are grateful.

So the idea is: whatever happens, let it happen. You are not particularly looking for pleasure or for pain. If diving into an ice-cold swimming pool in the middle of winter is what is best for your constitution, you go ahead and do it. It is a very direct approach, a simple and direct link with reality without any scheming. In particular, if there is any desire or fear, you act in the opposite way. That is, you jump into your fear and you refrain from your desire. This is the same approach as taking on other people's pain and giving them your pleasure. It should no longer be any surprise that we have such a strange way of dealing with things, but it usually works. We could almost say that it works one hundred percent.

You also accumulate merit by creating statues, building stupas (dome-shaped Buddhist shrines), or making offerings to the sangha. You can donate your money and at the same time try to let go of your possessiveness. So the idea of donation goes further than surrendering only your money. You are letting go and opening yourself completely to the situation. You may regard this approach as naive, but in fact it is extremely intelligent. Basically, you are not accumulating anything for your own ego, but you are trying to relate with what is sacred or holy. You are connecting with the sacred areas of reality, with the very idea of the teachings, the dharma, and basic sanity. That sacred quality is represented by works of art, images, statues, paintings, books, and all kinds of symbols and colors. By associating yourself with that kind of thing and by veneration, you are creating merit.

In letting go of your holding back, intelligence is very important. You cannot just have blind faith; you need intelligent faith. Holding back creates a kind of business mentality: "If I don't get my money's worth, then I will have to sue the Buddha, the dharma, and the sangha. If I don't get something in return, then I have been cheated." But in this case, it is not tit for tat. Instead when something comes up, you think, "Whatever has happened, I would like to let go of this problem of holding back." It is extremely simple and realistic.

You cannot accumulate merit if you have pride and arrogance. It is not that you have collected a pile of virtue and you are going to collect more. You have to be humble and willing to give rather than to collect. The more you are willing to give, that much more effective is the accumulation of merit.

Laying Down Evil Deeds

The second of the four practices is laying down your evil deeds. As a result of accumulating merit, and because you have learned to block out hope and fear, you develop a quality of gentleness and sanity. Having done so, you look back and you say, "Good heavens! I have been so stupid and I didn't even realize it!" Because you have reached a certain level of sophistication, when you look back you see how sloppy and embarrassing you have been. The reason you didn't notice it before is because of stupidity of some kind. So with this application, the point is to look back and realize what you have been doing and not make the same mistake all over again.

This practice is sometimes described as the confession of sins. However, the word *sin* has all kinds of connotations for people raised in the

Judeo-Christian traditions. In the world of Christianity, in particular, the concept of sin is all-pervasive. The Tibetan word *dikpa* does mean "evil deeds," or "sin," but its meaning is more psychological than ethical. Therefore, we have at times translated *dikpa* as "neurotic crimes," since neurosis is its backbone, and frivolity is its activities. It is because of neurosis that you end up with all kinds of crime and destruction. So basically what we are confessing is the underlying neurosis. In the Buddhist style of confession, there is no church to go into and no priest to hear your confession. It is not quite like the Christian idea of confession, but more a way of relieving yourself of your own neurotic crimes.

Traditionally, confession is done in a fourfold style: regret, refraining from evil actions, taking refuge in the Buddha, dharma, and sangha, and letting go of hope and fear.

The first step of confession is *regret*. It is getting tired of your own neurosis. That is important, for if you were not tired of doing the same thing again and again, if you were thriving on it, you probably would not have a chance to do anything about it. But once you begin to get tired of it, you think, "I shouldn't have done that" or "Here I go again" or "I should have known better" or "I don't feel so good." These are the kinds of remarks you make, particularly when you wake up in the morning with a heavy hangover. That's good. It is a sign that you are actually ready to confess your neurotic crimes. When you can come back and remember what you did, it is so embarrassing and you feel so terrible. You feel like not getting out of your bed. You don't want to go outside or face the world. That real feeling of total embarrassment, that feeling that your whole gut is rotten, is the first step. That kind of regret is not just social regret, but it is also personal regret. That shameful feeling begins to creep through your marrow into your bones and hairs. The sunshine coming through the windows begins to mock you. Such regret is regarded as a very healthy first step.

The second step of confession is *refraining from evil actions*. You say that from this time onward you are not going to do such actions. You think about what you have done and how it made you feel. Although you might still want to do it or think it is fun, you decide that it is better not to. So you refrain from it and prevent yourself from doing it again.

The third step of confession is *taking refuge in the Buddha, dharma, and sangha,* which means completely surrendering. You have to give up the crime rather than hoping that the crime will be forgiven. You have to give up your self, your stronghold. Nobody can wipe out your neurosis by saying, "I forgive you." The criminal has to give up rather than the crime being forgiven.

When someone forgives you for a wrong you have committed against them, it does not help, and it may even encourage you to sin further. Alternatively, if you are attacked and you forgive your attacker, although that person may not harm you again, they may try to harm somebody else. So from the Buddhist perspective, forgiveness is not all that helpful, and it may even lead to further crimes. It does not help unless the whole crime has completely subsided. The actions themselves are less important than the factors that lead a person to commit a crime. So if people are in jail, they need to be reformed so that they do not go back to their crimes. However, Buddhists do not usually have jails. It is said that the Buddhist emperor Ashoka actually denounced the use of them.

The fourth step of confession is *letting go of hope and fear*. At this point, you are completing the surrendering process, you are giving and opening completely. That action has the power to relieve your neurotic crimes. It is said that you should make supplications to prevent hope and fear by saying, "If there is hope, let my hope subside; if there is fear, may my fear subside as well." By transcending both hope and fear, you begin to develop the confidence that you could go through the whole process.

So the first step is feeling disgust with what you have done. The second step is refraining from that activity. The third step is offering your neurosis by taking refuge in the Buddha, dharma, and sangha, and committing yourself as a traveler on the path. And in the fourth step, all those processes are connected together, and there is no longer hope or fear.

Offering to the Döns

The third practice is to offer *torma* or food to the döns. A dön is a neurotic attack; we experience such neurotic attacks throughout our life. *Torma* is a Tibetan word that means "offering cake." A torma represents a gift or token. If you have watched a Tibetan ceremony, you may have seen little offerings of butter and dough. A similar concept in the West is the birthday cake with its decorations.

Laying down evil deeds is based on getting tired of your continual neurosis, tired of doing the same things again and again. But in this practice you are dealing with a sudden earthshaking situation, a big attack, something that makes you think twice. So the former practice is more like a camel's hump, whereas this one is a sheer drop. A sudden incident hits you, and suddenly things begin to happen to you. The döns attack suddenly, and they possess you immediately. They attack you by surprise, and suddenly you are in a terribly bad mood even though everything is okay.

Döns seem to attack us from outside and suddenly make us unreasonably fearful, unreasonably angry, unreasonably horny and passionate, or unreasonably mean. Being attacked by a dön is like catching a flu, like being possessed. Without any reason, we are suddenly terrified; without any reason, we are angry and uptight; without any reason, we are lustful; without any reason, we are suddenly so proud. Such neurotic attacks or döns always occur. They seem to come from outside us. It seems that external forces or phenomena make us do such neurotic things, as if we were possessed by ghosts.

Döns are said to steal your life force. Everything is fine and smooth and nothing is problematic, but then one day you are suddenly uptight and another day you are so down. Even though you have not done anything different and everything is smooth and ordinary, there are those ups and downs, those little punctures in your life. Little leaks, little upsurges, take place all the time. Hidden neuroses keep popping up. Suddenly, without any reason, we break into tears; we cry and cry and break down completely. Suddenly we would like to destroy the whole world and kick everybody out. We go to extremes.

Döns are unpredictable. Sometimes a dön doesn't go along with what we have started, so it pulls back. We have our fist extended in midair on the way to somebody's eyes, but suddenly there is nobody to encourage us, and our hand just drops down.

Döns pop up all the time, especially when you are careless. You go out without a coat and you catch a cold, or you don't watch your step and you slip and break your back. Döns come up in those ways. Your carelessness begins to affect you psychologically, and you get a sudden attack. Usually such upsurges coincide with a physical weakness of some kind, which is an interesting point not mentioned in the textbooks.

When you lose control, your problems take control and you lose your mindfulness, and with a loss of mindfulness, döns can attack you. But if you are working with mindfulness twenty-four hours a day, you will not have döns. Whenever there is a little gap in your mindfulness, döns could slip in. You have to face that fact. But with mindfulness, such problems can be avoided absolutely. That is an advertisement for being mindful. When you lose your mindfulness, you could welcome the döns as reminders. You could be grateful that they are telling you how unmindful you are being, so they are always welcome—but at the same time, you could continue with your mindfulness.

We do not regard feeding the döns as though once is enough. It is not like trick or treat, where they are going to go away. They come back again—and we should invite them back! However, inviting the ups and downs of those sudden attacks of neurosis is quite dangerous. Wives might be afraid of getting black eyes, and husbands might be afraid of being unable to enter their home and have a good dinner. But it is still important to invite the döns and to realize their possibilities. We are not going to get rid of them. We have to acknowledge that and be thankful for that.

According to this practice, we should feed the döns with torma. However, if we tried to do that literally, probably we would still have the same fits all the time. The idea of feeding the döns is somewhat symbolic. I don't think we can get rid of our ups and downs by giving them little Tibetan offerings. That would be far-fetched. Forgive me, but that is true. It needs more of a gesture than that. If you had a real feeling about offering, and were able to offer something that represents your existence as an expression of your opening and giving up, that could be okay. But that requires a high level of understanding.

Most people in the modern Western environment are not trained in that kind of ritualistic world, so they have very little feeling for such things. Ritualism becomes more a superstition than a sacred ceremony, which is problematic. Few people have experienced anything of that nature and found it meaningful. Genuine ritual means that we actually have to commit ourselves, rather than just having somebody sprinkle water on us, trying to make us feel good and happy. Most people have not experienced the depth of ritualism to the extent that they could actually put out cakes for the döns so that they will not attack them again. In order to do that, we would need immense sanity. So I don't suggest that you put out doggie bags for anybody, although it might be good for the local dogs and cats.

The idea of feeding the döns is to tell them how grateful you feel that they have caused you harm in the past. You would like to invite them back again and again to do the same thing to you. You are so grateful that they have awakened you from your sleepiness and slothfulness. So you ask the döns to wake you up as much as they can. Whenever any difficult situation comes along, you feel grateful. You appreciate anything that provides you with the opportunity for mindfulness or awareness, anything that shocks you. Rather than trying to ward off problems, you regard anything that can wake you up as the best.

The idea of giving offerings to those who create harm to us, those who are an evil influence on us, is quite complicated. It means more than just trying to feed little ghosts who spook us so that they will go away. The idea of offering to the döns is highly influenced by tantra.

Offering to the Dharmapalas

The fourth practice is asking the dharmapalas, or the protectors of the teachings, to help you in your practice. This is not quite the same thing as praying to your patron saint, asking them to make sure you can cross the river safely. It is a very ordinary and basic. The idea is that you have your root teacher who guides you and blesses you so that you could become a worthy student. Then at a lower level, you have protectors of the teachings, who will push you back to your discipline if you stray into any problems. The protectors are sort of like shepherds: if one sheep decides to run away, the shepherd drives it back into the corral. Likewise, you know that if you stray, the protectors will teach you how to come back. They will give you all sorts of messages. For instance, when you are in the middle of a tremendous fit of anger and aggression, and you have become a completely non-dharmic person, you might slam the door and catch your finger in it. That teaches you something. It is the dharmapala principle corralling you back to the world where you belong. If you have the slightest temptation to step out of the dharmic world, the protectors will herd you back—hurtle you back—to that world. That is the meaning of asking the dharmapalas or protectors to help you in your practice.

The dharmapalas or protectors represent your basic awareness. They take care of you not so much while you are absorbed in the meditative state of being, but during the postmeditation experience. That is why it is traditional to recite chants both at the end of the day, or at the end of a day's practice sessions, and when it is time to wake up in the morning. The idea is that from morning to evening, your life is secured purely by practice and learning, so your life is sacred. Toward the end of your day, quite possibly you might take a break from sacred activity and meditation. At that time, neuroses beyond measure could attack you, so that is the most dangerous time. The darkness is connected with evil, but it is not like the Christian concept of Satan. Instead, evil is regarded as a kind of hidden neurosis that might be indulged and thereby create obstacles to realization. So although you may be taking a break from your practice, in order not to create a complete break, you could ask the protectors of the dharma to work with you. But the protectors are no more than yourself. They are expressions of your own intelligence, which happens constantly.

The job of the protectors is to destroy any violence or confusion that takes place in you. Confusion is usually connected with aggression, which is *adharma,* or anti-dharma. Dharma does not have aggression; it is simple truth, but truth can be diverted or challenged by all kinds of concepts. Truth can be cut into pieces by one's own individual aggression. That aggression may be dirty aggression, or it could be very polite aggression smeared with honey and milk. But any such aggression is an expression of ego and needs to be cut through.

It is very necessary to work with the energy of aggression, and there are various levels and ways of doing so. In the vajrayana, there are many protector chants invoking great wrathful figures, or *mahakalas,* whose job is to cut through bloodthirsty subconscious gossip that does not allow any openness, simplicity, peace, or gentleness. The idea is to relate with gentleness, but in order to bring that gentleness into effect, you first have to cut through aggression. Otherwise, there would be no gentleness. So protector chants represent the idea that anybody who violates gentleness has to be cut through by means of gentleness. When gentleness becomes harsh, it becomes very powerful and can cut right through—and that cutting through creates further gentleness. It is like when a doctor says that a shot is not going to hurt you—just one little prick, and you are cured.

A further understanding of the dharmapalas or protectors is connected with the presentation of the dharma and how it can be handled properly in an individual's mind. That is my biggest concern. By inviting the dharmapalas, we are taking a lot of chances—not physically but spiritually. If the true teachings are not properly presented, if they are presented in the wrong way or a cowardly way, we could be struck down. So we are asking the dharmapalas to give us help and feedback—through mishaps, bankruptcies, windfalls, or any situation at all. That seems to be the basic point of offering to the dharmapalas.

16

Whatever you meet unexpectedly, join with meditation.

This slogan is about dealing with sudden occurrences. It says that you should join whatever comes up with meditation. What comes up is not regarded as a surprise, a threat, or an encouragement, but simply as an aspect of your discipline, awareness, and compassion. If somebody hits you in the face, that's fine, and if somebody decides to steal your Coca-Cola, that's fine too. That may be somewhat naive, but at the same time it is very powerful. It is not just a love-and-light approach. It is more than that. The idea is simply to be open and precise and to know your own territory, so you can relate with your own neurosis rather than expanding that neurosis to others.

"Whatever you meet" could be pleasurable or painful, but it always comes in the form of a surprise. You think that you have settled your affairs properly. You have your little apartment and you are settled in New York City. Your friends come around, and everything is okay, business is fine. Suddenly, out of nowhere, you realize that you have run out of money! Suddenly, your boyfriend or girlfriend is giving you up, or your patron is dead, or the floor of your apartment is falling down. Even simple situations could come as quite a surprise. You are in the middle of a peaceful, calm sitting practice and everything is fine—and somebody says, "Fuck you!" An insult comes out of nowhere. Or maybe somebody says, "You're fantastic!" You might suddenly inherit a million dollars just as you are fixing up your dilapidated apartment. "Whatever you meet" refers to any sudden occurrence; the surprise could go either way.

This slogan says that whatever you meet should be joined immediately with meditation. The idea is not to react right away to either painful or pleasurable situations. Instead, immediately apply the exchange of sending and taking, or tonglen. If you inherit a million dollars, you give it away, saying, "This is not for me. It belongs to all sentient beings." If you are being sued for a million dollars, you say, "I will take the blame, and anything positive that comes out of this belongs to all sentient beings."

When you first hear good news or bad news, you might gasp, "Aah!" That "Aah!" is a form of ultimate bodhichitta. But after that, you need to cultivate relative bodhichitta in order to make the whole thing pragmatic. Therefore, you practice sending and taking of whatever is necessary. The important point is that when you take, you take the worst, and when you send, you send the best. So don't take any credit—unless you have been blamed.

Sending and taking does not have to become martyrdom. When you actually begin to settle down to this kind of practice, to the level of being decent and good, you begin to feel very comfortable and relaxed in your world. It actually takes away your anxiety altogether, because you don't have to pretend. You don't have to be defensive and you don't have to attack others. What you say begins to make sense to others. There is so much accommodation taking place in you, and out of that comes some kind of power. The whole thing works very beautifully and wonderfully.

Point Four: Showing the Utilization
of Practice in One's Whole Life

The two slogans of the fourth point of mind training are instruc-
tions for completing your training. They are instructions on how to
lead your life from now until your death—about what you can do
while you are alive and what you can do when you are dying.

T HE FOURTH point of the seven points of mind training is connected
with the paramita of exertion. Exertion means freedom from laziness. In this case, laziness means a lack of mindfulness and a lack of joy
in discipline. When your mind is mixed with the dharma and you have
become a dharmic person, the connection has already been made, so you
have no problem dealing with laziness. However, if you have not yet made
that connection, laziness might still be a problem.

Exertion comes from developing joy and appreciation for what you
are doing. When you are about to take a holiday trip, you are inspired to
wake up in the morning because you are expecting to have a tremendous
experience. You trust that you are going to have a good trip, but you also
know that you will have to put effort into it. Likewise, with exertion, there
is a quality of celebration and joy, free from laziness.

It has been said in the scriptures that without exertion you cannot journey on the path. Even if you have the legs of discipline, without exertion
you cannot take any steps. You need to push yourself step-by-step, little by
little. In doing so you are actually connecting yourself to the path as you
are walking on it. Nevertheless, you will also experience resistance. That

resistance could be quelled by ceasing to dwell in the entertainment of your subconscious gossip, discursive thoughts, and emotionalism.

The two slogans of the fourth point of mind training are instructions for completing your training. They are instructions on how to lead your life from now until your death—about what you can do while you are alive and what you can do when you are dying.

17

Practice the five strengths, the condensed heart instructions.

According to this slogan, in order to practice your bodhisattva discipline throughout your whole life, you need five types of energizing factors, or five strengths: strong determination, familiarization, seed of virtue, reproach, and aspiration.

Strong Determination

With strong determination, you do not waste your time. You recognize that you and the practice are one, and that practice is your way of strengthening yourself. You may be feeling very feeble and uncertain, but with the strength of strong determination, as soon as you open your eyes and look out the window, as soon as you wake up, you reaffirm your commitment to continue with your bodhichitta practice. You also do so when you lie down on your bed at the end of the day, as you reflect back on your day's work and its problems, its frustrations, its pleasures, and all the good and bad things that happened. As you are dozing off, you think with strong determination that as soon as you wake up in the morning, you are going to resume your practice and maintain continual exertion and joy. So when you wake up in the morning, you have an attitude of looking forward to your day.

Strong determination is almost like falling completely in love with your practice. When you are in love, you long to go to bed with your lover and you long to wake up with your lover. You have appreciation and joy. With this strength, your practice does not become torture or torment. It does not become a cage, but it becomes a way of constantly cheering up. It might require exertion, a certain amount of pushing yourself, but you are well connected, so you are pleased to wake up in the morning and you are pleased to go to bed at night. Even your sleep becomes worthwhile, and you sleep in a good frame of mind. Strong determination is based on waking up basic goodness, the natural goodness of the alaya. You realize that you are in the right spot, in the right practice, so there is a feeling of joy.

Familiarization

Because you have developed strong determination, everything becomes familiar and natural. If you are mindless and lose your concentration or awareness, situations naturally remind you to go back to your practice. In the process of familiarization, your dharmic subconscious gossip begins to become more powerful than your ordinary subconscious gossip. When discursive thoughts become bothersome, you substitute dharmic thoughts. When you reflect on dharmic themes, such as the four noble truths, you are not producing passion, aggression, or ignorance. So your ordinary thinking is suspended, and beyond that, you might even begin to understand something about the topic. That is why we recite chants. While you are chanting, you don't say, "I hate my parents. I don't like my world"—you say something better than that. So at least at that point you are suspended. During meditation, when discursive thoughts arise, you could replace them with dharmic thoughts—but having noticed that you are thinking, you should always come back to your breath.

As with strong determination, the process of familiarization is also like falling in love. When somebody mentions your lover's name, you feel both pain and pleasure. You are excited by that person's name and by anything associated with them. In the same way, once the concept of egolessness has evolved in your mind, the natural tendency of mindfulness-awareness is to flash on that, to familiarize yourself with it.

Familiarization means that you no longer regard the dharma as a foreign entity. You begin to realize that the dharma is a household thought, a household word, and a household activity. Each time you uncork your bottle of wine, or unpop your Coca-Cola can, or pour yourself a glass of water, it reminds you of the dharma. Whatever you do becomes a reminder of the dharma. You can't get rid of it. The dharma has become natural, and you have learned to live with your sanity. At the beginning, that may be very hard to do, but once you have realized that your sanity is a part of your being, there should not be any problem.

Of course, you may occasionally want to take a break. You may want to run away and take a vacation from your sanity, to do something else. But as your strength becomes more powerful, your wickedness and insanity is changed into mindfulness and realization. Through the strength of familiarization, your wickedness is changed into wakefulness.

Seed of Virtue

The next strength is seed of virtue. In this case, virtue means that your body, speech, and mind are all dedicated to propagating bodhichitta in yourself. With the seed of virtue, you have tremendous yearning all the time, so you no longer want to take a rest from your wakefulness. You don't feel that you have had enough of it, or that you have to do something else instead.

At that point, however, your neurosis about individual freedom and rights might come up. You might think, "I have a right to do anything I want! I want to dive to the bottom of hell. I love it!" When that kind of reaction happens, you should pull yourself back up for your own sake. You should not just give in to the feeling that your sanity is claustrophobic but continue propagating the seed of virtue. You should not be content with what you are doing, and you should not take a break.

Reproach

This strength is based on reproaching your ego. You are encouraged to say to your ego, "You have created tremendous trouble for me, and I don't like you. You have caused me so much trouble by making me wander in the lower realms of samsara. I have no desire at all to hang around with you. I'm going to destroy you, this 'you.' But who are you, anyway? Go away! I don't like you." If you ever want to talk to yourself, you should talk in this way. In fact, sometimes talking to yourself in that way is highly recommended and very helpful. It is even worth talking to yourself in that way while taking a shower or sitting on the toilet seat. When you are driving, instead of turning on the radio, you could turn on your reproach to your ego. If you are accompanied by somebody, you might feel embarrassed, but you could still whisper to yourself. That is the best way to become an eccentric bodhisattva.

Aspiration

Because you have experienced joy and celebration in your practice, it does not feel like a burden to you. Therefore, you aspire further and further. You would like to attain enlightenment. You would like to free yourself from neurosis. You would also like to serve all other sentient beings throughout all times and all situations and at any moment. You are willing to become a rock or a bridge or a highway. You are willing to serve any worthy cause that will help the world. This is the basic aspiration in taking the bodhisattva vow. It is also general instructions on becoming a very pliable person—a person that the rest of the world can use as a working basis for their enjoyment of sanity.

As an expression of your aspiration, when you practice meditation, you should end each session with three aspirations: to save all sentient beings by yourself single-handedly; not to forget twofold bodhichitta, even in your dreams; and to apply bodhichitta in spite of whatever chaos and obstacles may arise.

18

The mahayana instruction for how to die is the five strengths.*

The second slogan of the fourth point of mind training has to do with the future—your death. Like the previous slogan, it is based on the five strengths. The question of death is very important. The realization of the truth of suffering and impermanence is an essential first step in realizing the Buddha's teaching altogether. All of us will die sooner or later. Some of us will die very soon, and some of us might die somewhat later, but that is not a reason for relaxing. Instead, we need to learn how to make friends with our death.

According to the tradition of ego-oriented culture, death is seen as a defeat and an insult. Theistic disciplines teach us to believe in eternity, but the Buddhist tradition, particularly the mahayana, teaches us that death is a fact. Because we have been born, we have to die. That is a very obvious

---

* This is an earlier translation of this slogan. A later and more literal translation is "The mahayana instruction for ejection of consciousness at death / Is the five strengths: how you conduct yourself is important."

and sensible thing to say. But beyond that, we can make friends with our death and see how we can die as we are.

People usually try to ignore their death completely, particularly if they have incurable diseases. Even healthy people ignore their death. If you say to somebody, "Do you realize that you could die tomorrow?" that person will say, "Don't be silly! I'm okay." That attitude is an attempt to avoid something within us that is seen to be fundamentally ugly. But death need not be regarded as ugly. It could be regarded as a way of extending ourselves into the next life. Death could be seen as an invitation to allow this thing we cherish so very much, called our body, to perish.

On the whole, we try to take very good care of this pet called our body. We shave, we take showers and baths, and we clothe ourselves quite beautifully. It is like having a little puppy. We don't want our puppy to die, so we feed it with the very best food we can come up with. When I was in England, I even heard a story about a rich person who left lots of money in their will for their little Pekingese, so that when they died their Pekingese would be well housed and well fed. But this little pet called our body will leave us sooner or later!

We have to realize that anything could happen to any one of us. We could be very healthy, but we might not die from ill health—we might die from an accident. We might die from a terminal disease, and sometimes we die without any reason at all. We have no external or internal problems; we just suddenly perish. We run out of breath and drop dead on the spot. So the point of this slogan is to familiarize ourselves completely with our own death.

You may find that you are unable to relate with the dharma because you are trying so hard to hang on to your life. Any attack that comes to you, even a little splinter in your finger, means death. You immediately become alarmed. Although it is not at all reasonable to get emotional about a splinter, somehow you associate it with the destruction of your body and the idea of your death. You want to live so much, and in order to live, you can't do this and you can't do that. You take certain medications, follow certain programs, eat certain diets, or even follow certain ways of clothing yourself. Your fear of death is so strong that you can't even sit on your meditation cushion properly because you think the circulation in your legs might be cut off. You are so afraid to die.

We have to make a big transformation in our approach to death. To begin with, we have to get rid of the idea that death is ugly, that it has bad connotations. Then we will be able to establish a new ground for relating with death. Relating with our own death is very individual and personal. It is connected with how we relate with our life, how we relate with the gap between that and this. In many vajrayana texts, it is said that the moment of orgasm is the same as the moment of death. It is said that in both cases, a twist takes place in your state of mind, and you leave your body and enter into another world. It is very helpful to realize that the moment of death is the same as the moment of orgasm, because we see that death is not necessarily a condemnation.

Usually we regard death as the final threat. We have been trying to build ourselves up all along, but finally we drop dead. You may think, "What happens to my shampoo? And the razor blades, hundreds of thousands of them? What about the drink and food that I have been taking into myself for fifty years? The whole thing is going down the drain. I'm dropping dead!" That is not the best attitude. It would be better to appreciate that death is not a condemnation or a final negation of anything. Instead, it is continuity, going further. Your mind still exists; it is continuous. You can't get rid of your mind so easily, even though it might cause you trouble. Pain continues, unfortunately, and pleasure continues, fortunately. So death is just another transition, the same as the transition from one moment to any other moment. There is really no difference. But it is an interesting transition—you might end up as a dog.

The point is to realize that death is imminent and that you should talk about death freely. You should realize or imagine that you are dying and reflect on that. That would be very helpful. Doing so is like rehearsing a trip to Europe by going to Berlitz and learning how to speak Spanish or French. In this case, you are trying to learn death language. You have to prepare for death—you already booked your flight when you were born!

The instruction on how to die is not only about how to die when death comes to you. It is also a question of realizing that death is always there. One of the Kadampa teachers always put his drinking bowl upside down on his table when he went to bed. Traditionally, that means you are not going to be at home. You put your cup upside down so it won't get dusty, to keep it clean and pure so that somebody else can use it. That teacher always thought he might die that night, so he turned his bowl upside down.

You might think that is rather an eccentric way of going about things, but you should think twice or thrice when you say good night to somebody. You don't really know whether or not you are going to see them tomorrow. That may sound somewhat grim, if you view death as a disaster. But saying good night nicely to somebody is a great way to get out of your life and your body. It is a very glorious and humorous way of ending your life. You don't need to die filled with remorse. If you have practiced as much as you can in this life, with exertion and joy, you could die happily. When you are about to die, if somebody says, "Look here, it is going to be very difficult for you to go on. May I pull the plug for you?" you are able to say, "Yes, of course." Plug pulled out.

Death is not that grim. It is just that people are embarrassed to talk about it. Nowadays, people have no problem talking about sex or going to porno movies, but they have difficulty talking about death. Although we may have seen all sorts of gory things in the movies, we are still embarrassed. Thinking about death is a big deal for us. We have never wanted to reflect on death, and we have chosen to disregard the whole thing. We prefer to celebrate life rather than to prepare for death, or even to celebrate death. We try to block the message of death by beautifying ourselves, entertaining ourselves, and following this and that diet. We refuse to relate to death, and we try so hard to protect our health and our body that we become like living corpses. The idea of a living corpse may seem contradictory, but if we don't want to die, that is what we become. In contrast, this slogan tells us that it is important to include death as part of our practice. Since we are all going to die, we are all going to relate with death in any case.

Applying the five strengths to dying is very simple and straightforward. In this context, strong determination means taking a very strong stand to maintain your egolessness and sanity, even in your death. You should concentrate on twofold bodhichitta, repeating to yourself: "Before death and during the intermediate state, or *bardo*, and in all my births, may I not be separated from twofold bodhichitta."

Familiarization means developing your mindfulness and awareness so that you don't react with panic because you are dying. You remind yourself repeatedly of bodhichitta.

The seed of virtue means not resting or taking any break from your fear of death. When you are facing death, you need to overcome your attachment to your belongings.

Reproach is based on realizing that this so-called ego does not actually exist. Therefore, you could ask, "What am I afraid of, anyway? Go away, ego!" Recognizing that all problems come from ego and recognizing that all death is caused by ego, you develop revulsion for the ego and vow to overcome it.

With aspiration, you realize that you have tremendous strength, and you desire to continue to open yourself up so you have nothing to regret when you die. You have already accomplished everything that you can accomplish. You have become a good practitioner and developed your practice completely. You have realized the meaning of shamatha and vipashyana and of bodhichitta.

When you are dying, if possible you should practice the seven mahayana exercises: prostrations, offering, confession/acknowledging what you have done, rejoicing in the virtues of others, asking your teachers to turn the wheel of the dharma, requesting your teacher to remain and not pass into nirvana, and dedicating the merit of your practice for the benefit of all beings.* If you cannot do that, you should make this aspiration: "Throughout all my lives, may I practice the precious bodhichitta. May I meet a guru who will teach me. May the three jewels bless me so that I may do that."

Pith Instructions

Beyond all that, there is an interesting twist. The key instruction on death is to try to rest your mind in the nature of ultimate bodhichitta. You should rest your mind in the nature of alaya, and continue in that way with every breath you take until you are actually dead.

---

* If you are not capable of doing so yourself, it is also possible to have another person chant this sevenfold service for you as you are dying.

Point Five:
Evaluation of Mind Training

Whether teachings are based on the hinayana or mahayana, all of them agree that the purpose is simply to overcome ego. Otherwise, there is no purpose at all. . . . All the sutras, scriptures, or commentaries on the teachings of Buddhism you read should be understood as ways of taming your ego.

T HE FIFTH category of mind training, known as the evaluation of mind training, contains four slogans. The paramita of meditation, or dhyana, permeates this section of lojong. Meditation is a somewhat futuristic practice. Although you are sitting on your cushion as a regular person, you have the potential of sitting on the vajra throne as an enlightened one. The possibility of being fully realized is always there.

Through meditation, you are beginning to catch a possibility of prajna. You have the fever of prajna already; therefore, you begin to develop tremendous awareness and mindfulness. It has been said that shamatha-vipashyana protects you from the lethal fangs of wild animals, which represent the kleshas or neuroses. Without mindfulness and awareness, you have no way of protecting yourself from those attacks. Without them, you also have no facility to teach others or to work for the liberation of sentient beings. So intelligence is a guard against the kleshas. You are ready for them, ready to deal with them.

19

All dharma agrees at one point.

Whether teachings are based on the hinayana or mahayana, all of them agree that the purpose is simply to overcome ego. Otherwise, there is no purpose at all. In fact, this is one of the main differences between theism and nontheism. Theistic traditions tend to build an individual substance of some kind, so that you can then step out and do your own version of so-called bodhisattva actions. But in the nontheistic Buddhist tradition, we talk in terms of having no being, no characteristics of egohood. Therefore, we are able to perform a much broader version of bodhisattva action. All the sutras, scriptures, or commentaries on the teachings of Buddhism that you read should be understood as ways of taming your ego.

The hinayana version of taming ego is to cut through sloppiness and wandering mind by the application of shamatha discipline. Shamatha practice undermines the fundamental mechanism of ego, which is that ego has to maintain itself by providing lots of subconscious gossip and discursive thoughts. Beyond that, vipashyana brings awareness of the whole environment into our discipline. That allows us to become less self-centered and more in contact with the world around us, so there is less reference to "me" and "my-ness." Vipashyana allows us to cut through our ego. When we enter the bodhisattva path and begin to practice bodhichitta, our concern is more with warmth and skillfulness, with karuna and upaya. We realize we have nothing in ourselves to hang on to, so we can give away our attachment each time it arises.

In the hinayana, our ego begins to get a haircut. In the mahayana, the limbs of ego are cut, so there are no arms and legs. We even begin to open up the torso of ego. With ultimate bodhichitta, we take away the heart, so nothing of ego remains. Then with relative bodhichitta, we utilize the leftover mess of cut-off arms, legs, heads, and hearts. We find a lot of this mess, along with lots of blood on the floor, and we make use of it. We don't throw that away. We don't want to pollute our world with our leftover ego. Instead, we bring it onto the path of dharma by examining it and making use of it. So our progress on the path depends on how much we are able to shed our limbs, torso, and heart. According to another Kadam saying: "The shedding of ego is like a scale that measures the practitioner." The shedding of ego is the measure of how much meditation and awareness have developed and how much mindlessness has been overcome.

The amount of reality that is presented to you depends on how much the lesson of the subjugation of ego has taken hold in you. And the extent to which you are able to give up your personal project of ego aggrandizement and achieve the impersonal project of attaining enlightenment depends on how heavy-handed or open you are. In this particular journey, you and your commitment can be put on a scale and measured. If your ego is very heavy, you go down, and if your ego is light, you go up. All the dharmas that have been taught are based on that. There is no other dharma in the teachings of Buddha.

Bodhichitta practice is based on groundlessness or egolessness. When groundlessness becomes a continuing and natural part of discipline, we understand that we are not fighting our own war for our own victory. We are just giving up and going along with the general understanding of things as they are. Bodhichitta practice is not a personal project. It is beyond personal projects, so any further projects become nobody's projects. We do not possess any ground, and we do not need to build ourselves up. With groundlessness, there is an absence of personal projects or ego aggrandizement. With groundlessness there is compassion.

The basis of compassion is nonterritoriality, non-ego, no ego at all. Further warmth, workability, and gentleness take place as well. If there is no ego-clinging, then all dharmas are one. All the teachings are one teaching, which is compassion. But in order to develop an affectionate attitude to somebody else, you have to begin by experiencing the nonground quality of compassion. Otherwise, you become an egomaniac, and try to attract people with your seduction or arrogance. So emptiness and compassion work together. It is like sunning yourself at the beach: you do it because there is both sunlight and heat, and a beautiful view of the sea. Compassion arises because you have nothing to hold on to, nothing to work with, no project, no personal gain, and no ulterior motives. Therefore, whatever you do is a clean job. Once there is groundlessness, there is no notion of choosing compassion—whatever you do is compassion.

20

Of the two witnesses, hold the principal one.

In the phrase "Of the two witnesses," the "two" are you and the other. When you do something, you would like to get feedback from your world. You have your own opinion of yourself and how well you have done, which you usually keep to yourself, and you also have other people's opinions of how well you have done. But even though you have your own opinion, you branch out and ask somebody else, "Was that all right? How do you think I'm doing?" That is a traditional question that comes up in meetings between teachers and students.

This slogan says that of the two witnesses, or two judges, you should hold the principal one. The actual, authentic witness is you. If you have been raised in the Judeo-Christian tradition, you may associate the idea of judging yourself with guilt. But we do not acknowledge concepts like original sin, and from our point of view you are not basically condemned. Your naughtiness is regarded as only temporary—but at the same time, it is witnessed.

You are the only person who knows yourself. People may be very impressed by you because you look fit and cheerful, and you seem to know what you are doing. Sometimes you receive a lot of compliments, and sometimes you hear a lot of criticism from people who do not properly and fully know what is actually happening within you. But you are the only person who has been with yourself since you were born. And even before that, you carried your own great karmic baggage with you. You decided to enter the womb of somebody or other, and you came out of it, and you still carry your baggage along with you. You feel your own pain and pleasure. You are the one who experienced your infancy, the pain and pleasure of it. You are the one who went through your teenagehood, the pain and pleasure of it, and you are the one experiencing your adulthood, the pain and pleasure of it. You may be beginning to experience your middle-age years, the pain and pleasure of it, and finally you will experience getting old and dying, the pain and pleasure of it. So you have never been away from yourself for even a minute.

You know yourself so well; therefore, you are the best judge of yourself. You know how naughty you are. You know how you try to be sensible, and you also know how you sometimes try to sneak things in. Usually you are talking to yourself: "I" is talking to "am." "Am I to do this? Am I to do something naughty? If I do, nobody will know." Only we know, so we could do it and we might get away with it. There are lots of tricks, projects, and activities that you and yourself do together, hoping that nobody will actually find out. If you had to lay the whole thing out in the open, it would be embarrassing. You would feel so strange. Of course, it is also possible that you are trying to be very good. You could be trying to be good so that somebody will be impressed with you and with how much effort you put into yourself. But if you had to spell the whole thing out, nobody would actually believe how good you were trying to be. People would think it was just a joke.

Only you really know yourself. You know that at every moment. You know the way you do things—the way you brush your teeth, the way you comb your hair, the way you take your shower, the way you put on your clothes, the way you conduct yourself in talking to somebody else, the way you eat. During all of those things, "I" and "am" are still carrying on a conversation about everything else. So there are a lot of unsaid things happening to you all the time. Therefore, the principal witness is you. The judgment of how you are progressing in your lojong practice is yours. You know best about yourself, so you should work with yourself constantly.

This slogan is based on trusting your intelligence rather than trusting your self, which could be very selfish. It is trusting your intelligence by knowing who you are and what you are. Because you know yourself so well, any deception could be cut through. You should come back to your own judgment, to your own knowledge of the tricks you play on yourself and others. So relying on the principal witness is not self-centered. Instead, it is self-inspired from the point of view of the nonexistence of ego. You just witness what you are without being judgmental. You are simply witnessing and evaluating the merit, rather than analyzing or psychologizing it.

21

Always maintain only a joyful mind.

The mahayana experience of reality and how mahayanists work with reality completely and fully is bounded by several categories. But these categories all combine into one basic point—the notion of compassion, or karuna. In fact, that is the hidden continuity that goes through the entire path right from the beginning. The hinayana aspect of compassion is based on nonaggression, on doing no harm to others; the continuation of that compassion in the mahayana is doing good for others.

Compassion is being both soft to oneself and disciplined with oneself. Although you may not yet have achieved twofold egolessness or one-and-a-half-fold egolessness, if you have compassion, you are actually able to practice the mahayana completely and fully. In interpersonal relationships—sexual relationships, business relationships, or whatever relationships you have—mahayana practice is very applicable. It helped me a lot personally, and it could also help you.

There is a sense of delight, as well as of egolessness, in the discipline of compassion. That sense of delight is present right from the beginning of the hinayana and mahayana paths, when we begin to feel a quality of joy, purpose, and strength. You take joy in having the right teacher to work with you, the right discipline, and the right conviction or faith. You have a genuine appreciation of the teachings and you are delighted with the whole thing, almost high. In other words, you feel fundamentally good. That feeling comes from no longer having any little pockets of deception. In fact, you have become bankrupt of reserves of any kind. You have been squeezed by the dharma, and fundamentally you have given up.

When I was about ten years old, I was studying the Kadampa slogans with my teacher. In spite of the overwhelming presence of my tutors, who were usually very nasty, I felt relieved that I had nothing to do but take pride in the dharma. There was no other entertainment for me. I felt extremely relieved that I could be gentle. I realized that if I pushed, I would be pushed back. I felt very good about the whole thing, and I have felt that way ever since. I feel extremely good that I am a practitioner, that I am following the path of the bodhisattva, and that I am a nontheistic Buddhist. I feel eternally grateful and good, and I would like you to share that feeling. You should know firsthand how it feels to be captured by the dharma, to be squeezed into the dharmic world. Obviously, you have more choices than I did, but that same situation of being cornered by the dharma could also happen to you. So I am sharing with you what I experienced. And later on, when students came to me, I began to realize that I was now the corner, and it was the students who were being pushed in.

The slogan "Always maintain only a joyful mind" means that you should maintain satisfaction and joyfulness in spite of all the little problems and hassles that take place in your life. In fact, every mishap is good, because it is encouragement for you to practice the dharma. Other people's mishaps are good also, as the continuity of their practice and discipline. You should share those mishaps as well, and bring them into yourself. It is a joy to feel that way; you feel so good. I felt that way myself. I felt so strong and strengthened by the dharma—so grateful, so good, and so joyful.

The warmth and sympathy of compassion has that same quality of joyfulness. You begin to take a very cheerful attitude toward the practice of mahayana. You are no longer pushed into the depths of the ghetto of human punishment, and you are transcending any kind of "Oy vey!" approach. You are getting out of Brooklyn, metaphorically speaking.

Cheerfulness has a lot of guts. It is an expression of buddha nature, or tathagatagarbha. Cheerfulness can be found in the compassion of people like Avalokiteshvara, Manjushri, Jamgön Kongtrül, Milarepa, Marpa, and all the rest of the gang. They have already experienced such a thing, and so could you.

The other day I was talking to a close friend of mine. She said that because her mother was insane, she felt that she had the kernel of insanity in herself as well, so she didn't want to push too hard. She thought that if she pushed too hard, that kernel of insanity would begin to grow and become gigantic, and she would become a monster, just like her mother. But out of that feeling of wretchedness, something positive can begin to grow. When you begin to feel wretched, terrible, absurd, stupid, and mean, that is a very good starting point for the discovery of buddha nature.

My friend had enough guts to tell me how she felt, which I thought was the essence of tathagatagarbha. She was willing to relate with somebody and to communicate that. My friend felt that her experience was pointing her to something that she used to believe and that quite possibly she could rediscover. She thought that kernel of insanity might have something else inside it, that it might turn out actually to be a kernel of sanity or buddha nature. My friend was afraid of that possibility, and at the same time she was ripe for it. It was as if she were having cramps, and was about to give birth to a baby.

That kernel of neurosis in the depth of the depths of my friend's being was softness, which is all-joyful. At that point, pain and pleasure are mixed together, and pleasure is more powerful than pain. I felt quite proud of my friend. It was very good that she said that; it meant that there was a working basis. Usually people philosophize everything, and you can't actually get a hold on anything. But she was able to say, "This is happening in me, and I feel terrible." I was able to hold on to that as a working basis, and she was able to hold on to it as well. That was the basis of our communication, and buddha nature was the pith of it. And that buddha nature keeps growing hour by hour, day by day, right now.

Since you are not condemned, you could apply a joyful mind. You do not have to be startled by sudden wretchedness or, for that matter, by sudden upliftedness. Instead, you could maintain your cheerfulness all along. To start with, you could maintain a sense of cheerfulness because you are on the path. You are actually doing something about yourself. Many sentient beings have no idea what to do with themselves, but at least you have a lead on it, which is fantastic. You might have heard a lot about the bodhisattva ideal already and become familiar with the whole thing, but if you step out into Brooklyn or into the Black Hole of Calcutta, you will realize that what you are trying to do with yourself on the bodhisattva path is incredible. Most people do not have the slightest idea about that possibility. The bodhisattva path is an incredible, fantastic idea. You should be tremendously excited and feel wonderful that somebody ever thought of such a thing.

Whenever you feel depressed, whenever you feel that you do not have enough in the environment to cheer you up, or whenever you feel that you do not have the feedback you need in order to practice, you can refer back to that quality of joy and celebration. Whether it is a rainy day, a sunny day, a very hot day, or a very cold day; whether you are hungry, thirsty, or full; whether you are healthy or sick—you can maintain cheerfulness. Constantly applying only a joyful mind allows you to wake yourself up.

22

If you can practice even when distracted, you are well trained.

According to this slogan, whenever extraordinary situations come up— your pot boils over, or your steak is turned into charcoal, or you suddenly slip or lose your grasp—a sudden memory of awareness should take place. It is like a well-trained, powerful horse that loses its balance, and in the middle of doing so, suddenly regains it. This is like an athlete who slips, and in the process of slipping, regains their balance by using the momentum of the slipping process. It is like skiing, where by using the force of gravity and letting yourself slide through the snow, you develop balance and attention. But this slogan is not about becoming chauvinistic about practice; there is a need for renunciation. You are not trying to be a fantastically powerful and strong person who has mindfulness taking place all the time. But when something hits you as a result of unmindfulness, suddenly that unmindfulness itself automatically creates a reminder of mindfulness. So you are able to get back on track, so to speak, and you are able to handle your life.

If you are a good rider, even if your mind is wandering, you do not fall off your horse. You have been trained already, so you will not have any problem in continuing. So when either pleasurable or painful circumstances hit you, you do not become the slave of those situations. You have learned how to reflect suddenly, on the spot, on shinjang, tonglen, and bodhichitta, so you are not subject to extreme pleasure, extreme pain, or depression. If you become uptight and lose your awareness, at the same time you regain it. And whenever there is a sudden surprise in your life and the fear of seeming to lose your grip on reality, it could be included in your practice. In our tradition, any chaos that comes up is regarded as an opportunity for holiness, for some kind of help, blessing, or prayer. In ordinary life as well as in the theistic traditions, when something shocking happens, we yell, "Goodness!" or we shout sacred names. Traditionally, that was supposed to be a reminder for awareness, but these days we utter such phrases and swear words in a more degraded way.

When you meet with a situation, it affects your emotions and your state of mind. But suddenly, because of that jolt, the situation itself becomes your awareness and mindfulness, so there is less need for you to put effort into it from your end. You don't have to try to project, to understand, or to be watchful. But that does not mean that you should give up trying, and things will come to you all the time. This slogan is connected with the paramita of meditation, and there is obviously a need for you to develop awareness and mindfulness and to be alert. In fact, that alertness could become your fundamental frame of mind.

This slogan is about realizing that you can practice in spite of your wandering thoughts. Let me give a personal example of that. At Surmang Monastery I was terribly hurt, psychologically depressed, and pushed into dark corners by my good tutors and my administration. When I felt remorseful, sad, and helpless—but carefully helpless, deliberately helpless—I used to think of my guru Jamgön Kongtrül and weep. My yearning for him was so great that I wept, but I didn't weep because I was deprived. In fact, I felt great about that weeping. I was weeping at my discovery of something new and good. I used to say to all my attendants, "Go out! I don't need to observe teatime. I'm going to read." Then I would lie back and just cry for thirty minutes or more. They became very worried, thinking that I was sick, but I would say, "Send them away! I don't need any more tea."

But I found that the approach of devotion and longing alone was not very effective. It was too early to introduce vajrayana devotion because we had not done enough basic training. So I developed a new tactic, which was purely in accordance with this slogan.

After Jamgön Kongtrül departed from Surmang, I kept thinking of him, and it actually cheered me up. When I visited him at his monastery, if there was any problem or chaos happening, I told Jamgön Kongtrül about it. And when I came back to Surmang, whenever anything happened, whether it was problems and chaos, or goodness and celebration, I would just come back to my existence and my memory of him, as well as my memory of the path and the practice. In doing so, I began to experience a quick and very direct awareness. That awareness was not particularly related with the memory of Jamgön Kongtrül. It was the awareness that comes when you are just drifting off, and the process of drifting brings you back. That is what this slogan is all about. When you are drifting off, if that process of drifting off brings you back, that is the mark of perfect practice.

The main logic of this section of the slogans, or the evaluation of mind training, is quite straightforward—it is not to let yourself be wounded by the fangs of the kleshas. The way to begin is by realizing that the point of all dharma is the taming of one's ego. That is the scale on which practitioners can be weighed. Then, rather than relying on the opinions of others, you rely on your own judgment as to how you are doing. Then you develop cheerfulness because you are not trapped in heavy-handed discipline. Whenever extremely evil situations or extremely joyful situations occur, you can experience joy. Finally, the mark of all this training is that you can practice even when distracted.

41

Point Six: Disciplines of Mind Training

[On the bodhisattva path,] with the help of shamatha and vipash-
yana, you learn how to consolidate yourself as a mahayana prac-
titioner—how to be in a state of compassion, kindness, openness,
and gentleness. At the same time, you experience a state of egoless-
ness in which there is no clinging. When you reach the point where
you are not dwelling on anything connected with ego, atman, or
soul, the activities described in the lojong text begin to manifest and
to permeate your life.

T HE SIXTH point of mind training contains sixteen slogans about
the discipline or ethics of mind training. Once more we are trying
to crack our ego, this time by means of prajna, the sixth paramita. In the
mahayana, as in the hinayana, prajna is regarded as the sword that cuts
the bondage of ego, and the way to develop prajna is through vipashyana
practice. So the prajna of vipashyana is what realizes egolessness.

Vipashyana is particularly connected with postmeditation experience.
It is a way of relating to your world and to a larger sense of your life.
By means of vipashyana, you are sharpening your intelligence in order
to work with yourself, so that whatever occurs in your life is governed
by prajna. Prajna cuts through habitual or potential neurosis. It is like
a sword that cuts you into pieces, or a surgeon who cuts into you and
examines you. If you are arrogant, you won't allow anybody to dissect
you, because arrogance is a form of solidifying. But in this case, you give

in to the surgeon and let their knife cut through you. You don't try to hold yourself together, and you are not afraid of your ego being exposed. Getting sewn up afterward is not particularly your concern, either. Dissecting is the important point.

Tremendous mindfulness and awareness develop through the bodhisattva path. With the help of shamatha and vipashyana, you learn how to consolidate yourself as a mahayana practitioner—how to be in a state of compassion, kindness, openness, and gentleness. At the same time, you experience a state of egolessness in which there is no clinging. When you reach the point where you are not dwelling on anything connected with ego, atman, or soul, the activities described in the lojong text begin to manifest and to permeate your life. You realize that there is no "I" to rely on, and no "am" to propagate your existence. Because of that, you are able to exchange yourself for others. By first sacrificing yourself, you are able to overcome obstacles and relate with the rest of the world. You learn how to deal with your journey on the path by means of the sword of prajna. So prajna brings you to one of the most crucial and important points of the mahayana path: the realization of twofold egolessness.

23

Always abide by the three basic principles.

This slogan is based on maintaining three basic principles: keeping the refuge and bodhisattva vows, refraining from outrageous actions, and developing patience.

Keeping the Refuge and Bodhisattva Vows

The first of the three principles is keeping the promises you made when you took the refuge and bodhisattva vows. It is quite straightforward: you should keep these promises completely. In practicing the buddhadharma, you keep the discipline of all three yanas. You practice hinayana mindfulness, mahayana benevolence, and vajrayana crazy wisdom—all at the same time.*

---

* *Yeshe chölwa,* or "wisdom gone wild," is a term for a level of realization that completely transcends the limits of conventional mind.

Refraining from Outrageous Actions

The second principle is refraining from outrageous actions. When you practice lojong, you realize that you should put others before yourself, so you try to act in a self-sacrificing manner. However, your attempt to manifest selflessness may become exhibitionism. You think that you are manifesting your unselfish actions because of your so-called convictions, but your actions are still based on the idea of your being a decent person. You have less sense of protecting *this*, but you might act on a whim and become very crazy. You might try to demonstrate your unselfishness by getting involved in outrageous actions such as getting arrested, going on long fasts, or lying down in the street in the name of bodhisattva activity. Many people have done just those things. However, that kind of activity should be regarded as exhibitionism rather than the accomplishment of bodhisattva action. If you begin to behave in a crazy style, unfounded in tradition, you may decide to disregard the dignity of other traditions and disrupt whole social setups. That is not supposed to happen. You should restrain yourself from doing such frivolous things.

Developing Patience

The third principle is developing patience. There is often some confusion about patience. You can be patient with your friends, but you cannot be patient with your enemies. You can be patient with people you are trying to cultivate, or your protégés, but you can't be patient with those who are outside of your circle of protégés. That approach is a form of personality cult, the cult of yourself, which is not a good idea.

At the prajna level, you realize how much you are trying to become something. When you have become somewhat accomplished in lojong practice, you may feel that it is time for you to branch out and become a leader or a hero, but you should watch out for that. With prajna, you are aware of such conduct and what you are doing. You are constantly watchful of all that.

Spiritual practice based on your own self-snugness and self-delight is most dangerous. You have your viewpoint worked out, your philosophy worked out, even your quotations. You have your grammar and your language already set up. But after all that, you still do not want to give up your ego, which is problematic. You do not want to give up your most sacred and secret property. With that approach, you are not actually following the journey properly, but maintaining some kind of ground. The dharma should not be perverted on the basis of such self-happiness or personal confirmation.

24

Change your attitude, but remain natural.

This slogan applies to the attempt to impose your power and authority on others. You usually practice gentleness and tenderness toward yourself, and the opposite of that toward others. First you want to preserve your own ground—others come afterward. But you need to reverse your attitude of always wanting to protect your own territory, so that you reflect on others first, and on yourself later.

You also try to get away with things. If you want something from outside, you send someone else to get it for you, instead of going and getting it yourself. You don't wash the dishes, hoping that somebody else will do it. Changing your attitude means reversing your attitude altogether, so that instead of making someone else do something for you, you do it yourself.

Having changed your attitude, the slogan then says to be natural and to relax. Because you are taming your basic being and your mind altogether, you do not constantly push other people around. Instead, you take the opportunity to blame yourself. You are changing your attitude so that instead of cherishing yourself, you cherish others—and then you just relax. It is very simple.

25

Don't talk about injured limbs.

Because of your arrogance and aggression, you might like to talk about other people's defects as a way of building yourself up. The point of this slogan is not to do so. "Injured limbs" can refer to a psychological defect or to a physical defect such as being blind, dumb, or slow. You may realize that a person is having problems dealing with their life, but you do not have to exaggerate that by making remarks about it. Instead of taking delight in their defect, you could simply accept it. Instead of regarding it as an ugly defect, you could recognize that it is just that person's response to reality. This same general approach is also found in Christianity. According to both Christianity and Buddhism, nobody is considered disreputable or condemned on account of their physical defects, but everybody is regarded as a worthy person.

26

Don't ponder others.

Because you have labored through your tonglen practice and worked so hard, you may develop tremendous arrogance. You feel that having gone through so much effort makes you more worthy than others. When you meet somebody who has not accomplished what you have, you like to put them down. You like to point out other people's little misgivings and problems. When somebody does something to you that violates your principles, you keep picking on that. You would like to make sure that person is subject to attacks, problems, and unhealthiness. The point of this slogan is simple: don't do that.

27

Work through the greatest defilements first.

Whatever is your greatest obstacle—whether it is aggression, passion, pride, arrogance, jealousy, or what have you—you should work with that first. You shouldn't say, "I will sit and meditate first, and I will deal with that later." Philosophical, metaphysical, poetic, artistic, or technological hang-ups are always related with your own neurosis. You should bring that out first rather than last. When you have a problem, you should work with that problem. All means should be applied in trying to tame it. But you should not try to arrive at certain results. The idea is to work on the highlights that come up, rather than regarding them as just junk. Whatever problem arises in your state of mind, you should work on it simply, directly, and straightforwardly. You do not just want to work with the chicken shit; you want to work with the chicken itself.

Calligraphy by Chögyam Trunpga Rinpoche.
"Always meditate on that which is most difficult. If you do not start right away,
the moment a difficulty arises, it is very hard to overcome it."

28

Abandon any hope of fruition.

You should give up any possibility of becoming the greatest person in the world by means of your training. You may quite impatiently expect that lojong practice will make you a better person. You may hope that you will be invited to more little clubs or gatherings by your protégés and friends, who are impressed with you. The point of this slogan is that you have to give up any such possibilities; otherwise, you could become an egomaniac. In other words, it is too early for you to collect disciples.

By relating properly to reality, you may have been able to achieve something. But in the buddhadharma, we are not looking for temporary revelation, and we are not saying that you have to achieve something. You may have become a great speaker, or a great psychologist who can cure people's neuroses. You may have become an accomplished literary figure who has written important books, or a famous musician who has produced successful song collections. But your connection with reality has been based on trying to subjugate the world in your own particular style, however subtle and sneaky it may be—and you may hope to attain enlightenment in the same way.

As a professional achiever, you think you can approach practice in the same way, using the same kind of tricks. You think that you can actually con the buddha mind within yourself and sneakily attain enlightenment. But according to this slogan, any pursuit of this life's happiness, joy, fame, or wisdom, as well as the hope of attaining some state of glorious liberation in the life hereafter, could be regarded as a problem.

29

Abandon poisonous food.

This is a very powerful slogan. It means that no matter what practice you do, if that practice is based on your own personal achievement, it is spiritual materialism. If your practice is for your own individual glory, it is poisonous. And if you think, "If I sit properly, with the greatest discipline and exertion, then I will become the best meditator of all!"—that too is a poisonous attitude. Likewise, thinking that you are in the right and others are wrong, or that you would like to conquer their wrongness or evil because you are on the side of God, is also like eating poisonous food. Such food may be presented to you beautifully and nicely, but when you eat it, it begins to stink.

If the practice of egolessness begins to become just another way of building up your ego—building your ego by giving up your ego—it will not take effect. In fact, rather than providing an eternally awakened state of mind, it will provide you with death, because you are still holding on to your ego. So whether you are sitting or doing postmeditation practice, if you are practicing for the purpose of self-improvement, it is like eating poisonous food.

30

Don't be so predictable.

Usually everything we do is predictable. If someone brings us a bottle of champagne, we repay that kindness by inviting them to dinner. And when someone does something bad to us, we repay them as well. Slowly we build up society in that way. But when somebody is about to inflict pain on you, rather than strategizing or waiting until that person actually attacks you, you could communicate immediately and directly.

As ordinary worldly people, we have relationships with both enemies and friends. We understand the debt we owe to our friends, and we hold resentment for our enemies. When somebody inflicts pain on us, we keep our resentment in long-term storage because we would eventually like to strike back at that person. We do not forget that insult in even twenty years. It is all very predictable.

This slogan has an interesting twist. Some people are trustworthy: when you become friends with people like that, they always remember your friendship, and the trust and commitment between you lasts for a long time. You should always remember your mutual connection with such trustworthy friends. But some friends are untrustworthy: they give you a bad deal and a lot of conflict. You should not constantly hold a grudge against them, and should not always remember that person's bad dealings with you. You need to give up your long memory of antagonism.

31

Don't malign others.

Disparaging people is a way of showing off your own virtue. When you talk about other people, it may be pleasantly coated with sugar and ice cream, but underneath you are trying to put them down. You think that your virtues seem stronger when the virtues of other people are lessened, so you want to show that they are less virtuous than you are. For instance, you might have better training in meditation, so you think, "Somebody else has a shorter attention span in shamatha practice than I do. Therefore, I am better." Or you may be well educated in the dharma, so you think, "Somebody else knows fewer dharma terms than I do. Therefore, I am better." Fundamentally, you are saying that other people are stupid and that you are better than them. You should not disparage or malign people in that way.

32

Don't wait in ambush.

This slogan is about attacking people when they are weak. If you are having a disagreement with somebody, you don't usually attack them right away because you don't want to be in a powerless position. You wait for them to fall apart, and then you attack. Sometimes you pretend to be their adviser, and you attack them in that disguise, pointing out to them how wretched they are. You say, "I have been waiting to tell you this. Now that you are falling apart completely, I am going to take the opportunity to tell you that you are not so good, and that I am in much better shape than you are." That is opportunism, a bandit's approach. That bandit's approach of waiting in ambush actually happens quite frequently. You wait for somebody to fall down so that you can attack; you wait for that person to fall into a trap. You want them to experience misfortune, and you hope that misfortune will take place in a way that will allow you to attack.

33

Don't bring things to a painful point.

This slogan means not to humiliate people. The bodhisattva approach is to encourage people on their path. However, you may try to discourage people and slow down their journey so that you can stay ahead of them. You may try to relate to them in a way that you think will help you progress much faster on the path than they do. But according to this slogan, instead of doing that, you should do the opposite—you should come along behind the others. You should not blame your own dissatisfaction, pain, and misery on anybody else, and you should not try to impose your power on others.

34

Don't transfer the ox's load to the cow.

This slogan is similar to the last one. The idea is that it is very easy to say, "It's not my fault, it's your fault. It's always your fault." But that is questionable. You have to think about your problems personally, honestly, and genuinely. If there were no "you" to initiate situations, there would be no problems. But since you exist, there are problems. You do not want to transfer that load. An ox is more capable of carrying heavy burdens than a cow, so the point is that you don't transfer your heavy load to someone who is weaker than you.

Transferring the ox's load to the cow is based on not wanting to deal with anything on your own. You don't want to take on any responsibilities—you just pass them on to your secretary, your friends, or anybody you can order about. Passing the buck in that way is a bad idea. You are supposed to be cutting down and creating less traffic in the samsaric world. You are supposed to be reducing chaos and administrative problems. You are supposed to be trying to sort things out. So although you could invite other people to be your helpers, you should not just pass the buck.

35

Don't try to be the fastest.

When you begin to develop your own understanding and appreciation of the dharma, you may fall into a sort of racehorse approach. You may become concerned with who is the fastest, who can best understand the highest meaning of tantra, who has the highest understanding of ultimate bodhichitta, who has understood any hidden teachings. You are concerned with who can sit better, who can eat better, who can do this and that better. You are always trying to race with other people. But if the path is regarded purely as a race, it is a problem. The whole thing becomes a game, rather than actual practice, and there is no seed of benevolence and gentleness in you. So you should not use your practice to get ahead of your fellow students. The point of this slogan is not to try to achieve fame, honor, or distinction through your practice.

36

Don't act with a twist.

Acting with a twist means that since you think you are going to get the best in any case, you might as well volunteer for the worst. That is very sneaky. You could act with a twist in dealing with your teacher or with anything else in your life. You could pretend to be a completely benevolent person who always takes the blame, realizing all along that you are going to get the best.

Acting with a twist is a form of spiritual materialism. You always have the ulterior motive of working for your own benefit. For instance, you may temporarily take the blame for something in order to get good results for yourself, or you may practice lojong with the idea of protecting yourself from sickness. The idea of this slogan is to drop that attitude of looking for personal benefits from practice either as an immediate or a long-term result.

37

Don't make gods into demons.

This slogan refers to the tendency to dwell on pain and go through life with constant complaints. By doing so, you make painful that which is inherently joyful. Likewise, through your arrogance, you make dharma into anti-dharma.

You may have achieved a certain level of taming yourself. Having developed tonglen and practiced exchanging yourself for others, you feel that your achievement is real. But you are so arrogant about the whole thing that your achievement begins to become evil. Because of your intention to show off, dharma has become adharma. Your achievement may be the right kind of achievement, and you may have a very good experience. But if you regard that as a way of proving yourself or building up your ego, it is not so good.

38

Don't seek others' pain as the limbs of your own happiness.

This slogan is about hoping that somebody else will suffer so that you can benefit. For instance, you may know that if a friend of yours dies, you might inherit something. Although you may benefit from that person's misfortune, you should not wish for that and dream about what you can get out of such a situation. Happiness that is built on pain is spurious and only leads to depression in the long run. The point is that you should not build your own happiness on the suffering of others.

42

Point Seven: Guidelines of Mind Training

By understanding and practicing lojong, you begin to become both humble and visionary. Smallness and bigness combined brings the possibility of overcoming ego in the fashion of absolute bodhichitta, and developing the softness, gentleness, and openness of relative bodhichitta. With that combination of humbleness and vision, you will be able to practice and follow the instructions of mind training properly and fully.

POINT SEVEN contains twenty-one slogans or guidelines. These slogans are instructions in how to proceed further in everyday life, and conduct yourself properly in your relationships and in the general postmeditation experience.

As you practice lojong, or mind training, you should become softer and more willing to adapt yourself to the rest of the world. All the slogans tell us the same thing: the problem is ego. If you become hard-nosed and individualistic, if you become aggressive toward your practice, if you develop self-righteousness or religiosity, if you think you are becoming the greatest practitioner of lojong ever, the problem is that your egotism is coming back. You would always like to prove yourself one way or the other, but that is problematic. Therefore, it is necessary to have appreciation and gratitude for the spiritual friend and the sangha. You should appreciate that without a practice environment, without a teacher, and without the dharma, you cannot practice. So appreciation and thankfulness seems to be most important.

You might think that you have tamed your unworkable ego and that your mind is completely soaked in the dharma, but it is still possible for you to become egotistical. In order to save yourself from that, a sense of gratitude toward the circumstances that brought you to the dharma is necessary. Gratitude humbles you, and at the same time uplifts you. Without gratitude, it is impossible to give rise to bodhichitta.

In order to arouse bodhichitta in your basic state of being, you have to learn to give and to open up. At the same time, you have to be visionary. You need to think, "The tathagatas, bodhisattvas, and buddhas of the past have gone through this journey. Therefore, I too would like to share this vision and journey in that same way." In order to do that, you have to relate with somebody who has done it already, which is the principle of the spiritual friend. Your relationship should not rest on the personality of the spiritual friend alone—the spiritual friend is simply a reflection of the teachings. You have to develop immense yearning, dedication, and appreciation for the teachings.

By understanding and practicing lojong, you begin to become both humble and visionary. On one hand, you are reduced in size; on the other hand, your size becomes larger. You are so small and so big. We could say that you are like a grain of sand with gigantic eyes. You are not arrogant, because you are as tiny as a grain of sand, but you have tremendous vision, because you have a pair of eyes the size of pots and pans. Smallness and bigness combined brings the possibility of overcoming ego in the fashion of absolute bodhichitta, as well as developing the softness, gentleness, and openness of relative bodhichitta. With that combination of humbleness and vision, you will be able to practice and follow the instructions of mind training properly and fully.

39

All activities should be done with one intention.

Your one intention should be to have gentleness toward others and a willingness to always be helpful. In whatever you do, whether sitting, walking, eating, drinking, and even sleeping, you should always take the attitude of being of benefit to all sentient beings. That seems to be the essence of the bodhisattva vow.

40

Correct all wrongs with one intention.

When you experience increasing kleshas, or you are in the midst of perverse circumstances such as serious illnesses, economic or domestic crises, court cases, or resistance to practice, you should develop compassion for all sentient beings, who also suffer like this—and you should aspire to take on their suffering yourself through the practice of lojong.

The problems you experience should be overcome right when they occur. If your practice becomes good when things are good for you, but nonexistent when things are bad, that is not the way. Instead, whether situations are extremely good or extremely bad, you should continue to do your practice. You need to stamp on obstacles. Whenever you don't want to practice, whenever any bad circumstance comes up, stamp on it! With this slogan you are deliberately, immediately, and very abruptly suppressing the kleshas.

41

Two activities: one at the beginning, one at the end.

The point of this slogan is to begin and end each day with twofold bodhichitta. In the morning, you should remember bodhichitta and take the attitude of not separating yourself from it. At the end of the day, you should examine what you have done. If you have not separated yourself from twofold bodhichitta, you should be delighted, and you should vow to take the same attitude again the next day. If you were separated from bodhichitta, you should vow to reconnect with it the next day. In this way, your life will be sandwiched by bodhichitta.

Because of your commitment and the vow you have taken to put others before yourself, at the beginning of the day, as soon as you wake up, you promise yourself that you will work on twofold bodhichitta and develop gentleness to yourself and others. You promise not to blame the world and other sentient beings, and you promise to take their pain on yourself. And at the end of the day, when you go to bed, you do the same thing. In that way, both your sleep and the day that follows are influenced by that commitment.

42

Whichever of the two occurs, be patient.

Whether you are in the midst of extreme happiness or extreme suffering, you should be patient. You should regard your suffering as the result of previous karma, but there is no need to feel remorseful. Instead, you should simply try to purify any evil deeds and obscurations. Your happiness is also the result of previous karma, so there is no reason to indulge in it. Instead, you should donate any riches to virtuous causes, and resolve to use your personal authenticity and power for virtue.

Whether a joyful or a painful situation occurs, your practice should not be swayed. You should maintain continual patience and continual practice. When things are disturbing or problematic for you, you may lose your sense of perspective and try to find some kind of scapegoat. You may try to justify your own inability to practice by coming up with all sorts of excuses and complaints—the environment is not right, the other practitioners are not right, the organization of the dharmic environment is not right. This pattern happens quite a lot among dharma students. In extreme cases, you may go back and take refuge in non-dharmic people and find situations in which your individual ego might be acknowledged. But patience means taking your time and being forbearing. It means that, whether situations are bad or good, you maintain your practice.

43

Observe these two, even at the risk of your life.

This slogan is about keeping your commitment to the two vows you have taken: the refuge vow and the bodhisattva vow. It means that you should maintain your hinayana and mahayana disciplines even at the risk of your life. To begin with, you should maintain the general lifestyle of being a decent Buddhist. Beyond that, the special discipline and practice of lojong should become a very important part of your life. You should keep the hinayana and mahayana disciplines, and the practice of lojong in particular.

44

Train in the three difficulties.

The three difficulties are the difficulty of recognizing your kleshas, the difficulty of overcoming them, and the difficulty of cutting through them. In order to deal with these difficulties, you need to recognize the kleshas, overcome them, and take a vow never to re-create them. So altogether there are six categories: three difficulties and three things to do about them.

Dealing with your own kleshas or neuroses is difficult. It is very difficult to recognize the point at which you are tricked by your neuroses, it is very difficult to overcome them, and it is very difficult to cut through them. So when a klesha arises, first you need to recognize it as neurosis. Secondly, you need to overcome it. Since neurosis comes from selfishness, from placing too much importance on yourself, the way to do that is to cut through your ego. Thirdly, you need to cut the continuity of the klesha, and vow never to re-create such a neurosis again. You should develop the determination to stop feeding the neurosis or being attracted to it. In order to overcome the kleshas, you need to take an abrupt approach.

45

Take on the three principal causes.

What causes you to be a good dharmic person or a bodhisattva? According to this slogan, the three causes are: having a good teacher, cultivating a mind and demeanor applicable to the dharma, and having the right practical circumstances for practicing the dharma.

The first cause is having a good teacher. You realize the necessity of the teacher, someone who introduces you to the dharma.

The second cause is cultivating a mind and demeanor applicable to the dharma. You realize that your mind should be tamed, but you may have all kinds of funny ambitions about your life and the dharma. You might get into the dharma in order to become a teacher, or to write a book, or to start a business. That kind of ambition was not all that prominent in the days when Jamgön Kongtrül wrote *The Great Path of Awakening,* but today there are more choices. You might think that by becoming a Buddhist, you could be a great hunter, a great author, a great bodhisattva, a great salesperson, or a great prostitute. But that kind of ambition is not all that good. Instead, you should reach the point where you say, "I would like to devote myself to the dharma completely and fully."

The third cause is having the right practical circumstances for practicing the dharma. You realize that you need to take an open attitude toward your life, and develop some kind of livelihood so you can economically afford to practice. Your food, clothes, and shelter need to be taken care of, and you need to have a roof over your head.

You should try to maintain those three causes and take delight that you have such an opportunity.

46

Pay heed that the three never wane.

The three that should never wane are devotion to your spiritual friend, delight in practice, and keeping the hinayana and mahayana disciplines. First, your mental attitude of admiration, dedication, and gratitude toward the spiritual friend should not diminish. Second, you should maintain a delightful attitude toward lojong. Your appreciation for receiving such teachings should not diminish. Third, you should maintain your conduct and the hinayana and mahayana vows you have taken. Your practice of the hinayana and mahayana disciplines should not diminish. At this point in mahayana practice, it is necessary to rouse an attitude of strength and energy.

There is a connection between the last three slogans. The slogan "Train in the three difficulties" is how to begin. The second slogan, "Take on the three principal causes," is how to proceed. The third slogan, "Pay heed that the three never wane," is what you are finally getting into.

47

Keep the three inseparable.

Your practice of lojong should be wholehearted and complete. In your three faculties of body, speech, and mind, you should be inseparable from lojong.

48

Train without bias in all areas.
It is crucial always to do this pervasively
and wholehcartcdly.

The practice of lojong includes everyone and everything. It is important to be thorough and impartial in your practice, excluding nothing at all that comes up in your experience.

49

Always meditate on whatever
provokes resentment.

Always meditate on that which is most difficult. If you do not start right away, the moment a difficulty arises, it is very hard to overcome it.

50

Don't be swayed by external circumstances.

Although your external circumstances may vary, your practice should not be dependent on that. Whether you are sick or well, rich or poor, have a good or a bad reputation, you should practice lojong. It is very simple. If your situation is right, breathe that out, and if your situation is wrong, breathe that in.

51

This time, practice the main points.

"This time" refers to this lifetime. You have wasted many lives in the past, and in the future you may not have the opportunity to practice. But now, as a human being who has heard the dharma, you do have that opportunity. So without wasting any more time, you should practice these three main points: the benefit of others is more important than yourself; practicing the teachings of the guru is more important than analytical study; and practicing bodhichitta is more important than any other practice.

52

Don't misinterpret.

In your practice, you may twist or misinterpret things. The six primary things that we tend to misinterpret are: patience, yearning, excitement, compassion, priorities, and joy. It is a misinterpretation of patience to be patient about everything in your life except for the practice of dharma. Misinterpreted yearning is to foster yearning for pleasure and wealth, but not to encourage the yearning to practice dharma thoroughly and properly. Misinterpreted excitement is to get excited by wealth and entertainment, but not to be excited by the study of dharma. Twisted compassion is being compassionate to those who endure hardships in order to practice dharma, but being unconcerned and uncompassionate to those who do evil. Twisted priorities means to work diligently out of self-interest for whatever benefits you in the world, but not to practice dharma. Twisted joy is to be happy when sorrow afflicts your enemies, but not to rejoice in virtue and in transcending samsara. You should absolutely and completely stop all six of those misinterpretations.

53

Don't vacillate.

You should not vacillate in your enthusiasm for practice. If you sometimes practice and other times do not, that will not give birth to certainty in the dharma. Therefore, don't think too much. Just concentrate one-pointedly on mind training.

54

Train wholeheartedly.

Trust yourself and your practice wholeheartedly. Train purely in lojong— single-mindedly, with no distractions.

55

Liberate yourself by examining and analyzing.

Simply look at your mind and analyze it. By doing those two things, you should be liberated from kleshas and ego-clinging. Then you can practice lojong.

56

Don't wallow in self-pity.

Don't feel sorry for yourself. If somebody else achieves success or inherits a million dollars, don't waste time feeling bad that it wasn't you.

57

Don't be jealous.

Don't be jealous if somebody else receives praise and you do not.

58

Don't be frivolous.

It is frivolous to be jealous of your friend's success. If an acquaintance is wearing a new tie or a new blouse that you yourself would like, don't capriciously point out its shortcomings to them. You could say, "Yes, it's nice, but it has a stain on it," but that will only serve to irritate them. It won't help either their practice or your own. Don't engage in such frivolity.

59

Don't expect applause.

Don't expect others to praise you or raise toasts to you. Don't count on receiving credit for your good deeds or good practice.

CONCLUDING VERSES

When the five dark ages occur,
This is the way to transform them into the path of bodhi.
This is the essence of the amrita of the oral instructions,
Which were handed down from the tradition of the sage
    of Suvarnadvipa.*

Having awakened the karma of previous training
And being urged on by intense dedication,
I disregarded misfortune and slander
And received oral instruction on taming ego fixation.
Now, even at death, I will have no regrets.

[These two verses are the concluding comments of Geshe Chekawa
Yeshe Dorje, the author of *The Root Text of the Seven Points of Training the
Mind*.]

---

* *Suvarnadvipa* (Skt.) means "golden land." A reference to Sumatra, where Atisha received
the lojong teachings from Serlingpa.

43

Additional Mind-Training Instructions

Happiness usually is considered the high point of experience, and suffering is usually considered the bottom, so you are trying to roll up those two ends of experience. This is what the dharma is all about, very simply and basically. Happiness and suffering could meet together properly.

When you want to go, you want to stay.
When you want to stay, you want to go.

In addition to the fifty-nine Atisha slogans, the various commentaries have further slogans that are very colorful and beautiful, such as this one. This slogan, from Jamgön Kongtrül's commentary, is about conflicting emotions. When you are here, you want to be there, and when you are there, you want to be here. That kind of conflict is absolutely silly, and this problem has become heightened in modern times because we have so much freedom, so many options. We have rental cars all over the place, airports all over the place, taxis everywhere. We can do anything we want as long as we have money. Even if we do not have money, we can hitchhike. We can go anyplace we want, and we have the freedom to do anything we want.

Too much freedom can be a problem. It may cause you to panic and institutionalize yourself in a mental hospital where you can be given drugs, get food and shelter, and nobody will bother you. At the same time, there is always the possibility of indulging in your freedom, which is absolutely sickening. You want to go when you stay, and you want to stay when you go. You want to have a change. You want to move out to California. You want to join the Peace Corps and go to Africa instead of staying in your townhouse. You want to be a great poet instead of doing your plumbing. You want to change your life and make it brighter or more valid. But all those possibilities become questionable. There are all kinds of choices, but they are not real choices, simply superficial demonstrations of freedom. All kinds of absurdities come out of that approach, which is especially strong in the Western world. Providing all kinds of conveniences provides all kinds of neurosis at the same time.

Atisha never had any idea of that kind of thing, nor did Jamgön Kongtrül, but what they had to say is completely right on the dot. Your wanting to go when you want to stay and your wanting to stay when you want to go is an expression of the restlessness of mind, which takes place all the time. When your disposition is like that, the best place by far is right where you are sitting. Your present state is the most pleasant—you cannot get any better than this. It is the best you can get. You are alive here, and you can handle yourself here. Moreover, because you have gone through your discipline, your study, and your practice, you can make friends with your discomfort.

> *It is fortunate that you are not born in hell.*
> *It is fortunate for you that you are not*
> *being cooked and burnt.*

In this slogan, from a commentary attributed to Serlingpa entitled *Stages of the Heroic Mind,** the idea is that this is the best place you can be, so don't complain, just go along. You should be grateful that you have not actually gotten into a worse situation. Considering how you are handling yourself and how your neurosis is expanding all the time, you could have gotten into a much more terrible situation—but since you have not, you should be grateful. Where you are is best. Thinking in this way is supposed to be a way of cheering up. It is good attitude to take, although it may be very hard to do so.

In summarizing the lojong teachings, and to conclude his commentary, Jamgön Kongtrül gives four instructions: bring down happiness, cheer up suffering, understand that everything is a dream, and invite bad omens as

---

* This commentary can be found in *Mind Training: The Great Collection*, translated and edited by Thupten Jinpa (Boston: Wisdom Publications, 2006).

wealth. The first instruction is to create a counterweight for happiness. The second is to create a great terminator of suffering. The third instruction is to understand that everything is just a dream, that nothing relevant is taking place. It is to realize that everything is just an upsurge of your neurosis, desires, and wrong conclusions about things as they are. Your thinking, your considering what to do or what not to do, is a waste of your time. You understand what is irrelevant and what is not irrelevant. The fourth instruction is to invite bad omens as wealth. It is to regard anything that goes wrong, any mishaps and problems that take place in your life, as a treasure. You invite unwanted ego collections as wealth.

The four instructions are extraordinarily wise and powerful remedies to deal with strong emotions and to correct mistakes. Such instructions are said to be necessary in these deteriorating times or dark ages in order to subjugate misunderstandings and spiritual materialism. They are a way to roll up suffering and roll down happiness. Happiness usually is considered the high point of experience, and suffering is usually considered the bottom, so you are trying to roll up those two ends of experience. This is what the dharma is all about, very simply and basically. Happiness and suffering could meet together properly.

Usually our expectations are the opposite of these four dharmas. We expect that we can increase our happiness, kill our suffering, and not invite bad omens. We believe that reality is solid. But those particular expectations are irrelevant. Instead, the point is to realize that such experiences are actually workable.

Part Eight

THE BODHISATTVA'S JOURNEY

44

The Paths and Bhumis

Altogether on the bodhisattva path, there are ten stages, or bhumis.
At each of the ten stages you are loosening up and getting more
inspired, because there is less bondage of samsaric confusion or
aggression. However, there is more to the bodhisattva path than
purely engaging in peaceful activities or being a "goody-goody."

THE TEN BHUMIS:
STAGES OF THE BODHISATTVA PATH

Having practiced mahayana meditation and understood mahayana philosophy in terms of the shunyata experience, as you go through the process
of the mahayana path you get to various spiritual levels, which are called
bhumis in Sanskrit. Such states of being are permanent. They are not just
temporary experiences, or *nyam*.* Altogether on the bodhisattva path,
there are ten stages, or bhumis. Each stage has various attributes, virtues,
and styles of dealing with the world.† The Tibetan word for bhumi is *sa*,
which means "level," "earth," or "ground." At each of the ten stages you

---

* For a discussion of temporary meditative experiences called *nyam*, see volume 1 of the
Profound Treasury, chapter 42, "Mindfulness of Mind."
† The *ten bhumis* are (1) very joyful, (2) spotlessness, (3) illuminating, (4) radiating light,
(5) difficult to accomplish, (6) becoming manifest, (7) far gone, (8) immovable, (9) good
intellect, and (10) cloud of dharma. The birth of enlightenment is referred to as the eleventh bhumi, complete radiance.

are loosening up and getting more inspired, because there is less bondage of samsaric confusion or aggression. However, there is more to the bodhisattva path than purely engaging in peaceful activities or being a "goody-goody."

The paramitas are the contents of the bhumis. Each of the ten bhumis is associated with a particular paramita. The paramitas are what you practice, and the bhumis are what you get out of that practice. It is like going through the educational system: first you learn how to spell, how to read, and how to do math, and later those skills become the basis of your business or profession. It is very simple.

THE FIVE PATHS

The mahayana journey can also be described in terms of the five paths: the paths of accumulation, unification, seeing, meditation, and no more learning. The first two paths—the path of accumulation and the path of unification—are usually associated with the hinayana. The last three paths—the path of seeing, the path of meditation, and the path of no more learning—are usually associated with the mahayana.*

The Path of Accumulation

From the mahayana perspective, the path of accumulation, which is the first path, establishes your journey on the enlightened path of the bodhisattva right from the beginning. The background of egolessness, compassion, and trust provides a starting point and a general motivation. With that starting point, and on the basis of the evolution of your practice experience through an understanding of shila, samadhi, and prajna, you can enter onto the path of the bodhisattva very simply and directly.

The path of accumulation itself is divided into three stages: the lesser, medium, and greater paths of accumulation.

ATTITUDE LIKE THE EARTH. On the first stage of the path of accumulation, which is the lesser path of accumulation, your attitude is very respectful.

---

* For a discussion of the *five paths* from a hinayana perspective, see volume 1 of the *Profound Treasury*, part 5, "The Hinayana Journey," chapters 63 to 66.

You would like to enter the path. You begin to experience the sacredness of your world, and whatever you perceive or do becomes trustworthy and ordinary. You have respect for reality, and you do not confuse things. You work with your life in accord with the four elements of fire, earth, water, and air. There is a quality of rightness about interacting with your world in this way. You are not upset by the sunrise and sunset, by shadows, by snow falling, by raindrops, or by gusts of wind. Changing weather conditions do not affect your state of mind. The analogy for such an attitude is the earth. You are like the earth, which is very solid, sits through the four seasons, and has evolved for millions of years.

INTENTION LIKE GOLD. On the second stage of the path of accumulation, which is the medium path of accumulation, your intention is like gold. As a decent person, a good citizen of the bodhi path, you trust the process of the path. Because of that, you never change your mind, but remain solid in your practice. The analogy for intention is gold: gold remains pure, and that quality never changes, even over millions of years. Likewise, until the attainment of enlightenment, the quality of good intention never changes. It is like a trustworthy friend who never gives up on you.

WHOLESOMENESS LIKE THE FULL MOON. On the third stage of the path of accumulation, which is the greater path of accumulation, your wholesomeness is like the full moon. Your intentions are clear and your attitude is good, and you are not trying to be devious or tricky in order to escape. You develop generosity, discipline, and all the rest of the paramitas on a small scale, and you feel that you can act appropriately. The analogy for wholesomeness is the full moon: wholesomeness is like the full moon because you accumulate and expand various good dharmas.*

---

* The Jewel Ornament of Liberation lists twenty-two similes for bodhichitta, which are related to the paramitas and to the stages of the bodhisattva path: (1) the earth, (2) gold, (3) the moon, (4) fire, (5) a treasure, (6) a jewel mine, (7) the ocean, (8) a diamond, (9) a mountain, (10) medicine, (11) a teacher, (12) a wish-fulfilling jewel, (13) the sun, (14) a song, (15) a king, (16) a treasury, (17) a highway, (18) a carriage, (19) a fountain, (20) a lute, (21) a river, and (22) a cloud. The first three—the earth, gold, and the moon—apply to the three stages of the path of accumulation. For a list of similes and their relationship to the paths and bhumis, see the chart on page 396, "Stages of a Bodhisattva's Development and Corresponding Similes."

The Path of Unification

On the second path, the path of unification, your willingness is like a burning fire. Having already experienced the three stages of the path of accumulation, you are looking forward to the possibility of entering the mahayana. At this stage, you see that obstacles to the path of dharma can be burnt. You regard them as fuel rather than as barricades.*

The meditation experience of the path of unification is called *nampar mitokpa*. *Mitokpa* is "nonconceptualization," and *nampar* means "completely" or "properly"; so *nampar mitokpa* is "complete nonconceptualization." It is the final realization of the desolateness of the meditative state. Based on your shamatha-vipashyana experience, you begin to enter into shunyata practice and realization.

FOUR STAGES OF DISCRIMINATION. It is also said that on the path of unification, you develop four stages of discrimination: heat, crest, patience, and higher dharma.

Heat: a hint of mahayana. The path of unification is complete preparation for the mahayana. It is not the mahayana as such, but you get a hint of mahayana, a hint of shunyata. This is called *trö*, or "heat." It is like getting a fever before becoming seriously ill. With trö, you sense the possibility of treading on the path of the bodhisattva, and being a mahayanist who is fully dedicated to working with sentient beings. You are excited that you might attain the first bhumi at some point.†

Crest: terrifying sharpness and conviction. With crest, or *tsemo*, you develop terrifying sharpness and conviction. *Tsemo* means "peak," or "crest," as in the growing tip of a tree or plant. You are beginning to touch a sensitive point of your development, a once-in-a-lifetime experience. Tsemo is very penetrating. You feel a sharpness inside you, as if you had swallowed a razor blade. There is the possibility for the first time of becoming superhuman. But that cannot be achieved unless you relate with that insight and are willing to live with it.

The combination of heat and crest leads into a further process, the development of five perceptions and five powers.

The first perception is *faith* in your discovery.

---

* *Fire* is the fourth of the twenty-two similes for bodhichitta (see previous footnote).
† The first stage of the mahayana path. See chapter 45, "Very Joyful: The First Bhumi."

The second perception is *energy*. You are not tired of what you are trying to do, but you are highly energized and interested. The third perception is *mindfulness,* or *trenpa*. Mindfulness is twenty-four-hour work; you are completely at the mercy of the dharma. Trenpa brings egolessness because your only interest is in awakening bodhichitta. You have no personal interest in anything else.

The fourth perception is *samadhi,* or meditative absorption. With samadhi, even ordinary thoughts such as fantasies of aggression or sex become sources of inspiration on the bodhisattva path.

The fifth perception is *prajna,* or knowledge. You begin to discover all kinds of subtleties in the world—subtleties of colors and shapes, and implications of energy exchange—and whatever happens in your life becomes tremendously sharp. Life reveals itself on its own, not according to your own preconceived ideas, or ego's version of things.

All five perceptions are based on selflessness and the recognition that you are advancing on the path.

Along with the five perceptions, five powers develop at this point. The five powers are that faith never needs to be sought; energy never needs to be sought; mindfulness never needs to be sought; meditative absorption never needs to be sought; and prajna, or knowledge, never needs to be sought. With the five powers, you have complete command. You have developed the five perceptions, and you are confident about those abilities.

Patience: complete identification with the teachings. With patience, the teachings are a part of your system, so you are not impatiently looking forward to the next excitement, but you are willing to wait. Because you have identified with the teachings completely and thoroughly, you feel that you have the right to expound the teachings. The result of patience is that you develop the mental power to memorize the words you read or hear from the teacher. Forgetfulness is based on trying to preserve things for yourself. In contrast, an egoless approach toward sentient beings brings a tremendously sharp memory and powerful recollection.

Higher dharma: becoming a part of the lineage. Having developed conviction and powerful mental recollection, you begin to have the idea that you are a holder of the dharma. Although you may not yet have become a teacher, you feel that you are becoming a part of the lineage.

On the path of unification, you realize that your mind and body can be synchronized independent of the kleshas, or conflicting emotions. You have begun to take on an attitude that allows you to burn up the fuel of the kleshas. This change of attitude is based on joining mind and body; it is based on joining the very tranquil and the very active. You accumulate physical merit at the level of the ayatanas, or sense perceptions, and you join that with a pure state of mind, achieved by shamatha-vipashyana. By joining together the very tranquil and the very active, you are joining your intention and your action. That is what you do when you take the bodhisattva vow. Combining skillful means and prajna comes much later on the path, although it could happen even at this point, since it is a natural tendency already.

The path of unification links the past, or the path of accumulation, with the future, or the path of seeing. The path of seeing is forward vision, the fever of what you might do, and the path of accumulation is what you have already done. So on the path of unification, forward vision and what you have already experienced are joined.

The Path of Seeing

Traditionally it is said that the mahayana journey begins with the third path, the path of seeing, which is connected with the first bhumi. But that is not completely accurate, because each of the ten bhumis is a mixture of the path of seeing and the path of meditation. The mahayana begins with the path of seeing because you begin to have constant forward vision. Because you have forward vision, you begin to be pensive and have a quality of reserve.

The Path of Meditation

On bhumis two through ten, you are said to be on the fourth path, the path of meditation. So as you evolve through the paramitas to the level of jnana, you are on the path of meditation.

The Path of No More Learning

Finally, with the attainment of enlightenment, you are on the fifth and last path, the path of no more learning.

45

Very Joyful: The First Bhumi

The coming together of the hook of compassion and the ring of devotion is based on the idea that what you are doing is real. I think that is what the great joy of the first bhumi really means: what you are doing is real.

T HE FIRST bhumi is connected with the third path, the path of seeing. At this level the dharma is actually seen. You could say that the first bhumi is the loss of ego's virginity. It is as if until now you have only heard stories about the pleasures of sex, but now you are actually experiencing it. There is both apprehension and openness. It is very powerful and personal.

At the level of the first bhumi, a hint of meditation in action begins to develop. Your intellectual approaches to life and your personal experiences of life become one huge awareness. You no longer discriminate between the experiential and the intellectual—the whole thing becomes completely one. Having gone through that process, there is enormous joy and celebration.

The ground of the mahayana path is an attitude of openness, and the willingness to communicate and work with both yourself and others. Such an attitude comes about through training in the hinayana path of shamatha and vipashyana, which automatically evolves into compassion. You don't hold a grudge against anybody, whether you think your grudge is right, good, or logical, but you maintain a peaceful attitude, if we could use such a term as *peaceful attitude*.

In the mahayana, a basic understanding of shunyata is important. Shunyata is like the breath—if you don't have breath, you are dead. Shunyata is where we begin. With shunyata, you may go beyond the layperson's level of the bodhisattva path and become professional mahayanists, otherwise known as bodhisattvas. The first bhumi is called very joyful. It is analogous to a treasure mine, where you might find jewels such as diamonds, rubies, and emeralds embedded in the coal. It is like digging jewels from the earth.*

On the first bhumi, the path is both philosophical and experiential. You do not go to either extreme, for if you become sharp in one point, you lose the other. As the *Tao Te Ching* says: "If your knife is sharpened too much, it can quickly get dull." Buddhism teaches you how to be a good citizen, a good straightforward samsaric person. Dharma is accurate from the point of view of samsara, so to begin with, you have to develop samsaric logic thoroughly and completely—nirvanic logic comes afterward.† That is why the Buddhist path is called the middle way. It is not called the middle way because it is devoid of samsara or nirvana—and therefore it is safe—but because it is committed to samsara and nirvana at the same time.

There is enormous potential to raise the consciousness of all sentient beings, and particularly human beings. All the abilities of human beings, who are in the land of karma, all their intellect and intuition, could be raised up to the level of being immaculately clean, pure, powerful, and energetic. They could develop spontaneously, without straining. Buddhism is regarded as humanism because it develops human abilities.

The discoveries made in the first bhumi are fantastic. On the first bhumi, for the first time you begin to feel that you have been caught, like a ring caught by a hook. There is a sense of saving grace, as if somebody threw down a hook and pulled you up out of the turbulent, greasy ocean of samsara. Something is actually happening in your path. Because of that understanding, this bhumi is called *raptu gawa*. *Raptu* means "very," and *gawa* means "joy"; so *raptu gawa* means "extremely joyful." The myth

---

* A treasure is the fifth simile for the stages of the bodhisattva's development; it is connected with the first bhumi and the path of seeing. The closely related simile of a jewel mine is usually associated with the second bhumi.

† Trungpa Rinpoche often uses the phrase *thoroughly and completely*. In explaining his repeated emphasis on these two qualities, he points out that in the way he uses the terms, *completely* means that you have gone to the extreme of exposing yourself, and *thoroughly* means that you lose your reference point.

begins to become reality. Something is beginning to work. At the level of the first bhumi, you have no choice. What you have seen is fantastic and beautiful, so how could you go back to the dark dungeon of samsara?

The coming together of the hook of compassion and the ring of devotion is based on the idea that what you are doing is real. I think that is what the great joy of the first bhumi really means: what you are doing is real. You thought there could be a hook, but now you find that your ring is actually caught by somebody's hook, that it is actually functioning. For example, when I was living in Tibet, I was surprised to hear that such a thing as an airplane exists. When I first heard about airplanes, I wondered if they were real. But one day we were in our tutorial course out in a meadow studying "Prajna," the sixth chapter of Shantideva's book on the bodhisattva path,* when suddenly there was a roar up in the sky and somebody said, "It must be an airplane!" Somebody else said, "Oh no! There's no such thing!" Then we looked up and we saw this glittering, shiny, aluminum bird. It was very birdlike, but it was very solid and it didn't wave its wings. So airplanes do exist, and nobody can argue about that. It is reality, not a myth.

UNBIASED GENEROSITY

Because something is beginning to work, your practice automatically becomes that of the paramita of generosity. You are so relieved, confident, and overjoyed that you have found your own path that you wouldn't mind giving away anything. Having arrived at the other shore, what you arrive with is material, psychological, and spiritual generosity. Generosity is unbiased; you give without discrimination. It is a bit like being a drunken generous person, but if you are drunk, you regret your generosity along with your hangover the next day. In this case, there is no hangover—it is continual joy.

There is a way to practice generosity that may be unknown to you: you could just behave in a way that is generous, rather than being generous for a reason. You could develop the kind of unconditional discursive mind that triggers this kind of attitude. That is precisely what is brought out by the shunyata experience. You could be generous to somebody because

---

* A reference to the classic text *The Way of the Bodhisattva*, or the *Bodhicharyavatara* of Shantideva.

you are intelligent enough to see that the person needs help—not because it is a good thing to do, but as a natural, almost a physical, reflex. And if you feel like a do-gooder, you could acknowledge that, and work with your shunyata discipline.

FAINT SUGGESTION OF GOD REALM

The tremendous pleasure and appreciation of the first bhumi still has a faint suggestion of the realm of the gods, or *brahmaloka*. You have not yet cut through the cause and effect of the god realm. By relating with the absorptions, or jhanas,* you reach the level called *Tsangpa,* the realm of pure brahma. But this is not the same as the mahayana concept of pure land, which transcends the brahmaloka. Pure lands, such as the realm of Amitabha, are said to be at the seventh bhumi level, not the first.

Being in the realm of the gods is nice, but not quite freedom. There is still some self-consciousness to the experience of joy, due to the very fact that the idea of joy is conditional. There is a sense of completeness, a quality of absorption, and so much appreciation that you are almost hypnotized. You would like to sit back and relax. The joy and appreciation that everything is sharp and clear and beautiful is okay—but as a kind of delayed reaction you begin to hold on to it, or try to find some way of sneaking back. That little attempt to hang on to that quality of joy is where the quality of the god realm begins to come in—not as the first message, but in the faint watcher that develops. With true absorption, there are no gaps; it is total. Absorption is ineffable. There is no need to communicate this experience to people. Instead, bodhisattva activity is communicated by itself spontaneously. A bodhisattva does not have to make their enlightenment confessions to everybody.

REEXAMINING THE FOUR NOBLE TRUTHS

The four noble truths are (1) suffering, (2) the origin of suffering, (3) the cessation of suffering, and (4) the path. Until you reach the first bhumi and a sense of complete conviction develops, you will be unable to hear the dharma properly and thoroughly. Although you may have been work-

---

* *Jhanas* (Pali; Skt.: dhyanas) are subtle and progressively more refined states of meditative absorption, usually divided into four form jhanas and four formless jhanas.

ing very hard, you will not really understand the four noble truths. It is said that ordinary sentient beings hear the Buddha only partially, whereas bodhisattvas hear him completely. So once you attain the first bhumi, you become the true audience of the Buddha.

At the hinayana level, we talked about how suffering should be understood, the origin should be felt, and so forth. And at the mahayana level, you are examining the teaching of the four noble truths all over again. However, you now have a fantastically clear and precise way of looking at that teaching because you are able to hear Buddha speak. Your approach to the four noble truths is much greater, more sophisticated and powerful, because the isness of the dharma is utterly felt.

When you become a bodhisattva, because you have an understanding of openness, not only do you become perceptive enough to see the truth of suffering, but you develop enormous patience. Because you are patient, you are willing to wait and wait and wait to receive inspiration. You take a nonviolent approach, with no aggression or speeding, and with enormous patience and clarity you examine the truth of suffering as true dharma. And having realized the truth of suffering as true dharma, you see it simply as truth. You begin to develop a complete and full understanding of your state of mind. It is the full impact, as when you eat a meal, feel satisfied, and burp.

Finally, you reach complete understanding without being particularly patient or impatient, but simply by remaining in the state of beingness, or isness. You go through each of the four noble truths in that way. If you do so, this automatically has the quality of shamatha and vipashyana. However, until you are able to experience shamatha-vipashyana completely, until mahavipashyana is achieved, you will not have the faculty to understand the real meaning of the truth of suffering, the origin of suffering, the path, and the goal. With mahavipashyana, there is an appreciation of the teachings, and it is needless to push or discipline yourself, because discipline comes along with you.

THE SEVEN LIMBS OF A BODHISATTVA

At the level of the first bhumi, you begin to develop the seven limbs of a bodhisattva: (1) awareness, (2) discrimination, (3) effort, (4) joy, (5) shinjang, (6) samadhi, (7) equilibrium. In Tibetan this is called *changchup kyi yenlak*. *Changchup* means "enlightenment," *kyi* is "of," and *yenlak* is "limb"; so *changchup kyi yenlak* is "limbs of enlightenment."

Awareness

The first limb is called trenpa, which means "mindfulness," or "recollection." In Sanskrit it is *smriti*. Recollection loosens ego's hold on your psychology so you become joyful. It is as if you are in love for the first time. There is a romantic quality based not on egohood, but on an appreciation of dharmas. The tathagatas, sugatas, and buddhas seem to be singing along with your romantic songs. There is an enormous sense of celebration, and everything becomes part of your dharmic activity.

Discrimination

The second limb is called completely pure discrimination of dharmas, or *chö-je yang tak* (Skt.: dharmapravichaya). *Chö* is "dharma," *je* is "discrimination," *yang* is "perfect," and *tak* is "pure"; so *chö-je yang tak* means "perfectly pure discrimination of dharmas." You are fully in love with your own dharmas and you have developed enormous sensitivity. You see blueness and whiteness and redness; you see flowers, mountains, streams, bridges, highways, clouds, the sun, and the moon—everything that goes on in the realm of your mind—as visual bodhisattva demonstrations. You become highly discriminating, not in a biased way, but by seeing clearly with great precision. Without bias, things are seen to be more complementary to one another. We could say that the first bhumi experience is almost the equivalent, on the bodhisattva level, of the mahamudra experience of vajrayana. It is necessary and very powerful.

Effort

The third limb is tsöndrü. In Sanskrit it is *virya*, or "effort." Because such a magnificent display of the new world is revealed to you, you are willing to work hard.

Joy

Effort is followed by the fourth limb, which is *gawa*, or "joy" (Skt.: priti). There is a quality of celebration, joy, pleasure, and happiness. Because you have been being willing to work hard, with no punishment or guilt complex, a sense of joy takes place. You are not being persecuted, but you are being invited to become a bodhisattva. There is tremendous hospitality coming from the teacher and the teaching and the whole dharmic path.

Shinjang

The fifth limb is shinjang, which means "thoroughly processed" (Skt.: prashrabdhi). First you have awareness, then discrimination, then energy, then joy—and shinjang is further joy. Your whole system has no hang-ups: your body has no hang-ups, and your speech has no hang-ups. Your behavior, your relatives, your parents, your puppy dog, your car—whatever you have in your life is without hang-ups. Such things may seem to be problematic, but fundamentally they do not present you with any threat of real chaos at all. The whole process is perfectly smoothed out.

Samadhi

The sixth limb is tingdzin, or samadhi in Sanskrit. Tingdzin is beyond words; it is ineffable. There is no way of referring to your fantastic experience of the first bhumi—the joy, pleasure, excitement, smoothness, and uncomplicatedness. It is like getting out of your prison and being treated as a VIP who is bathed, fed with good food, and dressed in beautiful clothes. For the first time you have come out of prison into the real world. And it is actually true; that is what is happening.

Equilibrium

The last limb, number seven, is tang-nyom (Skt.: upeksha), which means "equilibrium," or "equality." Tang means "let go," or "let loose," and nyom is "equalizing"; so tang-nyom is "equilibrium." The reason equilibrium is the last limb is that there is no indulgence. Everything is so direct and obviously open that there is no threat. So you can relate with the rest of your environment and radiate joy, rather than keeping it to yourself.

The point of discussing these details of the bodhisattva's path is that the entire path becomes very real. You know the logic, how the psychology changes, how somebody could become a bodhisattva, and what that actually means.

Stages of a Bodhisattva's Development and Corresponding Similes

	Stages of a Bodhisattva's Development	Bhumi	Path	Paramita	Simile
1.	Hinayana		Accumulation (lesser)		Earth
2.			Accumulation (medium)		Gold
3.			Accumulation (greater)		Moon
4.			Unification		Fire
5.	Mahayana	1. Very Joyful	Seeing	Generosity	Great Treasure
6.		2. Spotlessness	Meditation	Discipline	Jewel Mine
7.		3. Illuminating		Patience	Great Ocean
8.		4. Radiating light		Exertion	Diamond
9		5. Difficult to accomplish		Meditation	King of Mountains
10.		6. Becoming manifest		Prajna	Medicine
11.		7. Far gone		Skillful Means	Spiritual Friend
12.		8. Immoveable		Aspiration	Wish-Fulfilling Gem
13.		9. Good intellect		Power	Sun
14.		10. Cloud of dharma		Wisdom / jnana	Dharma Song
15.	Buddhahood	11. Complete radiance	No more learning		King
16.					Treasury
17.					Highway
18.					Carriage
19.					Fountain
20.					Echo
21.					River
22.					Cloud

46

The Second through Tenth Bhumis

The details of the ten bhumis are definite, but the journey is guess-work. Supposedly, some people stay in a certain bhumi longer and others pass through quickly. . . . But for most people, the experience of the bhumis is an extremely gradual process. Nonetheless, enlightenment is possible, and traditionally one tends to get certain warnings of that possibility.

SPOTLESSNESS: THE SECOND BHUMI

The second bhumi is *trima mepa*. *Trima* means "spot," or "dirt," and *mepa* means "not"; so *trima mepa* means "purity," or "spotlessness." On this path, passive sitting and active awareness in everyday life become one. In terms of the five paths, the second through the tenth bhumis are connected with the fourth path, the path of meditation.

The Paramita of Discipline

Although the bodhisattva practices all ten paramitas, the emphasis in the second bhumi is predominately on shila paramita, or discipline. Usually the idea of discipline or morality is based on rules and regulations, and not following the rules inflicts guilt. But in this case, discipline is self-existent, and there is no guilt. So discipline becomes pure rather than a threat.

The practice of generosity could be tainted by a belief in the self and a quality of self-indulgence. You may feel that you are resourceful already, so you don't have anything to purify. So along with generosity, discipline is necessary. Discipline brings out and cleanses any germs you have collected. With discipline, you do not indulge in the sense pleasures. You are interested in understanding the meaning of dharma, and you are interested in how the world functions. You are working for the benefit of sentient beings, but you do not have a particular scheme, and you don't keep a diary of how many people you have saved or how great a social worker you are. Instead, there is a quality of simplicity. That simplicity is the key to helping other people as well as yourself.

Transcending the Realm of the Gods

The purpose of developing the second to the tenth bhumis is to completely transcend the realm of the gods. At this point you have already transcended the world of passion, or desire, which includes the hell realm, hungry ghost realm, animal realm, human realm, jealous god realm, and a lower portion of the realm of the gods, called the realm of Indra. But there are higher form and formless god realms, connected with the realm of Brahma.

On the path of meditation, you are not only transcending the karmic cause of being reborn in one of the six realms, but you are also transcending the highest experience of the god realm. You are transcending the absorptions, or jhana states.

The absorption states of the god realm are largely based on a sense of ego-oriented joy. The blissfulness of the god realms is connected with a state of being high and losing contact with reality. You are losing contact with your energy, your emotions, and your body. It is a realm of intoxication and vague pleasure, and with each of the four jhanas, you get higher and higher. From the bodhisattva's point of view, it is a kind of indulgence, a sort of jhana opium den. As you go through the bhumis, you transcend such god-realm experiences. That is what distinguishes the remaining bhumis from the first bhumi, which still has a faint connection with the god realm. In the first bhumi, experiences are very festive. However, your discriminating awareness is still functioning, and there is a pervasive quality of earthiness. So the feeling of joy and appreciation is still coming from a view of basic sanity, whereas there is actually very little joy in the blissful god realms.

The purpose of the path of meditation is to transcend the three worlds—the world of desire, the world of form, and the formless world—

totally and completely. On this path, you examine the mental attitude in such meditative absorptions. You examine the degree of the watcher. By doing so, you see that although you might experience a state of absorption or bliss, it is not joy, but pleasure.

The Eightfold Path

Bodhisattvas are able to keep away from the absorptions of the god realm and develop sanity because they practice the eightfold path: (1) right view, (2) right understanding, (3) right speech, (4) right action, (5) right livelihood, (6) right effort, (7) right recollection, or mindfulness, and (8) right meditation. The eightfold path plays an extremely important part throughout the ten bhumis of a bodhisattva's experience.

The right view of dharma is passionlessness. The purpose of dharma is not to fulfill one's desire, but to transcend one's desire.

Right understanding is not intellectual understanding alone, but intuitive precision. The phenomenal world can be regarded as a guideline to the bodhisattva's path.

Right speech means that a bodhisattva's approach to communication is gentle. Speech is no longer self-centered, and is true rather than false. A bodhisattva's speech is an expression of the needlessness of aggression. You have nothing to lose and nothing to gain. The path is open and you act freely, in accordance with your wisdom.

With right action, discipline or morality is not an attachment or an accessory, but an integral part of your whole body.

With right livelihood, you are not hassled by lack of money, too much money, or looking for a job. There is a feeling of confidence. Bodhisattvas may not always find good jobs or have lots of money, but they not hassled by a lack of balance in their daily existence.

With right effort, you are not tied to living in this world, but you are still constantly open to it. The world demands a lot of your attention and responsibility. There could be millions of things happening at once in your life, or in one moment of your life, but you are not hassled and there is a desire to exert yourself further. It is transcendental efficiency.

With right recollection or right mindfulness, the practice of awareness is not self-centered or paranoid. Awareness is spontaneous; it just happens. When a bodhisattva is absentminded, or forgets to give their bare attention to what they are doing, the forgetfulness itself acts as a reminder.

With *right meditation*, the bodhisattva is able to cut through the three worlds—the world of desire, the world of form, and the formless world—and is completely freed.

Overcoming Fear

The bodhisattva's attitude toward life at the second bhumi level is one of enormous power and energy. You are not afraid of taking responsibility. You also begin to comprehend the meaning of *dharmadhatu*, the space of dharma. You understand the meaning of it, and you see such a discovery as worthy of respect. It is a deepening of the shunyata experience of the first bhumi, in which you see emptiness and fullness simultaneously existent in the experience of the phenomenal world. You see the formlessness and fullness of reality. Both the spaciousness and active manifestation happening in the realm of experience are clearly comprehended, and doubts as to the nature of reality are cleared. That is the experience of dharmadhatu, and that is why this bhumi is called spotless.

It is said in the scriptures that a bodhisattva of the second bhumi will become a king or queen, a leader, or a wise person. You begin to regard yourself as a *dharmaraja*, a righteous sovereign of dharma. The joyful experience of the first bhumi leads to a sense of relaxation, and you understand completely the needlessness of fear. There are no dark corners. Your discipline is spotless, and your experience becomes open, powerful, and immaculate.

ILLUMINATING: THE THIRD BHUMI

The third bhumi is called *öjepa* in Tibetan. Ö means "light," and *jepa* means "creating," or "activating"; so *öjepa* means "illuminating." It is creating a quality of awakening. With each new level of the bodhisattva path, you have a sense that you are leaving the frontier, where things are not all that sophisticated, and approaching the capital, where the highest civilization exists. There is a feeling that as you get closer to the capital, that much more sophistication is taking place. Just as when rivers get closer to the ocean, a slow expansion takes place and they become bigger.

On the third bhumi, you begin to demonstrate your understanding and discipline without tiring and without aggression. You identify with the teachings. You are tremendously eager to comprehend the meaning of dharmadhatu, the nature of reality, and shunyata. In order to hear even four lines of dharma and transmit it to others, you would sacrifice your body. You are falling in love with the dharma and eager to learn it all.

The Paramita of Patience

The paramita for the third bhumi is patience, or söpa. You are patient with yourself, with the various practices required, and with the study and understanding of the dharma. Patience is a form of bravery: you are willing to jump in and let yourself be soaked in the dharma. You are willing to take a leap.

Patience is being without anger. It is the absence of a short temper. If you are teaching, you do not tire of relating the meaning of dharma to others. You are not bothered by students, but you are generous with the teachings. You are not bored by repeating the same verse or the same idea over and over again. You are also not discouraged by your own ignorance, but you keep wanting to learn more. You are able to prolong the threat of dissatisfaction in order to seek further dharma.

Experiencing the Truth of the Dharma

Dharma is a very personal experience. Sometimes what you learn from the teachers or the teachings makes sense to you, and sometimes you disbelieve the teachings, so you begin to play with the dharma, testing whether it is true or not. It is like you are a little child who has been told not to put your finger on the electric burner. When you quietly turn it on and touch it, sure enough you get burned. Likewise, by personally testing the teachings, a kind of transmission takes place. The bodhisattva experiences the truth of the dharma.

At the bodhisattva level, discursive thoughts regarding such concepts as nonduality or egolessness are considered to be valid, and even encouraged. Your whole being is beginning to become dharma. You begin to catch dharma fever, to be obsessed with dharma, even in your dreams. You are so much into it that everything becomes teaching. Ordinary things like going to a movie, watching people talk to each other, or seeing hot water boiling, all mean something to you. When we say that whatever you hear is the voice of dharma, it does not mean that somebody is reciting sutras. It means that you are learning from what is happening around you. You are obsessed with that, which seems to be fine.

RADIATING LIGHT: THE FOURTH BHUMI

The fourth bhumi is called *ötrowa,* which means "radiating light." Ö means "light" and *trowa* means "radiate," so *ötrowa* means "radiating light." It is like rays of fire, like a flame or a beam of light that destroys any desire for further achievement and further indulgence in spiritual development. At this point, the bodhisattva becomes highly competent, so they are willing to disregard their desire for the dharma. They begin to see through that. Even devotion to the Buddha is seen as desire and is disregarded.

The Paramita of Exertion

The paramita that goes with the fourth bhumi is exertion, or tsöndrü. It is energy, working hard. There is no hesitation in cutting your own spiritual materialism. You no longer regard yourself as a leader or an important person, and you are willing to mingle with simple people. You no longer preach the dharma, but just simply teach.

The patience of the third bhumi provides a lot of energy and power, and on the fourth bhumi, you develop sharpness and penetration. You know how to handle your laziness and you are willing to work. At the same time, you have a desire for simplicity. There is still the drive to teach others, but there is also the desire to be alone. Due to the element of cutting and destroying spiritual materialism, even the bodhisattva's desire to save all sentient beings is seen as self-aggrandizement. You want to pull back from that, and you are almost willing to retire.

When you work very hard, you cannot help feeling that you have achieved something. You feel proud, so there is a need for humbleness. Humbleness is important not only for your own development, but also to demonstrate that a bodhisattva of the fourth bhumi is not athletic in their bodhisattvahood. Exertion can be very harsh. But if there is no egolessness, no humility, and no softness, it is very difficult to practice the paramita of exertion. You need to be both communicative and humble.

In the paramita of exertion, hard work comes from joy. You have the right situation psychologically, physically, and environmentally, and you are not afraid of anything. You are not seduced into indulging the emotions or using them as a form of entertainment. You aren't thrown by sudden changes in your situation, such as your husband being killed in a car crash, or inheriting a billion dollars. You remain steady.

DIFFICULT TO ACCOMPLISH: THE FIFTH BHUMI

The fifth bhumi is called *shintu jangkawa,* which means "very difficult to accomplish."* *Shintu* means "very," *jong* means "to accomplish" or in this context "to conquer," and *kawa* means "difficult"; so *shintu jangkawa* means "very difficult to accomplish or to conquer." This bhumi provides a lot of challenges. You need to work with people who do you a disservice—even those who are your enemies. No one is excluded. You need to develop the quality of never being tired of working with fellow sentient beings.

The fifth bhumi combines practice and action, which is why it is difficult. You do not separate wisdom and experience, but realize that they are one. Dharmadhatu becomes completely one with your basic being.

On the fifth bhumi, you have to shift your mind in a slightly different angle than you were used to in the first four bhumis. Things become so powerful that it is like holding a thunderbolt in your hand and not knowing what to do. It is completely bewildering. You need more compassion and more shunyata to bring things together. There is a need for coordination. In the earlier bhumis, it was somewhat lopsided because different aspects of yourself were working on different paramitas. It was like training your right arm and leg separately from your left arm and leg, with no thought of putting them together and walking. But you need to coordinate your right and left sides as you walk. Likewise, you need the paramita of meditation to bring together the other paramitas.

The Paramita of Meditation

With the paramita of meditation, or *samten* paramita, there is a sense of comfort. You feel at home with shamatha and vipashyana. Your medi-

---

* Traditionally the *fifth bhumi* is called "difficult to conquer," implying that a bodhisattva at this level cannot be defeated by any worldly deity.

tation becomes completely identified with your own experience, to the level of welcoming the quality of cool boredom.* Having made yourself at home, you continue to cultivate knowledge and to work on the experience of shunyata, and you sharpen the meditation-in-action aspect as well. You need both shunyata and compassion. There is a kind of coexistence: you work with other people, you meditate, you work with other people, you meditate. It is as natural as breathing in and breathing out.

Unbiased Commitment to Others

On the fifth bhumi, you are beginning to turn around: you change your direction toward working with others, seeing that they really *are* more important than you. Until this point, although you have taken the bodhisattva vow, there is still self-orientation. You have been working with other people, but it is not really one hundred percent. You keep to yourself, or hope that others will be able to learn from you, rather than actually committing yourself to them. Up to this point, that kind of commitment has been very difficult to develop because you have been so preoccupied with what you were doing.

But at the fifth bhumi, you can work with sentient beings without bias. When you teach others, you don't act like a veteran who has come back from a war and is trying to tell everyone what it was like. That is a very heavy-handed approach. You still have not recovered from your own experiences, so you cannot really communicate them to somebody else. In teaching others, rather than being heavy-handed, the idea is that you should provide a space or a gap.

BECOMING MANIFEST: THE SIXTH BHUMI

The sixth bhumi is called *ngöndu kyurpa*, which means "something that becomes real, or manifest." *Ngön* means "visible," "complete," or "real," and *kyurpa* means "becoming"; so *ngöndu kyurpa* means that the first five

---

* *Cool boredom* is a term Trungpa Rinpoche uses to refer to a meditation experience that is at once solid and transparent. Such an experience is one of both absolute hopelessness and well-being. See volume 1 of the *Profound Treasury*, chapter 26, "Breathing Out."

paramita practices or the first five bhumis become real. You are less blind, and there is a more personal—or more impersonal—experience of prajna.

On this bhumi, you realize more and more that the idea of abandoning samsara and achieving nirvana is meaningless. Your prajna begins to cut through that dualistic notion and all other dualistic discriminations thoroughly and completely. Finally you end up nowhere, and from there you can develop a real approach to comprehending the dharma. You can sharpen your intellect at the highest level of prajna. So at this stage, the paramita practice of the bodhisattva is prajna, or transcendent knowledge.

Prajna Paramita

It has been said in the sutras that without the eye of prajna, the first five paramitas are blind. They cannot touch the bodhi mind. Prajna prepares you for all the remaining bhumis; it is a very essential practice and experience. With mundane prajna, you have been educated in the ordinary sense, so you have a way of linking yourself with other people. With supreme prajna, or prajna paramita, you transcend the ego of self and the ego of dharmas. You can relate with the phenomenal world intelligently, without ego orientation.

Prajna paramita is the mother who bore the buddhas of the past, present, and future. With prajna, you begin to find the origin of your basic being, at the same time knowing that you have no beginning, no end, and no middle. You discover shunyata. Nowness and endlessness are one in the perspective of prajna. In the discovery of shunyata, there is openness and endlessness. A million becomes zero. Because of the nonexistence of relative reference, the nonexistence of both *this* and *that,* the bodhisattva has very clear perception.

In the first five bhumis, you tried this way and that way, and you achieved a certain state of accomplishment. But with the sixth bhumi and prajna paramita, you finally discover the real way to view the dharma. It is like the acquisition of a good microscope: clear, precise, and penetrating. You are able to separate false dharma from true dharma. Your meditation is in the state of prajna, which is a very interesting state. In the previous bhumis, your experience of dharmadhatu had an element of peacefulness, but at this point your experience of dharmadhatu becomes a state of action. Meditative absorption is no longer passive, but it is very active and sharp, like the sword of Manjushri.

Before the sixth bhumi, prajna is sort of passive. It is like an inactive grandfather sitting in the back and encouraging you to unmask. That inactive aspect of prajna and the notion of shunyata are present from the first bhumi onward. But when you are on the seventh bhumi, upaya, or skillful means, becomes more active. The prajna of the sixth bhumi is like the acquisition of weapons, and the upaya of the seventh bhumi is like having the army that could use those weapons to destroy the twenty mountains of ego.* So from the sixth bhumi onward, prajna functions as a weapon or ornament. At this point, there are so many things happening that ego is completely bewildered. It has no role to play, so ego just slips back, and its functions become irrelevant. In tantra, the passive quality of prajna could be considered masculine, and the sword or active aspect of prajna could be regarded as feminine.

The fifth bhumi is analogous to a king of mountains because a mountain is unshakable; it conquers the whole environment. Once you are on the top of it, you can see the entire continent. Likewise, at the level of the sixth bhumi, there is both vision and solidity. Joining prajna and shunyata, joining learning with practice and experience, makes sense.

FAR GONE: THE SEVENTH BHUMI

The seventh bhumi is the last bhumi in which the bodhisattva has to go forward deliberately with diligence and effort. Therefore the name of this bhumi is *ringdu songwa*. *Ring* means "long," and *ringdu* means "longness," or "far away," *songwa* means "become," or "gone,"; so the translation of *ringdu songwa* is "far gone." The reason it is called "far gone" is because this is the last conventional bhumi.

---

* The *twenty mountains of ego* refer to the five components or backbone of ego, or the five skandhas, interpreted and reinterpreted four different ways—as the self, as the possession of the self, as within the self, and as the environment for the self—thus totaling twenty aspects altogether. Also referred to as twenty elements of samsara, or twenty things to be abandoned. These twenty are (1) grasping at self, (2) grasping at others, (3) grasping at one's life force, (4) grasping at people as active agents, (5) grasping at the impermanence of sentient beings, (6) grasping at the permanence of sentient beings, (7) grasping at duality, (8) grasping at various causes, (9) grasping at the five skandhas, (10) grasping at the dhatus, (11) grasping at the ayatanas, (12) grasping at the three worlds, (13) grasping at the kleshas, (14) discouragement with the path of dharma, (15) grasping at the Buddha and the attainment of nirvana, (16) grasping at the dharma, (17) grasping at the sangha, (18) clinging to morality and ethics, (19) dissension with emptiness, and (20) grasping at the conventional and emptiness as contradictory. See *The Jewel Ornament of Liberation*.

On the seventh bhumi, the bodhisattva has finally managed to destroy the twenty great mountains of ego.*

The Paramita of Skillful Means

The paramita practice related with this particular bhumi is upaya, or skill-ful means.†

Skillful means has two aspects: knowing your own skill, and knowing how to use your skill to work with sentient beings. You need to know what other people need, and you need to know your own strengths and weak-nesses. It is like knowing how much medicine to take yourself, and how big a dosage to give to others. With skillful means, you do not get carried away. You know that you have enormous resources and that you can use your effort, energy, and inspiration to help other people and yourself, but you do not use everything at once. You are very economical and careful.

It is quite clearly stated in the scriptures, particularly by Nagarjuna, that in the end, the ego is not acceptable. Up to a certain point, we might

---

* In *The Jewel Ornament of Liberation*, this is referred to as abandoning twenty kinds of attachment to self. You finally destroy that whole landscape. Previously you were still putting your own dwelling place in that landscape, but at this point you destroy all that completely.

On this bhumi, you begin to see that a hinayana understanding of the three marks of existence—suffering, impermanence, and egolessness—is still perpetuating ground, still supporting ego. You realize that you can use your understanding of suffering, imperma-nence, and egolessness as a way of establishing dharmic ground. You see through all that completely. Instead of using your understanding in that way, you use the three marks of existence as a bomb to explode the mountain ranges of ego, as a kind of mantric power. You begin to realize that even the understanding of the nonduality of dharmadhatu, or no subject-object division, is flawed, and that the idea of nonduality is also part of ego's mountain ranges. You see through that falsification as well.

† In discussions of the six paramitas, the first five combined are also referred to as *skill-ful means*, and the sixth, or prajna, is referred to as knowledge. According to Trungpa Rinpoche, skillful means as the particular paramita connected with the seventh bhumi is no longer simply a technique or a device, but a state of total understanding. The paramita of skillful means needs to be taken in and become a part of your body, a part of your basic being. It is like medicine: when you take medicine, it cures you, but it must be taken internally. You have to swallow it, chew it, or drink it. Once the medicine becomes part of your body, it begins to cure your sickness. It is the same with the paramita of skillful means: it must be taken in and become part of you rather than used as an embellishment. The traditional simile for the seventh bhumi is the spiritual friend; medicine is usually associated with the sixth bhumi.

make ego workable. We might work with it, tease it, and play with it—but in the end, ego has a philosophy that is unacceptable to the enlightened mind. So you have to attack it and kill it. That seems to be the heroic approach of the bodhisattva's way. There is definitely the notion of warfare and destruction. It is not particularly passive, but more like launching an attack. In this attack, prajna is used as a sword, and skillful means is the soldier. At the tantric level, we talk about the transmutation of ego, but transmutation is not all that kind and accepting a gesture. It is based on using the corpse of ego and bringing it to life, but in a very enlightened way.

IMMOVABLE: THE EIGHTH BHUMI

The eighth bhumi is called *miyowa*. *Yowa* means "moving," and *mi* is "negation"; so *miyowa* means "not moving." At this level you cease to be an ordinary bodhisattva and begin to touch the level of *mahasattva,* or "great being." Up through the seventh bhumi, you still have a feeling of journey, a sense of proceeding somewhere. But the mahasattva level is perpetual. You are like fully ripened fruit.

You could visualize the bodhisattva path as a journey in which you set sail from a huge continent, namely the samsaric world, and cross the ocean to get to an island you have seen. That island consists of the first seven bhumis and the corresponding paramitas. But then, having crossed that particular island and achieved the seven conventional paramitas—generosity, discipline, patience, exertion, meditation, prajna, and upaya—you take another boat. Now you are on an endless journey, a final journey. You have no more islands to cross. You have left the samsaric world, and you have completed the first seven bhumis. You have gone through the process necessary in order to go beyond into the larger ocean, the greater end-ness—or begin-ness, for that matter.

On the eighth bhumi, you are not moved by either the relative or absolute understanding of the phenomenal world. At the same time, you develop an enormous comprehension of other people. You see through people, you know them, and you understand completely what dharmic approach you might take with them. Tremendous communication takes place, which goes beyond the physical and verbal level to the environmental level.

At this stage, the bodhisattva has cut through the mentality of the formless gods, as well as the mentality of the gods of form and desire. Up to the seventh bhumi, spiritual materialism is a problem, as well as basic materialism and poverty. But the closer you get to enlightenment, the higher you go in the paths and bhumis, and the less spiritual materialism you have. However, psychological materialism and the need for basic security keep coming back.* Because you feel you are getting close to something, you are more concerned with your security. But at the eighth bhumi, spirituality is simply part of your behavior, so spiritual materialism is not a problem.

The Paramita of Aspiration

The eighth bhumi is connected with the paramita of aspiration. In Sanskrit, aspiration is *pranidhana,* and in Tibetan it is *mönlam. Mön* is often misinterpreted as "prayer," or "good wishes," and *lam* is "path"; so *mönlam* may seem to mean "wishful thinking." However, in this case, and particularly in the context of the bodhisattva path, *mönlam* is more like "aspiration," or "inspiration."

Aspiration is connected with vision. Generally what happens to us is that we cannot think bigger. We think that if we think bigger we are foolish, that we are speaking nonsense. We think that we cannot have a vision of something expanded, elaborate, open, and workable.

A personal experience of such a problem took place when we hosted the sixteenth Gyalwa Karmapa for his first visit to North America in 1975. We had no idea what to expect. Everybody was concerned that we might do the wrong thing, and some people thought that the visit might be too exorbitant and costly, and should be canceled. Small thinking is based on that kind of unfamiliarity and uncertainty. You are just about to approach something beyond your conception of what you can handle, and you begin to panic. When that panic happens, you become smaller and smaller, more and more practical, economical, and sensible. Because those are the only resources you have, having great vision is seen as madness and terrifying. You think that somebody who has great vision must be mad.

---

* Trungpa Rinpoche discusses materialism in terms of three levels: basic materialism, psychological materialism, and spiritual materialism. In the first, you cling to objects; in the second, you cling to ideas, identities, and ideologies; and in the third, you cling to religiosity and spiritual accomplishment.

Eighth-Bhumi Vision

Eighth-bhumi vision cannot be moved or changed. It is always there. By remaining immovable, you can expand. If you actually do not move, you accomplish everything at once—but if you try to move, you miss a lot of things. While you are there, you miss this, and while you are here, you miss that. The highest speed of all is not to move. You stay completely still. Immovability is good advice.

The eighth bhumi has two types of vision: temporary and permanent. Temporary vision means that whenever you need to be resourceful in working with sentient beings, a vision of how to help will arise. Mahasattvas do not have to think in terms of strategy—the situation comes to them. Permanent vision means that you do not step back. You never give up on your long-term projects, whatever they may be, but you expand your work infinitely and constantly. You are not panicked by expansion. The eighth bhumi is like a good friend who constantly encourages you to be brave and to expand.

On the eighth bhumi, the bodhisattva begins to give up the concept of deep understanding. The dharma is no longer regarded as understanding, and it is not even a state of being—it is just *there*. You do not attempt to confirm or not confirm anything. All those processes become meaningless. You do not destroy such false notions deliberately—they just leave you. They become irrelevant.

Ten Powers

On the eighth bhumi, the bodhisattva is the embodiment of peace and nonaggression, and begins to develop what are called the ten powers: power over life, mind, belongings, karma, birth, desire, aspiration, miracles, wisdom, and dharma. You are not imprisoned by anything, even your dedication to the paramitas. You are enormously inspired by the total needlessness of any conceptual pigeonholing, either spiritual or worldly. Enormous freedom is developed, and because of that, you achieve these ten powers.

Power over life, the first power, means that you are not threatened by life. You are no longer concerned with survival, physical or psychological threats, health concerns, or any form of discomfort.

Power over mind, the second power, means that you approach your mental activity as inspiration, rather than as something uncontrollable that takes you over.

Power over belongings, the third power, means that you do not become a slave to your belongings, for the very reason that you do not renounce anything—because once you begin to give something up, you become possessed by it at the same time.

With power over karma, the fourth power, because mental volitional action is being transmuted into aspiration, or pranidhana, you do not have hopes and fears of future karmic consequences.

With power over birth, the fifth power, your birth is not subject to national neurosis or national psychology, and it is not biased by genetics. You have free choice of rebirth: you have control over where you will be born and who your parents will be. Only the bodhisattva of the eighth bhumi has this major mark of spiritual achievement.

The sixth power is power over desire, or longing. This power has more of a pragmatic aspect, whereas power over aspiration has a more visionary quality.

The seventh power, power over aspiration, again refers to pranidhana, or mönlam. With pranidhana there is enormous openness, vision, and future orientation. You are bringing the future into the present. For instance, you might say that you are going to have a nice party this evening. When you project that idea of having a fantastic party and inviting lots of guests and providing good food and drink, your mind becomes open. It is as if you are already actually having the party, even though it is still in the future. It is like a great leader of a country having a vision of how the country should develop, or a good architect having a vision of a fantastic building complex. That kind of aspiration and future orientation is a form of capturing the future in the present by magical power. You are bringing the future into the present and executing your wishes accordingly. So your approach becomes up-to-date, rather than future-oriented dreaming, and your execution becomes accurate.

The eighth power is power over miracles. The general idea of a miracle is that it is like turning water into fire, or sky into earth, but in this case miracles are based on taking advantage of a situation rather than fighting against it. We may think that if we had power over miracles, we could conjure up a million dollars if we were poor, but that goes directly against our karmic inheritance. It is said that even the Buddha cannot change the law of karma, so miracles do not go against the karmic flow. A miracle is karmically lawful. Situations provide the source of miracles, like flint and stone create the spark to produce fire.

In a story about Milarepa, Milarepa appeared to his disciple Rechungpa inside a yak horn, without either changing or appearing to change size. That was a true miracle. It is said that Milarepa never become smaller, and the yak horn never became bigger, but Milarepa was still singing a song and sitting in the yak horn. How could Milarepa fit in a yak horn if he didn't become smaller and the yak horn didn't become bigger? That's a direct contradiction. But a person who is awake, up-to-date, and present can take advantage of situations and create seeming miracles. That kind of miracle brings you into the present. The purpose of a miracle is to stop your mind. Because your logic no longer functions, you have to stop and look twice. A miracle is not regarded as a gimmick, a game, or trickery.

The ninth power is power over wisdom. With this power, the source of wisdom is endless; the bodhisattva achieves inexhaustible wisdom, or jnana.

The tenth power is power over dharma. With this power, the bodhisattva becomes the holder of the dharma. Your approach and your way of relating with the teachings, yourself, and students is such that you become a dharmaraja, a king of dharma.

GOOD INTELLECT:
THE NINTH BHUMI

The bodhisattva of the eighth bhumi has achieved so much that it seems there is nothing left to do, but somehow there is still more—and we have not even gotten to the tantric level, or vajrayana. The ninth bhumi is called *lek-pe lodrö*. *Lek-pe* means "good," and *lodrö* means "intellect"; so *lek-pe lodrö* means "good intellect." On this bhumi, the epitome of discriminating wisdom is achieved. Good intellect has a nonflinching quality, and it is powerful. Once you begin to realize your own strength, you see that good intellect is much higher than ordinary intellect. The bodhisattva's penetration is more powerful and speedy, so powerful in fact that nobody can stop you from fulfilling your power properly.

Paramita of Power

The paramita connected with the ninth bhumi is power: the power of fearlessness and rejoicing. Conventionally, the word *power* has the sense of trying to gain victory. In a theistic approach to enlightenment, power is a victory over something, but in the nontheistic approach, power is based on rejoicing and fearlessness, rather than trying to conquer the world. It is being in the state of power, rather than having power over something or somebody.

The bodhisattva at this level has enormous ability to discriminate between this and that without dualistic neurosis. They know all the languages of the universe. The bodhisattva is able to comprehend the languages and approaches of people in many different worlds, including the realm of the gods.

Four Types of Discriminating Awareness

On the ninth bhumi, the bodhisattva develops four types of discriminating awareness: dharma, meaning, purpose, and confidence. In Tibetan this is called *soso yang-dak-par rikpa. Soso* means "individually" or "discriminating," *yang-dak-par* means "correct" or "true," *rikpa* means "insight"; so *soso yang-dak-par rikpa* means "true discriminatory awareness."

With the discriminating awareness of dharma, or *chö,* the bodhisattva understands the doctrines, customs, and cultures developed over the ages by the human race. They understand the customs of all six realms.

With the discriminating awareness of meaning, or *tön,* the bodhisattva understands the meaning of words rather than just the letters. They understand that the customs of various societies have tremendous meaning behind them. Nothing is seen as adharma or non-dharma, but everything becomes dharma. The bodhisattva is very open-minded, and all traditions and customs are seen as an expression of buddha nature. There is that kind of faith and trust in universality.

With the discriminating awareness of definition, or *ngetsik,* in addition to understanding the meaning, the bodhisattva also understands the significance. *Nge* means "certain" or "definite," and *tsik* means "word"; so *ngetsik* means "certain word" or "definition." They understand the function, or the pragmatic aspect of things, such as that the purpose of a sword is to cut, or the purpose of fire is to burn.

The last category, confidence, or *poppa*, is a very important one. Poppa is the particular type of confidence connected with Manjushri, the bodhisattva of wisdom. Manjushri has a knowledge aspect and a confidence aspect, and of the two aspects, the confidence aspect is much more important. Confidence does not just mean being unafraid or being able to handle things. It means you are able to communicate with your own basic treasury. It means you have no notion of poverty at all. The ninth-bhumi bodhisattva possesses eight great treasures,* which represent your basic potential. They represent fundamental confidence that does not need any help or encouragement. You realize that you have these treasures and that you are the treasurer. That sense of fundamental wealth and richness has never been questioned.

CLOUD OF DHARMA: THE TENTH BHUMI

Last, but not least, is the tenth bhumi, called *chökyi trin*. *Chö* means "dharma," *kyi* means "of," and *trin* means "cloud"; so *chökyi trin* means "cloud of dharma." This is the highest achievement of the bodhisattva experience, the final stage before the attainment of enlightenment. In this case, the image of a cloud is not regarded as an obstacle, like a cloud hiding the sun. Instead it implies the richness of a cloud, slowly rising, inexhaustible, basically pure, clean, and white.

At this point, you have gone so far and so completely that you are just about to approach enlightenment. Your power and confidence are great. At the same time, it is like a nearsighted universal monarch saluting his troops from the balcony: such a monarch has the power and the energy to appear as a king, but he can't quite make out the details of the vision.

It is said in the scriptures that on the tenth bhumi, you can emanate millions of buddhas and bodhisattvas from your pores, become king of the gods, or turn the earth upside down. It is true that you could churn out millions of buddhas from the pores of your skin if you were filled with dedication and inspiration, but this does not mean buddhas literally pop out of your skin. For instance, my teacher Jamgön Kongtrül woke up one morning and saw a huge fresco of buddhas wherever he looked. He was very excited about that, and thought maybe he was having some kind

---

* The *eight great treasures* are (1) recollection, (2) intellect, (3) realization, (4) retention, (5) brilliance, (6) doctrine, (7) enlightenment, and (8) accomplishment.

of bodhisattva vision, experiencing the phenomenal world as the realm of the buddhas. But when he asked his guru whether it was real, his guru said, "I haven't been deluded like that for a long time."

The Paramita of Wisdom

The paramita connected with the tenth bhumi is jnana, or wisdom. But this wisdom is not quite at the level of the five buddha-family wisdoms of the vajrayana.* With jnana, even the slightest notion of a journey is finally freed, except for a faint recollection. That faint sense of recollection remains until one attains enlightenment, which is the eleventh bhumi.

Wisdom does not seem to have any categories. It is free from the kinds of psychological problems that exist within even the subtlest level of samsara. In the earlier bhumis, bodhisattvas still have a path to achieve, a journey to make—but this bhumi is journeyless. There is only a faint memory left over, like the fragrance left in an empty bottle of perfume.

According to the scriptures, at this stage the bodhisattva sees the phenomenal world in a very brilliant way, like the brilliance of a full-moon night, or seeing the mountains in the moonlight. It seems to me that sunlight would be much more brilliant, but that is the traditional image. The idea is that what you have seen previously is partial, and finally you are able to see fully, as in full-moon light. Ironically, this particular bhumi is also often symbolized by the sun, because the quality of wisdom is all-pervasive, all-comprehensive, and open.†

Empowerments

The tenth-bhumi bodhisattva receives all kinds of *abhishekas,* or empowerments. You are enthroned by the buddhas or by your spiritual friend, and empowered with omniscient wisdom and enormous confidence. Since you were a samsaric person for a long time, you still need to be encouraged, initiated, and enthroned. The final enthronement is called the enthronement of the light, in which it is proclaimed that the bodhisattva

---

* The *five buddha-family wisdoms* represent different styles of awakened mind. They include the wisdom of all-encompassing space, mirrorlike wisdom, the wisdom of equanimity, discriminating-awareness wisdom, and the wisdom of all-accomplishing action.

† The simile for this bhumi is the song of dharma.

is a great being, a mahasattva. You are proclaimed to be a child of Buddha and a would-be buddha.

At this point, the only thing you have left to develop is your confidence. The last problem before the attainment of enlightenment is poverty mentality. It is not having the confidence to work with your inspiration. The bodhisattva has ground and knows their heritage and their richness. But like ordinary successful people who have a fear of being unsuccessful in spite of their fame and wealth, there is a faint fear that they might go wrong. There is still fear of losing one's ground, so the development of confidence becomes very important and powerful. That is why empowerment is necessary.

On the tenth bhumi, the bodhisattva is completely prepared and willing to take responsibilities. You have some idea of how it should be done, but the question is where to begin. It is like a young professor giving a talk to their class for the first time, not knowing how to handle it or what to say first. That kind of shyness, that leftover from past experience, that desire to hold on to security, remains an obstacle until the bodhisattva achieves vajra-like samadhi.

THE JOURNEY THROUGH THE BHUMIS

The details of the ten bhumis are definite, but the journey is guesswork. Supposedly, some people stay in a certain bhumi longer, and others pass through quickly. Particularly up to the eighth bhumi, your journey is very slow, because the first seven bhumis are still impure. The bhumis from the eighth bhumi on are called pure bhumis, and you advance much more quickly. Because psychological time is less strained, you go faster. But for most people, the experience of the bhumis is an extremely gradual process. Nonetheless, enlightenment is possible, and traditionally one tends to get certain warnings of that possibility.

Although the bodhisattva path can be divided into levels, you cannot really distinguish exactly where you are within each bhumi. However, as a person goes through the bhumis, there is a very slow and ordinary, almost insignificant, change. But you only become aware of that change when you look back at what was, rather than by what you see at any one point.

You might feel the bhumis are on the level of storytelling. But even if you are only a beginner, you can still experience how they work. On the other hand, you might feel that you already have some experience of the bhumis, but that does not mean that you have overcome the fetters of the kleshas, or achieved realization. Nonetheless, things are happening constantly, even at an ordinary person's level, let alone the bodhisattva's level.

In the mahayana, enormous suggestions of vajrayana begin to happen. Although it may feel as if the whole path is programmed, there is the possibility of joy. Such joy is the vanguard of the *mahasukha,* or great bliss, described in the tantras. The more you develop on the path, the more you have such warnings or vanguards. The vajrayana approach to the bhumis is that you could achieve buddhahood on the spot, and at the same time you have to go through a process. But that process is not so drastic. You do not have to change your behavior patterns or your physical shape, and you don't have to glow with light or perform miracles. The bhumis represent an extension of the human condition, so you can actually do it. Tathagatagarbha, or buddha nature, is possible. It is not just possible; it is so.

In Tibet one day, when we were discussing the reality of all this, someone asked Jamgön Kongtrül if any of us could do this, or were the bodhisattvas just mythical people? I remember Jamgön Kongtrül saying that you can get a glimpse of the tenth bhumi when you are on the first bhumi. He said that even if you are on the path of accumulation, you may get an occasional glimpse. But those glimpses are not a sign that you have actually reached that state. As a beginner, you may find such glimpses reassuring. You could identify them from your own experience, but that does not mean that you are at that level. You must not get carried away. However, once you join the path, the attainment of enlightenment is becoming a strong possibility.

As ordinary lay mahayanists, or potential bodhisattvas, the way to work on the bhumis is by practicing the paramitas. For instance, whenever any stinginess comes up, you do the opposite: you are generous. For impatience, you have patience; for laziness, you have exertion; for distraction, you have meditation; and if you feel stupid, you have prajna. But the opposites of the paramitas are not regarded as pitfalls. Instead, those seeming pitfalls are regarded as reminders that come from working with reality. They act as messengers. In fact, there are no pitfalls, there is only continual growth. It is like aging: you can never return to being sixteen years old, and you cannot suddenly regress to age one. It would be physically and psychologically impossible to do so.

In general, you try to practice whatever is called for by the situation. Paramita practice is like military training, in which you pretend to be attacked by somebody in a tropical area, and then you pretend to be attacked in the mountains or in a city. So rather than seeing the paramitas as a linear development, which becomes very limited, you try to apply all of them at once. A bodhisattva evolves in that way. It is not a question of deliberate, conscious effort, but it becomes very natural. Bodhisattvas do not have to check their notes.

Each time you go up to the next step of the path, there is a layperson's level and a professional's level. By layperson, I am not simply referring to someone who is not a monk or a nun—not at all. Basically, I believe that anybody who has taken the refuge and bodhisattva vows is no longer a layperson. When practice is no longer just a part-time job, it becomes real practice, and a person ceases to be a layperson. So a professional is somebody whose life is involved full-time with practice. The distinction between layperson and professional is very subtle. The more sane you are and the less distracted, that much more professional you become.

On the bodhisattva path, you are constantly being helped by the spiritual friend, or kalyanamitra, so the journey is no longer one short journey made by one individual. From the time you take refuge, you are relating with a spiritual friend, so the bodhisattva path is a mutual journey between your teacher and yourself. Buddha was very clever. He realized that physical manifestations are very tricky and can be easily faked. So he did not say that as you progress on the path your face will be glowing or you will perform miracles. He never mentioned such things. Instead, he talked about psychological development, and in the psychological development of the bodhisattva path, you have your kalyanamitra working along with you all the time. Someone at the level of the seventh bhumi no longer needs the spiritual friend's heavy-handed approach, but until you reach the tenth-bhumi level, you still need the watchful eye of the kalyanamitra. The sambhogakaya buddhas will take over from there.*

---

* In the mahayana and the vajrayana, it is said that in order to teach sentient beings buddhas manifest in terms of three bodies, or kayas: nirmanakaya, sambhogakaya, and dharmakaya. The kalyanamitra would be an example of an "embodied buddha," or nirmanakaya. *Sambhogakaya* is translated as "bliss body," or "energy body," and dharmakaya as "truth body." This reflects the fact that teachings can be transmitted through physical connection, through speech or energy, and through a meeting of minds (body, speech, and mind). As one progresses on the path, it becomes possible to access teachings at all three levels.

The teachings describe the process of sickness and recovery, rather than the treatment, which is very good. It is a fantastic approach, in that there is no possibility of following the whole thing completely and totally by yourself, no possibility of latching onto spiritual materialism. The whole thing is so beautifully worked out—and it was thought of twenty-six hundred years ago!

47

Complete Radiance:
The Eleventh Bhumi

The completely radiant and luminous path of this particular bhumi is backless, and there are no hidden corners, so you see in all directions simultaneously. It has no front, because there is no manipulation of perception whatever you see is seen as the working base for dealing with the phenomenal world. It is all-pervasive enlightenment without direction.

HAVING GONE through the ten bhumis and the first four paths, you finally reach the fifth path, the path of no more learning. The fifth path is buddhahood. It is the level of breaking through the vague and nearsighted vision of the tenth-bhumi bodhisattva. At this stage, the bodhisattva of the tenth bhumi decides to give up the ascetic approach to life and development. You begin to let go of your nearsightedness, the punishment of your body, and the restriction of your emotions.

The eleventh bhumi, or *küntu ö*, means "always luminous," or "complete radiance." *Küntu* means "always," or "all," and *ö* means "light," or "luminosity"; so *küntu ö* means "always luminous." The eleventh bhumi is the equivalent of buddhahood. On the tantric level, higher levels of spiritual achievement and further aspects of buddhahood are described, but at this point we are just touching on the eleventh bhumi. On the tenth bhumi, you were still a journeyer. You were inspired to sit and to practice, but you had not settled down—you were still maintaining your traveler's approach.

The Birth of Enlightenment

The enlightenment flash of the eleventh bhumi does not take place by acting, but by sitting. Previously you may have focused on actions, on working with sentient beings, and on developing a compassionate attitude, and so forth. But at the actual time the birth of enlightenment takes place, you decide to sit, just like Gautama Buddha. The point at which enlightenment occurs is not so much while you are sitting as a discipline, but when you begin to sit for relaxation. For instance, after Gautama Buddha was offered rice pudding, he decided to make himself more comfortable by collecting *kusha* grass to make a mat to sit on. He sat underneath a shade tree called a pipal tree and began to relax—and with that level of relaxation, enlightenment took place instantaneously.* Gautama Buddha, or Prince Siddhartha, achieved enlightenment at that point.

For the young Buddha, who just became Buddha that morning, it was a shock. So much was cut through, and so many changes took place in him as he discovered his new abilities and existence and being. Gautama Buddha was completely amazed at his achievement. After such struggle and effort, he was amazed to find himself enlightened one morning. He then spent seven weeks thinking about the best way to proceed from that day onward. Maybe he was thinking about how he could communicate with other people, how he could explain his experience. Maybe he was wondering how to show that it is workable and that people could understand it. Or maybe he was thinking that he should just retire and resign from the whole thing. He spent a week walking up and down the Nairanjana River, and another week gazing at the site of his enlightenment.

Enlightenment is such a shock—it is not a shock of the present, but a shock of the past. Somehow, after so much expectation, suddenly nothing happens, and everything is right there in your hands. Suddenly you become a king or queen, a universal monarch. The question of how to proceed from that day onward seems to be very challenging.

It is said that there is only going to be one buddha in each kalpa, but that raises a lot of questions. Does that mean that you could never become a buddha, never attain enlightenment? How about the one-lifetime attainment of buddhahood in tantric discipline? How about the sudden enlightenment of the bodhisattva path? It is also said that in the reign of one

---

* After the Buddha's enlightenment, this tree became known as the bodhi tree, and the variety of ficus is now known as *Ficus religiosa*.

buddha, there cannot be a second buddha. In our era, Shakyamuni became the Buddha without first becoming a Buddhist. He made his whole journey and attained enlightenment with no label or discipline. There may be millions of buddhas after that, but they are Buddhist buddhas who follow the path that he taught.

It was Gautama Buddha who proclaimed the truth, no one else. He has the copyright, so to speak. But many buddhas have been churned out from Shakyamuni's teaching—many dharmakaya buddhas, in fact, let alone nirmanakaya ones. Such enlightened beings did not manufacture the doctrine, however, which is good. Otherwise they could become like so many little gurus, trying to figure something out by taking a pinch of Hinduism, a pinch of Buddhism, or a pinch of Zen, and trying to make their own enlightenment programs. Since practitioners of Buddhism cannot become the primordial leader of this spiritual discipline, that takes away a lot of unnecessary egotism.

INDESTRUCTIBLE MEDITATION

Generally, there is so much tension and pressure in one's state of being. You have a sense of working hard and taking a journey—and finally, you give up. You don't exactly give up, but you begin to relax. That is when the attainment of enlightenment takes place. That attainment is called *vajropama-samadhi*, or "vajra-like samadhi." *Vajra* means "indestructible," *upama* means "like," and *samadhi* means "meditative state"; so *vajropama-samadhi* means "indestructible meditative state." In this case, vajra-like samadhi does not refer to the practice of meditation as such, but to a basic state of mind that is tuned in to a meditative state forever.

The achievement of enlightenment is characterized as knowing and seeing. Knowing does not mean becoming a great scholar or a person who knows facts and figures. It means having a fundamental understanding of the world we live in, its basic principles, and how it functions psychologically. Seeing means knowing how to operate, or how to relate with that knowledge. You are able to see completely and fully. Those are the two characteristics of the enlightened state of mind—you know and you see. As a result of vajra-like samadhi, you are fully aware in relating with students or with your own behavior.

In the earlier bhumis, you may have picked up the habit of trying to imitate buddha-like behavior. Because it is an imitation, rather than a real expression, that approach is somewhat distorted. It is a copy rather than the original, and at this stage, copying from the original has become an obstacle one has to overcome. You may have adopted an ethical and moralistic approach at the beginning as a means to develop high spiritual levels. But in the end, the ethical moralities of the bodhisattva's discipline become obstacles to becoming enlightened. Concerns about how to handle your life, how to handle your emotions, how to be a perfect bodhisattva on the path have become a problem. Although you have achieved the necessary discipline of spontaneity, you realize that the means themselves have become a hang-up.

The attainment of vajra-like samadhi, or indestructible meditation, overcomes the only remaining obstacle to the attainment of enlightenment, which is the hesitation and mannerism of concerns about ethics. Vajra-like samadhi is the way to cut through that final deception, that final layer of hesitation based on tradition and belief. In other words, the bodhisattva attains the final realization of enlightenment by cutting through the hesitations arising from their own discipline.

FOUR QUALITIES OF VAJRA-LIKE SAMADHI

Vajra-like samadhi has four qualities: toughness, stability, one flavor, and all-pervasiveness.*

Toughness

The first quality, toughness, means that vajra-like samadhi never surrenders. There is no confusion, veil, or obstacle that can overpower it. That quality of toughness is symbolized by the vajra scepter held by King Indra to defeat the *asuras,* or jealous gods.† According to Hindu myth, this vajra was made from a half-human, half-god Hindu saint, or rishi, who meditated in a cave on Mount Meru. When he passed away and achieved oneness with the god Brahma, his body became the essence of adamantine. All his bones became super-diamond, the most precious stone one could

---

* In *The Jewel Ornament of Liberation,* there are said to be five qualities of *vajra-like samadhi:* unobstructedness, hardness, stability, one flavor, and all-pervasiveness, whereas Trungpa Rinpoche only lists four qualities.

† A reference to a mythical battle between the gods and the demigods, or *jealous gods.* In Buddhism, the *vajra,* or weapon of Indra, is a powerful symbol of indestructibility. The term *vajra* (Tib.: dorje), also refers to a ritual instrument used in tantric ritual practices.

ever find in the three realms of the world, and completely indestructible. Indra discovered this material and he made a weapon out of it, and the weapon and the material itself are both called vajra.

Traditionally, a vajra has five points, but Indra made a vajra with one hundred points as a weapon to destroy the asuras, or jealous gods. In creating such a powerful weapon, he made three promises. First, he would never use it unless necessary. Second, once he decided to use it, the vajra would fulfill its purpose and destroy the enemy. Third, having destroyed the enemy, the vajra would return to its owner's hand. His vajra was made in such a way that it closed its points when it was held by its owner. But when it was invoked as the destroyer of the enemy—when Indra held it and waved it and let it go—the vajra would spring out all its points, destroy the enemy, and come back.

The vajra is powerful not only because it is made from extraordinary material, but also due to the spiritual power and energy of the meditator. It represents the idea of an independent intelligence that destroys confusion and returns to you. Buddhists have taken up the symbol of the vajra as a symbol of indestructibility. It has powerful meaning, especially in the vajrayana, which is named after that particular symbol.

Stability

The second quality of vajra-like samadhi is stability. Vajra-like samadhi is unmoved by the wind of thoughts. There may be thoughts, but they are no longer confused thoughts. Therefore, they do not move as the ordinary wind moves; they just persist.

One Flavor

The third quality of vajra-like samadhi is one flavor. It is similar to a concept in tantra called *rochik,* which means "one flavor." In this case, one flavor means that without confused thoughts, the mental approach becomes very direct and simple, highly open and spacious, in the style of the five wisdoms, or the five buddha-families. You could say that the different buddha-families have one flavor, which is the awakened quality.*

---

* A reference to a description of five aspects of enlightened wisdom, displayed as a mandala of deities in vajrayana Buddhism. See volume 3, chapter 26, *"The Five Buddha-Family Mandala."*

All-Pervasiveness

Fourth, and last, vajra-like samadhi is all-pervasive. At this level of spiritual achievement, you develop an enormous ability to comprehend all that is knowable, anything that is subject to confusion or clarity.

THE THREE KAYAS

Enlightenment means that you are not here and you are not there; therefore, you have achieved an understanding of something. You can call it consciousness, if you like, but it is not consciousness as a reference point—it is just being. That being manifests as the three kayas: dharmakaya, sambhogakaya, and nirmanakaya.*

Dharmakaya: Body beyond Reference Point

At this point, we could say that a buddha actually sees their own world or the world in general—the entire world—from a nonreference point of view. They see that the world can exist without a reference point, that reference points are no longer applicable. When you possess such an enlightened view, you attain the dharmakaya, the body of nonreference point. *Dharma* means the "highest norm of the universe," which is nonreference point. *Kaya* means "form" or "body," and it refers to the achievement of that particular experience; so *dharmakaya* means "dharma body."

Dharmakaya has no categories; dharmakaya is simply being awake. It is the first achievement of a buddha, the first glimpse of vajra-like samadhi. Vajra-like samadhi means cutting through with a vajra blade or diamond sword. It means to cut through everything completely and thoroughly. It goes beyond the level of a tenth-bhumi bodhisattva's vague vision of perfection. On the eleventh bhumi, you achieve the fullest cutting through—you cut through psychological and spiritual materialism, and you cut through the notion of perfectionism as well. You are able to see *this* and *that* as one—and at the same time there is also the clarity that *this* does exist and *that* does exist. However, their existence does not serve as a reference point, but more as the working basis for skillful means.

---

* In some contexts, the kayas are described as fourfold: (1) dharmakaya, (2) sambhogakaya, (3) nirmanakaya, and (4) svabhavikakaya. For a discussion of the four kayas, see chapter 38, slogan 14.

The dharmakaya is referred to as a nonphysical body, and the remaining two kayas, the sambhogakaya and nirmanakaya, are known as physical bodies (Skt.: rupakaya). The dharmakaya does not have any background or connection to *how*, but only to *what is*. Only after that do you begin to have *how* and *why* and *when* to conduct activities. With the sambhogakaya and nirmanakaya, you begin to relate with the world and with conduct.

Sambhogakaya: Body of Complete Joy

Having already achieved the first glimpse of enlightenment and attained the dharmakaya state, a buddha would also experience something beyond that: a sense of vow, promise, and concern. Having gone through the constant struggle and discipline of practicing the bodhisattva's work of compassion, this compassion brings the very predictable world of the sambhogakaya buddha. *Sambhoga* means "complete joy," and *kaya* means "body"; so *sambhogakaya* means "body of complete joy." The sambhogakaya is beyond any kind of inhibition. With the sambhogakaya, there is freedom to relate with whatever you have understood. Whatever you feel can be communicated or taught.

When suddenly the bottom of the barrel of the world drops out and you cannot hold on to anything, it is very shocking. In fact, it is remarkable that Shakyamuni Buddha took it so very lightly. However he did spend time recuperating from the hard work of the past ten bhumis, partly spacing out in the dharmakaya and partly planning the next move. After attaining enlightenment, it took Gautama Buddha seven weeks to finally grow the confidence to articulate what he had experienced. But there is a need for articulation. Once you are a buddha, you have to say something to the world. You have to do something; you have to proclaim. It is a process of growth.

Having removed your inhibition, what are you going to do? You can't just say, "Come and look at me." You have to be very skillful, particularly if you proclaim yourself as an enlightened person, for then you have a heavier burden. It is hard to present yourself to the world, so at the sambhogakaya level it is very important to work with what are known as the five ways of teaching: (1) you choose a particular place to teach, (2) you know who you are as a teacher, (3) you know what you are going to teach, (4) you know what kind of audience you have, and (5) you know what time of the day you are going to teach. So the sambhogakaya involves a sense of relationship. You know the place, you know what kind of crowd you're going to get, and you know what you are going to say. You do not just want to proclaim yourself, you want to proclaim the dharma—something other than yourself. Since you have no fear, you seem to know everything in the very highest sense. Fearlessness equals learnedness—you can churn out information, and you know how to handle things.

Nirmanakaya: Emanation Body

The last kaya is the nirmanakaya, the buddha who actually takes form as a human individual. Nirmanakaya buddhas are living people who relate with their students. They eat with them, sleep with them in the same jungle, and share their life with them. That is their function.

Nirmana means "emanation" and *kaya*, again, means "body," so *nirmanakaya* means "body of emanation." It is the physical body that actually exists on earth as an emanation of the dharmakaya. It can be a human form or a representation.* So there are two types of nirmanakaya buddhas: actual nirmanakaya buddhas like Gautama Buddha, and the buddhas represented by books, statues, and images. Historically, people first began to represent the Buddha in books, so what the Buddha said came first. What Buddha looked like and how he behaved were secondary, so images of the Buddha did not appear until the late Ashoka period.

It is very moving to know that twenty-six hundred years ago, a person called Siddhartha became the Buddha. He actually did that, and he made an enormous impact and impression on people—so enormous that we still continue to follow his way and share his ideas. It is very powerful that somebody actually achieved enlightenment and went so far as to proclaim it, to teach, and to share his life with his students from the time of his enlightenment until his death when he was over eighty years old. Siddhartha showed us how to behave and how to handle ourselves with other people. He showed us that enlightenment is not a myth or concept, but something that actually took place. That is the basis of our conviction as Buddhists. And from that time onward, successive people have done the same thing. They have followed the same path and attained enlightenment.

---

* According to Trungpa Rinpoche, the term *nirmanakaya* in this context relates directly to the buddha level rather than to the level of ordinary tülkus (the Tibetan translation of *nirmanakaya*), which seems to be slightly different.

It is necessary for Buddhists to identify with that particular living situation, to see that it is real. You can visit Bodh Gaya and see the tree that the Buddha sat under when he attained enlightenment, and you can visit Sarnath where he gave his first sermon. They are very inspiring places. It is very powerful and important to identify with the historical Buddha, the nirmanakaya buddha who actually lived and walked on our earth. Many Buddhists do not pay much attention to Gautama Buddha, the present Buddha. We take for granted that somebody did this thing, and tend to be more concerned with what we have gotten from the Buddhist tradition than with who started it and what kind of lifestyle he had. I am not suggesting hero worship, but a humanizing of Buddhism. It is not a Superman story—it is the story of someone who lived where we do, on this earth. That person took a particular journey, and we are trying to follow his example. His impact has gone on continuously for twenty-six hundred years, and it is getting stronger. And the Buddha is supposed to be coming back constantly—driven by compassion to return, not as the Buddha again, or as a proclaimed buddha, but as a human being.

Three Kayas as Individual Experience

The three-kaya principle is based on the body, speech, and mind of an ordinary person. Simultaneously you have the dharmakaya version of yourself, the sambhogakaya version of yourself, and the nirmanakaya version of yourself. You can also look at an element such as water in terms of the three-kaya principle: basic waterness is like the dharmakaya, its wetness is like the sambhogakaya, and the fulfilling of its functions, such as quenching thirst and irrigation, is like the nirmanakaya. So you can apply the three kayas as a way of looking at one body from three different perspectives.

The dharmakaya is your nonphysical manifestation. You have a nonphysical aspect of yourself that others cannot see or communicate with. That basic state of being is ungraspable, but you know that it is within yourself and everybody else. You also possess a semigraspable state of being, or sambhogakaya, which is the communication between your nonmanifested and manifested levels. That semigraspable state is symbolized by speech, but it includes all forms of communication, such as physical gestures, facial expressions, and how you present yourself in all kinds of ways. Then there's the nirmanakaya, which means that you actually have a body. Even if you are a great teacher or a buddha, you still have a body, and that body behaves more or less the same as other people's bodies. The necessities of eating, shitting, wearing clothes, and combing your hair are basically the same as anybody else's. So the three kayas are the subtle world, the direct world, and that which goes back and forth between the subtle and direct worlds in order to survive on earth.

Nonattainment

The eleventh bhumi is the bhumi of nonattainment. You do not have any paramitas to practice, and you are not concerned with the other shore or this shore at all. This particular bhumi no longer has the reference point of a journey. On the path of no more learning, the eightfold path is also in the form of nonattainment. To understand the idea of nonattainment, you need to get a feeling for the near purposelessness of this state of being, as opposed to the purposefulness of the bodhisattva.

TEN DHARMAS OF NONATTAINMENT. The nirmanakaya buddha of the eleventh bhumi—the new buddha—attains what are called the ten dharmas of nonattainment.* These dharmas are largely based on the three principles of discipline, meditation, and knowledge, and on the eightfold path.

In terms of discipline, right speech becomes the speech of nonattainment, right action becomes the action of nonattainment, and right livelihood becomes the livelihood of nonattainment.

In the area of meditation, right mindfulness becomes the mindfulness of nonattainment, and meditative absorption becomes the samadhi of nonattainment.

At the level of knowledge, or prajna, right view becomes nonattainment view, right understanding becomes nonattainment understanding, and right effort becomes nonattainment effort. Those are the first eight dharmas of nonattainment.

The ninth dharma falls outside the principles of discipline, meditation, and knowledge. It is the state of complete liberation, which is a pathless state. You are actually being liberated without bondage or binding factors related with your discipline, your learning, or your notion of saving sentient beings.

---

* A more literal translation is the "ten dharmas of nonlearning" or the "ten dharmas of no more training."

429

The tenth dharma is perfect wisdom, or jnana. It is a state of hundreds of millions of awarenesses and interests and sense perceptions. You experience life with great interest, completely exposed and unchallenged, with no prohibitions. It is as if hundreds of jnanas spring out like the rays of the sun, touching every aspect of the physical world. But at the same time, that multiplicity of bodhisattva experiences has a feeling of oneness. There is a sense of complete energy, power, and understanding. You are no longer threatened, and you no longer have to keep a record of those millions of experiences. It is like a hundred bowls of water reflecting one moon. It is like the sun, which has no desire to shine on every flower and every bit of greenery, yet the greenery and flowers still receive the sun's rays. On one hand, you could say the sun is keeping a good record of its projection; on the other hand, the sun is completely careless. It does not care about anything at all, but simply by being the sun—the brilliant sun shining—it becomes a part of the spontaneity.

Back to the Beginning

The ten dharmas of nonattainment are inspired by the complete understanding of the four noble truths. It all starts with the truth of suffering. Everything else follows—the awful confusion and chaos and uncertainty and panic, and occasional hopes that something might be happening or something might not be happening. The minute you get back to this point, there is not much struggle. Even though it is the eleventh bhumi, it is the same "you" experiencing reality. You do not see a green world or a blue world, but you see a black-and-white world. Suffering is seen as a reality, as truth.

On the eleventh bhumi, the four noble truths are not just truths in terms of ethical understanding and discipline, but they become wisdom, or jnana. You experience their absolute truth. You have actually understood at last what you began with as a student on the path of accumulation. You have made a complete circle, but in this case you have done it with more understanding. Previously, you were just tossed and challenged by the consequences of the truth, rather than understanding it as jnana, or higher truth. That process is very important; it makes the whole thing very real. In the end, you have not bypassed anything, but you are returning to the origin—to the source of your original inspiration at the level of the first path. Tantric scriptures say that you might feel enormously resentful that the journey was a complete put-on, a sort of pacifier. Nevertheless, you did make a journey, and you did get somewhere.

On the eleventh bhumi you are not taking the journey anymore, but you have a very definite memory of it. It feels somewhat different, but that difference is not based on attaining a new state of being. Although you have come back to where you began, the memory of the journey makes it somewhat different. As an example, I regard my escape from Tibet, from the communists, as a memory, but it is a very impressionable memory. I was able to get out of Tibet and just be myself once more—which I was, anyway—but I could not be myself if I did not escape.

The attainment of enlightenment means joining your world completely, and letting go of any reservations. We usually don't want to join the rest of our world. We want to maintain ourselves as individuals, so we call the world outside "bad," or a bad influence on us. We never join our world properly, completely, thoroughly, and fully. It is like the story about a king who heard a prophecy that a rain was going to fall on his country that would cause everyone to go mad. So he saved up his own reservoir of fresh water. At some point, all the inhabitants of his country became mad, while he continued to be sane. But eventually, he decided to drink the water of madness with them.

The eleventh bhumi is considered to be the first level of nirmanakaya buddhahood. You are wholeheartedly willing to join the world. In turn, instead of the confused world that you used to see, you begin to see a complete world, a sane world. You can communicate with confused people—who are also very complete people from your enlightened point of view.

On the eleventh bhumi, having gone through all the other bhumis, the bodhisattva has become a universal monarch. You have achieved all-pervasive awareness like Vairochana, the buddha with four faces looking in four directions. The completely radiant and luminous path of this particular bhumi is backless, and there are no hidden corners, so you see in all directions simultaneously. It has no front, because there is no manipulation of perception whatever you see is seen as the working base for dealing with the phenomenal world. It is all-pervasive enlightenment without direction.

APPENDIX 1:
NEVER FORGET THE HINAYANA

This spontaneous short talk was given at the 1986 Seminary at Shambhala Mountain Center in Red Feather Lakes, Colorado, late at night at the beginning of the mahayana section of the Seminary. The students were scattered about in their tents and sound asleep, and Chögyam Trungpa Rinpoche had them awakened and brought together to hear what he had to say.

GOOD EVENING. Ladies and gentlemen, it is a very profound time and a profound experience for us to realize how important is the hinayana teaching. It is very important to us, and inseparable from our lives and our existence as individuals. It is to be understood as the life force that carries on whether you are going through the hinayana, mahayana, or vajrayana. It is our substance and our sustenance.

It is for us to understand that basic life, that basic strength, which goes on continuously. The hinayana teaching should not be regarded as something that you can just carry out, and then get rid of or discard. The hinayana teaching is the life force that carries out our own practice and discipline, which goes on continuously. From that point of view, the hinayana should be regarded as life's strength.

Okay. That's that.

NEVER FORGET HINAYANA!

[Laughter and applause]

APPENDIX 2:
THE PRACTICE OF ORYOKI

Oryoki, a Zen monastic-style eating practice, was first introduced as a practice for Vajradhatu Seminary participants beginning in 1979. The form of oryoki used at seminaries was a modification that included elements drawn from the Tibetan Buddhist tradition as well. In subsequent seminaries and at other intensive meditation retreats, this mindful eating practice continued to be shaped and refined. The following brief description of oryoki is compiled from a variety of instructions given at Vajradhatu Seminary by Chögyam Trungpa Rinpoche.

THE DISCIPLINE of oryoki is based on the way that the Buddha taught his disciples to eat food: eating simple food with mindfulness and awareness. Oryoki is an ancient practice, based on the 250 rules of Buddhist monastic discipline, which includes almost forty rules for eating.

After ordination, a disciple was given a bowl, a robe, and a seat. Such begging bowls, fashioned after the Buddha's own begging bowl, were not received by anyone who had not taken the refuge vow. Traditionally, oryoki is done only in monastic communities. However, in the Japanese tradition it is sometimes extended to the lay community, which is the approach I am using as well.

In oryoki practice, you are served your meals and you eat in the shrine hall. You eat the way the Buddha ate. In your oryoki set you have a wrapping cloth, a wiping cloth, and a lap cloth; you have a *setsu*, or cleaning utensil, a spoon, and chopsticks; you have a case for these instruments; and you have a set of nested bowls. As you prepare for the meal, you chant the liturgy, and as you are chanting, you unwrap your oryoki set, take out your bowls, and set each one in its particular place. You appreciate that you are going to eat your food properly and mindfully, paying attention to the details of the practice. That is the ground. The path is raising your bowl to receive food, and the fruition is actually eating the food.

After eating, you finish your oryoki properly. You wipe your bowls clean, and you also fold the cloths and tie them up properly. That gesture is applicable to any situation: you can clean your entire world properly and fully. The logic is that at the beginning there is no praise, and at the end there is no blame.

During oryoki practice you and the server bow to one another. It is a question of recognizing the sacredness and also of being mindful of one another. When the servers lose their awareness, by bowing you could remind them to be aware; and if you lose your awareness, by bowing they could remind you to come back to your awareness as well.

In oryoki practice, everything is looked at and everything is very much cared for. Whenever there is a speck of dust in your oryoki bowl, you look at it; whenever there is a badly folded oryoki napkin, you see it. You begin to expand your world in that way, so your world is not stuck. At that point, your intelligence is so sharp and quivering that your awareness is almost bursting out onto the energy level.

By synchronizing study, sitting practice, and oryoki, you do not create the schizophrenia of taking time off. In that way, you become a true dharmic practitioner. Even though sitting posture may seem very difficult and even painful to maintain, there is upliftedness and a sense of enjoyment, and the same is true in oryoki. When you begin to eat oryoki style, you begin to appreciate every grain of rice and every pinch of vegetables. They become delicious. It is not that the food has changed or been blessed by the "up-above"; it is simply a matter of how you relate with the phenomenal world.

APPENDIX 3:
THE HEART SUTRA

THUS HAVE I heard. Once the Blessed One was dwelling in Rajagriha at Vulture Peak mountain, together with a great gathering of the sangha of monks and a great gathering of the sangha of bodhisattvas. At that time the Blessed One entered the samadhi that expresses the dharma called profound illumination, and at the same time noble Avalokiteshvara, the bodhisattva mahasattva, while practicing the profound prajnaparamita, saw in this way: he saw the five skandhas to be empty of nature.

Then, through the power of the Buddha, venerable Shariputra said to noble Avalokiteshvara, the bodhisattva mahasattva, "How should a son or daughter of noble family train, who wishes to practice the profound prajnaparamita?"

Addressed in this way, noble Avalokiteshvara, the bodhisattva mahasattva, said to venerable Shariputra, "O Shariputra, a son or daughter of noble family who wishes to practice the profound prajnaparamita should see in this way: seeing the five skandhas to be empty of nature. Form is emptiness; emptiness also is form. Emptiness is no other than form; form is no other than emptiness. In the same way, feeling, perception, formation, and consciousness are emptiness. Thus, Shariputra, all dharmas are emptiness. There are no characteristics. There is no birth and no cessation. There is no impurity and no purity. There is no decrease and no increase. Therefore, Shariputra, in emptiness, there is no form, no feeling, no perception, no formation, no consciousness; no eye, no ear, no nose, no tongue, no body, no mind; no appearance, no sound, no smell, no taste, no touch, no dharmas; no eye dhatu up to no mind dhatu, no dhatu of dharmas, no mind consciousness dhatu; no ignorance, no end of ignorance up to no old age and death, no end of old age and death; no suffering, no origin of suffering, no cessation of suffering, no path, no wisdom, no attainment, and no nonattainment. Therefore, Shariputra, since the bodhisattvas have no attainment, they abide by means of prajnaparamita. Since there is no obscuration of mind, there is no fear. They transcend falsity and attain complete nirvana. All the buddhas of the three times, by means of prajnaparamita, fully awaken to unsurpassable, true, complete enlightenment. Therefore, the great mantra of prajnaparamita, the mantra of great insight, the unsurpassed mantra, the unequaled mantra, the mantra that calms all suffering, should be known as truth, since there is no deception. The prajnaparamita mantra is said in this way:

OM GATE GATE PARAGATE PARASAMGATE BODHI SVAHA

Thus, Shariputra, the bodhisattva mahasattva should train in the profound prajnaparamita."

Then the Blessed One arose from that samadhi and praised noble Avalokiteshvara, the bodhisattva mahasattva, saying, "Good, good, O son of noble family; thus it is, O son of noble family, thus it is. One should practice the profound prajnaparamita just as you have taught, and all the tathagatas will rejoice."

When the Blessed One had said this, venerable Shariputra and noble Avalokiteshvara, the bodhisattva mahasattva, that whole assembly and the world with its gods, humans, asuras, and gandharvas rejoiced and praised the words of the Blessed One.

Lotsawa bhikshu Rinchen De translated this text into Tibetan with the Indian pandita Vimalamitra. It was edited by the great editor-lotsawas Gelo, Namkha, and others. This Tibetan text was copied from the fresco in Gegye Chemaling at the glorious Samye vihara. It has been translated into English by the Nalanda Translation Committee, with reference to several Sanskrit editions.

APPENDIX 4:
PRAJNA DIALOGUES

The following short interchanges between Chögyam Trungpa Rinpoche and his students, taken from Vajradhatu Seminary question-and-answer periods, illustrate the use of dialogue to sharpen a student's prajna. In these dialogues, students were encouraged to question what they were being taught and to wrestle with the material in order to develop a deeper and more personal understanding of concepts such as shunyata. They were challenged to discover the link between such seemingly abstract philosophical teachings, their meditation practice, and their daily lives.

SHUNYATA: DEAD MAN TALKING

Question: Is there a knower of shunyata?

Chögyam Trungpa Rinpoche: No. Otherwise, it wouldn't be shunyata.

Q: Okay. Then what sense can it be said to exist, independent of idea or concept?

CTR: Because it is independent of concept, nobody is at home. It is very simple when you realize that nobody is at home.

Q: Yeah, but "nobody is at home" is a statement that is bounded by concepts.

CTR: Sure. Definitely so.

Q: So we are not talking about shunyata, but are we talking about something that we substitute for shunyata?

CTR: At this point, we are not talking about shunyata from the point of view that nobody is home, but we are talking about the possible *fever* of shunyata. Hearing that there is nobody at home to help you and that the house is completely empty, you could be panicked. There is no ground, although you are on some kind of ground. There is a fever of shunyata. From there we go on.

Q: In that case, you would not really say that shunyata exists?

CTR: That is the whole idea. You cannot say shunyata exists: that would be a contradiction. And you cannot even say that it nonexists, because you have no idea whether it exists or not. It is total experience.

Q: Does the concept of shunyata come from shunyata occurring in somebody's life and then going away, after which they have sort of a flavor of the memory, and then try to describe what it was? Is that how the concept of something that doesn't exist or nonexist arise?

CTR: No.

Q: No?

CTR: No. It is like a dead man telling us a story. It is like a dead man describing to you what it is like being dead.

Q: Well, as someone who is telling us about shunyata, isn't that what you are doing?

CTR: Yeah, I suppose so.

Q: Well, that makes it rather frightening.

CTR: People died [when the Buddha taught about shunyata]. They had heart attacks. All kinds of drama about shunyata took place.

DOES BODHICHITTA EXIST?

Q: How does bodhichitta relate to tathagatagarbha?

CTR: It is tathagatagarbha. Is that all?

Q: That's all.

Q: Is bodhichitta self-existing?

CTR: Since it is a goalless approach, therefore, it is self-existing. If it were goal oriented it could not exist. That is why it is called unconditional.

Q: In what sense do we mean "exist" then?

CTR: It doesn't really mean very much. Bodhichitta is unconditionally there, but we cannot actually say "exist," as such. We can't say that it exists as the JFK Airport exists in New York City.

Q: So it could be a construct of mind, actually.

CTR: Yes.

Q: It could be simply something that we agree is there.

CTR: That is the point. If we agreed something was there, it would be goal oriented. But we have not agreed about anything at all. It just suddenly appeared. It is like the analogies of Shantideva, such as discovering a jewel in a heap of refuse, or being a beggar with a universal monarch in her stomach about to give birth. Those things apparently come about by chance, which makes the whole thing neither eternal nor unconditional. Bodhichitta comes about purely by chance. In fact, we could say that the idea of having bodhichitta in us was a big mistake from ego's point of view. But that mistake turned out to be good from the enlightened point of view.

JUST A TOOTHBRUSH

Q: Rinpoche, when the experience and the experiencer are both cut through, it sounds like there is nothing left to function. And it also sounds very scary.

CTR: Nothing left to function. You're right. The question of function is actually what the whole of Buddhism is all about. What do you mean by "function"?

Q: Brushing your teeth.

CTR: Yes, that's fine. That's very common. But do you expect that in order to brush your teeth you have to assume a certain particular state of mind?

Q: Well, I expect that I have to be able to pick up my toothbrush and—

CTR: But where does that come from?

Q: How do you mean?

CTR: You have to have some philosophical belief in order to pick up your tube of toothpaste and your brush and put your toothbrush in your mouth. Does that come from an attitude of real ego-orientation alone?

Q: I suppose it comes from the belief that the toothbrush is a solid thing.

CTR: Not necessarily. That's the trick about the whole thing. A toothbrush is just a toothbrush, rather than anything particularly solid. It's just a toothbrush doing its function. Because of its function, it is very light, so you are not holding this clunky thing in your hand, which helps you to be less nervous about your arm muscle. Holding your toothbrush is not a heavy thing: [changes to somber monotone] "Now I'm going to brush my teeth."

Little by little, any pressure or tension is relieved by experiencing egolessness. Your shoelaces become tighter, your nails become brighter, and your toothbrush becomes lighter. When you take the attitude that the toothbrush does not exist and the brusher does not exist, you can brush your teeth much more easily. You can experience the whole thing. That is why we talk about a double-edged sword. The brusher has been cut along with the brush, so the toothbrush can brush properly and fully.

Q: This isn't something that happens real quickly or all of a sudden, necessarily, I hope.

CTR: Fat chance, I would say. Fat chance.

APPENDIX 5:
FORTY-SIX WAYS IN WHICH
A BODHISATTVA FAILS

THIRTY-FOUR CONTRADICTIONS
TO EMBODYING VIRTUE

Contradictions to the Paramita of Generosity

Contradictions to Generosity with Regard to Material Things

1. Not offering to the three jewels
2. Giving in to possessiveness

Contradictions to the Generosity of Protection from Fear

3. Not respecting more experienced people
4. Not answering questions

Those That Prevent the Generosity of Others

5. Not accepting invitations as a guest
6. Angrily refusing gifts

Contradiction to Generosity with Regard to Dharma

7. Not teaching the dharma to those who want it

Contradictions to the Paramita of Discipline

Contradictions Mainly to Benefiting Others

1. Rejecting those who do not keep their discipline
2. Not developing learning, which inspires others' faith
3. Making little effort for the benefit of sentient beings

4. Not performing evil actions even though it is permitted when one has compassion and there is a need

Contradictions Mainly to Benefiting Oneself

5. Willingly taking up any of the five kinds of wrong livelihood
6. Mindlessly indulging
7. Due to desire and attachment, remaining in samsara

Contradictions to Benefiting Both Oneself and Others

8. Not preventing getting a bad reputation
9. Not controlling the kleshas

Contradictions to the Paramita of Patience

1. Not practicing the four dharmas of a practitioner (not returning curses for curses, anger for anger, blow for blow, or insult for insult)
2. Not working peacefully with, but rejecting, people who are angry at you
3. Refusing to accept another's apology
4. Giving in to anger

Contradictions to the Paramita of Exertion

1. Collecting followers for fame and fortune
2. Not overcoming laziness and so forth
3. Indulging in busyness and chatter

Contradictions to the Paramita of Meditation

1. Not seeking instruction in samadhi
2. Not abandoning obscurations to meditation
3. Viewing the experience of meditation as good and being attached to it

Contradictions to the Paramita of Prajna

Faults Related to Lesser Things

1. Not respecting the shravakayana, and therefore rejecting it
2. Having abandoned one's own tradition, the mahayana, and instead exerting oneself in the shravakayana
3. In the same way, studying non-Buddhist literature
4. Although exerting oneself in the mahayana, preferring shravaka and non-Buddhist literature

Faults Related to Excellent Things

5. Not taking interest in the distinctive features of mahayana
6. Not seeking the holy dharma due to pride, laziness, and so forth
7. Praising oneself and disparaging others
8. Relying on the words rather than the meaning

TWELVE CONTRADICTIONS TO BENEFITING SENTIENT BEINGS

General Application

1. Not helping those in need
2. Not caring for the sick
3. Not removing the suffering of others
4. Not correcting those who are heedless

Specific Application

Faults of Not Being Helpful

1. Not repaying kindness
2. Not removing the pain of others
3. Not giving to those in need even though you can
4. Not benefiting those around you
5. Not acting in accord with the customs of others
6. Not praising those who have good qualities

Faults of Not Overpowering

1. Not overpowering those on a perverted path
2. Not taming with miracles and higher perceptions those who must be tamed in that way

Translated by the Nalanda Translation Committee from the compilation of Jamgön Kongtrül the Great in his Treasury of Knowledge.

445

APPENDIX 6:
THE ROOT TEXT OF THE SEVEN
POINTS OF MIND TRAINING

POINT ONE

The Preliminaries,
Which Are a Basis for Dharma Practice

1. First, train in the preliminaries.

POINT TWO

The Main Practice,
Which Is Training in Bodhichitta

2. Regard all dharmas as dreams.
3. Examine the nature of unborn awareness.
4. Self-liberate even the antidote.
5. Rest in the nature of alaya, the essence.
6. In postmeditation, be a child of illusion.
7. Sending and taking should be practiced alternately. These two should ride the breath.
8. Three objects, three poisons, and three seeds of virtue.
9. In all activities, train with slogans.
10. Begin the sequence of sending and taking with yourself.

POINT THREE

Transformation of Bad Circumstances into the Path of Enlightenment

11. When the world is filled with evil, transform all mishaps into the path of bodhi.
12. Drive all blames into one.
13. Be grateful to everyone.
14. Seeing confusion as the four kayas is unsurpassable shunyata protection.
15. Four practices are the best of methods.
16. Whatever you meet unexpectedly, join with meditation.

POINT FOUR

Showing the Utilization of Practice in One's Whole Life

17. Practice the five strengths, the condensed heart instructions.
18. The mahayana instruction for ejection of consciousness at death is the five strengths: how you conduct yourself is important.

POINT FIVE

Evaluation of Mind Training

19. All dharma agrees at one point.
20. Of the two witnesses, hold the principal one.
21. Always maintain only a joyful mind.
22. If you can practice even when distracted, you are well trained.

POINT SIX

Disciplines of Mind Training

23. Always abide by the three basic principles.
24. Change your attitude, but remain natural.
25. Don't talk about injured limbs.
26. Don't ponder others.
27. Work through the greatest defilements first.
28. Abandon any hope of fruition.
29. Abandon poisonous food.
30. Don't be so predictable.

31. Don't malign others.
32. Don't wait in ambush.
33. Don't bring things to a painful point.
34. Don't transfer the ox's load to the cow.
35. Don't try to be the fastest.
36. Don't act with a twist.
37. Don't make gods into demons.
38. Don't seek others' pain as the limbs of your own happiness.

POINT SEVEN

Guidelines of Mind Training

39. All activities should be done with one intention.
40. Correct all wrongs with one intention.
41. Two activities: one at the beginning, one at the end.
42. Whichever of the two occurs, be patient.
43. Observe these two, even at the risk of your life.
44. Train in the three difficulties.
45. Take on the three principal causes.
46. Pay heed that the three never wane.
47. Keep the three inseparable.
48. Train without bias in all areas. It is crucial always to do this pervasively and wholeheartedly.
49. Always meditate on whatever provokes resentment.
50. Don't be swayed by external circumstances.
51. This time, practice the main points.
52. Don't misinterpret.
53. Don't vacillate.
54. Train wholeheartedly.
55. Liberate yourself by examining and analyzing.
56. Don't wallow in self-pity.
57. Don't be jealous.
58. Don't be frivolous.
59. Don't expect applause.

From a text by Chekawa Yeshe Dorje, translated by the Nalanda Translation Committee.

APPENDIX 7:
OUTLINE OF TEACHINGS

The numbered lists of teachings in this book have been organized into outline-style here as a study aid. The lists are in order of appearance in the text.

PART ONE. AWAKENING THE HEART

Chapter 1. A Glimpse of Wakefulness
Two Types of Bodhichitta / Awakened Heart or Mind
  1. Relative bodhichitta
  2. Absolute or ultimate bodhichitta

Chapter 2. Love, Vision, and Warriorship
Two Aspects of Love
  1. Maitri (champa)/ being kind and gentle to oneself
  2. Karuna (nying-je) / nobility of heart, being compassionate to others

Chapter 3. Doubt and Delight

PART TWO. BUDDHA NATURE

Chapter 4. Enlightened Genes
Two Types of Buddha Nature
  1. Stained or conditional / covered by veils and yearning toward wakefulness
  2. Unstained or unconditional / spontaneous, beyond concept or limitation without reference to the past or future

Obstacles to Awakening Enlightened Genes
  1. Intrinsic slavery
  2. Being without awareness
  3. Taking part in evil activities
  4. Sleepiness

Situations Conducive to Awakening Enlightened Genes
  1. Waking up at the right time (outer situation)
  2. Taking an interest in dharma practice (inner situation)

Methods for Awakening Enlightened Genes
  The Four Brahmaviharas
  1. Love
  2. Compassion
  3. Joy
  4. Equanimity

The Four Limitless Ones / Beyond Ego Intention
  1. Love/Loving-Kindness
  2. Compassion
  3. Joy
  4. Equanimity

Aims of the Four Limitless Ones
  1. Loving-kindness: to experience peace and cause others to be peaceful
  2. Compassion: to separate the cause of pain from the pain itself
  3. Joy: to help people experience pleasure without causing themselves pain
  4. Equanimity: to free people from passion and aggression so they can see beyond the bias of close and distant

Causes of the Four Limitless Ones
  1. Root cause / buddha nature (from within)
  2. Spiritual friend (from without)
  3. Confidence
  4. Discriminating awareness / prajna

Natural Progression of the Four Limitless Ones
  1. Liking oneself
  2. Beginning to like others

3. Celebration
4. Settling down and working with others

Three Levels of Accomplishment
  1. The four brahmaviharas
  2. The four limitless ones
  3. Twofold egolessness

Chapter 10. The Spiritual Friend
Three Attitudes toward the Spiritual Friend
  1. Guide / goes before
  2. Escort / accompanies
  3. Ferryman / follows behind

Analogies for Four Types of Student
  1. Upright container / open to the teachings
  2. Upside-down container / nothing penetrates
  3. Leaky container / nothing sticks
  4. Poisonous container / dharma is polluted

PART FOUR: MAKING A COMMITMENT

Chapter 11. Indestructible Wakefulness
Threefold Purity
  1. No actor
  2. No action
  3. No one acted upon

Chapter 12. Planting the Moon of Bodhi in Your Heart

Chapter 13. Cultivating a Mahayana Mentality
Four Factors of Mahayana Mentality
  1. Affection for the world
  2. Faith in the right situations
  3. Compassion for sentient beings
  4. Bravery

Chapter 14. The Seven Mahayana Exercises
  1. Prostrations
  2. Offering
  3. Confession / acknowledging what you have done
  4. Adoration / rejoicing in the virtues of others

Chapter 27. Generosity
  Three Levels of Generosity
    1. Material generosity
    2. Fearlessness
    3. Dharma

Chapter 28. Discipline
  Three Types of Discipline
    1. Binding yourself
    2. Gathering virtuous dharmas
    3. Benefiting sentient beings

Chapter 29. Patience
  Four Types of Maras
    1. Devaputra-mara / mara of seduction
    2. Klesha-mara / mara of kleshas
    3. Skandha-mara / mara of skandhas
    4. Yama-mara / mara of the god of death

  Three Categories of Patience
    1. Overcoming other people's destructiveness
    2. Realizing the nature of other people's aggression
    3. Individually examining

Chapter 30. Exertion
  Three Categories of Laziness, the Main Obstacle to Exertion
    1. Casualness / slothfulness
    2. Losing heart
    3. Degraded laziness

  Three Qualities of Exertion
    1. Suit of armor
    2. Action
        a. Overcoming the kleshas
        b. Developing virtue
            i. Perseverance
            ii. Joy
            iii. Immovability
            iv. Not changing your mid
            v. Nonarrogance
        c. Working with others
    3. Never being satisfied

Three Poisons (Slogan 8)
1. Passion
2. Aggression
3. Ignorance

Three Virtuous Seeds (Slogan 8)
1. Absence of passion
2. Absence of aggression
3. Absence of ignorance

Chapter 38: Point Three: Transformation of Bad Circumstances into the Path of Enlightenment
The Four Kayas (Slogan 14)
1. Dharmakaya (truth body) / basic openness
2. Nirmanakaya (form body) / clarity
3. Sambhogakaya (bliss body) / the bridge between dharmakaya and nirmanakaya
4. Svabhavikakaya / the totality, total panoramic experience

Four Practices (Slogan 15)
1. Accumulating merit
   Three Lines of Encouragement
   a. Grant your blessing so if it is better for me to be sick, let me be sick
   b. Grant your blessing so if it is better for me to survive, let me survive
   c. Grant your blessing so if it is better for me to be dead, let me die
2. Laying down evil deeds
   Fourfold Confession
   a. Regret
   b. Refraining from evil actions
   c. Taking refuge in the Buddha, dharma, and sangha
   d. Letting go of hope and fear
3. Offering to the döns
4. Offering to the dharmapalas

Chapter 39: Point Four: Showing the Utilization of Practice in One's Whole Life
The Five Strengths (Slogans 17 and 18)
1. Strong determination
2. Familiarization

461

3. Seed of virtue
4. Reproach
5. Aspiration

Chapter 40: Point Five: Evaluation of Mind Training

Two Witnesses (Slogan 20)
 1. Yourself
 2. Other

Chapter 41: Point Six: Disciplines of Mind Training

Three Basic Principles (Slogan 23)
 1. Keeping the refuge and bodhisattva vows
 2. Refraining from outrageous actions
 3. Developing patience

Chapter 42: Point Seven: Guidelines of Mind Training

Two Activities (Slogan 41)
 1. Beginning the day by remembering bodhichitta
 2. Ending the day by examining what you have done

Two Forms of Patience (Slogan 42)
 1. Patience with extreme suffering
 2. Patience with extreme happiness

Two Vows to Observe (Slogan 43)
 1. Refuge vow
 2. Bodhisattva vow

Three Difficulties (Slogan 44)
 1. Difficulty of recognizing your kleshas
 2. Difficulty of overcoming your kleshas
 3. Difficulty of cutting through your kleshas

Three Things to Do about the Three Difficulties (Slogan 44)
 1. Recognize your kleshas
 2. Overcome the kleshas
 3. Take a vow never to re-create the kleshas

Three Principal Causes (Slogan 45)
 1. Having a good teacher
 2. Cultivating a mind and demeanor applicable to the dharma
 3. Having the right practical circumstances for practicing the
    dharma

The Five Paths
  1. The path of accumulation
    Three Qualities of the Path of Accumulation
      a. Lesser path of accumulation / attitude like the earth
      b. Medium path of accumulation / intention like gold
      c. Greater path of accumulation / wholesomeness like the full moon
  2. The path of unification
    Three Qualities of the Path of Unification
      a. Willingness like a burning fire
      b. Completely nonconceptual meditation
      c. Increasing discrimination
        Four Stages of Discrimination
          i. Heat / a hint of mahayana
         ii. Crest / terrifying sharpness and conviction
           Five Perceptions Developed by Heat and Crest
             a. Faith in your discovery
             b. Energy
             c. Mindfulness
             d. Samadhi / meditative absorption
             e. Prajna
           Five Powers Developed by Heat and Crest
             a. Faith never needs to be sought
             b. Energy never needs to be sought
             c. Mindfulness never needs to be sought
             d. Meditative absorption never needs to be sought
             e. Prajna never needs to be sought
         iii. Patience
         iv. Higher dharma
  3. The path of seeing / entry into the mahayana
  4. The path of meditation / mahayana practice
  5. The path of no more learning / mahayana attainment

Chapter 45. Very Joyful: The First Bhumi
The Four Noble Truths
  1. Suffering
  2. The origin of suffering
  3. The cessation of suffering
  4. The path

The Seven Limbs of a Bodhisattva
1. Awareness
2. Discrimination
3. Effort
4. Joy
5. Shinjang
6. Samadhi
7. Equilibrium

Chapter 46. The Second through Tenth Bhumis
The Eightfold Path
1. Right view
2. Right understanding
3. Right speech
4. Right action
5. Right livelihood
6. Right effort
7. Right recollection, or mindfulness
8. Right meditation

The Twenty Mountains of Ego
1. Grasping at self
2. Grasping at others
3. Grasping at one's life force
4. Grasping at people as active agents
5. Grasping at the impermanence of sentient beings
6. Grasping at the permanence of sentient beings
7. Grasping at duality
8. Grasping at various causes
9. Grasping at the five skandhas
10. Grasping at the dhatus
11. Grasping at the ayatanas
12. Grasping at the three worlds
13. Grasping at the kleshas
14. Discouragement with the path of dharma
15. Grasping at the Buddha and the attainment of nirvana
16. Grasping at the dharma
17. Grasping at the sangha
18. Clinging to morality and ethics
19. Dissension with emptiness
20. Grasping at the conventional and at emptiness as contradictory

Two Aspects of Skillful Means
1. Knowing your own skill
2. Knowing how to use your skill to work with sentient beings

The Ten Powers
1. Power over life
2. Power over mind
3. Power over belongings
4. Power over karma
5. Power over birth
6. Power over desire
7. Power over aspiration
8. Power over miracles
9. Power over wisdom
10. Power over dharma

Four Types of Discriminating Awareness
1. Dharma
2. Meaning
3. Definition
4. Confidence

Eight Great Treasures
1. Recollection
2. Intellect
3. Realization
4. Retention
5. Brilliance
6. Doctrine
7. Enlightenment
8. Accomplishment

Five Buddha-Family Wisdoms of the Vajrayana
1. Wisdom of all-encompassing space
2. Mirrorlike wisdom
3. Wisdom of equanimity
4. Discriminating-awareness wisdom
5. Wisdom of all-accomplishing action

Chapter 47. Complete Radiance: The Eleventh Bhumi
Four Qualities of Vajra-Like Samadhi
1. Toughness
2. Stability
3. One flavor
4. All-pervasiveness

Three Bodies / Trikaya
1. Dharmakaya / body beyond reference point / mind
2. Sambhogakaya / body of complete joy / speech
Five Ways of Teaching
a. Choosing a particular place to teach
b. Knowing who you are as a teacher
c. Knowing what you are going to teach
d. Knowing what kind of audience you have
e. Knowing what time of the day you are going to teach
3. Nirmanakaya / emanation body / body
Two Kinds of Nirmanakaya Buddhas
a. Actual nirmanakaya buddhas like Gautama Buddha
b. Buddhas represented by books, statues, and images

Ten Dharmas of Nonattainment
Discipline
1. Speech of nonattainment
2. Action of nonattainment
3. Livelihood of nonattainment

Meditation
4. Mindfulness of nonattainment
5. Samadhi of nonattainment

Knowledge / Prajna
6. Nonattainment view
7. Nonattainment understanding
8. Nonattainment effort

Beyond Discipline, Meditation, and Knowledge
9. Complete liberation
10. Perfect wisdom or jnana

GLOSSARY

This glossary includes terms in English, Tibetan (Tib.), Sanskrit (Skt.), Pali, Chinese (Chin.), and Japanese (Jpn.). Tibetan terms are spelled phonetically, followed by the transliteration in parentheses. Tibetan equivalents of Sanskrit words are first written phonetically, then transliterated.

abhidharma (Skt.). Superior or higher dharma. The Buddhist teachings can be divided into three parts, called the "three baskets," or Tripitaka: the sutras (general teachings of the Buddha), the vinaya (teachings on conduct), and the abhidharma (teachings on philosophy and psychology). According to Trungpa Rinpoche, abhidharma can be thought of as the "patterns of the dharma."

abhisheka (Skt.; Tib.: wang; dbang). Sprinkling. An empowerment ceremony in which a student is initiated into a particular vajrayana practice.

alaya (Skt.; Tib.: künshi; kun gzhi). The fundamental ground that gives rise to both samsara and nirvana, or the basic split. Not to be confused with alayavijnana, or alaya consciousness, the eighth consciousness.

alayavijnana (Skt.; Tib.: künshi nampar shepa; kun gzhi rnam par shes pa). The base, or storehouse consciousness; the basis of duality and of all mental activities, also referred to as the eighth consciousness.

anapanasati (Pali). Mindfulness of the coming and going of the breath. A traditional form of Buddhist meditation.

arhat (Skt.; Tib.: drachompa; dgra bcom pa). In Sanskrit, "worthy one." In Tibetan, "one who has conquered the enemy" of conflicting emotions and grasping at a self-entity. A fully accomplished practitioner of the hinayana path who has achieved liberation from the sufferings of samsara.

Asanga (ca. 300–370 CE). An exponent of the Yogachara school of Buddhist philosophy.

aspiring (Tib.: mön-pe sem-kye; smon pa'i sems bskyed). The first aspect of taking the bodhisattva vow, which is the desire to enter the bodhisattva path. It is followed by the second aspect, or entering (Tib. juk pe sem-kye; jug pa'i sems bskyed), the actual entry into the disciplines and practices of a bodhisattva. *See also* entering.

ati (Skt.; Tib.: dzokpa; rdzogs pa). Completion, perfection. Ati, which is also referred to as *maha ati* (Tib.: dzokchen; rdzogs chen) or "great perfection," refers to the highest vajrayana teaching, according to the Nyingma school of Tibetan Buddhism.

Atisha Dipankara (982–1054 CE). A renowned Indian Buddhist scholar and teacher, and founder of the Kadam ("oral instruction") school of Tibetan Buddhism. Atisha was invited to bring the teachings of lojong, or mind training, to Tibet, where he taught for thirteen years until his death.

Avalokiteshvara. One of the most important bodhisattvas of the mahayana, the embodiment of limitless compassion.

ayatana (Skt.; Tib.: kye-che; skye mched). Sense field. The collection of six sense organs and their corresponding objects. The twelve ayatanas are comprised of the sense organs of eyes, ears, nose, tongue, body, and mind; and the sense objects of sights, sounds, smells, tastes, touchable objects, and thoughts. The Tibetan translation, *kye-che*, literally means "arising and spreading."

bhumi (Skt.; Tib.: sa; sa). Stage, level; the progressive stages on the path of the bodhisattva that lead to enlightenment.

Black Crown Ceremony. A ceremony unique to the Kagyü tradition, performed only by the supreme lineage holder, or Karmapa. In the Black Crown Ceremony, the Karmapa holds on his head a black crown, a replica of the crown given to the fifth Karmapa by Yung-lo, Emperor of China. The original was said to have been made from the hairs of dakinis (female deities who protect the teachings) after Yung-lo had a vision of the crown on the fifth Karmapa's head. As the Karmapa holds the crown on his head, he slowly recites the mantra of Avalokiteshvara, the bodhisattva of compassion. It is said that during those few minutes, the Karmapa brings to earth the transcendent form of Avalokiteshvara and radiates the bodhisattva's pure egoless compassion.

bodhi (Skt.; Tib.: changchup; byang chub). Awake. Full illumination or enlightenment.

bodhichitta (Skt.; Tib.: changchup kyi sem; byang chub kyi sems). Enlightened heart / mind. Ultimate, or absolute, bodhichitta is the union of emptiness and compassion, the essential nature of awakened mind. Relative bodhichitta is the tenderness arising from a glimpse of ultimate bodhichitta that inspires the practitioner to train in working for the benefit of others.

bodhisattva (Skt.; Tib.: changchup sempa; byang chub sems 'dpa). Awake being. In Tibetan, literally "hero of the enlightened mind." A person who has largely overcome confusion and who is committed to cultivating compassion and wisdom through the practice of the six paramitas (transcendent actions or perfections) in order to free all beings from suffering. *See also* paramitas.

bodhisattva path (Tib.: changchup sem-pe tekpa; byang chub sems dpa'i theg pa). The path of awakened beings, the mahayana. The practices and attitudes of those who dedicate their lives to awakening and to freeing all beings from suffering. *See also* bodhisattva.

bodhisattva vow. The vow to attain enlightenment for the benefit of all beings, marking one's aspiration to enter into the mahayana path of wisdom and compassion, and one's intention to practice the bodhisattva discipline of the six paramitas.

Brahma (Skt.). The first god of the Hindu trinity of Brahma, Vishnu, and Shiva. God in the aspect of creator of the universe.

brahmaloka (Skt.). Realm of the gods. One of the six realms of samsaric beings.

brahmavihara (Skt.). Literally, the "dwelling place of Brahma." The four brahmaviharas are a meditation practice in which the practitioner contemplates four positive states of mind and radiates them out. The four states are love toward all beings, compassion toward those who are suffering, sympathetic joy, and equanimity or unbiasedness.

buddha / Buddha (Skt.; Tib.: sang-gye; sangs rgyas). Awakened one. In a general sense, "buddha" may refer to the principle of enlightenment or to any enlightened being. In particular, "the Buddha" refers to the historical Buddha Shakyamuni.

chakpa mepa (Tib.: chags pa med pa). Passionlessness.

champa (Tib.: byams pa; Skt.: maitri). Love, loving-kindness.

Chandrakirti. Seventh-century Indian madhyamaka (middle way) teacher and author of a well-known commentary on Nagarjuna's *Root Stanzas on the Middle Way* (Skt.: Mulamadhyamaka-karikas) entitled *Introduction to the Middle Way* (Skt.: Madhyamakavatara).

Changchup Shunglam (Tib.: byang chub gzhung lam). *The Great Path of Awakening,* Jamgön Kongtrül's commentary on the lojong slogans and a classical guide to working with them. One of the main sources used by Trungpa Rinpoche for his presentation of lojong, or mind-training, teachings.

chö-je yang dak (Tib.: chos 'byed yang dag). Perfect discrimination of dharmas. Second of the seven limbs of a bodhisattva.

chökyi trin (Tib.: chos kyi sprin). Cloud of dharma. The tenth bhumi and the final stage before the attainment of enlightenment.

dagdzin (Tib.: bdag 'dzin). Conception of a self; ego-clinging.

dana (Skt.; Tib.: jinpa; sbyin pa). Generosity. First of the six paramitas. *See also* paramita.

denpa nyi (Tib.: bden pa gnyis). Two truths; the relative and the absolute truth.

dharma (Skt.; Tib.: chö; chos). Truth, law, phenomena. Specifically, the bud-dhadharma, or teachings of the Buddha. Lower dharma is how things work on the mundane level: for example, how water boils. Higher dharma is the subtle understanding of the world: how mind works, how samsara perpetu-ates itself, how it is transcended, and so on. The plural form *dharmas* simply refers to phenomena. First of the four types of discriminating awareness.

dharmadhatu (Skt.; Tib.: chökyi ying; chos kyi dbyings). Sphere of dharma, or sphere of reality. All-encompassing space in which all phenomena arise, dwell, and dissolve.

dharmakaya (Skt.; Tib.: chöku; chos sku). Dharma body; truth body. One of the three kayas. *See also* kayas, three.

dharmapala (Skt.; Tib.: chökyong; chos skyong). An enlightened emanation or a being bound by oath to protect practitioners and the integrity of the dharma. Aid to practitioners in taming of inner and outer obstacles.

dharmaraja (Skt.). Sovereign of dharma.

dharmata (Skt.). "Dharma-ness," "isness"; true nature of reality.

dhyana (Skt.; Tib.: samten; bsam gtan). Meditative stabilization, concentration. The fifth of the six paramitas. *See also* paramita.

dikpa (Tib.: sdig pa). Karmic deeds; evil actions; neurotic crimes.

dompa (Tib.: sdom pa; Skt.: samvara). Binding; vow.

dom-pe tsültrim (Tib.: sdom pa'i tshul khrims). Binding oneself to the disci-pline of dharma. First of three types of discipline.

dön (Tib.: gdon). A sudden attack of neurosis, an emotional upheaval, or kle-sha, that seems to come from outside oneself. *See also* klesha.

dug-ngal kyi ngowo söpa (Tib.: sdug bsngal kyi ngo bo bzod pa). Patience toward the fact of suffering; realizing how others' impatience is caused by their pain. The second of the three types of patience.

duhkha (Skt.; Tib.: dug-ngal; sdug bsngal). Suffering. Physical and psychologi-cal suffering of all kinds, including the subtle but all-pervading frustration experienced with regard to the impermanence and insubstantiality of all things. The truth of suffering is the first of the four noble truths.

eightfold path. Fundamental components of the Buddhist path as expounded by Gautama Buddha. The path that leads to the cessation of suffering. The eightfold path consists of (1) right view, (2) right understanding, (3) right speech, (4) right action, (5) right livelihood, (6) right effort, (7) right recollec-tion or mindfulness, and (8) right meditation.

entering (Tib.: juk-pe sem-kye; jug pa'i sems bskyed). The second aspect of the bodhisattva vow, the actual application of the disciplines and practices of a bodhisattva. This follows the first aspect, the aspiration or desire to enter the bodhisattva path (Tib.: mön-pe sem-kye; smon pa'i sems bskyed). *See also* aspiring.

four noble truths. The four noble truths are (1) suffering, (2) the origin of suffering, (3) the cessation of suffering, and (4) the path.

gawa (Tib.: dga' ba). Joy. Fourth of the seven limbs of a bodhisattva.

Geluk (Tib.: dge lugs). One of the four major schools of Tibetan Buddhism, characterized by an emphasis on scholarship and intellectual analysis.

Geshe Chekawa Yeshe Dorje (1101–1175 CE). A Kadam master renowned as the author of the *Seven Points of Mind Training*, a summary of Atisha's lojong teachings.

gewa (Tib.: dge ba). Virtue.

ge-wa chödü (Tib.: dge ba'i chos sdud). Gathering virtuous dharmas, or gathering goodness. The second of three types of discipline.

gomden (Tib.: sgom gdan). A block-shaped meditation cushion designed by Trungpa Rinpoche.

gyi-luk-pe lelo (Tib.: sgyid lug pa'i le lo). Losing heart; the second of the three categories of laziness.

Heart Sutra. Short for *Sutra of the Heart of Transcendent Knowledge* (Skt.: Prajnaparamita Hridaya Sutra). An important and beloved sutra, studied and recited by many schools of Buddhism. A concise encapsulation of prajnaparamita teachings and an essential discourse on emptiness.

hinayana (Skt.; Tib.: thekpa chung; theg pa chung). Lesser or narrow vehicle. The spiritual path of individual salvation, based on meditation practice and an understanding of basic Buddhist doctrines such as the four noble truths. Also known as the foundational vehicle, it provides the essential instruction and training that serves as a basis for both the mahayana and the vajrayana.

Jamgön Kongtrül Lodrö Thaye (1813–1899 CE). One of the most prominent Buddhist masters of nineteenth-century Tibet, credited as one of the founders of the Ri-me, or nonsectarian, movement. Jamgön Kongtrül achieved great renown as a scholar and writer, and authored more than one hundred volumes of scriptures. Trungpa Rinpoche used Jamgön Kongtrül's commentary on slogan practice, *The Great Path of Awakening*, and his monumental work, *The Treasury of Knowledge*, as primary references for his presentation of the three yanas.

jangkawa (Tib.: sbyang dka' ba). Difficult to accomplish. The fifth bhumi.

jhana (Pali; Skt.: dhyana; Tib.: samten; bsam gtan). State of meditative absorption. According to Trungpa Rinpoche, attachment to such absorption states is an obstacle that can lead to becoming trapped in the god realm, and therefore it is better not to seek out such states.

jinpa (Tib.: sbyin pa; Skt.: dana). Generosity. The first of the six paramitas, or transcendent actions. *See also* paramita.

jnana (Skt.; Tib.: yeshe; ye shes). Wisdom. The wisdom activity of enlightenment, transcending all dualistic conceptualization. Spontaneous wisdom that need not be sought. Primordial knowing.

ka (Tib.: bka'). Sacred command.

Kadam/Kadampa (Tib.: bka' gdams pa). Oral instruction. School of Tibetan Buddhism founded by Atisha and noted for its emphasis on lojong, or mind-training teachings.

Kagyü (Tib.: bka' brgyud). One of four main sects of Tibetan Buddhism. Kagyü means "command" lineage. Due to its emphasis on meditation and on direct experience, it is referred to as the "practice lineage." As the eleventh Trungpa tülku, Chögyam Trungpa Rinpoche was a Kagyü lineage holder, although he also studied within the Nyingma tradition.

kalpa (Skt.). An endlessly long period of time; world cycle, world age.

kalyanamitra (Skt.; Tib.: ge-we shenyen; dge ba'i bshes gnyen). Spiritual friend. The mahayana teacher, who guides students through wisdom, compassion, and skillful means.

karma (Skt.; Tib. le; las). Action. The chain-reaction process of action and result, or cause and effect, arising from the habit of ego fixation. According to this doctrine, one's present experience is a product of previous actions and volitions, and future conditions depend on what is done in the present. Virtuous actions leads to positive results, and nonvirtuous actions to negative results. Ultimately, the goal is to break the karmic chain and free oneself from the destructive habit of ego by means of wisdom and skillful means.

Karmapa. The spiritual head of the Karma Kagyü school and the oldest tülku lineage of Tibetan Buddhism. The appearance of the Karmapa as an embodiment of compassion was prophesied by both the Buddha and Padmasambhava. In seventeen incarnations, the Karmapa has worked for the welfare of all sentient beings. In the Black Crown Ceremony, performed since the fifteenth century, the Karmapa shows himself as the embodiment of Avalokiteshvara. The sixteenth Karmapa, Rikpe Dorje (1924–1981), was the Kagyü lineage holder during Trungpa Rinpoche's lifetime. The current, or seventeenth, Karmapa is Ogyen Trinley Dorje (b. 1985). *See also* Black Crown Ceremony.

karuna (Skt.; Tib.: nyingje; snying rje). Compassion; noble heart. The second of both the four brahmaviharas and the four limitless ones.

kayas, four (Skt.). The four kayas are dharmakaya (body of nonreference point), sambhogakaya (body of complete joy), nirmanakaya (body of emanation), and svabhavikakaya (the totality of panoramic experience). In context of the lojong slogan, "Seeing confusion as the four kayas is the supreme shunyata protection," the four kayas are the four mental processes of perception: openness, clarity, joining the two, and the totality of panoramic experience. *See also* kayas, three.

kayas, three (Skt.). The three bodies, or forms, of a buddha: dharmakaya (body of nonreference point); sambhogakaya (body of complete joy); and nirmanakaya (body of emanation). *See also* kayas, four.

khorsum yangdak (Tib.: 'khor gsum yang dag). Threefold purity. The three purities are no action, no actor, and no object of the activity.

klesha (Skt.; Tib.: nyönmong; nyon mongs). Defilement or conflicting emotions, also referred to as poison. Kleshas are properties that dull the mind and lead to unwholesome actions. The three main kleshas are passion, aggression, and ignorance or delusion.

kshanti (Skt.; Tib.: söpa; bzod pa). Patience, forbearance. The third of the six paramitas or transcendent actions. *See also* paramita.

kündzop (Tib.: kun rdzob). Relative or conventional truth. This is contrasted to töndam, or "absolute truth," in the teaching of the two truths. *See also* töndam.

künshi ngangluk kyi gewa (Tib.: kun gzhi ngang lugs kyi dge ba). The natural virtue of the alaya. A natural state of goodness, or basic goodness. *See also* alaya.

küntak (Tib.: kun brtags). Random labeling; false conceptions.

küntu ö (Tib.: kun tu 'od). Always luminous; complete radiance. The last of the ten bhumis, the equivalent of buddhahood.

lakshana (Skt.). Permanence. One of the four aspects of ultimate truth; the others are joy, purity, and being.

lamkhyer (Tib.: lam khyer). Carrying all life circumstances to the path.

lek-pe lodrö (Tib.: legs pa'i blo gros). Good intellect. The ninth bhumi.

lelo (Tib.: le lo). Laziness.

lhakpa (Tib.: lhag pa). Supreme.

lobur gyi trima (Tib.: glo bur gyi dri ma). Temporary stain.

lodrö (Tib.: blo gros). Intellect.

lohan (Chin.; Skt.: arhat). A close disciple of the Buddha.

lojong (Tib.: blo sbyong). Mind training; specifically the practice of cultivating loving-kindness and compassion by working with the slogans of *The Seven Points of Mind Training,* a teaching compiled by Geshe Chekawa and attributed to Atisha.

madhyamaka (Skt.). The "middle-way" school, a philosophical school based on the dialectical approach of undercutting any attempt to establish a solid logical position, developed by the great logician Nagarjuna (second to third century CE).

Madhyamakavatara (Skt.). Chandrakirti's commentary on Nagarjuna's *Root Stanzas on the Middle Way.*

mahakaruna (Skt.; Tib.: nyingje chenpo; snying rje chen po). Great love, great compassion. First of the four aspects of great compassion.

mahamudra (Skt.; Tib.: chaggya chenpo; phyag rgya chen po). Great symbol. The meditative transmission handed down especially by the Kagyü school, from Vajradhara Buddha through Tilopa up to the present lineage holders. A tradition of systematic meditative training leading to a direct nonconceptual understanding of the vivid-empty nature of phenomenal reality.

mahasattva (Skt.). Great being.

mahasukha (Skt.; Tib.: bde ba chenpo; bde ba po'i). Great bliss.

mahavipashyana (Skt.). Panoramic awareness that is both precise and all-encompassing. A greater form of vipashyana that leads to a glimpse of shunyata and the realization of the four noble truths. *See also* vipashyana.

mahayana (Skt.; Tib.: thekpa chenpo; theg pa chen po). Great vehicle. The stage of Buddha's teaching that emphasizes the practice of compassion and the realization of both the self and phenomena as vast openness, or emptiness. It is the path of the bodhisattva, the practitioner whose life is dedicated to helping others on the path to liberation.

maitri (Skt.). Love, or loving-kindness. The first of the four brahmaviharas, as well as the four limitless ones.

Manjushri (Skt.). "He who is noble and gentle." The bodhisattva of wisdom, often depicted holding a two-bladed sword and a prajnaparamita text, symbolizing the cutting of twofold ego and the power of prajna.

Mara/maras (Skt.; Pali). Literally "death" or "destruction." Mara is the demon who tempted Buddha with seductive visions. He is the embodiment of death who symbolizes the passions that overwhelm beings, as well as everything that hinders the arising of wholesomeness and progress on the path. More generally, maras refer to evil, seductive forces.

Marpa (1012–1097 CE). Renowned Tibetan Kagyü yogi and translator; principle teacher of Tibet's poet saint Milarepa.

mepa lelo (Tib.: smad pa le lo). Degraded laziness. The third of the three categories of laziness.

mik-che kyi nying-je (Tib.: dmigs bcas kyi snying rje). Deliberate compassion.

Milarepa (1040–1123 CE). One of the forefathers of the Kagyü lineage. A student of Marpa who attained enlightenment in one lifetime, he is the most famous of Tibetan saints and is known for his spontaneous spiritual songs, or *dohas* (Skt.).

mi-lob-lam (Tib.: mi slob lam). Path of no more learning. Fifth of the five paths

Mind-only school. *See* Yogachara school.

miyowa (Tib.: mi gyo ba). Not moving. The eighth bhumi.

mönlam (Tib.: smon lam; Skt.: pranidhana). Aspiration, vision, or prayer.

mudita (Skt.). Joy. The third of the four brahmaviharas, as well as the third of the four limitless ones.

Nagarjuna (second to third century CE). A great Indian teacher of Buddhism, the founder of the Madhyamaka school of Buddhist philosophy. He contributed greatly to the logical development of the doctrine of shunyata and was the author of many key texts. According to tradition, he was also the guru of various important Buddhist teachers.

nampar mitokpa (Tib.: rnampar mi rtog pa). Complete nonconceptualization; the experience of the first bhumi.

namtok (Tib.: rnam rtog). Concept; conceptualization.

namdrang ma-yin-pe töndam (Tib.: rnam grangs pa'i don dam). "Uncountable" töndam. Vast experience beyond fixation. One of two types of töndam. *See also* nam-drang-pe töndam.

nam-drang-pe töndam (Tib.: rnam grangs ma yin pa'i don dam). "Countable" or categorized töndam. A partial transcending of fixation. One of two types of töndam. *See also* namdrang ma-yin-pe töndam.

ngetsik (Tib.: nges tshig). The discrimination of definition, the third of four types of discriminating awareness of the ninth bhumi.

ngöndu kyurpa (Tib.: mngon du gyur pa). Becoming manifest. The sixth bhumi.

nidana (Skt.). One of the twelve links of interdependent origination: ignorance, formation, consciousness, name and form, six sense faculties, contact, feeling, craving, clinging, becoming, birth, and death. The web of mutually conditioned psychological and physical phenomena that constitute individual existence, and entangle sentient beings in samsara.

nirmanakaya (Skt.; Tib.: tülku; sprul sku). Form body or emanation body. *See also* kayas, three.

nirvana (Skt.; Tib.: nya-ngen ledepa; mya ngen las 'das pa). Extinguished. The Tibetan translation means "gone beyond suffering"; a state of no more suffering achieved when one is enlightened. Used in contrast to *samsara*.

nyam (Tib.: nyams). Temporary experience.

nying-je (Tib.: snying rje; Skt.: karuna). Compassion; literally, "noble heart."

Nyingma (Tib.: rnying ma). The ancient ones. The oldest of the four principal schools of Tibetan Buddhism, focusing on the early transmission of Buddhist teachings brought from India to Tibet by Padmasambhava, as well as monks and scholars such as Vimalamitra and Vairochana in the eighth century.

nyom-le kyi lelo (Tib.: snyom las kyi le lo). The first category of laziness. Casualness and attachment to leisure. Slothfulness.

öjepa (Tib.: 'od byed pa). Illuminating. The third bhumi.

öselwa (Tib.: 'od gsal ba). Luminosity. Second of four aspects of great compassion.

ötrowa (Tib.: 'od phro ba). Radiating light. The fourth bhumi.

pagyang (Tib.: bag yangs). Naiveté.

pagyö (Tib.: bag yod). Bare attention, heedfulness.

pandita (Skt.). Scholar.

paramita (Skt.; Tib.: pharchen; phar phyin). Perfection; in Tibetan "gone to the far shore." The six paramitas are the transcendent virtues of generosity, discipline, patience, exertion, meditation, and prajna (knowledge).

pharöl tu chinpa (Tib.: pharol tu phyin pa; Skt.: paramita). Transcendent virtue. In condensed Tibetan style referred to as pharchen (phar phyin). *See* paramita.

poppa (Tib.: spobs pa). Confidence. The fourth of the four types of discriminating awareness.

postmeditation. Follow-up to formal sitting practice. Bringing the practice of mindfulness and awareness into all the activities of one's daily life.

prajna (Skt.; Tib.: sherap; shes rab). Perfect knowledge, meaning wisdom, understanding, or discrimination. Ordinary prajna is understanding the world and how things work on a mundane level. In the beginning of the path, higher prajna encompasses direct experience of the mind and its processes; in later stages, it means penetrating insight that discovers both the world and the self to be illusory. Sixth of the six paramitas.

pranidhana. *See* mönlam.

pratyekabuddha (Skt.). Solitary realizer. A term for a person who has realized one-and-a-half-fold egolessness (egoless of self and a partial realization of the ego of phenomena) due to insight into dependent arising, without relying on a teacher.

pratyekabuddhayana (Skt.). The path of the "solitary realizer" of the hinayana.

rapkar gewa (Tib.: rab dkar dge ba). White virtue. Unstained basic goodness.

raptu gawa (Tib.: rab tu dga' ba). Very joyful. The first bhumi.

refuge vow. The vow marking one's formal entry into the Buddhist path, and one's commitment to the Buddha, the dharma, and the sangha.

rikpa (Tib.: rig pa). Knowing; insight.

ringdu songwa (Tib.: ring du song ba). Far gone. The seventh bhumi.

rochik (Tib.: ro gcig). One flavor, or one taste. A mental approach that is very open, spacious, and direct. Seeing all phenomena as one flavor: awake.

samadhi (Skt.; Tib.: tingdzin; ting 'dzin). One-pointedness, meditation. Sixth of the seven limbs of a bodhisattva. The third of the three supreme disciplines.

Samadhiraja Sutra (Skt.). King of Samadhi Sutra. A mahayana sutra on wisdom and emptiness, viewed in the Kagyü tradition as establishing a foundation for the practice of mahamudra.

sambhogakaya (Skt.; Tib.: longku; longs sku). Enjoyment body. *See also* kayas, three.

samsara (Skt.; Tib.: khorwa; 'khor ba). Cyclic existence; the continual repetitive cycle of birth, death, and bardo that arises from ordinary beings' grasping and fixating on a self and experiences. All states of consciousness in the six realms, including the god realms, are bound by this process. Samsara arises out of ignorance and is characterized by suffering.

samten (Tib.: bsam gtan; Skt.: dhyana). Meditative stabilization, concentration. Fifth of the six paramitas.

sattvic (Skt.). Purified, or blessed. For example, sattvic food refers to food that is pure, clean, and wholesome.

sem (Tib.: sems). Mundane mind.

semchen tön-che (Tib.: sems can don byed). The third type of the three types of discipline. The discipline of benefiting sentient beings.

semjung (Tib.: sems byung; Skt.: samskara). Mental factor; the fifty-one mental events arising from the mind. In the context of the five categories of mind, samjung refers to the thinking or watching process as the mind relates to the phenomenal world.

sending and taking. *See* tonglen.

Seven Points of Mind Training. A compilation of lojong or mind-training teachings in the form of fifty-nine slogans divided into seven main points composed by the Kadampa master Geshe Chekawa Yeshe Dorje.

shamatha (Skt.; Tib.: shi-ne; zhi gnas). Peaceful abiding. Mindfulness practice; taming and stabilizing the mind. The central practice of the hinayana path and a key component of the practice tradition throughout all three yanas.

shamatha-vipashyana (Skt.). The union of mindfulness and awareness, in which the concentration, stillness, and precision of shamatha is in harmonious balance with the expansiveness, inquisitiveness, and clarity of vipashyana, or awareness practice.

shengyi nöpa la söpa (Tib.: gzhan gyi gnod pa la bzod pa). Patience with other people's destructiveness. The first of the three types of patience.

shepa (Tib.: shes pa). Consciousness.

sherap (Tib.: shes rab; Skt.: prajna). Knowledge, superior knowing.

shikantaza (Jpn.). Zen formless meditation practice of just sitting.

shila (Skt.; Tib.: tsültrim; tshul khrims). The first of the three supreme disciplines. It comprises generosity, discipline, and patience, the first three paramitas.

shinjang (Tib.: shin sbyang). Thoroughly processed or trained through meditation practice. The fifth of the seven limbs of a bodhisattva.

shiwa (Tib.: zhi ba; Skt.: shanti). Peace. Fourth of the four aspects of great compassion.

shravaka (Skt.). Hearer; a practitioner of the shravakayana.

shravakayana (Skt.; Tib.: nyenthö; nyan thos). The path of the "hearer" of the hinayana.

shunyata (Skt.; Tib.: tongpanyi; stong pa nyid). Emptiness. A completely open and unbounded clarity of mind characterized by groundlessness and freedom from all conceptual frameworks. Emptiness does not mean voidness or blankness, but an openness that is inseparable from compassion and all other awakened qualities.

six realms. Realms of samsaric existence. The three lower realms of hell beings, hungry ghosts, and animals; and the three higher realms of humans, jealous gods, and gods.

skandha (Skt.; Tib.: phungpo; phung po). Heap or basket; aggregate. The five skandhas describe the aggregates or collection of phenomena that we take to be a self. The five aggregates are: form, feeling, perception / impulse, formation or concept, and consciousness.

söpa (Tib.: bzod pa; Skt.: kshanti). Patience, forbearance. The third of the six paramitas, or transcendent actions. *See also* paramita.

soso rangrik (Tib.: so so rang rig). Discriminating awareness; seeing things as distinct entities, just as they are.

soso yang-dak-par rikpa (Tib.: so so yang dag par rig pa). Discriminating awareness or intelligence.

sosor tok-pe sherap (Tib.: so sor rtog pa'i shes rab). Discriminating awareness, individually seeing things as they are as separate entities.

sosor tok-pe söpa (Tib.: so sor rtog pa'i bzod pa). Individually examining. The third of three types of patience.

spiritual friend (Tib.: ge-we shenyen; dge ba'i bshes gnyen; Skt.: kalyanamitra). A mahayana teacher. *See* kalyanamitra.

sugata(s) (Tib.: dewar shekpa; bde bar gsheg pa). One who has gone beyond with joy; a buddha.

sugatagarbha (Skt.; Tib.: dewar shek-pe nyingpo; bde bar gshegs pa'i snying po). Buddha nature, basic wakefulness. The essence of those who have passed into liberation joyfully and easily.

sutra (Skt.; Tib.: do; mdo). Thread, string, cord. Sutras are hinayana and mahayana texts in the Buddhist canon that are attributed to the Buddha. The term *sutra* means a meeting point or junction, referring to the meeting of the Buddha's enlightenment and the student's understanding. A sutra is usually a dialogue between the Buddha and one or more of his disciples elaborating a particular topic of dharma.

Sutra of the Heart of Transcendent Knowledge (Skt.: Prajnaparamita Hridaya Sutra). *See* Heart Sutra; appendix 3, "The *Heart Sutra*."

svabhavikakaya (Skt.). The totality of panoramic experience. Fourth of the four kayas. *See* kayas, four.

tang-nyom (Tib.: btang snyoms). Equanimity. Seventh of the seven limbs of a bodhisattva.

tantrayana (Skt.). Also referred to as tantra. A synonym for vajrayana, the third of the three yanas or vehicles. *Tantra* means continuity, and refers both to the root texts of the vajrayana and to the systems of meditation they describe.

Tao Te Ching (Chin.: Tao [the Way]; Te [strength or virtue]; Ching [scripture]). A classical text on Taoism attributed to Lao-tzu.

tathagata (Skt.; Tib.: teshin shekpa; de bzhin gshegs pa). Thus come or thus gone; an epithet for the Buddha.

tathagatagarbha (Skt.; Tib.: teshek nyingpo; de gshegs snying po). Buddha nature. The intrinsic state of wakefulness inherent in all human beings.

tendrel (Tib.: rten 'brel). Coincidence. The twelve nidanas; interdependent origination. *See also* nidana.

thapla khepa (Tib.: thabs la mkhas pa). Skillfulness. Third of the four aspects of great compassion.

thekpa (Tib.: theg pa; Skt.: yana). Vehicle. *See also* yana.

three jewels. The Buddha, the dharma, and the sangha. Also called the "triple gem."

tokpa (Tib.: rtog pa). Realization, understanding.

tön (Tib.: don). Meaning. Understanding the meaning of the dharma, and not just the words. Second of the four types of discriminating awareness.

töndam (Tib.: don dam). Ultimate truth or nature; higher understanding. This is contrasted with relative truth, or kündzop, in the teaching of the "two truths." *See also* kundzöp.

tonglen (Tib.: gtong len). Sending and taking; the practice of exchanging oneself for others.

tongphö (Tib.: gtong phod). Daring to let go. A quality of generosity.

torma (Tib.: gtor ma). Ritual barley cake used in vajrayana feast practice.

trenpa (Tib.: dran pa; Skt.: smriti). Mindfulness; recollection. First of the seven limbs of a bodhisattva.

tren-she (Tib.: dran shes). Recollection and knowing; mindfulness and awareness. The kind of recollection that joins past and present together.

trima mepa (Tib.: dri ma med pa). Spotlessness. The second bhumi.

trö (Tib.: drod; Skt.: ushman). Heat; an increased degree of realization. A whiff or hint of mahayana on the path of unification.

tsemo (Tib.: rtse mo). Crest. A penetrating sharpness and conviction developed on the path of unification.

tsöndrü (Tib.: brtson 'grus; Skt.: virya). Exertion. Third of the seven limbs of a bodhisattva. Fourth of the six paramitas.

tsültrim (Tib.: tshul khrims; Skt.: shila). Discipline; proper conduct. The second of the six paramitas. *See also* paramita.

tülku (Tib.: sprul sku; Skt.: nirmanakaya). Emanation body; a person who is recognized as the reincarnation of a previously deceased enlightened being. *See also* kayas, three.

two truths. Relative truth and absolute, or ultimate, truth. An understanding of the two truths is an essential component of madhyamaka teachings.

upaya (Skt.). Method; skillful means.

upeksha (Skt.). Equilibrium. The fourth of the four brahmaviharas, as well as the fourth of the four limitless ones.

Uttaratantra (Skt.). A classical text on buddha nature by Maitreya, recorded by Asanga.

vajra (Skt.; Tib.: dorje; rdo rje). Ritual scepter, used in tantric practice. The term *vajra* means "indestructible" or "adamantine."

vajra-like samadhi (Skt.: vajropama-samadhi). An indestructible meditative state of mind that occurs with enlightenment. *See also* vajra.

vajrayana (Skt.; Tib.: dorje thekpa; rdo rje theg pa). The indestructible or adamantine vehicle. Also referred to as tantra or tantrayana. The third of the three stages of the path (hinayana, mahayana, and vajrayana). *See also* vajra.

vijaya (Skt.). Victorious one, an epithet of the Buddha.

vipashyana (Skt.; Tib.: lhakthong; lhag mthong). Awareness. In Tibetan, it is "higher" or "superior" seeing. Insight arising from direct meditative experience or contemplative analysis. An open expansive quality of meditative practice complementary to the stability and groundedness of shamatha.

virya (Skt.; Tib.: tsöndrü; brston 'grus). Exertion. The fourth paramita. *See also* paramita.

yana (Skt.; Tib: thekpa; theg pa). Path or vehicle that carries the practitioner to liberation.

yang-dak-pe nying-je (Tib.: yang dag pa'i snying rje). Absolute compassion.

yeshe (Tib.: ye shes; Skt.: jnana). Wisdom. In the vajrayana teachings, the term *yeshe* or *jnana* refers to a primordial, fruitional state of knowing. *See also* jnana.

yogachara (Skt.). Literally the "application of yoga." The Mind-only school of mahayana Buddhism. The term *yoga* refers to this school's emphasis on developing direct insight by means of meditative practice.

yul la sem pena sem (Tib.: yul la sems pas na sems). A definition of mind as that which can think of the other.

SOURCES

THE MATERIAL in this volume is primarily taken from a series of programs taught by Chögyam Trungpa Rinpoche called Vajradhatu Seminaries. (For further information, see "Editor's Introduction" in volume 1 of the *Profound Treasury*.) Thirteen Seminaries were held between 1973 and 1986, at the following locations:

1. 1973: Jackson Hole, Wyoming. September–November.
2. 1974: Snowmass Village, Colorado. September–November.
3. 1975: Snowmass Village, Colorado. September–November.
4. 1976: Land O' Lakes, Wisconsin. September–November.
5. 1978: Dixville Notch, New Hampshire. March–May.
6. 1979: Lake Louise, Alberta, Canada. March–May.
7. 1980: Lake Louise, Alberta, Canada. January–March.
8. 1981: Lake Louise, Alberta, Canada. January–March.
9. 1982: Bedford Springs, Pennsylvania. January–April.
10. 1983: Bedford Springs, Pennsylvania. January–March.
11. 1984: Bedford Springs, Pennsylvania. January–March.
12. 1985: Shambhala Mountain Center, Red Feather Lakes, Colorado. June–August.
13. 1986: Shambhala Mountain Center, Red Feather Lakes, Colorado. June–August.

More details on the primary sources for each chapter are given below. When the source is a Vajradhatu Seminary, the talk name is given, followed by the year and the talk number.

PART SIX. BODHISATTVA ACTIVITY

PART EIGHT. THE BODHISATTVA'S JOURNEY

RESOURCES

For information about meditation instruction or to find a Shambhala-affiliated practice center near you, please contact one of the following:

Shambhala International
1084 Tower Road
Halifax, Nova Scotia
Canada B3H 2Y5
phone: (902) 425-4275, ext. 10
website: www.shambhala.org

Karmê Chöling
369 Patneaude Lane
Barnet, Vermont 05821
phone: (802) 633-2384
website: www.karmecholing.org

Shambhala Mountain Center
4921 Country Road 68C
Red Feather Lakes, Colorado
80545
phone: (970) 881-2184
website: www.shambhala
mountain.org

Gampo Abbey
Pleasant Bay, Nova Scotia
Canada B0E 2P0
phone: (902) 224-2752
website: www.gampoabbey.org

Dechen Choling
Mas Marvent
87700 St. Yrieix sous Aixe
France
phone: +33 5-55-03-55-52
website: www.dechencholing.org

Dorje Denma Ling
2280 Balmoral Road
Tatamagouche, Nova Scotia
Canada B0K 1V0
phone: (902) 657-9085
website: http://dorjedenmaling.org
e-mail: info@dorjedenmaling.com

NAROPA UNIVERSITY

Naropa University is the only accredited, Buddhist-inspired university in North America. For more information, contact:

Naropa University
2130 Arapahoe Avenue
Boulder, Colorado 80302
phone: (303) 444-0202
website: www.naropa.edu

OCEAN OF DHARMA QUOTES OF THE WEEK

Ocean of Dharma Quotes of the Week brings you the teachings of Chögyam Trungpa Rinpoche. An e-mail is sent out several times each week containing a quote from Chögyam Trungpa's extensive teachings. Quotations of material may be from unpublished material, forthcoming publications, or previously published sources. Ocean of Dharma Quotes of the Week are selected by Carolyn Rose Gimian. To enroll go to OceanofDharma.com.

THE CHÖGYAM TRUNGPA LEGACY PROJECT

The Chögyam Trungpa Legacy Project was established to help preserve, disseminate, and expand Chögyam Trungpa's legacy. The Legacy Project supports the preservation, propagation, and publication of Trungpa Rinpoche's dharma teachings. This includes plans for the creation of a comprehensive virtual archive and learning community. For information, go to ChogyamTrungpa.com.

SHAMBHALA MEDIA

For publications from Vajradhatu Publications and Kalapa Recordings, including both books and audiovisual materials, go to www.shambhalamedia.org.

SHAMBHALA ARCHIVES

For information about the archive of the author's work, please contact the Shambhala Archives: archives@shambhala.org.

ABOUT THE AUTHOR

THE VENERABLE Chögyam Trungpa Rinpoche was born in the province of Kham in eastern Tibet in 1940. When he was just thirteen months old, Chögyam Trungpa was recognized as a major tülku, or incarnate teacher. According to Tibetan tradition, an enlightened teacher is capable, based on his or her vow of compassion, of reincarnating in human form over a succession of generations. Before dying, such a teacher may leave a letter or other clues to the whereabouts of the next incarnation. Later, students and other realized teachers look through these clues and, based on those, plus a careful examination of dreams and visions, conduct searches to discover and recognize the successor. Thus, particular lines of teaching are formed, in some cases extending over many centuries. Chögyam Trungpa was the eleventh in the teaching lineage known as the Trungpa Tülkus.

Once young tülkus are recognized, they enter a period of intensive training in the theory and practice of the Buddhist teachings. Trungpa Rinpoche, after being enthroned as supreme abbot of Surmang Dütsi Tel Monastery and governor of Surmang District, began a period of training that would last eighteen years, until his departure from Tibet in 1959. As a Kagyü tülku, his training was based on the systematic practice of meditation and on refined theoretical understanding of Buddhist philosophy. One of the four great lineages of Tibet, the Kagyü is known as the Practicing (or Practice) Lineage.

At the age of eight, Trungpa Rinpoche received ordination as a novice monk. Following this, he engaged in intensive study and practice of the traditional monastic disciplines, including traditional Tibetan poetry and monastic dance. His primary teachers were Jamgön Kongtrül of Shechen and Khenpo Gangshar—leading teachers in the Nyingma and Kagyü lineages. In 1958, at the age of eighteen, Trungpa Rinpoche completed his studies, receiving the degrees of *kyorpön* (doctor of divinity) and *khenpo* (master of studies). He also received full monastic ordination.

The late fifties was a time of great upheaval in Tibet. As it became clear that the Chinese Communists intended to take over the country by force, many people, both monastic and lay, fled the country. Trungpa Rinpoche spent many harrowing months trekking over the Himalayas (described later in his book *Born in Tibet*). After narrowly escaping capture by the Chinese, he at last reached India in 1959. While in India, Trungpa Rinpoche was appointed to serve as spiritual adviser to the Young Lamas Home School in Delhi, India. He served in this capacity from 1959 to 1963.

Trungpa Rinpoche's opportunity to emigrate to the West came when he received a Spalding sponsorship to attend Oxford University. At Oxford he studied comparative religion, philosophy, history, and fine arts. He also studied Japanese flower arranging, receiving a degree from the Sogetsu School. While in England, Trungpa Rinpoche began to instruct Western students in the dharma, and in 1967 he founded the Samye Ling Meditation Center in Dumfriesshire, Scotland. During this period, he also published his first two books, both in English: *Born in Tibet* (1966) and *Meditation in Action* (1969).

In 1968 Trungpa Rinpoche traveled to Bhutan, where he entered into a solitary meditation retreat. While on retreat, Rinpoche received a pivotal *terma* text for all of his teaching in the West, "The Sadhana of Mahamudra," a text that documents the spiritual degeneration of modern times and its antidote, genuine spirituality that leads to the experience of naked and luminous mind. This retreat marked a pivotal change in his approach to teaching. Soon after returning to England, he became a layperson, putting aside his monastic robes and dressing in ordinary Western attire. In 1970 he married a young Englishwoman, Diana Pybus, and together they left Scotland and moved to North America. Many of his early students and his Tibetan colleagues found these changes shocking and upsetting. However, he expressed a conviction that in order for the dharma to take root in the West, it needed to be taught free from cultural trappings and religious fascination.

During the seventies, America was in a period of political and cultural ferment. It was a time of fascination with the East. Nevertheless, almost from the moment he arrived in America, Trungpa Rinpoche drew many students to him who were seriously interested in the Buddhist teachings and the practice of meditation. However, he severely criticized the materialistic approach to spirituality that was also quite prevalent, describing it as a "spiritual supermarket." In his lectures, and in his books *Cutting Through Spiritual Materialism* (1973) and *The Myth of Freedom* (1976), he pointed to the simplicity and directness of the practice of sitting meditation as the way to cut through such distortions of the spiritual journey.

During his seventeen years of teaching in North America, Trungpa Rinpoche developed a reputation as a dynamic and controversial teacher. He was a pioneer, one of the first Tibetan Buddhist teachers in North America, preceding by some years and indeed facilitating the later visits by His Holiness the Karmapa, His Holiness Khyentse Rinpoche, His Holiness the Dalai Lama, and many others. In the United States, he found a spiritual kinship with many Zen masters, who were already presenting Buddhist meditation. In the very early days, he particularly connected with Suzuki Roshi, the founder of Zen Center in San Francisco. In later years he was close with Kobun Chino Roshi and Bill Kwong Roshi in Northern California; with Maezumi Roshi, the founder of the Los Angeles Zen Center; and with Eido Roshi, abbot of the New York Zendo Shobo-ji.

Fluent in the English language, Chögyam Trungpa was one of the first Tibetan Buddhist teachers who could speak to Western students directly, without the aid of a translator. Traveling extensively throughout North America and Europe, he gave thousands of talks and hundreds of seminars. He established major centers in Vermont, Colorado, and Nova Scotia, as well as many smaller meditation and study centers in cities throughout North America and Europe. Vajradhatu was formed in 1973 as the central administrative body of this network.

In 1974 Trungpa Rinpoche founded the Naropa Institute (now Naropa University), which became the first and only accredited Buddhist-inspired university in North America. He lectured extensively at the institute, and his book *Journey without Goal* (1981) is based on a course he taught there. In 1976 he established the Shambhala Training program, a series of seminars that present a nonsectarian path of spiritual warriorship grounded in the practice of sitting meditation. His book *Shambhala: The Sacred Path of the Warrior* (1984) gives an overview of the Shambhala teachings.

In 1976 Trungpa Rinpoche appointed Ösel Tendzin (Thomas F. Rich) as his Vajra Regent, or dharma heir. Ösel Tendzin worked closely with Trungpa Rinpoche in the administration of Vajradhatu and Shambhala Training. He taught extensively from 1976 until his death in 1990 and is the author of *Buddha in the Palm of Your Hand*.

Trungpa Rinpoche was also active in the field of translation. Working with Francesca Fremantle, he rendered a new translation of *The Tibetan Book of the Dead*, which was published in 1975. Later he formed the Nalanda Translation Committee in order to translate texts and liturgies for his own students as well as to make important texts available publicly.

In 1979 Trungpa Rinpoche conducted a ceremony empowering his eldest son, Ösel Rangdröl Mukpo, as his successor in the Shambhala lineage. At that time he gave him the title of Sawang ("Earth Lord").

Trungpa Rinpoche was also known for his interest in the arts and particularly for his insights into the relationship between contemplative discipline and the artistic process. Two books published since his death—*The Art of Calligraphy* (1994) and *Dharma Art* (1996) [a new edition appeared in 2008 under the title *True Perception: The Path of Dharma Art*]—present this aspect of his work. His own artwork included calligraphy, painting, flower arranging, poetry, playwriting, and environmental installations. In addition, at the Naropa Institute he created an educational atmosphere that attracted many leading artists and poets. The exploration of the creative process in light of contemplative training continues there as a provocative dialogue. Trungpa Rinpoche also published two books of poetry: *Mudra* (1972) and *First Thought Best Thought* (1983). In 1998 a retrospective compilation of his poetry, *Timely Rain,* was published.

Shortly before his death, in a meeting with Samuel Bercholz, the publisher of Shambhala Publications, Chögyam Trungpa expressed his interest in publishing 108 volumes of his teachings, to be called the Dharma Ocean Series. "Dharma Ocean" is the translation of Chögyam Trungpa's Tibetan teaching name, Chökyi Gyatso. The Dharma Ocean Series was to consist primarily of material edited to allow readers to encounter this rich array of teachings simply and directly rather than in an overly systematized or condensed form. In 1991 the first posthumous volume in the series, *Crazy Wisdom,* was published, and another seven volumes followed in the ensuing years. Carolyn Gimian gathered many of these published materials, along with a great number of previously unpublished articles, into the eight-volume set, *The Collected Works of Chögyam Trungpa.* Plans continue for many future volumes of his teachings to be published.

Trungpa Rinpoche's published books represent only a fraction of the rich legacy of his teachings. During his seventeen years of teaching in North America, he crafted the structures necessary to provide his students with thorough, systematic training in the dharma. From introductory talks and courses to advanced group retreat practices, these programs emphasized a balance of study and practice, of intellect and intuition. *Chögyam Trungpa* by Fabrice Midal, a biography, details the many forms of training that Chögyam Trungpa developed. *Dragon Thunder: My Life with Chögyam Trungpa* is the story of Rinpoche's life as told by Diana Mukpo. This also provides insight into the many forms that he crafted for Buddhism in North America.

In addition to his extensive teachings in the Buddhist tradition, Trungpa Rinpoche also placed great emphasis on the Shambhala teachings, which stress the importance of meditation in action, synchronizing mind and body, and training oneself to approach obstacles or challenges in everyday life with the courageous attitude of a warrior, without anger. The goal of creating an enlightened society is fundamental to the Shambhala teachings. According to the Shambhala approach, the realization of an enlightened society comes not purely through outer activity, such as community or political involvement, but from appreciation of the senses and the sacred dimension of day-to-day life. A second volume of these teachings, entitled *Great Eastern Sun,* was published in 1999. The final volume of these teachings, *Smile at Fear,* appeared in 2009.

Chögyam Trungpa died in 1987, at the age of forty-seven. By the time of his death, he was known not only as Rinpoche ("Precious Jewel") but also as Vajracharya ("Vajra Holder") and as Vidyadhara ("Wisdom Holder") for his role as a master of the vajrayana, or tantric teachings of Buddhism. As a holder of the Shambhala teachings, he had also received the titles of Dorje Dradül ("Indestructible Warrior") and Sakyong ("Earth Protector"). He is survived by his wife, Diana Judith Mukpo, and five sons. His eldest son, the Sawang Ösel Rangdröl Mukpo, succeeds him as the spiritual head of Vajradhatu. Acknowledging the importance of the Shambhala teachings to his father's work, the Sawang changed the name of the umbrella organization to Shambhala, with Vajradhatu remaining one of its major divisions. In 1995 the Sawang received the Shambhala title of Sakyong like his father before him, and was also confirmed as an incarnation of the great ecumenical teacher Mipham Rinpoche.

Trungpa Rinpoche is widely acknowledged as a pivotal figure in introducing the buddhadharma to the Western world. He joined his great appreciation for Western culture with his deep understanding of his own tradition. This led to a revolutionary approach to teaching the dharma, in which the most ancient and profound teachings were presented in a thoroughly contemporary way. Trungpa Rinpoche was known for his fearless proclamation of the dharma: free from hesitation, true to the purity of the tradition, and utterly fresh. May these teachings take root and flourish for the benefit of all sentient beings.

CREDITS

INDEX

Bodh Gaya, 428
Bodhicharyavatara
   (Shantideva), 75
bodhichitta
  aggression as danger to, 230
  buddha nature and, 31–34
  definition, 4
  dialogues on, 440–41
  ego shedding through, 348
  importance of, 374
  in paramita practice, 226
  similes for, 385n, 396
  skillful means and, 12–13
  tenderness of, 92
  three components, 107
  threefold purity of, 93
  twofold, 94–96, 345, 370
   (*See also* relative bodhi-
    chitta; ultimate
    bodhichitta)
  viewpoint of, 180–81
bodhisattva fever, 293
bodhisattva path, 3, 61
  basic goodness and, 44
  bodhichitta on, 348–49
  commitment to, 97
  emptiness on, 188–89
  enlightenment on, 193
  entering, 116–17
  inspiration for, 111–12
  joy in, 354
  meditative approach to, 282
  nature of, 25–26
  stages of (*See* bhumis)
  theory and practice, differences between, 273–74
  youthfulness of, 138
  See also mahayana
bodhisattva vow, 72, 108–9,
   112–14, 371, 388, 455, 462
  aspiration and application,
   114–15, 322, 342
  bodhichitta, role of in, 274
  discipline of, 120
  egolessness in, 125, 137–38,
   195–96
  inspiration for, 99, 369
  intention in, 201–2
  maintaining, 358
  motivation for, 148, 194
  suitability for, 117
bodhisattvas
  activity of, 195–96, 392,
   457–59

  (*See also* paramitas)
  approach of, 108
  attitudes of, 23, 26, 104,
   121–23, 455
  communication of, 147
  conduct of, 188
  definitions, xi, 3
  fearlessness of, 10
  heroism of, 8–9, 91
  limitations of, 168, 319,
   443–45
  seven limbs of, 393–95, 465
  six realms and, 284
  as spokespeople, 105–6
  three causes of, 372–73
  as warriors, xi, 10, 19, 61,
   279, 316
boredom, 52, 241, 404
Born in Tibet, 496
brahmaviharas, four, 71–73,
  76–77, 454
bravery, 99, 101–2, 401, 454
breathing practice, riding the
  breath, 284–85, 304–6
  See also tonglen
Buddha (Gautama,
  Shakyamuni), 263
  on destruction of dharma,
   312
  devotion to, 101
  on emptiness, 139
  enlightenment of, 35–36,
   421–22
  epithets for, 34
  hinayana/mahayana views
   of, 21
  sugatagarbha and, 41
  teaching of, 426, 427–28
buddha nature, xi, 451–52
  alaya and, 298
  causes of, 76
  cheerfulness as, 353–54
  conditional and unconditional, 36–39, 89–91
  emptiness and, 170, 183
  as inner wound, 293
  mahayana view of, 24–25,
   140
  maitri and, 16
  path, role on, 282
  prajna and, 148
  self-existing, 160–61
  shamatha-vipashyana and,
   21–23

  spiritual friend's role in
   development of, 78–79
  split from, 176
  terms for, 31, 41–42, 440
  ultimate truth and, 173
buddhahood, 420
  See also enlightenment
buddhas
  three bodies of, 418n,
   425–29, 467
  views on, 421–22
Buddhism
  death, view of in, 342–44
  historical Buddha, role of
   in, 428
  logic of, 92
  as middle way, 390, 456
  nontheism of, 38, 60–61,
   74, 348
  philosophical traditions of,
   143, 150
  self-respect in, 63–64
  in Tibet, 274–76
  vows in, 120, 358, 371
  worldliness, views on, 177

Changchup Shunglam
  (Kongtrül), 275, 276,
  277, 378
chanting, purpose of, 340
Chekawa Yeshe Dorje, Geshe,
  xii, 275, 377
Chögyam Trungpa (Midal), 498
Christianity, 330, 361
*Collected Works of Chögyam
  Trungpa*, 498
comfort, attachment to, 101–2
coming as you are, 138–39
commitment, 349, 454
  to dharma, 70
  joy, role of in, 245
  of mahayana, 112–14
   (*See also* bodhisattva
    vow)
  unbiased, 404
compassion (Skt.: karuna), xii
  bodhichitta and, 9, 94–95,
   107, 278, 291–92
  brahmavihara of, 72, 74
  continuity of, 351–53
  cutting quality of, 125
  deliberate and
   nondeliberate, 284–86,
   288, 460